The
Accidental Constitution

To Janice

The
Accidental Constitution

The Story of the European Convention

Peter Norman

EuroComment • Brussels

Published by
EuroComment
Avenue Louise 113
1050 Brussels
Belgium

For further information regarding any aspect of this publication, please contact; info@eurocomment.be

ISBN 90-77110-05-4

Cover photograph provided by A/P Reporters

Table of Contents

Preface

When, early in 2002, Peter Ludlow suggested I might like to write a book about the Convention for EuroComment, his new publishing venture, neither of us realised that the Convention would be as big an event as it turned out to be.

The result is a book that is also a good deal bigger and more ambitious than either of us envisaged at the time. I have set out not just to chronicle the Convention, its unexpected twists and turns and the caprices of the conventionnels. I have also tried to explain and analyse this unique event in the broader context of a European Union that increasingly affects the lives of the citizens of its member states, old and new.

I hope this will give the book relevance that endures beyond the present Intergovernmental Conference. As I write, the IGC has been meeting somewhat inconclusively for just under a month with the aim of turning the Convention's draft into a constitutional treaty that all 25 members of the soon-to-be enlarged EU can accept.

Because I believe passionately that one of the Union's great failings is its inability to explain its purpose and its actions, I have tried to write a book that can reach out to the lay reader. I have taken my cue from the Convention's president, Valéry Giscard d'Estaing, who said he wanted the outcome of the Convention to be understandable to an educated teenager. As the book contains an annex with extracts from the constitutional treaty agreed by the Convention, the reader will be able to judge how far we have succeeded in our separate endeavours.

I have also tried to write a book that is ideologically neutral. This is no easy task when writing about the EU and I often thought how much easier my life would be if I were to tackle the themes of the Convention from an extreme europhile or eurosceptic or integrationist or non-integrationist viewpoint. Because it is so complex and bewildering, the EU invites commentaries from all manner of zealots who can run amok with the truth, confident that informed opinion lacks the resources for reasoned rebuttal. I will be content if this book and, for that matter, the constitutional treaty spread a little more understanding.

That said, neutral is not the same as neutered. I have views on the EU and it is only right that the reader knows my underlying position before embarking on this book. I consider myself a 'good European' but one who regrets many aspects of the European Union as it exists today. Having lived and worked during the past 35 years at different times in Britain, Germany and Belgium, and spent altogether roughly the same length of time in each of these countries, it probably could not be any other way. But in writing this book, my aim has been to put my opinions to one side. I have tried to treat the facts as sacred. I hope the judgements are measured. They are, however, my own.

A note on sources appears after this preface. At this point, however, I would like to thank John Willman, the Financial Times' chief leader writer, for graciously accepting the protracted absence of one of his writers; Jo Mulcaire of the FT's Brussels office for keeping me aware of events, and John and Carla Wyles for their unstinting hospitality during my frequent visits to Brussels.

Special thanks go to Valerie Polding, for her quiet professionalism while editing this book; to Peter Ludlow, for his support, encouragement and guidance, and to my wife, Janice, to whom this book is dedicated, for her support, encouragement and patience.

Peter Norman, London, 28 October 2003.

Note on Sources

The European Union's leaders decided at their summit in Laeken that the European Convention's discussions and all official documents would be in the public domain. As a result, much but by no means all of the material that has informed this work is readily accessible for readers who wish to discover more.

One of the first acts of the Convention secretariat was to set up an Internet site, http://european-convention.eu.int, which is a treasure trove of information. More than 850 documents were posted during its proceedings in a series labelled CONV. These include background notes of the secretariat and Praesidium, draft articles, the contributions of individual conventionnels, the various versions of the constitutional treaty and the final draft that was submitted to the Italian presidency of the EU on 18 July. Many of these documents are cited in the text of this book and acknowledged in footnotes. The site also carries material that informed the discussions in the Convention's working groups, the 6,000 or so amendments to draft articles that were submitted during the process of crafting the constitutional treaty between February and July 2003 and speeches, including several by the Convention President Valéry Giscard d'Estaing. Although the Convention is now over, the website will remain unchanged and open for consultation for at least five years. The archives of the Convention will also be deposited at the Secretariat of the Council.

Although I attended all plenary sessions of the Convention, apart from two extra one-day meetings in March 2003, I cannot pretend to have listened to or noted every word of the debates. But from April 2002, the European Parliament came to my aid, and doubtless to that of other researchers, by publishing verbatim accounts of the Convention's debates in the language used by the individual speakers. Some six months later, the Parliament began to produce summaries of the debates. Together these proved an invaluable checking tool. They can be read on http://www.europarl.eu.int/Europe2004 the Future of Europe page on the Parliament's website, under the heading 'Debates at the Convention'.

I also consulted on a less systematic basis the EU's 'Forum' and 'Futurum' websites and the websites of governments, foreign ministries, the European political party groups, broadcasting organisations and newspapers. I have included references to websites in the footnotes in cases where I am reasonably sure that they will be accessible for some time. A list of websites referred to in the text also follows this note. Where articles or interviews in newspapers have served as primary source material, they are acknowledged in footnotes.

Attending the Convention plenary sessions gave me access to the conventionnels, their assistants, other followers of the Convention, press conferences and briefings. While the documentary sources cited above provided the bones of the story, personal contacts on the margins of the Convention and elsewhere added the flesh.

The Convention press service was always helpful beyond the call of duty, particularly after my move from Brussels to London during the life of the Convention. I am greatly indebted to Nikolaus Meyer-Landrut and Christine Priol.

I owe special thanks to many people who cannot be named or more closely identified. Although the Convention was an exercise unique in its openness, many of the most interesting developments took place away from public scrutiny, in the Praesidium, in bilateral discussions among the protagonists and in national capitals. Such insights as I have gained into such developments, I owe to the help and candour of many people, some in the Convention and some elsewhere, who were kind enough to give me their time and their trust. A final acknowledgement and word of thanks must go to former colleagues in the Brussels press corps, who in the traditions of the place, were typically generous in sharing information during the 18 months and more of covering developments from the Laeken European Council to the Convention's final day.

Excerpts from the 'Draft Treaty establishing a Constitution for Europe' are reproduced in this book with the kind permission of the European Communities. The text is as published in the Official Journal of the European Union, 'Information and Notices' series, C 169 of 18 July 2003. Responsibility for the contents of the Draft Treaty establishing a Constitution for Europe lies entirely with the European Convention, an independent body which was set up to reflect on the future of Europe.

List of Websites

- http://european-convention.eu.int
  The European Convention.

- http://www.europarl.eu.int/Europe2004
  The European Parliament's 'Future of Europe' page.

- http://www.auswaertiges-amt.de
  The German foreign ministry website.

- http://www.elysee.fr
  The French President's website.

- http://www.premier.fgov.be
  The Belgian prime minister's website.

- http://www.number-10.gov.uk
  The UK prime minister's website.

- http://www.government.fi
  The Finnish government's website.

- http://www.d-s-f.net
  The French Socialist delegation in the European Parliament.

- http://europa.eu.int/futurum/comm/documents/penelope_en.htm
  The Penelope document.

- http://europa.eu.int/futurum
  The EU's 'Futurum' website.

- http//ue.eu.int
  The Council of Ministers website.

- http://www.fco.gov.uk
  The UK foreign office website.

- http://www.eu2003.gr
  The Greek presidency website.

- http://www.europa.eu.int
  The European Union's web portal through which its institutions, and policies may be accessed.

Part I

Europe at a Crossroads

CHAPTER 1
A New Way to Reform the Union

The tall, elderly gentleman was working the room. Elegant, in an immaculately tailored slate grey suit and sober maroon tie, he appeared unconscious of the video camera men who jostled around him.

But a light application of stage make-up showed that Valéry Giscard d'Estaing had prepared for a moment in history. The former President of France, voted out of office some 20 years before, was back – and in charge of a great experiment that could change the destiny of Europe.

The 76-year-old elder statesman was preparing to preside over the first constituent assembly of a continent uniting after a century of carnage and division. Around him in the packed plenary hall of the European Parliament in Brussels were another 206 members of a Convention that had been called to consider the future of the European Union and its relationship with 28 present and future member states.

No one knew, on that last day of February 2002, what the Convention would produce. Men and women from the 28 democracies were gathered in Brussels because the leaders of the European Union's member states had determined that Europe was 'at a cross roads.'[1] They wanted the Union to be more democratic, transparent and efficient and to this end had created a novel assembly of 105 full members and 102 alternates to ponder its constitutional future for more than a year.

The Convention was a first. Never before had the European Union been subject to such intense scrutiny from such a large and diverse group of people. The 'conventionnels,' as Giscard called them, were representatives of an area stretching from Finnish Lapland, north of the Arctic Circle, to the toe of Italy in the south, and from the Portuguese Azores islands far to the west of the European mainland to Turkey's eastern frontier with Iraq, close to the cradle of civilisation.

Never before had EU governments gone so far in sharing the tasks of plotting constitutional change as in the Convention. Hitherto, preparing

---

[1] The Lacken Declaration, December 2001.

reform of the EU was the jealously guarded preserve of member state administrations, whose ministers and senior officials negotiated behind closed doors in 'intergovernmental conferences'. For the first time, the representatives of national leaders would discuss proposals for change with national parliamentarians from the 15 present and 13 applicant states of the European Union and members of the European Parliament and the European Commission. The great majority of conventionnels were elected representatives of Europe's citizens with delegates from the 28 national parliaments making up more than half of their number.

The members of the Convention were to meet in unprecedentedly open conditions. Its plenary sessions were held in public and broadcast on the Union's satellite television channel. A vast number of documents were posted on the Internet. Inevitably, the Convention was not quite as open as many, including the author, would have liked. The discussions in the Praesidium, the 13 member body charged with pushing the Convention forward, took place behind closed doors and the minutes released since the Convention's close are – intentionally – not particularly illuminating. Published information gave only occasional insights into the negotiations in the back rooms and corridors away from the Convention hall, while Giscard and his aides sought to draw a veil over his bilateral talks with Union leaders in his travels around the capitals.

But compared with past intergovernmental conferences, the Convention was remarkably transparent. A counterpart to diversity and openness was unpredictability. When the Convention started, it was far from clear that it would discuss, let alone draft. In its early months, it was open whether it would result in a written constitution, a constitutional treaty, a series of treaty amendments or just recommendations. There were many, mainly concentrated in national capitals, who thought it would be no more than a high-level talking shop. There was a widespread expectation that it would, at best, come up with a series of options, which would allow the governments in the intergovernmental conference, or IGC, that would follow the Convention largely to ignore its results and carry on as before.

The Convention's chemistry was always volatile. Many of its turning points were unpredictable. This was as true on the eve of the Convention's final day in July 2003 as it was in February 2002, when – in an atmosphere rather like that on the first day at school – the conventionnels crowded into the debating chamber of the Parliament in Brussels and sat in alphabetical order to hear Giscard and European Union's leaders speak.

The first part of this book briefly describes the pressures for change that led to the decision to set up the Convention. The second part covers the period from the Nice and Laeken declarations, which gave the Convention its instructions, to the first outline 'skeleton' treaty produced by its Praesidium or steering body. The third part discusses the issues addressed by the Convention and the role of the working groups of Convention members, in so far as these shaped the 'building blocks' of the future constitutional treaty. The fourth part describes the period of changing dynamics in late 2002 and splits among member states in early 2003 that buffeted the Convention as it attempted to hammer out precise constitutional texts. The fifth part, the End Game, is a description and analysis of events in the Convention's final, frantic weeks, ending with an evaluation of the process and its outcome. The documentary annex contains the articles, with brief comments attached, of the first 'constitutional' part of the text that was handed over to the Italian presidency for negotiating among the member states of the soon to be enlarged Union of 25 nations. Also included in the annex are selected articles with comments from parts II, III and IV of the draft constitutional treaty and the controversial draft articles on the institutions which Giscard produced on 22 April 2003.

Knowing 'how' the European Union's draft constitutional treaty came about is crucial to understanding the 'what' of its contents. This book, written from the standpoint of an observer who followed the Convention from beginning to end, sets out to describe the process of 'how' and consider the 'what' of the constitutional treaty that the Convention produced. It is a tale of people and policies, but above all of the unexpected. That is why the book is called *The Accidental Constitution*.

CHAPTER 2
Pressure for Change

2.1 THE UNCERTAIN GIANT

The European Union entered the 21st century plagued by doubts. Viewed in the broad sweep of history, it was a huge success. In the fifty years since Robert Schuman, the French foreign minister, proposed the creation of a European Coal and Steel Community on 9 May 1950 it had brought peace and prosperity to countries previously hell bent on mutual destruction in two world wars. It had grown from six to 15 member states and was negotiating entry terms with another 12 candidates. Its changes of name reflected growing ambition, from the European Economic Community of 1957, through the European Communities of 1965 to the European Union of 1992. Internal borders between member states had disappeared throughout most of its area. It was the world's biggest trading entity. It aspired to a common foreign and security policy. Its common market acted as an engine to integration, involving ever more Union decisions in the lives of the citizens of its member states whether they liked it or not.

The Union had formidable and historic tasks in hand. Its prospective enlargement to include the former Communist countries of central and eastern Europe would put a line under the post-Second World War division of Europe by the Iron Curtain. The recognition, in addition, of Turkey as an applicant amounted to a promise to bridge ancient divisions that had split Europe since the fall of Constantinople to the Turks in 1453. Among the existing 15 member states, 12 were engaged in an unprecedented and bold experiment to create a single currency, the euro, without first achieving political union or harmonising their economic and fiscal policies. All 15 were committed to forging a single market for goods and services. The Lisbon European Council in March 2000 added the target of creating 'the most competitive and dynamic knowledge based economy in the world' by 2010.

Yet as the Union hatched ever greater ambitions and became ever more important in the lives of its citizens, it failed to develop its full potential on the world stage or find a place in peoples' hearts.

The Union's weak international profile partly reflected collateral damage from its two great projects of the 1990s: the euro and the single market. Both were motors of greater integration and intended to advance the EU. But they required large scale adjustment of rules, legislation and habits at the Union and national levels. The EU therefore looked inwards in the decade after the collapse of communism, when pressures mounted for it to play a bigger global role. The gap between the Union's economic strength and ambitions and its ability to project power outside its territory was cruelly exposed in the wars of the Yugoslav succession, where the resolution of conflict in Bosnia and Kosovo required US intervention. The Union began to address these deficiencies at its December 1999 European Council in Helsinki with plans for a 60,000 strong rapid reaction force. But the world did not stand still to let the EU catch up. The terrorist attacks on New York and Washington on 11 September 2001 and their effect in turning the US, the world's sole superpower, into a still more assertive force on the global stage, stepped up the challenges facing Europe as it tried to develop its foreign and defence policies.

The Union's rapport with Europe's citizens was weak. Voter participation in the June 1999 European Parliament elections dropped below 50 per cent for the first time. A Danish referendum on whether to join the euro in September 2000 and an Irish referendum in June 2001 on adjustments to the Union's governance in the Treaty of Nice resulted in damaging defeats for supporters of more integration. These setbacks were to continue, as when Sweden voted in September 2003 to stay out of the euro. In national politics, far right politicians such as Jörg Haider in Austria and Jean Marie le Pen in France made gains on platforms that included hostility to the Union. The regular meetings of member states' leaders in the European Council sometimes became an excuse for riots, stirred up by a small hard core of anarchist-inspired anti-globalisation protesters and hooligans. Eurobarometer surveys in spring 2000 and 2001 showed overall support for the EU in its 15 member states, dip below 50 per cent. The fractured relationship between Union and citizen was not helped by a sense of institutional malaise in Brussels. The mass resignation of the European Commission headed by Jacques Santer in March 1999 amid allegations of mismanagement, nepotism and fraud tainted the image of what headline writers called 'Brussels'.

Beneath the surface, the ideas of what constituted the Union were in flux and had been for some years. In the 1950s, the original six members had embarked on a federal project to create 'an ever closer union among the peoples of Europe.' This was swiftly balanced in the following decade by the vision, made flesh in France's president Charles de Gaulle, of a Europe anchored in the nation state. Very much the goal of the continental west-European post-war elite, federalism reached its provisional climax with agreement in the 1992 Maastricht Treaty to pool sovereignty over monetary policy and create the single currency. However, in that same treaty, the member states set political limits to integration elsewhere by placing the new areas of foreign and security policy and justice and home affairs in separate 'pillars', where they would decide actions by cooperating among themselves on an intergovernmental basis.[1]

This ambivalence towards integration continued through the 1990s as a younger generation of politicians in EU member states took over and began to question the 'top down' prescriptive approach towards the Union's development adopted by the European Community's founding fathers and the 1980s generation dominated by Germany's chancellor Helmut Kohl and French president Francois Mitterrand. Not that they rejected the Community out of hand. When it was found that the intergovernmental methods failed to deal with a sharp increase in the numbers of asylum seekers and illegal immigrants, the leaders decided at their June 1997 Amsterdam summit, gradually to bring these parts of the justice and home affairs pillar under the community umbrella. But the 'Community method' of conducting affairs through specially designed European institutions was only one of several ways forward. When the leaders met in Lisbon in March 2000 to relaunch the single market, they relied on an elaborate system of benchmarking national policies, dubbed the open method of coordination, to push the project ahead.

Little wonder, therefore, that the Union developed complex structures as it grew. It was far from being a classic federation. There was no central elected government or any great central bureaucracy, as in the US, to manage foreign policy, defence, justice or macroeconomic policy. These remained the responsibility of the member states. Instead, the Union was entrusted with exclusive competences in remarkably few areas and which reflected its origins as a 'common market' or 'European Economic Community'. These were competition rules in the internal market, a common commercial policy, the customs union, the conservation of fish stocks under the common fisheries policy and, from 1999, monetary policy for those member states which adopted the euro. In most areas of economic and political activity, the Union and the member states worked together, following many and varied rules that had been devised and modified over decades in the course of complex and frequently confused negotiations.

The differing levels of engagement of Union and member states were reflected in its institutional structure. There was an 'institutional triangle',

---

[1] These were the second and third pillars respectively, which became titles V and VI of the treaties of Maastricht, Amsterdam and Nice. The first pillar embraced the existing European Communities and detailed Community policies and institutions.

comprising a Commission of appointed officials, a Council of Ministers[2] with a secretariat which represented the member states and a directly elected European Parliament. These institutions secured the Union's objectives in the areas of pooled sovereignty that constituted the European Community. The Commission, representing the European interest, had the right to propose legislation. The Council, consisting of ministers from member states meeting in various different formations, and the Parliament, representing Europe's citizens, would approve, amend or reject the legislation in the process known as the 'Community method'. Also part of the Community structure were the Court of Justice which enforced Community law and the independent, Frankfurt-based European Central Bank running monetary policy.

Giving strategic direction to the three participants in the Union's 'institutional triangle' was the European Council of heads of state and government, which met at least twice a year and frequently more often. It was chaired by a different national leader every six months under a system of rotating presidencies that applied also to the Council of Ministers. The European Council grew greatly in importance as member states resorted increasingly to coordinated national policies to obtain their objectives in the Union rather than pool sovereignty using the Community method.

The Union's relatively simple architecture was greatly complicated from the beginning of the 1990s when its leaders decided to develop a common foreign and security policy and cross-border initiatives in justice and home affairs without pooling sovereignty in the traditional community manner. The result, summarised in the Treaty on Union agreed at Maastricht, was the creation of the two new intergovernmental pillars with their own decision-making practices alongside the traditional Community structure. Ironically, given its name, one of the main objectives of the Maastricht Treaty on Union was to keep the pillars apart.

The European Union was therefore a hybrid with two sources of political legitimacy: the Community and the member states with the citizen

---

[2] The Council of Ministers, as an institution, is easily confused with the European Council, mentioned in the next paragraph, and the Council of Europe, which is an intergovernmental body based in Strasbourg and which has nothing to do with the European Union. The references in this book to the Council of Ministers, the Council and the Council Secretariat identify the same institution, or elements of it, representing the Union's member states in the 'institutional triangle'. The European Council is defined as a separate institution in the constitutional treaty and is given its full title when it appears in this book. However, there are some quotations where the speaker says 'Council' when meaning 'European Council'. In these cases, either the word 'European' is inserted in parentheses or an effort has been made to put the quotation in a context that makes it clear the speaker is referring to the European Council.

represented in both. The inbuilt tension between those parts in which sovereignty was pooled and decisions reached through the Community method, and those parts in which the member states retained their sovereignty and cooperated on an intergovernmental basis spawned a quasi-religious divide among their adherents that at times was reminiscent of the divisions among the early Christians as described by Edward Gibbon in his *Decline and Fall of the Roman Empire*. Having grown a structure unlike any other in history, the European Union spent much of the 1990s trying to adjust it to make it work more effectively.

Complex negotiations aimed at changing or augmenting the Union's founding treaties became frequent. The Maastricht Treaty was followed after five years by the Treaty of Amsterdam which made modest progress, notably in extending citizens' rights and in prescribing the transfer of asylum and immigration policies to the community pillar. Just three months after the fall of the Santer Commission, the European Council in Cologne decided to reach out to citizens by bringing together the fundamental rights applicable at Union level into a Charter. This task, designed to give the Union a more human face, was entrusted to a novel body comprising government representatives, European and national parliamentarians plus one commissioner, which called itself a convention.

But important issues relating to the Union's institutions went unresolved and there was an unmistakeable sense that as far as reforming the Union was concerned, the law of diminishing returns had set in, just as it was facing the unprecedented challenge of enlarging to the east.

As the 21st century dawned, it became clear that the remedy in the planning stage – another intergovernmental conference of the member states that would be held in 2000 and conclude in Nice in December that year – lacked the breadth and ambition necessary to tackle the accumulation of challenges facing the Union. The IGC that culminated in the Nice Treaty of December 2000 had the narrow brief of tackling technocratic 'leftovers' from the previous attempt at revising the Union's founding treaties at the Amsterdam summit of June 1997.

The Nice negotiation had the laudable aim of avoiding a paralysis of decision making caused by institutional gridlock in an EU that was now set to grow to 25 or more member states. But the issues seemed paltry compared with the historic tasks the Union had taken on. The Nice agenda was all to do with the distribution and use of power among the member states as a preliminary for the enlargement to encompass the former communist states of eastern and central Europe and the Mediterranean island states of Malta and Cyprus. The main points of contention were the future size and composition of the European Commission, the weighting of member states' votes in the Council of Ministers and the possible extension of votes by qualified majority in place of unanimity. During the course of 2000, the member states added 'enhanced cooperation' to the list. Enhanced cooperation, by which a small number of member states could forge ahead with integration in specific areas of policy, was emblematic for the Nice agenda. It was a policy that was approved at Amsterdam, with a purpose that its title left unclear, that had never been used, and which stirred strong passions inside the Brussels beltway. It had zero resonance with voters in the Union.

Those politicians who listened to the people found Europe's voters were not necessarily hostile to the Union playing a bigger role in the world. Opinion polls testified to a growing appetite for European-wide solutions to tackle the ongoing problems reverberating after the collapse of Soviet Communism or the failure of distant states in an increasingly globalised world. When asked, voters in most member states wanted what the 2002 Spanish EU presidency defined as 'more Europe' to tackle problems that individual member states were no longer powerful enough to deal with or which had cross-border ramifications. Their concerns included aspects of foreign and defence policy and such intra-Union problems as cross-border organised crime or the movements of asylum seekers and illegal migrants, environmental disasters, food safety and, because epidemics had never respected national boundaries, the spread of diseases of humans and animals. It appeared early in 2000 that the ordinary voter had a better idea about the future demands on the Union than many politicians.

2.2   A NEW DEBATE ON EUROPE'S FUTURE

In was in this environment that Joschka Fischer, Germany's foreign minister, launched the debate on Europe's future through a speech at Humboldt University in Berlin on 12 May 2000.[3] Speaking, so he claimed, as a private individual, Fischer set out ideas to allow the Union to continue integrating while doubling its membership through enlargement. His prescription was to transform the EU from a union of states to a 'lean federation' which would be 'capable of action, fully sovereign yet based on self-confident nation states' and which citizens would understand. It would be a federation in which people would retain their national identities. The nation states would have 'a much larger role' than the states or *Länder* in the federal republic of Germany.

---

[3] 'From Confederacy to Federation: thoughts on the finality of European integration.' Available at http://www.auswaertiges-amt.de.

To achieve these goals, Fischer proposed a transition 'to full parliamentarisation as a European federation'. This would mean 'nothing less than a European Parliament and a European government which really do exercise legislative and executive power within the federation.' To avoid a strong centralised federation, he spoke of integrating Europe on the basis of a division of sovereignty between Europe and the nation state, drawing on the concept of subsidiarity[4] by which political decisions should be taken as closely to the citizen as possible. He thus proposed a second chamber of the European Parliament, which would contain elected members of national parliaments. He left open whether Europe's government should be developed from the intergovernmental European Council or the Commission, the agent of the Community approach, to which he would add a directly elected president 'with far-reaching executive powers'.

Fischer broached the idea of a constitution quite late in his speech and with the twin aims of securing democracy in the EU and distinguishing between what was to be regulated at the European level and what was still to be regulated at the national level. Europe, he said, would have to be 'established anew with a constitution' which would be centred around 'basic, human and civil rights, and equal division of powers between the European institutions and a precise delineation between European and nation-state level.' The division of sovereignty between the Union and nation states would be the 'main axis' for the European constitution. Fischer also pondered what might happen if not all countries wanted more integration. He suggested that a majority, or failing that, a small group of member states constituting an 'avant-garde' might want to push ahead with political integration, rather than face standstill by clinging to a federation of states. What ever happened, no European project would succeed 'without the closest Franco-German cooperation'.

Fischer's message came almost 50 years to the day after Schuman launched what would become the European Union. His speech was skilfully timed and, although hedged with ambiguities, lifted the debate on Europe's future to a new level. It provoked a wide range of responses, with two of the most significant coming from French president Jacques Chirac and Britain's prime minister Tony Blair.

It was also in Berlin that Jacques Chirac made his contribution to the budding debate on Europe. In the German Bundestag, during a state visit, just days[5] before the start of the French presidency, he looked beyond the

---

[4] Subsidiarity was first written into the 1992 Treaty of Maastricht but was rarely obeyed.
[5] 27 June 2000. This text is filed in the speeches section of the French President's website http://www.elysee.fr.

negotiation that would end in Nice in December to the 'first European constitution'.

Chirac's vision was less federal than Fischer's but the two were close on a large number of points. Chirac put stronger emphasis on the nation state and Europe's international role than Fischer, telling the German parliament that neither France nor Germany was 'envisaging the creation of a super European state which would supplant our national states and mark the end of their existence as players in international life'. According to Chirac, Europe's nations were 'the source of our identities and roots' and 'for the peoples who come after us, the nations will remain the first reference points'.

But he also wanted to see Europe 'as a world power' with strong institutions and an effective and legitimate decision-making mechanism, 'in which majority voting is the rule and which reflects the relative weight of the member states'. To ensure that Europe retained a capacity for greater integration after enlargement, he suggested that interested countries should forge a 'pioneer group' with Germany and France and, using the enhanced cooperation procedures agreed at Amsterdam, start in 2001 on improving economic policy coordination, strengthening defence and security policy and join together in fighting organised crime.

For Chirac, the Nice negotiation was just the beginning of a 'great transition' in which the Union would have to adjust to enlargement. He therefore suggested that immediately after the Nice summit, there should be a 'process' to address other important issues. It should look at reorganising the treaties to make them easier for people to understand; 'clearly define the division of responsibilities'; clarify the nature of the Charter of Fundamental Rights which, when he spoke, was being discussed in its specially created convention, and perhaps ponder the Union's ultimate geographical limits. Last but not least on Chirac's list of priorities came institutional adjustments to both the Union's executive and Parliament to strengthen the effectiveness and democratic control of the Union.

He proposed to prepare this new push for reform by way of an open discussion involving the member states' governments, the candidate countries and Europe's citizens through members of the European and national parliaments. Bringing the idea of a convention into the debate on Europe's future, Chirac added: 'There are several possible ways of organising, ranging from a committee of wise men to an approach modelled on the Convention which is drafting our Charter of Fundamental Rights.'

Tony Blair chose to outline his vision of Europe in Warsaw, capital of Poland, the biggest of the states negotiating to join the Union, and a memorial to a people's proud struggle to keep alive a national identity through more than two centuries of foreign oppression. Speaking just after the Danish 'no' vote, he was anxious to underline that Britain's future was 'as a leading partner in Europe'.[6]

On the federal-nation state spectrum, Blair was further towards the nation state vision of Europe than Chirac, but he was also adamant that Europe should be more than a free trade area.

> Europe is a Europe of free, independent sovereign nations who choose to pool that sovereignty in pursuit of their own interests and the common good, achieving more together than we can achieve alone. Europe will remain a unique combination of the intergovernmental and the supranational. Such a Europe can, in its economic and political strength, be a superpower – a superpower but not a superstate.

For Blair, the primary sources of democratic accountability in Europe were national parliaments and governments. On the other hand, Europe needed strong institutions such as an independent and strong Commission to protect smaller states and to allow Europe to overcome purely sectional interests.

Blair looked at the European reform agenda by asking the question: what do the people of Europe want and expect it to do? He outlined goals including completing the single market, reform of the common agricultural policy, fighting organised crime, obtaining a more coherent foreign policy, restoring full employment and protecting the environment and stopping Europe from interfering in what it should not do.

Blair's chosen instrument for promoting these aims was the European Council. This he said should set an annual agenda for the Union. The Commission, through its president, would play a role in this process and remain the independent guardian of the treaties. But 'we', meaning the European Council, 'would have clear political direction, a programme and a timetable by which all the institutions would be guided'.

Blair's government was open to reforming the way individual councils worked. He suggested team presidencies to give council leadership more continuity and weight, stressed how Javier Solana, the Union's high representative for foreign and security policy, should be able to play his full role in developing foreign and security policy, and cast doubt on whether the Union's six-month rotating presidency could survive enlargement. 'When

---

[6] On 6 October 2000. Speech to the Polish Stock Exchange available at http://www.number-10.gov.uk.

Europe is more than 25 members, can we seriously believe that a country will hold the presidency only every 12 or 13 years,' he asked.

He was sceptical whether a single constitution could emerge out of the Union's existing treaties and, invoking Britain's lack of a written constitution, invited other countries to realise that 'a constitutional debate must not necessarily end with a single, legally binding document called a constitution for an entity as dynamic as the EU'. But he did urge 'a statement of principles' to determine what would best be done at the European and national levels. Like Fischer, he called for a second chamber of the European Parliament, involving national parliamentarians. But it would have a controlling function. Its most important job would be to review the Union's work in the light of the statement of principles: in effect subjecting subsidiarity to political review. This, Blair said, would be preferable to judicial review of formal constitutional provisions through a European constitutional court.

Blair took a fairly relaxed view of enhanced cooperation providing the policies agreed by a smaller group of countries were open to the rest. It must not become 'a hard core' as suggested in the mid-1990s by senior German Christian Democrat politicians. Looking beyond the likely compromise of Nice, he warned that at some time the EU Commission would have to 'streamline considerably' because 'in the long run' a Commission of up to 30 members would be unworkable. Blair's government prided itself on 'joined up thinking'. His remarks in Warsaw amounted to an incipient, but not yet fully joined up, version of the UK's stance in the Convention.

These visions of European leaders broadly mirrored political conditions in their respective home countries. But while Europe's leaders were mulling over the Union's future, the negotiations leading up to Nice were going from bad to worse. In October 2000, about two months before their close, they were punctuated by a spectacularly bad tempered row between big and small member states at a special European Council meeting in Biarritz. The final conference of EU leaders in Nice was a gladiatorial cliffhanger of unusual bitterness that lasted four days and ended just before dawn on a December Monday morning.

Nice finally achieved messy compromises on the issues of the intergovernmental conference: the Commission's size, reweighting votes in the Council of Ministers, the allocation of seats in the European Parliament, the rules of enhanced cooperation and a limited extension of qualified majority voting in the Council to some 30 treaty articles where previously unanimity applied. Although Jacques Chirac, the summit host, closed the proceedings with a prediction that Nice would go down 'in the history books as one of the great summits because of the extent and complexity of the issues settled', the leaders recognised more would be needed. Blair spoke for nearly all the participants when he said: 'As far as Europe is concerned, we cannot do business like this in the future.'

Part II

The Convention:
From Conception to Skeleton

CHAPTER 3
Setting up the Convention

3.1 THE NICE AND LAEKEN AGENDAS FOR EUROPE

It was fortunate that before tempers really became frayed at Nice, the assembled EU leaders agreed a 'Declaration on the Future of the Union'. It called 'for a deeper and wider debate' about the EU's future development that would lead to a new intergovernmental conference (IGC) in 2004. They also proclaimed as a legally non-binding document, the EU Charter of Fundamental Rights that had been drawn up during 2000 by the EU's first ever Convention.

The debate was to address four important questions absent from the Nice agenda. These were:[1]

- 'How to establish and monitor a more precise delimitation of competences between the EU and the member states, reflecting the principle of subsidiarity.'
- 'The status of the Charter of Fundamental Rights of the EU proclaimed in Nice, in accordance with the conclusions of the European Council in Cologne.'[2]
- 'A simplification of the treaties with a view to making them clearer and better understood without changing their meaning.'
- 'The role of national parliaments in the European architecture.'

The agenda defined in Nice was a reaction to the debate on Europe's constitutional future triggered by Fischer's Humboldt University speech of May 2000 and picked up some of the points made later that year by Chirac and Blair. The declaration also took note of widespread disenchantment with the workings of the EU by identifying 'the need to improve and to monitor the democratic legitimacy and transparency of the Union and its institutions, to bring them closer to the citizens of the member states.' Although the four questions made no reference to a constitution, they would, if eventually transposed into the EU treaties, give the Union a governing architecture with

---

[1] Declaration on the future of the Union, http://europa.eu.int/futurum
[2] The Cologne summit of June 1999 decided to consolidate the fundamental rights applicable at Union level into a Charter and said that once proclaimed, it would 'have to be considered whether and, if so, how the Charter should be integrated into the treaties'.

many aspects of a constitution such as a bill of rights and a clear definition of who does what.

The competences question, or 'who does what' in Europe, was politically important in the light of a widespread feeling that faceless bureaucrats in Brussels were acquiring ever greater powers and usually by stealth. The wish to involve national parliaments more in EU affairs was the obverse side of this coin and linked to awareness that the European Parliament, by itself, could not plug the EU's widely perceived democratic deficit. Simplification of the treaties was a pure common sense, as anyone opening the existing 1,045 pages of jumbled and often incomprehensible articles, protocols and declarations could testify.[3]

That the Charter of Fundamental Rights should be placed back on the EU reform agenda at the same time as being proclaimed in Nice was a recognition that its newly established status was unsustainable. In Nice the Charter was proclaimed as a political declaration only because of British objections. The UK insisted it should not have legal status for fear that the social rights included among its 54 articles might become enforceable through UK courts. Germany, backed strongly by France, Italy and the Benelux countries, wanted the Charter incorporated into EU law as a bill of rights which would distinguish the Union as a community of values.

2001 was a year of definition in which two C words, 'constitution' and 'convention', gradually gained acceptance. Guy Verhofstadt, the restless, young Belgian prime minister and holder on the Union presidency in the second half of the year, played a key role in pushing forward the debate. A strong advocate of the Community method of decision making, Verhofstadt was at the same time the first Union leader to highlight the need for simpler and more transparent policy instruments.[4]

One year on from Nice, the European Council in Laeken agreed a declaration that combined soul-searching over where Europe had gone astray with a welter of possible remedies.[5] After 12 months of high-level speeches on Europe's future and several weeks of negotiation between Belgium and its EU partners, the four questions posed at Nice had ballooned to more than 50 detailed queries geared to improving the Union's institutions, its democratic life and working methods.

---

[3] *European Union: Selected instruments taken from the treaties.* Book I, Vol. I. Copyright European Communities, 1999.
[4] Speech to the 7th European Forum Wachau in Göttweig, Austria, 24 June 2001, filed among the speeches of the prime minister on http://www.premier.fgov.be.
[5] For a detailed account and analysis of the Laeken Council see Peter Ludlow, *The Laeken Council*, EuroComment, Brussels, 2002.

Europe, the Laeken declaration said, was 'at a cross roads.' It needed to become 'more democratic, more transparent and more efficient'. In doing so, it must resolve three basic challenges:

- How to bring citizens, and primarily the young, closer to the European design and the European institutions.
- How to organise politics and the European political area in an enlarged Union.
- How to develop the Union into a stabilising factor and a model in the new, multipolar world.[6]

To flesh out these challenges, the Laeken declaration added a mass of detail to the issues raised in the earlier declaration of Nice. The text was at times repetitive and confused and bore all the hallmarks of a difficult political compromise between proponents and opponents of greater integration. At various points it appeared to accept the need for greater activism at Union level as a given. 'How can we intensify cooperation in the field of social inclusion, the environment, health and food safety?' it cried, only to check itself in the following sentence by asking: 'But then, should not the day-to-day administration and implementation of the Union's policy be left more emphatically to the member states and, where their constitutions so provide, to the regions?'

However, it spelled out issues that were to be important for the Convention. It called for a better division and definition of competence in the EU, in particular between those exclusive to the Union, those of member states and those shared by the Union and member states. It asked whether there needed to be any reorganisation of competences, suggesting this could 'lead both to restoring tasks to the Member States and to assigning new missions to the Union'. It delved into the nitty-gritty, posing questions such as *whether* the EU should have a more integrated approach to police and criminal law cooperation and *how* it should develop a more coherent foreign and defence policy or improve economic policy coordination. It raised the question of simplifying the instruments used by the Union to implement its policies and asked, for example, whether there should be fewer ways of passing laws and whether to have a distinction between legislative and executive measures.

The declaration wondered how to increase the democratic legitimacy and transparency of the EU's three big institutions: the Commission, the Council and the European Parliament. Should the Commission president be elected, and if so by whom? Should Parliament be involved more in EU law making by extending cases where it has equal rights with the Council through the

---

[6] SN300/1/01 REV 1 Annex I.

process known as 'codecision'? Should citizens have better access to documents and should the Council of Ministers' meetings be in public, at least when making laws?

It looked at the possible future role of national parliaments, asking whether they should be represented in a new institution in Brussels or whether they should focus on policing subsidiarity.

When dealing with decision making and the EU institutions, Laeken went back over some of the ground covered at Nice and asked whether more decisions should be taken by qualified majority voting. It put a question mark against the Union's six-month rotating presidency and the role of the various Council formations. However, it made no reference to the Nice decisions on the future composition of the Commission and European Parliament or the complex sharing out of votes among present and future member states to determine a qualified majority in the Council, implying that one year on from Nice the leaders at Laeken wanted these questions left alone.

The issue of a constitution was raised with a notable degree of caution. The headline 'Towards a Constitution for European citizens' gave the clearest indication of where the text wanted to go. The following five paragraphs were less explicit.

Noting that the Union's objectives, powers and policy instruments were spread over four treaties (covering the Coal and Steel Community, the European Communities, Euratom and the European Union), the declaration asserted that simplification was essential to achieve greater transparency. It therefore wondered whether 'without changing their content' the distinction between the Union and the Communities should be reviewed.

It posed the question, 'What of the division into three pillars?' But it did not elaborate.

Picking up on preliminary work by the European University Institute in Florence, the declaration asked whether the treaties should be reorganised into a 'basic treaty', akin to a constitution, that would be separated from other, more technical, treaty provisions. This prompted the question whether the technical part should be subject to different, less rigorous, amendment and ratification procedures than those in force which required the ratification of each member state.

Developing an issue raised at Nice, the Laeken declaration asked whether the Charter should be incorporated into the basic treaty and whether the Union should accede to the European Convention on Human Rights.

When the Laeken declaration finally broached the issue of a constitution, it implied that this was something for the distant future. 'The question ultimately arises as to whether this simplification and reorganisation might not lead in the long run to the adoption of a constitutional text in the Union', it said. Then pondering its contents, it added in the haziest of terms: 'What might the basic features of such a constitution be? The values which the Union cherishes, the fundamental rights and obligations of its citizens, the relationship between member states in the Union?'

These questions, and any answers, were to be mulled over by a Convention. This would be made up of 'the main parties involved in the debate on the future of the Union'. It would start on 1 March 2002 and draw up a final document in preparation for the 2004 IGC agreed at Nice. The exact date of completion was a matter of some inexactitude reflecting a stand-off between Verhofstadt and the Italian prime minister Silvio Berlusconi.[7] In practice, however, the deadline was set for the summer European Council of the Greek presidency in June 2003.

The Convention would meet in Brussels. In marked contrast with the practice of IGCs, all its discussions and official documents would be in the public domain. For its final text, the Convention could either produce different options, or recommendations, if it were able to achieve a consensus. However, the leaders at Laeken made clear that the document would provide no more than a starting point for discussions in the IGC set for 2004, which would 'take the ultimate decisions'.

Nonetheless, Verhofstadt saw a vital role for the Convention. There must be 'no taboos'. It must address questions not normally asked by the member states in the Council of Ministers or their summits. It must consider fundamental reform of the treaties. Not all his fellow prime ministers were so enthusiastic. Jean-Claude Juncker, the Luxembourg prime minister, reported that some leaders had queried the need for a constitutional debate. He believed it was not necessary for the Convention to produce a detailed text and that there should be options. Juncker added that 'certain governments' would try to have as many options as possible to steer the IGC in the direction they desired.

Britain, a late convert to ideas of constitutions and conventions, said it would not stand in the way of the project, although it had reservations. 'If it is a question of clarifying a tangled web of treaties which are unintelligible, then we are up for that. But if it is a question of renegotiating some sort of

---

[7] See Ludlow, *The Laeken Council*, p. 71.

framework for a superstate, then No,' was how Peter Hain, Britain's minister for Europe, interpreted the message of Laeken.

3.2   THE CHOICE OF A CONVENTION

The decision to entrust preparation of the IGC to a Convention had emerged over the previous 12 months.

The Nice declaration was unclear about how to organise the debate on Europe's future. The Swedish and Belgian presidencies, 'in cooperation with the Commission and involving the European Parliament', were entrusted with encouraging 'wide ranging discussions with all interested parties' during 2001. The 'interested parties' were defined in a broad brush manner as 'representatives of national parliaments and all those reflecting public opinion; political economic and university circles, representatives of civil society, etc.' The sole element of innovation was that the candidate countries would 'be associated with this process in ways to be defined'. The aim was to agree a declaration at Laeken containing 'appropriate initiatives for the continuation of this process'.

Elsewhere, however, a Convention bandwagon had been gathering strength. The European Parliament in its resolution on the 1997 Amsterdam Treaty had registered its dissatisfaction with the IGC method of EU reform, saying future changes to the EU treaties should no longer be fashioned 'using the methods of classic diplomacy'. Reform, it said, should be driven by politics, with the European and member states' parliaments playing 'a full role in this respect'.

Politicians began to take up the idea of a convention to prepare Union reforms. Following Jacques Chirac's passing reference to the Charter convention in his speech to the German Bundestag in June 2000, Paavo Lipponen, Finland's prime minister, floated the idea[8] that a Convention should launch a 'constitutionalisation process' for the Union which would include the candidate states. Thereafter, similar proposals began to appear in speeches on Europe's future.

The Union's first ever convention, which in 2000 drew up the Charter of Fundamental Rights, was deemed a success – particularly when compared with the shambles that emerged at Nice from the IGC which preceded the summit.

---

[8] In a speech to the College of Europe in Bruges 10 November 2000, filed under EU Speeches on the Finnish government website, http://www.government.fi.

There was growing pressure during 2001 from the European Commission and the Parliament for a Convention to be set up. The UK, a long-term sceptic about its merits, accepted the idea during the summer.[9] Goaded on by Louis Michel, Belgium's foreign minister, the General Affairs Council agreed in October 2001 that a Convention should meet in 2002 to take forward the tasks set down at Nice and to be refined in Laeken. Its structure would be similar to the previous convention, which had agreed the Charter, with the important innovation that the candidate countries would participate.

Some vital decisions about the Convention were left for Laeken, however. The most important was who should be its chair.[10] Like all issues dealing with personalities and positions, the run-off for the post of Convention president was a telling reminder of the importance of national prestige and interests in the Union. By the time the leaders gathered there were two main candidates: Wim Kok, the widely supported and soon-to-retire prime minister of the Netherlands, and the former French president Valéry Giscard d'Estaing. To the surprise of many and the unconcealed dismay of Verhofstadt, Giscard was chosen. The odds on the summit appointing the septuagenarian elder statesman had been narrowing in the days ahead of the Laeken meeting.[11] But the clever tactics of President Chirac and the unwillingness of Kok to push himself forward clinched the deal.

Giscard's appointment was the first of many surprises that would characterise the history of the Convention. It had one very positive, unforeseen consequence. Acting on the spur of the moment, Verhofstadt decided Giscard should have two deputy chairmen and obtained the summit's agreement to appoint two men who had been members of the 'Laeken Group', a small, top-level team of advisers to the Belgian prime minister in the months ahead of the meeting. One of the two, Giuliano Amato, Italy's left of centre prime minister at the time of Nice, had also been a contender for the chairmanship of the Convention until Silvio Berlusconi, the centre-right incumbent in Rome, pulled back from supporting him. The other, Jean-Luc Dehaene, was Verhofstadt's predecessor as Belgian prime

---

[9] It was during a public debate in the General Affairs Council in Brussels on 16 July 2001 that Jack Straw, the UK foreign secretary, disclosed the UK government's acceptance of a Convention. He also tried to limit its scope, commenting: 'I think it is crucial that this Convention draws up only options and does not itself come down with prescriptions for what should be done because that would simply tend to confirm the view that our publics have that the institutions of the EU are dominated by people who want to tell the citizens of Europe what is good for them'.

[10] For a detailed account of how the choice was made, see Ludlow, *The Laeken Council*, pp. 68–70.

[11] The author, writing in the *Financial Times*, 14 December 2001, reported just ahead of the summit that the Convention presidency 'appeared to be heading towards' Giscard.

minister and, as a Christian Democrat, balanced Amato by coming from the centre-right.[12]

The leaders at Laeken then agreed the Convention would be composed of 15 representatives of the heads of state or government of the member states (one per member state), 30 members of national parliaments (two per member state), 16 members of the European Parliament and two Commission representatives.

The 13 candidate countries (including Turkey which was not yet negotiating membership) would be fully involved in the Convention's proceedings and represented in the same way as the member states with one government representative and two national parliament members each. The only restriction on the candidates was that they would be unable to prevent any consensus which might emerge among the member states.

The Convention would have a Praesidium composed of the chairman, the two vice-chairmen and nine members drawn from the Convention. The creation of the two vice-chairmen meant the Praesidium ended up bigger than originally planned. The nine would include representatives of Spain, Denmark and Greece, the three governments holding the six-month rotating presidency during the Convention's life. In addition, there would be two representatives each of the national parliaments, the European Parliament and the Commission.

The inclusion of two Commission representatives reflected another late decision that was to prove very beneficial to the work of the Convention. The Commission's representation was doubled from one to two. As a result, Romano Prodi, the Commission president, announced at Laeken that Antonio Vitorino, the Commissioner for Justice and Home Affairs, would join Michel Barnier, the Commissioner with the institutional reform portfolio, in the Convention and the Praesidium.

The Laeken declaration set out details for the first stages of the Convention's work. Its chairman would 'pave the way for the opening of the Convention's proceedings by drawing conclusions from the public debate', while the Praesidium would 'serve to lend impetus' and provide the Convention with an initial working basis. The Praesidium could consult Commission officials and experts on technical issues and given the go-ahead to set up ad hoc

---

[12] Dehaene's appointment had political ramifications inside Belgium. As far as European Union reform was concerned, it bound the opposition centre-right Christian parties to Verhofstadt's six party coalition of Flemish and Walloon Liberals, Socialists and Greens and ensured the Convention would not be a party political issue during the Belgian general election campaign of spring 2003.

working parties. It would be assisted by a Convention secretariat, which would be provided by the Council Secretariat, but which could include experts from the Commission and the Parliament. The Convention members would have alternates, to be designated in the same way as the full members. The Laeken text stipulated that members could only be replaced by alternates if they were not present.

There would be 13 observers: six representing the regions, six the Economic and Social Committee and the 'social partners', and the European Ombudsman. To continue the wider debate on Europe's future, there would be a Forum, representing civil society, defined as 'the social partners, the business world, non-governmental organisations, academia etc', which would receive regular information on the Convention and 'serve as an input to the debate'.

EU leaders would be kept informed of developments through oral progress reports from the Convention chairman at subsequent European Council meetings.

3.3 THE CONVENTION TRIUMVIRATE

Giscard was a controversial choice as chairman. The press immediately fastened on his age and his patrician ways and wondered if he was quite the man 'to bring citizens, and primarily the young' closer to Europe. Those with long memories recalled his injudicious acceptance of a gift of diamonds from the self-crowned 'Emperor' Jean-Bedel Bokassa of Central Africa that helped bring about his defeat by Francois Mitterrand in the French presidential election of 1981. Others suggested Giscard's nomination was a ruse by Chirac to remove a long-standing rival and potential critic from France's 2002 presidential election campaign. 'Chirac just wants him out of the way so he doesn't cause him trouble,' was the view of one senior minister from another member state.

But Giscard's credentials for presiding over the Convention were impressive. His spectacular and rapid rise to the pinnacle of French politics bore witness to a powerful intellect while his personal history gave him an emotional commitment to Europe. Although often branded as haughty, he could be extremely charming, particularly when talking to an attractive woman. While his tall slender frame, domed head and elegant suits signalled aristocratic aloofness, a pair of twinkly eyes indicated a lively sense of humour below the surface. Dismissive of those he considered his intellectual inferiors, Giscard could be a remarkably good listener, provided the speaker was making good sense. But as some members of the Convention would learn to their cost, Giscard was quick to spot and squash logical inconsistencies and verbal infelicities. A stickler for correct procedure, he displayed remarkable powers of concentration and stamina during the Convention's lengthy plenary sessions and expected the same from the conventionnels. Accustomed to exercising power, Giscard soon showed he could exercise authority over the 200 very different egos of the Convention members and their alternates.

In the weeks following his appointment, Giscard was to make frequent reference to America's 1787 Philadelphia Convention. His comments were a sign that he was doing his homework and looking back at historical precedents. They also gave him an opportunity to remind critics that Benjamin Franklin, one of the fathers of the US constitution, was 81 when the Philadelphia convention met.

Giscard was born on 2 February 1926 in Koblenz, Germany, the son of a French official in the French occupied Rhineland. He fought for France in the Second World War. Elected to the French National Assembly in 1956, he had been General de Gaulle's finance minister between 1962 and 1966, when he balanced the budget for the first time in 30 years. Blamed for causing a recession, he was sacked and went on to found his own right of centre party, the Républicains Indépendants. He returned to the finance ministry between 1969 and 1974 during the presidency of Georges Pompidou before going on to become the fifth republic's third President after winning the first of his contests with Mitterrand. When appointed to head the Convention, he was the last active member of that generation of European politicians whose support for European integration was rooted in their own experience of war. This alone guaranteed him a certain prestige among the 'conventionnels', as he called the Convention members.

His practical contributions to the European Union were also considerable. As French president between 1974 and 1981, Giscard, in partnership with West Germany's chancellor Helmut Schmidt, helped both to sustain the European Communities and promote European economic integration through the difficult years that followed the inflationary oil shock and recession of 1973. He was founder of the European Council, although it was unclear whether creating this exclusive 'club' of Union leaders gave him any extra leverage with the present members. He had also promoted the first direct elections to the European Parliament in 1979 and was an MEP between 1989 and 1993. With Schmidt, he founded the European Monetary System of semi-fixed exchange rates in the late 1970s, so starting the process of economic and monetary integration that culminated in the euro.

However, there were areas where his vision was more restricted, reflecting his fluctuating political fortunes at local, national and European levels after he descended from France's highest political office. He was not particularly interested in the Court of Justice or the European Central Bank. He was surprised, on meeting top businessmen a few months after the Convention started, to find that they regarded the Commission as a positive force that protected their interests in an integrated market rather than as an encroaching Brussels-based bureaucracy.

In the 1950s Giscard was influenced strongly by Jean Monnet, one of the founding fathers of today's EU. But by the time he was appointed to the Convention, his enthusiasm for a federal approach to Europe's future had waned. Early in 2002 he told the French daily *Le Monde* that neither a federal Europe nor the intergovernmental approach based on negotiation and cooperation among the member states would work in the soon to be enlarged Europe of more than 25 member states. The Union would instead develop as a hybrid, as a 'union of states with federal competences'.

Giscard had no blue print for reforming the Union. But he had a compass and he knew how to change course as circumstances dictated. As the founding father of the European Council, he was by experience and instinct more a Council than a Commission man. But he had concluded that the European Council in its existing format would not work with 28 member states, partly because of the problems posed by there being so many small member states in the enlarged Europe.

He took a dim view of the Commission and the ambition of its president, Romano Prodi, for it to be the 'government' of Europe. In a session with the European Parliament's constitutional affairs committee two months before Laeken, [13] Giscard recalled how the founding fathers of Europe had envisaged the Commission would turn into a European government. But in the 1970s, when he set up the European Council, Monnet had told him that this new body would be the future executive of Europe. Turning to the present, he argued that the European Council had a much clearer vocation to be the executive power in Europe. 'We would not be able to have a government with the present composition of the Commission,' he said.

In February 2002, before the Convention started, Giscard outlined two institutional priorities. He told Lamberto Dini, the former Italian prime minister and representative of the Italian senate on the Convention, that he wanted a stable presidency for the European Council and a smaller Commission. Around the same time, Giscard suggested in a conversation with MEPs that the Commission had served its purpose in establishing the single market. He made the same point to commissioners Vitorino and

---

[13] 10 October 2001.

Barnier at their first lunch together. When he returned to the Parliament's constitutional affairs committee at the end of March 2002, he was rather more diplomatic: he said the EU needed both the Commission and the Council with 'perhaps a more original cooperation between them'.

Twice prime minister of Italy and as such a veteran of Nice, Giuliano Amato was also a distinguished professor of constitutional law. Whereas Giscard oozed authority, Amato earned it through his knowledge, ingenuity and intellect. Amato had a subtle mind: indeed, it was so subtle that Tony Blair once told the British Labour Convention members that trying to work out what Amato stood for was like trying to follow a single strand from beginning to end in a dish of spaghetti. Aged 63 when the Convention began, Amato approached it as a pragmatic integrationist. In a response to Fischer's Humboldt speech, he had described the Union 'as still a bold joint venture between partner states: a Union which moves ahead by successive adjustments, combining integration and cooperation, common structures and classic intergovernmental compromises, standards to be achieved, authorities acting as umpires and mutual monitoring'. It summed up his undogmatic view of the Union.

Amato started work on the Convention with the advantage of having been in the 'Laeken Group' of Verhofstadt's advisers with Dehaene; Jacques Delors, the former Commission president; Bronislaw Geremek, a former Polish foreign minister, and David Miliband, a close aide of UK prime minister Tony Blair. A couple of months before Laeken, he had – with Dehaene – given his support to a manifesto of the EU establishment's great and good entitled 'Wake Up, Europe!' Among a *pot pourri* of ideas, it urged more qualified majority voting in the Council, the incorporation of the Charter of Fundamental Rights in the Treaty and linking the presidency and composition of the Commission to the results of European Parliament elections to boost the Commission's democratic credentials. Amato was keen to see national parliaments play a bigger role in EU affairs. But he was cautious as to whether the Convention would produce a constitution.

As a chairman of two working groups in the Convention, Amato was to find ways of solving two of the Union's most confusing constitutional conundrums. He made possible the creation of a single legal personality for the Union, getting rid of the three pillar structure in the process, and greatly simplified the Union's ultra-complex systems of legislating. He also became head of the Socialist 'political family' in the Convention. He was more successful in the Praesidium and Convention plenary than in his party role where some brute political power would have come in useful. During the Convention, the conventionnels belonging to the Party of European

Socialists (PES) were less disciplined than those of the Liberal and centre-right European People's Party caucuses.

Amato was feline. Giscard's other deputy, the 61-year-old Jean-Luc Dehaene, was a bulldozer of a man. Stocky, with a deal maker's rough and ready charm, Dehaene was Belgian prime minister and the country's pre-eminent political fixer from 1992 until 1999, when he lost office in a general election to Verhofstadt's 'rainbow' coalition of Liberals, Socialists and Greens after a spate of judicial, administrative and political scandals.

Dehaene was a keen federalist, who nonetheless always knew when to temper passion with pragmatism. He was in line for the presidency of the European Commission in 1994 until his candidacy was blocked by John Major, the UK prime minister at the time, who feared the Belgian was too federally inclined and too close to the German chancellor Helmut Kohl. One of Romano Prodi's first acts as Commission president was to appoint Dehaene, who had just lost power, to a three man high-level group to help him prepare for the negotiations that culminated in Nice summit. Dehaene added to his EU guru status by serving as Belgium's representative in the Charter convention and later as one of Verhofstadt's Laeken Group. One of Giscard's early decisions was to ask Dehaene to organise the 'forum' linking the Convention to civil society. As chairman of the working group on 'external action',[14] he was to make an important contribution to the draft constitution. His finest hour came in the Convention's closing weeks, when, thanks to his negotiation prowess, he ended a split in the Praesidium and restored it as an effective decision-making body. As the arch-federalist who knew when to accept a less than perfect deal, Dehaene pointed the way for others to embrace the final compromise.

Relations between Giscard, Amato and Dehaene were not easy at first. The three were very different personalities and Verhofstadt had contrived to foster suspicion among them. With the wry comment, 'He's well supported', Verhofstadt at Laeken had let slip that he saw the appointment of the two vice-chairmen as a way of circumscribing Giscard's power. It took time for reservations to die away, but when they did, the three proved to be a very effective team.

3.4   THE PRAESIDIUM FORMS

Michel Barnier and Antonio Vitorino, the Commission's conventionnels, were the two other Praesidium members confirmed at Laeken. Vitorino had

---

[14] Convention jargon for all aspects of foreign affairs except defence.

a fine legal brain and was to emerge as one of the Convention's key problem solvers. Fluent in several languages, his interventions in the plenary usually drew applause, even though sometimes listeners would be hard pressed afterwards to explain the point he was making. He had the important skill, in a body that was to operate by consensus, of knowing when to defer the resolution of a difficult issue to the point where it would gain general acceptance. Born in Lisbon in January 1957, Vitorino's politically formative period coincided with the dying years of the Salazar dictatorship and Portugal's 1974 Carnation Revolution. A socialist, he rose high in Portuguese politics to be deputy prime minister and defence minister before moving to Brussels in 1999 to take over the newly upgraded justice and home affairs portfolio in the Commission. His previous EU experience included five years at the European Parliament where he headed its civil liberties and internal affairs committee. Having been the Commission's representative in the earlier Charter convention, Vitorino was to take the chair of the Convention working group handling the Charter of Fundamental Rights.

Michel Barnier, the institutional affairs commissioner, was another veteran of Nice and had been French minister for Europe during the Amsterdam Treaty IGC. Born in January 1951, Barnier had built his political power base in the Savoie region of France in the Alps above Lake Geneva. This qualified him for his other Commission responsibilities in charge of regional policy. With the looks of a 1950s matinee idol – and often underestimated because of this – Barnier was never really part of the French European establishment. Unlike Giscard and many of the top French officials in European institutions, Barnier was not an *énarch*, a former student of the prestigious École Nationale d'Administration. His domestic political allegiance was to Chirac's brand of centre-right French politics, which also fostered certain coolness in his relations with Giscard. Nonetheless, Barnier turned down a senior French government post to stay in the Convention after Chirac's presidential election victory in 2002, and became an unexpectedly successful chair of the Convention working group on defence.

Both Commission representatives were to contribute significantly as individuals to the eventual success of the Convention. Their roles could have been more impressive had they been given coherent support by the rest of the college of Commissioners.

The next Praesidium members to be confirmed were those of the European Parliament. Because of a deal between the European Parliament's two big political families, the Spaniard Inigo Méndez de Vigo of the European People's Party, Parliament's biggest political group, and the German Social

Democrat Klaus Hänsch were widely tipped as the MEPs' representatives on the Praesidium even before the Laeken summit met.

Born in 1956, Méndez de Vigo was another politician whose formative years coincided with the end of dictatorship. But unlike Vitorino, Méndez de Vigo had built his career on the centre-right as a member of the Partido Popular of Spain's prime minister José Maria Aznar. A lawyer by training, Méndez de Vigo was charming, affable and ambitious and a prolific writer on EU affairs. He chaired the Parliament's delegation to the Charter convention and was to win his spurs early in Giscard's Convention as chairman of a working group that devised rules for the more effective application and control of subsidiarity, mainly by more closely involving national parliaments – an issue close to Aznar's heart. A skilful behind the scenes operator, Méndez de Vigo organised a discreet but influential dining club of 'movers and shakers' that would meet in the Brussels Hilton during each plenary session.

Hänsch, 63 when the Convention started, was a former president of the Parliament and the only German national in the Praesidium. It was his misfortune to chair one of the Convention's more difficult and therefore less successful working groups – that on economic governance. He nonetheless had his moments in the plenary. Ever inclined to see a glass half full rather than half empty, Hänsch was particularly useful for Giscard in rallying his fellow conventionnels behind the president's perception of consensus. His ability to sum up positively, powerfully and cogently some of the more crucial twists and turns as the Convention developed would elicit a muttered 'bravo' from Giscard high on the dais in the plenary hall. Both Hänsch and Méndez de Vigo were to come in for criticism from their fellow MEPs in the Convention as being too willing to succumb to Giscard's blandishments.

The three governments with places in the Praesidium opted for Brussels insiders. The result was a steering body including four MEPs, two commissioners and a former commissioner in its ranks and with an inherently integrationist bias.

Spain's prime minister José Maria Aznar chose MEP Ana Palacio, chair of the European Parliament's human rights and justice and home affairs committee, to be his representative. Palacio, who was 53 when appointed, had been a centre-right MEP since 1994 and was widely admired, not least because of the brave way in which she had seen off an attack of cancer earlier in the parliamentary session. She quickly became one of the Convention's most active and charismatic members. 'I'm really what the Convention is about,' she once said, 'taking different allegiances and making one project'. She proved so successful that in July 2002, Aznar appointed her foreign minister: a promotion that unfortunately meant she would have less time for the Convention and which prompted her to swap places with Alfonso Dastis, her alternate, in 2003. Although Spain was to suffer setbacks as the Convention's work developed, she remained an enthusiastic supporter of the Convention method of preparing EU reform. In particular, she praised its openness as a vital response to contemporary media democracy. The idea of changing EU treaties behind closed doors in an intergovernmental conference was 'a 19th century diplomatic approach unsuited to the 21st century'.

Denmark, which was to hold the rotating presidency in the second half of 2002, appointed Henning Christophersen, a former minister of finance and foreign affairs and a vice-president of the Commission between 1985 and 1995. The Praesidium's only Liberal, Christophersen was a Brussels-based consultant when, at age 62, he joined the Convention. He was given the unenviable task of trying to make sense of competences and came in for much criticism when he reported his conclusions, which left all confused except Christophersen himself. He was more effective later when addressing budgetary questions.

Greece's representative on the Praesidium was another MEP, George Katiforis. A stalwart of the Party of European Socialists in the Parliament, Katiforis had twice been head of the economic office of Andreas Papandreou, the Greek prime minister, before being elected to the Parliament in 1994. Katiforis, who was 66 when the Convention first met, had spent many years as an academic economist: an experience reflected in his often discursive interventions. His last major publication, *An Introduction to Marxist Economics* was published in 1989, which was unlucky timing as that year the Berlin Wall came down. Katiforis's good humour and interest in social affairs came to the fore when he chaired a working group on 'Social Europe' shortly before ceding his Praesidium place to George Papandreou, the Greek foreign minister and son of his former boss, in 2003.

The last Praesidium members to be named were those representing the diffuse, and initially badly organised, group of conventionnels from national parliaments.

Gisela Stuart, a British Labour MP, was one of two national parliamentarians elected to the Praesidium on 22 February by parliamentarians from the member states. The elevation of a British parliamentarian to the Praesidium had seemed likely ever since Verhofstadt, in a verbal *faux pas* at the end of the Laeken summit, had said David Miliband, his former adviser, could occupy the position. As it happened, Miliband did not join the Convention. But as one of the minority of women members, and German-born to boot, the 46-year-old Stuart appeared an ideal choice for an important role in the

Convention to the spin-oriented government in London. She symbolised the pro-European ideals of Tony Blair's New Labour party when she won the English constituency of Birmingham Edgbaston in the 1997 landslide election victory from Dame Jill Knight, a fierce Conservative populist. A former junior health minister in Blair's government, Stuart brought a legal training to the task of representing the British House of Commons in the Convention. The Convention, she once confided, was simply 'the most important job I've ever done,' although at times it seemed more a chore than a pleasure. She was to chair a working group which made some modest suggestions on how to enhance the role of national parliaments in the Union. But, perhaps because she was so wedded to the ways of Westminster, she never properly came to represent the very diverse group of conventionnels from national parliaments.

Stuart's task in the early months was made no easier by the distractions of her right-of-centre stable mate John Bruton. As a member of the parliament in Dublin, the former Irish prime minister had to contend with a general election and looming referendum on the Nice Treaty at home. Once free of these preoccupations, Bruton, who was 54 at the start of the Convention, was to prove an effective member of the Praesidium. He was to chair a successful working group which prepared the way for the section of the draft constitution defining the Union's 'area of freedom, security and justice' – that area of policy dealing with asylum, immigration, police cooperation and the fight against internationally organised crime. His role was crucial in brokering the final Convention compromise over France's demands that a national veto should be retained over trade policies covering cultural and audio-visual services. Bruton would occasionally remind the Convention of its need to connect with the citizens and raise important – but hardly constitutional – issues such as the looming threat of global pandemics. This commendable effort, however, could not save him from falling into the same trap as Stuart and failing to represent sufficiently the concerns and enthusiasms of the group of the national parliamentarians to the triumvirate heading the Convention.

The 12 strong Praesidium defined in the Laeken declaration was expanded in April to 13, with the addition of Alojz Peterle, the representative of the Slovenian parliament. Peterle's appointment, first as a 'guest' and eventually as a full member, followed heavy lobbying by the candidate countries which complained that they had no one in the Convention's decision-making body. Peterle, who was 53 when the Convention started, had risen from a poverty stricken childhood to hold office as Slovenia's first democratically elected prime minister between 1990 and 1992. As the representatives of the candidate countries decided not to form a distinct group in the Convention, Peterle's power base in the Praesidium was even more nebulous than those of its other two national parliamentarians. Politically, he was part of the EPP caucus, where he found a mentor in Méndez de Vigo.

3.5   BUILDING THE SECRETARIAT

Throughout January, Giscard was searching for someone to head the Convention secretariat. He later said that everyone he asked told him to take the best person available. He found his man in Sir John Kerr, who was named secretary general on 24 January, a month before his 60th birthday and just days after retiring as head of the British foreign office.

Kerr was no stranger to the European Union. A resourceful man and a wily and tough negotiator, he performed the now legendary feat of hiding under the table when officials were banished from the conference room during the closing hours of the Maastricht summit, so that he could continue advising his prime minister John Major on the British opt-out from the single currency.

He was also used to surviving difficult situations over longer periods. He was Britain's permanent representative to the EU between 1990 and 1995, when London's relationship with its European partners came under increasing strain as Major's government succumbed to the power of the Conservative party's eurosceptics. Yet, perhaps because he was Scottish rather than English, Kerr always believed in the importance of a constructive UK approach to the EU. It was a policy that bore fruit in what he considered his finest hour: the December 1992 Edinburgh summit, where he engineered a deal which saved several billion pounds in British contributions to the EU budget over the following seven years.

Pierre de Boissieu, the deputy secretary general of the Council and a contemporary of Kerr as an ambassador to the EU, is credited with encouraging Giscard to appoint the British diplomat to the secretary general's post. De Boissieu, a formidable operator in his own right, learned to appreciate the capabilities of his British opposite number in the weekly meetings of Coreper, the committee of EU ambassadors where most important decisions were pre-cooked. The UK government also weighed in with strong support for his candidacy.

As the Convention's *eminence grise*, Kerr was seen and not heard. He would sit next to Giscard on the dais, whispering in his ear, writing pencilled notes to be passed to individual conventionnels, making, whenever possible, a show of interest in the remarks coming from the plenary hall, and occasionally slipping down into the plenary to cut a deal or negotiate away a perceived misunderstanding. To the inevitable charges that he was Blair's 'mole', Kerr would quietly reply that he was appointed to serve the Convention as a whole – a claim frequently validated in later months by expressions of frustration about his activities from British officials. He defined the secretariat's task as providing logistical support for Giscard, his deputies and the Praesidium, and drawing up documents. In the Convention's early months, these would synthesise the debate over Europe's future: later they would be the drafts, first preliminary and later refined, of the constitutional treaty.

Kerr was quickly ensconced, with a trademark ashtray at hand, in the functional, sparsely furnished offices provided by de Boissieu in the EU Council of Ministers building in Brussels. It was from there that he and Giscard recruited a team of eager and talented young lawyers to form the secretariat.

On the same day as Kerr's appointment was announced, Giscard named Walpurga Speckbacher, an Austrian economist who worked for the Council, to head his private office and organise the Convention meetings. Annalisa Giannella, an Italian-born defence and foreign affairs expert, was recruited from the Council to be Sir John's deputy. Another important early appointment was Nikolaus Meyer-Landrut as the Convention spokesman. Meyer-Landrut, a career diplomat from the German foreign ministry, had been a successful spokesman for the German permanent representation to the EU.

Giscard and Kerr picked the other 15 members of the secretariat. They represented a blend of talents from different backgrounds. There were lawyers, diplomats, administrators and academics of UK, German, French, Spanish, Portuguese, Swedish, Belgian, Dutch and Polish nationality. The Laeken declaration said the secretariat would be 'provided by the general secretariat of the Council' and 'may incorporate' experts from the Commission and the European Parliament. The Parliament and Commission each provided two members of the secretariat so that all three institutions were represented. But enthusiastic federalists were kept at bay.

It was Kerr's job to turn the recruits into a team. This he did by making them all sit round a table, two days a week, and discuss the successive versions of the draft analytical papers that fuelled the Convention's debates in its early months. The same technique was applied later when the secretariat began to prepare draft articles. The resulting brainstorming allowed Kerr to learn the individual strengths of the secretariat staffers, enabling him to allocate the right people to assist the various working groups. The secretariat members learned to work with each other, creating a team spirit that paid off as the pressure of work mounted.

The secretariat became the powerhouse of the Convention. Speaking shortly after the very last session of the Convention, Giscard paid a handsome tribute to Kerr, describing him as 'one of the most brilliant men I have ever met'. Typically, Kerr declined to respond.

3.6 THE CONVENTIONNELS

The Convention gradually constituted itself during the early weeks of 2002. It was a big enterprise. There were 105 full members (including Giscard and his two deputies) and 102 alternates, making it bigger than many parliaments. Because of the involvement of the candidate countries, it was larger than the previous EU convention that agreed the Charter of Fundamental Rights. It was much bigger than the Philadelphia Convention which agreed the US constitution in 1787.

Not only had the Union's national leaders been willing for the first time to involve others in mapping the EU's future, they had set up a body in which government representatives would be in a minority. Leaving the triumvirate at the top to one side, there were 56 national parliamentarians, 28 government representatives, 16 MEPs and two commissioners, with an alternate for each of these. Although far more broadly based than any previous body charged with reforming the Union, the final assembly was not representative of the EU's population. As Giscard was wont to lament, there were too few women. Although the government conventionnels of Sweden, Finland, Poland and (later) Latvia were women, their low representation at the Convention (17 women members and 23 female alternates) provided a poor advertisement for the EU's policies of equal rights and 'gender mainstreaming'. The Union's eurosceptics, who were a substantial force in the UK, Denmark and Sweden, were still less well represented. Led by Jens-Peter Bonde, a veteran Danish MEP, and David Heathcoat-Amory, a British Conservative member of the House of Commons, they numbered just four conventionnels and four alternates.

By contrast, the European Parliament's presence was bigger than its official contingent of 32 full members and alternates. Like Greece and Spain, Luxembourg chose to be represented by an MEP – its former prime minister and, later, Commission president Jacques Santer. Proinsias de Rossa, one of two Irish parliament representatives, was also an MEP when the Convention started.

There were other former national leaders besides Giscard, Amato, Dehaene, Bruton, Peterle and Santer. One of the most influential was Lamberto Dini, a former Italian prime minister who represented the Italian senate. Dini was to become one of the decisive figures in the frantic politicking of the

Convention's final months. By contrast, Lennart Meri, the former Estonian president and a national hero, was appointed to represent his country but failed to appear after April 2002. The Convention appearances of Mesut Yilmaz, Turkish prime minister from 1997 to 1999, were cut short by the 2002 election defeat of the Turkish Motherland Party.

Among serving ministers were Peter Hain, the British minister for Europe, and Pierre Moscovici, his French counterpart. Moscovici was to be replaced in November 2002 after the Socialists' defeat in the French Presidential and National Assembly election by Dominique de Villepin, the foreign minister. Hain stayed the course, despite promotion, first to be minister for the UK principality of Wales (which bizarrely was a position of cabinet rank in Britain unlike minister for Europe), and later to be leader of the House of Commons. Louis Michel, the Belgian foreign minister who played a big part in securing member states' acceptance of the Convention, was to be a spasmodic attendant, reflecting the pressure of work to which all foreign ministers were subject, and the growing demands of Belgium's 2003 general election.

Several governments appointed academics, reflecting in some cases a belief that the Convention would be little more than a talking shop. Finland was represented throughout by Teija Tiilikainen, an EU expert from Helsinki University. Until autumn 2002, Gerhard Schröder's representative was Peter Glotz, a thoughtful 62-year-old Social Democrat professor for media and societal studies at the Swiss University of St Gallen who had quit German politics in 1996. He was to be replaced by Joschka Fischer, Germany's foreign minister, in a move which signalled Berlin's realisation that the Convention was a serious business. Fischer's arrival prompted other countries, including France, Greece and Slovenia, to follow suit, turning the Convention into a body that no government could afford to ignore.

CHAPTER 4
Early Days

4.1   DIFFICULTIES AFTER LAEKEN

Many predicted at Laeken that the Convention would be little more than a talking shop that would rapidly sink from view. In the first months of 2002, it appeared more a forum for squabbling with a capacity to generate negative headlines.

In mid-January, reports began to circulate in Brussels that Giscard wanted paying for the job of chairman and expected the going rate: around €20,000 a month, similar to the gross income of Romano Prodi, the European Commission president. Also on his wish list were a luxury suite of rooms in a top Brussels hotel and a hand picked team of 10 to 12 people to help him perform his task. Officials tried to deny the stories. But Giscard's requirements had been put on paper and had provoked a shocked reaction among member states' ambassadors when discussed informally at a 'Coreper' lunch.

At first sight, Giscard's requests seemed like pure greed. Here was a man who had not only pushed himself forward for the job. He was well endowed with pensions and emoluments as a former President of France, deputy in the National Assembly and·president of the regional council of the Auvergne. Moreover, Roman Herzog, the president of the EU's previous convention on the Charter and a former President of Germany, had been happy to draw expenses only. Giscard's demands were a blow for Pierre de Boissieu. Despite an extremely tight budget, the Council's deputy secretary general had moved fast to create space for the Convention's staffers, clearing a floor in the Justus Lipsius building of the Council of Ministers for its use. It looked as if he had invited a cuckoo into the nest.

The issue was not quite as clear cut as Giscard's critics claimed. Although the Laeken declaration was full of all manner of suggestions and questions, it was silent on the issue of payment for the Convention president and his deputies. It was assumed that the other conventionnels would be paid by their respective institutions. But unlike Herzog, who had been appointed to the Charter convention by the German government and then elected its president by his peers, Giscard had been appointed by the summit to act in the interests of the Union, its members and the applicant countries. An international elder statesman like Giscard would clearly need bodyguards. He also needed to sleep somewhere in Brussels. This would cost money. Was it appropriate for him to carry these costs himself? Should France, the country that put him forward, foot the bill or would that not subvert his independence? If there was a risk of the latter, should not the EU foot the bill somehow?

The issue was closed after Giscard issued a statement from his office[1] in the French National Assembly, as deputy of Puy-de-Dome, acknowledging his work would be unpaid. Rather than deny the reports, Giscard said his only request was that the payments should be 'appropriate and in line with the norm of the European institutions' because he had wished 'to position the Convention at a good level vis-à-vis other institutions.' Coreper agreed and foreign ministers, meeting in the General Affairs Council of 28 January, confirmed that Giscard and his two deputies would be paid expenses but no salary. Giscard would receive €1,000 a day, which would be expected to cover his accommodation in Brussels and that of two bodyguards. Amato would receive €750 per day, while Dehaene, who was mayor of Vilvoorde, an industrial suburb of Brussels, would be entitled to €200 daily to reflect his lack of need for overnight accommodation.

The Council also agreed a €10.5 million budget for the Convention in the 10 months that it would meet in 2002. This was sharply lower than a total of €35 million estimated at one point by Council officials. Cash outlays were held down by the Brussels institutions, member states and the candidate countries supplying €6.5 million 'in kind', mainly in the form of meeting rooms in the European Parliament and Justus Lipsius buildings and seconded staff. The Laeken summit had agreed the Convention would work in all the EU's 11 working languages, thus necessitating substantial translation and interpreting facilities. The three big Union institutions agreed to stump up €4 million in cash, with €2.6 million coming from the Commission, €1 million from the Parliament and €400,000 from the Council Secretariat. From these funds, nearly €340,000 were earmarked for the travel and accommodation expenses of Giscard and his deputies; €150,000 to cover representational costs and €375,000 to meet the costs of the Convention secretariat.

Giscard's other demand was easier to solve. Although, as Convention president, he would later fend-off unwelcome requests from individual conventionnels by quoting the terms of the Laeken declaration to them, there was one detail he wanted changing quickly. Laeken said the Convention should start on 1 March, a Friday. Giscard reasoned – correctly – that he

---

[1] Dated 25 January 2002.

would get more media coverage if the launch were moved forward to 28 February. He lobbied Spain, the new holder of the EU's rotating presidency, which consulted its partners and, somewhat reluctantly, agreed.

The declaration needed clarification in one other respect. Not for the first time after a European Council, there was uncertainty over what exactly had been decided. Verhofstadt's decision to create the two vice-chairmen was so sudden that the first Dehaene knew about his appointment was half an hour before it was announced. In the days after the summit, others began to revisit the decision and query its implications.

Announcing the move to the press at Laeken, Verhofstadt gave the clear impression that Amato and Dehaene would be among the 15 members of the Convention representing the EU leaders. However, confusion emerged with the publication of the final summit conclusions. Those in English and most other languages stated that the member states' leaders would have 15 representatives in the Convention 'in addition to its chairman and vice-chairmen'. The Dutch version reflected Verhofstadt's verbal account of the decision.

This divergence became a source of friction when Italy's premier, Silvio Berlusconi, bid for his own representative on the Convention alongside the left-leaning Amato. His nomination of Gianfranco Fini, deputy prime minister and leader of the post-fascist National Alliance party, prompted the Netherlands, Sweden and Germany to insist the verbal agreement at Laeken was the true version of events. Berlusconi, in turn, made clear that if Italy were to have only one representative in the Convention, Amato would have to go.

In the event, the opposition to Fini fizzled out when the three objecting countries decided not to pursue the issue at the General Affairs Council of 28 January. For his part, Berlusconi, who took part in the GAC for the first time as Italy's interim foreign minister following the abrupt departure of Renato Ruggiero from the Italian cabinet earlier that month, adopted an uncharacteristically low profile. Fini, who believed Europe should develop into a federation of nation states, went on to be a distinguished representative of his prime minister and a model of moderation throughout the life of the Convention.

4.2   TEETHING TROUBLES IN THE CONVENTION

The Convention faced other problems, concerning the candidate countries and the drafting of its rules of procedure.

The candidate countries complained of being treated as second class citizens, because the Laeken declaration made no provision for documents or proceedings to be translated into their languages and gave them no place in the Praesidium. At Laeken, Verhofstadt had expressed the hope that the national parliamentarians would choose a representative for the Praesidium from the candidate countries. He was too optimistic. The candidates' representatives were not even invited to the 22 February meeting of the Convention members designated by national parliaments, which, in a party political carve-up between the EPP and PES, elected Bruton and Stuart as their representatives. The candidates raised their complaints before and during the Convention's opening ceremony. They were taken on board by the secretariat in March[2] with the result that the candidates elected Alojz Peterle to attend Praesidium meetings with permanent 'guest' status. The secretariat recruited a staff member from a candidate country (Poland) and arrangements were made so that any candidate country speaker could provide an interpreter to translate his or her remarks into an EU language for translation into the other official languages.

While Giscard was flexible in addressing the candidates' concerns, he was stubborn in the dispute over the Convention's rules of procedure. There had been an inkling of trouble to come at Verhofstadt's press conference in Laeken. Sitting in the front row was Andrew Duff, a British Liberal Democrat MEP who was an ardent federalist and, as head of the Liberal caucus, was to be one of the Convention's leading figures. Listening to Verhofstadt announce the 12 strong Praesidium, Duff forecast a 'busy Christmas' spent drafting rules of procedure to prevent the Praesidium being 'too strong' and 'all powerful'.

As Duff predicted, the first drafts of the rules of procedure[3] envisaged a very powerful Praesidium with the sole right to draw up agendas for the Convention and even more muscular Convention president.[4] According to the 27 February draft, Giscard would have great freedom to orchestrate the Convention sessions: 'In particular, he shall arrange the order in which items are to be taken, determine the length of discussion on each item, decide who is to speak, and apportion and limit the length of each intervention'.

---

[2] CONV 10/02 and CONV 18/02.

[3] The difficult issues are still apparent in CONV 3/02 dated 27 February 2002, which brought the problems into the public domain on the Convention website after several weeks of drafting and discussion between designated Convention members and the secretariat.

[4] During 2002, the titles president and vice-president gradually supplanted the terms chairman and vice-chairman used in the English version of the Laeken text and will be used henceforth in this account of the Convention.

Giscard was also determined not to have the decisions of the Convention subject to votes and insisting that the alternates should play a very limited role in the Convention's proceedings. Duff, by contrast, wanted votes to settle procedural disputes and 'indicative votes' or straw polls to assess the levels of support for individual options should the Convention result in several different options.[5] During February he bombarded Hänsch and Méndez de Vigo with letters and draft rules to put to the Praesidium. In alliance with the Danish eurosceptic Bonde, he was also campaigning against proposals that would, in many cases, have excluded alternates from being able to address the Convention. One early draft, prepared on 21 February, had proposed that an alternate should only participate in a session of the Convention when the full member was absent and on condition that the member had advised the secretariat two days in advance.

Giscard's antipathy to the alternates partly reflected concern that the full Convention members would be less than diligent in attending the plenary sessions, and so fail to develop the necessary *esprit de corps*, if the alternates were practically their equivalents. But the secretariat's proposal was offensive on several counts. It imposed impossibly rigid rules, given the uncertainties and consequent need for flexibility in the lives of politicians. It would also have posed real problems for representatives of national parliaments with more than one chamber and some of the smaller political families, whose representation at the Convention was limited to an alternate only.

The British parliament, for example, had decided that its two full members of the Convention should come from the House of Commons and their alternates from the House of Lords. Excessive restrictions on alternates would have meant an inadequate participation in the Convention by the delegates from the House of Lords, a chamber with a high level of constitutional expertise. In the case of Sir Neil MacCormick MEP, an authority on legal and political theory and the only Scottish Nationalist Party member in the Convention, the proposed rules would have left him unable to do his job. He was the alternate of Johannes Voggenhuber, an Austrian Green MEP, who came from a different party with somewhat different interests. If the early draft proposals were applied, MacCormick would have been able to attend the Convention but unable to get across specific points of concern from a regional perspective, so long as Voggenhuber was in attendance.

---

[5] For example, Duff in a letter to Méndez de Vigo and Hänsch on 5 February 2002 and in a press statement with amendments to the Praesidium's seventh draft on 12 March 2002.

The disputes over the rules of procedure were not resolved by the opening of the Convention on 28 February. They rumbled on until the Praesidium produced revised proposals[6] on 14 March. These made clear that any member of the Convention could ask the Praesidium to add points to the draft agenda and limited somewhat the powers of the president to manage the plenary sessions. The revised rules continued to insist on consensus rather than votes. But alternates could be present in the hall and substituting for full members absent for the day – provided the member advised the secretariat by 9am that day.

The new proposals did not solve the alternates' problems in full, but offered hope of a compromise. The Praesidium's original proposals attracted much suspicion and no fewer than 347 amendments. By the time the issue came to the Convention floor in the 22 March plenary session, not only had Giscard made concessions, but most members were anxious to get on with the real business of the Convention. As Hänsch declared: 'The duty of the Convention is to draft a constitutional treaty, not rules of procedure.'

There was a tacit agreement between the Parliament representatives and Giscard that rules should be interpreted with some flexibility as the Convention bedded down. After an animated debate, Giscard uttered the two words *'Je constat',* which roughly translates as 'I determine that ...' before announcing there was a consensus. He declared the rules accepted and the squabbling subsided.

Although the wrangling appeared arcane, the row over the rules of procedure was an important episode. It showed to the Convention rank and file that Giscard could change his mind when presented with firmly presented and well argued counter proposals – an impression confirmed by his treatment of candidate country complaints. The compromise over the rules of the game also helped lift some of the mistrust with which the conventionnels viewed the Praesidium. The format and half the members of the Praesidium had been designated by heads of government. Yet it had served as the conduit for bringing the objections of the conventionnels to Giscard's attention.

As for Giscard, he came away from the dispute with a vitally important prize. The Convention had accepted that its decisions would be established by consensus and not by votes. Giscard had made clear in January that he would not accept voting, because the Convention did not reflect European demography and its component parts were of such different orders of magnitude that it would be impossible to devise a weighted system of votes to deal with the problem. On the other hand, consensus was a wonderfully

---

[6] CONV 9/02.

vague concept and as long as it was Giscard who determined consensus in the Convention he had great power. Consensus was Giscard's secret weapon and he made sure it stayed under his control until the Convention's final day.

4.3   THE OPENING CEREMONY

The body which first met on 28 February was a bold departure from the previous tradition of EU institutional reform behind closed doors. The Convention opened in the plenary hall of the European Parliament building in Brussels, with its proceedings open to the public, broadcast live on EBS – the EU's satellite broadcaster – and carried on the Internet.

The grumbles and doubts of recent weeks were replaced by a bustle of excitement as the 105 members and 102 alternates came into the hall and found their seats, with conventionnels at the front and alternates behind. Then respectful silence as they sat through a ceremonial opening with speeches from José Maria Aznar, the Spanish prime minister and president in office of the European Council; Romano Prodi, Commission president and Pat Cox, the recently elected president of the European Parliament. The massed ranks of suits testified to the lack of women among the Convention's members. Sir Neil MacCormick, resplendent in his Maclaine and Lochbuie tartan, was a rare flash of colour amidst the grey.

Giscard took the floor last. For once, the Convention president did not mention Benjamin Franklin or the 1787 Philadelphia Convention. Instead Giscard launched the Convention with a speech that invited the conventionnels to 'dream of Europe'.

He was both inclusive and emotional. After beginning with 'Ladies and Gentlemen' in the 11 official languages of the Union, and adding the Polish 'Szanowni Panstwo', he offered the Convention members a stark choice between the 'yawning abyss of failure' or the 'gate to success'. Failure would see what had been created in Europe over the previous 50 years 'reach its limit and be threatened with dislocation'. If the Convention failed, 'each country would return to the free trade system. None of us – not even the largest of us – would have the power to take on the giants of the world. We would then remain locked in on ourselves, grimly analysing the causes of our decline and fall.'

Success, 'if we agree to propose a concept of the European Union, which matches our continental dimension and the requirements of the 21st century', would allow the conventionnels 'to leave here and return home, whether you are Italo-European, Anglo-European, Polish-European – or any of the others

– with the feeling of having contributed, modestly but effectively, to writing a new chapter in the history of Europe'. Europe needed to overcome its shortcomings in its own interests and those of the world.

> If we succeed, in 25 years or 50 years – the distance separating us from the Treaty of Rome – Europe's role in the world will have changed. It will be respected and listened to, not only as the economic power it already is, but as a political power which will talk on equal terms to the greatest powers on our planet, either existing or future, and will have the means to act to affirm its values, ensure its security and play an active role in international peace keeping.

Giscard mapped out three phases for the Convention's work. First would be a phase 'of open, attentive listening' when the Convention would ponder what Europeans wanted of the Union at the start of the 21st century. The second 'study' phase would examine the questions raised at Laeken, the organization of European institutions resulting from the Treaty of Nice and the various ideas put forward for the future of Europe. He cited three: the plans for a Europe along federal lines put forward by Fischer and other German politicians; the ideas of the European Commission for modernizing the Community method, and the various solutions, from Chirac and Blair among others for a federation of nation states, 'whether or not they involve the creation of a second chamber'. Only after this examination would the Convention, in its third phase, be able to draw up recommendations or a proposal for the IGC, scheduled for 2004.

He reminded the Convention that it was neither an IGC nor a parliament. It was a unique opportunity – 'the first occasion since the Messina Conference in 1955'[7] – with both the resources and time to examine in detail the future of the EU.

There was only one spontaneous burst of applause, when he urged the Convention to 'achieve a broad consensus on a single proposal' for a constitutional treaty 'which we could all present' to the IGC. Consensus, he said, would 'open the way towards a Constitution for Europe'.

In a schoolmasterly manner, he told the members of the Convention's four components they 'must not regard themselves simply as spokespersons for those who appointed them'. Each conventionnel 'must make his or her personal contribution to the work'. The Convention could not succeed if views remained entrenched. 'It needs to become the melting-pot in which, month by month, a common approach is worked out.' In short, it needed to create a 'Convention spirit'. Giscard sought to calm those who feared most

---

[7] Which paved the way for the EEC and Euratom treaties.

of the work would be carried out in the Praesidium. Declaring that 'for me, the Convention is the Convention', he explained that the Praesidium would prepare and organise the Convention's proceedings but 'everything else' would depend on the Convention members and their contributions.

It was a confident performance, executed with charm and energy and designed to allay many of the suspicions and doubts that had surfaced since the Laeken summit. He lavished compliments on the previous speakers, and slipped occasionally from French into heavily accented English and German. His remarks, while generating respect rather than excitement, showed he was determined to be a strong leader. He was ambitious, with a real determination to leave his mark on history, and not just for a few years, but for the first half of the 21st century at least. His aim for the Convention to 'achieve a broad consensus on a single proposal for reform' showed he would not accept a lowest common denominator outcome. Whereas the Laeken declaration included the possibility of the final document containing different options, Giscard wanted to present the IGC and subsequent European Council with a proposal that would be very difficult to turn down. And to back up this drive for consensus, Giscard had already in his own mind ruled out the idea of votes in the Convention.

He wanted to develop an *esprit de corps*. The conventionnels should think for themselves without always referring back to the political factions and power structures from which they were drawn. The year-long convention should not be the place for negotiations among member states or EU institutions. Unremarked at the time, his reference to rethinking the organization of European institutions resulting from the Treaty of Nice hinted at radical proposals to come.

4.4   THE LISTENING PHASE

Giscard had appealed in the opening ceremony for the conventionnels to show enthusiasm for their mission. They did. Their meetings in the European Parliament building in Brussels were well attended, unlike plenary sessions of the Parliament itself where there were usually rows of empty seats. Between 70 and 80 speakers would take the floor in each of the working sessions.

The conventionnels demonstrated a strong desire to get down to serious business. The first full working session on 21–22 March was a diffuse affair, in which Convention members, each allocated three minutes to speak, tried to answer the question 'What do you expect from the European Union?' By the time the Convention next met on 15–16 April, to debate the EU's 'missions' there was strong support for these to include a more effective Union foreign policy. The April and 23–24 May meetings tackled the difficult issue of competences. By its 6–7 June meeting, the Convention was discussing in very practical terms how better to provide justice and security in the Union in the face of problems such as cross-border organised crime and the role of national parliaments in the EU.

But there were problems. Some reflected the different levels of expertise among the conventionnels. The MEPs, playing on their own turf and steeped in the mysteries and jargon of the EU, were impatient with Giscard's insistence on a listening phase, and aware of the huge volume of work ahead wanted to get on with drafting texts. This created friction with some of the national parliamentarians who needed time to feel their way in unfamiliar surroundings and complained of being underresourced and underinformed. After their initial successes in securing recognition of their languages and representation in the Praesidium, the applicant countries' conventionnels made little impact for several months as their governments focused on the enlargement negotiations. The member states' representatives also tended to be reticent, with some notable exceptions such as Spain's Ana Palacio and Britain's Peter Hain.

The high British profile in the Convention was one of the more striking phenomena of its early months. Indeed, Hain's faithful attendance and assiduous lobbying of fellow Convention members, notably from the applicant countries, was such a feature of the early sessions as to provoke suspicious grumbles from some other national representatives. In the March session, Hain impressed many pro-integrationists when he stated that the Convention's task was 'nothing less than the creation of a new constitutional order for a new Europe'. However, this apparently open minded approach was coupled with a warning that Britons 'only want Europe to act when it genuinely has something extra to add'. But for many, the UK approach was still a refreshing change. It showed Blair's government had learned its lessons from the EU's fundamental rights convention of 2000 when it was out of sympathy with the proceedings and became isolated. Also indicative of Blair's interest in the Convention was the frequent presence among the advisers at the back of the plenary hall of Roger Liddle, the prime minister's EU adviser, who liaised closely with Gisela Stuart, the Labour parliamentarian in the Praesidium.

The Convention's early months saw its organisers try to reach a broader public through the Forum and a special Youth Convention. The Forum was meant to bring the views of 'civil society' into the Convention and spread the Convention's message to Europe's citizens. Accordingly, Dehaene had adopted a 'multidimensional' approach to the broadly based debate envisaged in the Laeken declaration. This entailed a 'structured dialogue' on the Internet, for which 160 organisations registered; the organisation of national Forums in each of the member states and candidate countries; special meetings with the observers from the Economic and Social Committee, the Committee of the Regions, the social partners and non-government organisations (NGOs) and debate at the level of the Convention itself. A hearing of civil society was set for 24–25 June and preceded by a series of preparatory meetings in eight contact groups, each chaired by a Praesidium member. On 24–25 June, representatives from eight categories of NGO spoke to the Convention. Perhaps it was unavoidable that the participation was heavily tilted towards organizations from inside the Brussels ring road, but this exposed the exercise to attacks from the eurosceptics. Looking back a year later, a Convention official described its efforts at consultation as a 'gallant failure', which pleased the lobbies but failed to get through to the general public.

Giscard also wanted to involve young people in the Convention and the future of Europe and proposed a special Youth Convention in his speech at the opening ceremony. Plans were made for 210 young persons (aged between 18 and 25) to come to Brussels between 9 and 12 July and a hold a Convention to be modelled as closely as possible on the Convention proper, although with no distinction in this case between full and alternate members. The conventionnels representing national parliaments and governments chose 168 Youth Convention members, the European parliamentarians 32, the Commission representatives four and Giscard and his two deputies two representatives each. The Convention members were asked to ensure an appropriate diversity as far as the sex; occupation and geographical background of the delegates were concerned. They complied in terms of gender, with the result that half the Youth Convention delegates were female. The Youth Convention members were invited to join the proper Convention for part of its meeting on 11 and 12 July and report their findings to the Convention proper.

'You are here to enlighten us. We need your fresh ideas and your freedom of thought,' Giscard told the Youth Convention's opening session. He was to be disappointed. The Youth Convention proved to be a far more acrimonious version of the senior Convention and even had its own mini-scandal when a candidate for the chair was found to be over 25. It agreed a strongly federal text (including the idea of a 'welfare Europe' with 'common legislation in the fields of social policy and equal opportunity'), which was supported by three-quarters of its delegates. A minority report, signed by 51 eurosceptic and disenchanted rank and file members, accused the Youth Convention of 'limited legitimacy' and said it had been conducted 'in a manner that was unrepresentative, undemocratic and too concerned with vested interest and political factions'.

The concerns were shared by some members of the grown up convention. Johannes Voggenhuber, an Austrian Convention member, complained that the Youth Convention was an assembly of young bureaucrats, 'many of whom were already practiced in the clichés, jargon and fixed ideas of the parties that sent them'. He had hoped, perhaps tongue in cheek, that it would be a forum 'where the young Spanish seamstress might confer with the Finnish electrician, where the Hungarian engineering student might meet the Irish social worker'. Instead the politics student from Paris met the politics student from Berlin. 'It is not European youth that has come to Brussels, but the future bureaucrats of the EU institutions.'

Whatever their failings, the hearings of civil society and the Youth Convention showed how the Convention was turning into a much bigger enterprise than expected. The numbers in and around the Convention hall grew from month to month, swollen by advisers and assistants making up the sophisticated support systems on hand for MEPs and government representatives. Adding to the buzz were officials, diplomats, journalists, lobbyists and members of the NGOs that made up 'civil society'.

This burgeoning activity obliged the members of the Convention to become enthusiastic networkers. Their plenary meetings – held on an afternoon and following morning, usually once and sometimes twice a month – would be only part of their activities. The mornings before each plenary session began early and were spent caucusing in various overlapping groups. The evenings would be filled with more networking and working dinners. The ballooning workload of Convention members put a premium on able assistants, who were soon forming networks of their own.

The political families were of crucial importance in providing structured links between the members of the various component groups and would usually meet early on the first day of a plenary session. Benefiting from their relatively small numbers, the Liberal Democrats organized quickly and developed a cohesive caucus, headed by Andrew Duff. The PES or socialist group, under Amato, was less easily organized, in part because a shambolic selection of PES representatives for the Convention's group of MEPs had resulted in the exclusion of some of the more talented PES constitutionalists, such as Richard Corbett, a British MEP and authority on the Parliament, from the Convention. By contrast, Elmar Brok, the long-serving German Christian Democrat MEP and Convention member, turned the centre-right EPP members of the Convention into a formidable block.

Other fora cut across party lines. The conventionnels met in groups of *composantes* – as representatives of the component governments, national parliamentarians and European Parliament, usually after the meetings of the political families before each plenary session. There were also meetings of national contingents, eurosceptics, working dinners of the small to medium sized member states and 'federalist breakfasts'. While the federalist breakfasts petered out, the 'Hilton dinners' were an enduring institution.

The Hilton dinners were organised by Méndez de Vigo, with the financial support of Pat Cox, the European Parliament president, and modelled on informal dinners that Méndez had arranged during the Charter convention. At Méndez's invitation, a group of 'movers and shakers' met on the 26th floor of the Brussels Hilton after the first day of each two day plenary session to test ideas on a totally informal basis across the traditional demarcation lines of political party and component group. There were no officials present. Regulars were Hain, Hänsch, Brok, Bruton, Dini, commissioners Barnier and Vitorino and Poland's Danuta Hübner. As the government representatives of France, Germany and Spain came and went, so the *placement* changed. Pierre Moscovici handed his place to Pascale Andréani[8]; Peter Glotz to Hans Martin Bury[9] and Ana Palacio (although staying in the Convention as an alternate) to Alfonso Dastis. Jacques Santer, for the Luxembourg government, attended occasionally; Jean-Luc Dehaene and the Netherlands' Gijs de Vries attended when institutional issues dominated the agenda towards the end of the Convention. Hannes Farnleitner, the Austrian conventionnel and one of the 'shop stewards' of the small member states, was invited once.

4.5   MOVERS AND SHAKERS

The Convention in its listening phase was dominated by a strong cohort of federal thinkers who emerged alongside the members of the Praesidium as its early movers and shakers. Most of them were MEPs, who had the advantage of operating in familiar surroundings and with familiar material. One key figure was Elmar Brok, the leader of the conventionnels of the European People's Party. The EPP had a problem in that the 55-year-old cigar-chomping Brok and Méndez de Vigo were rivals and this sometimes got in the way of efficient communication with each other. But Brok, a political protégé of former German chancellor Helmut Kohl with a girth to match, was a tireless and effective operator with sharp political judgement

---

[8] de Villepin's visits to the Convention were too brief to allow attendance at the Hilton dinners.
[9] Similarly, Joschka Fischer's attendances at the Convention were limited in time.

who welded the EPP's national parliamentarians and MEPs into a cohesive body. In the Convention's final months, Brok emerged as one of its key power brokers and deal-makers.

Also from the EPP, Alain Lamassoure, a French MEP and former close aide to Giscard, was a constant and thoughtful contributor to the debates. A one man ideas factory over the life of the Convention, Lamassoure, 58, played an important part in the early debates on who should do what in the EU as the author of an influential parliamentary report on delimiting competences between the Union and member states. When Giscard praised the report, people took note, and not just because Lamassoure was once the Convention president's speech writer.

Andrew Duff, the leader of the Liberal caucus, was as prolific a producer of ideas and proposals as Lamassoure. Duff was a rare combination of UK citizen and convinced federalist and was not afraid to provide the grit for the Convention's oyster. The 51-year-old Liberal Democrat MEP for the east of England was described by one admirer, 'a good little Socrates in the system'. Duff was so enthusiastically federalist that a UK diplomat was once heard proposing that he should be tried for treason. Duff had served in the Charter convention. Impatient with the protracted listening period, Duff was the first to start submitting his own draft constitutional treaty texts to the Praesidium.[10] Duff's star role in the Convention was the more remarkable because he had to struggle with a speech impediment.

Seated next to Duff was another conventionnel who enjoyed creating a stir. Olivier Duhamel, 51, a French Socialist MEP, was the Convention's 'blogger', producing an entertaining diary of its happenings on the World Wide Web.[11] In the plenary, he saw himself as a picador, whose job it was to goad Giscard into candour. When newspapers were full of reports of Tony Blair's plans to strengthen the European Council, it was Duhamel who challenged Giscard to define his position. 'Did the chairman believe in Blair or Barnier (the Commissioner for institutional affairs)?' he asked. 'Neither', came the reply, 'but a little bit of Duhamel'. The good humour underlying the exchange bore witness to historic ties between the two men that transcended age and party affiliations: Duhamel's father was once a political ally of Giscard.

The fully paid-up member of the Convention's awkward squad was Johannes Voggenhuber, the Austrian MEP and one of the few Greens in the Convention. Voggenhuber, 51, a keen federalist and outspoken critic of Giscard's manner and methods, was one of the very few conventionnels who

---

[10] CONV 22/02.
[11] Obtainable on Duhamel's page via http://www.d-s-f.net.

would openly take the president to task in a plenary session. Sometimes, however, he would lose control of his rhetoric, as when he once disparagingly compared the proceedings to an 'Italian bazaar'. Giscard showed his skill as a chairman by delivering a mild rebuke to Voggenhuber before immediately handing the floor to Lamberto Dini, the representative of the Italian senate. Dini, a former Italian prime minister and foreign minister, then fulfilled his patriotic duty by upbraiding Voggenhuber in the most outspoken terms, leaving the hapless Green temporarily isolated from his supporters.

At 70 Dini was of an older generation than most of the Convention's influential players. He had spent much of his life as a senior monetary official, first at the International Monetary Fund in Washington and later at the Bank of Italy. His was a late career move into politics. It came in 1994 when he was appointed Treasury minister in Berlusconi's first, short-lived, coalition government. In 1995–96 he was caretaker prime minister of Italy. Dini was elected a member of the Italian parliament in 1996 and served as foreign minister from 1996 until 2001 after which he became a member of the senate. A member of the Convention's Liberal caucus, he impressed in the early sessions with his thoughtful interventions while building up links with Duff and other conventionnels that would enable him to play a key role in the Convention's final stages. Dini, a supporter of greater integration, carried an iron fist in a velvet glove and knew how to pull the levers of power.

Erwin Teufel, 62, was another influential national parliamentarian. As prime minister of the south-west state of Baden-Württemberg, he was the senior representative in the Convention of Germany's opposition Christian Democrats and represented the Bundesrat, Germany's second chamber, where the CDU and their Christian Social allies from Bavaria held the majority. While German government approval would be a necessary condition for the Convention's success, it would not be sufficient: the Convention's conclusions would also need the support of Teufel and those he represented. This put Teufel in a strong political position. He also had a clear agenda as an advocate of a catalogue of competences. He represented a traditionally Catholic region and, like many in Germany's south-west, had close ties with France. He was Germany's cultural representative under the Franco-German partnership from 1995 to 1998. Giscard made a point of establishing and maintaining good relations with Teufel. One of Giscard's early keynote speeches outside Brussels was in Stuttgart, the capital of Baden-Württemberg in May 2002.[12]

---

[12] The speech, given on 5 May 2002, is filed in the speeches section of the Convention website.

One of Giscard's most frequent complaints was about the poor representation of women in the Convention. Anne Van Lancker, a Belgian MEP, compensated through hyperactivity. The 47-year-old Flemish Socialist was a tireless advocate of changes that would lead to a federal 'Social Europe'. Another problem was the relative lack of prominence of applicant country representatives, especially in contrast to the well informed and assertive phalanx of MEPs. Going some way to redress this imbalance was Danuta Hübner, state secretary for European integration in the Polish foreign ministry who represented the Polish government. A former academic, Hübner, 53, prized the Convention because it gave the applicant countries a sense of ownership in the soon to be enlarged EU. Wooed by the UK as a potential ally, she steered a middle course between the Convention's integrationists and intergovernmentalists stressing Poland's interest in a strong Union, with greater transparency and full respect for subsidiarity.

Britain's Peter Hain had the highest profile of the government representatives during the first half of the Convention. Hain, 51 when the Convention started, was a rising star in Blair's government. As minister for Europe, he was in his fourth government job since the election of 1997. Born in Nairobi, educated partly in South Africa and a notable campaigner against apartheid, he had a Commonwealth rather than an EU hinterland. But he was a fast learner, naturally outward going, willing to speak his own mind and (unusually for a government representative) at times prepared to indicate to the plenary that he might be willing to shift policy. He was rapidly on first name, back slapping terms with a large number of his fellow conventionnels. That was just as well. He had to work harder than most Convention members because the British government had much it wanted to protect. A significant cohort of Convention members calling for greater European engagement in social and economic affairs posed a threat to the UK position on the Charter as adopted at Nice. The UK was deeply suspicious of any moves to 'communitarise' foreign and defence policy. Hain also had to consider a sceptical public and largely hostile eurosceptic press at home.

The eurosceptics in the Convention were a very small group that had to make up for their lack of numbers by prominence in the plenary. They were led by the president of the 'Group for Europe of Democracies and Diversity', the 53-year-old Jens-Peter Bonde, a maverick Danish MEP since 1979 who was consequently well versed in the ways of Brussels. British Conservative David Heathcoat-Amory, 52 at the start of the Convention, was an articulate advocate of the need to boost the EU's democratic credentials. Ever ready to take away the punch bowl from the celebrations, he dismissed the two day June hearing of NGOs as a staged event in which many of the contributors represented lobbies supported by EU funds rather than society at large.

4.6   THE LISTENING PHASE: AN EVALUATION

The listening phase enabled the 105 Convention members and their 102 alternates to learn to work together – an important matter in such a diverse body. It also set down some important markers. It moved the debate about Europe's future very decisively in the direction of a constitutional treaty, to be based on just one proposal for reform. This goal was unclear before the Convention's start on 28 February.

The Convention rejected the idea of a strict catalogue of competences, as urged by the German *Länder* ahead of Nice, because of the inflexibility this would entail. But, as Giscard made clear when he reported to EU leaders at their June 2002 European Council in Seville, there was a consensus on the need to clarify who does what. The debates suggested the EU should focus on core issues with better policing of subsidiarity. The Convention discussed in some detail whether subsidiarity should be vetted before or after legislation was proposed and whether this task should fall to a political committee, possibly involving national parliaments, or a judicial body such as the Court of Justice. These discussions matured in plans for national parliaments to be more engaged in EU affairs.

While there was no strong demand for the Union to have new competences, the early debates uncovered a strong wish for a more effective common foreign and security policy (CFSP) and more effective ways of combating cross-border crime as well as support among some conventionnels for greater coordination of economic policies. The Convention was less clear in its early months over whether there should be more European involvement in social policy. Public services, culture, social security and – for the most part – education were areas where speakers generally wanted the member states to stay in charge.

Giscard himself highlighted the need for simplification, stressing that the Convention must produce proposals to reduce the mind boggling complexity of the Union's systems, procedures and treaty texts so these could be easily understood by its citizens. He considered that the abstruse nature of decision making was a major cause of popular disaffection with the Union. Things had reached the stage that experts no longer knew what was going on, let alone citizens.

The hearing of civil society in June revealed strong support among NGOs and conventionnels for incorporation of the Charter in the treaties. But as Dehaene made clear, there was little enthusiasm among the Convention's leaders for any rewriting of the Charter.

The Convention was far from revolutionary. And Giscard seemed determined to keep it that way by steering it towards incremental reforms that maintained the Union as a unique hybrid with both 'community' and intergovernmental characteristics. Yet while there was no sign it would spawn a European 'superstate', there were clear differences between those who wanted a more integrated or federal Europe and those who saw political control resting primarily with Europe's nation states.

The choice was brought to the fore through the contrasting visions of the British, French and Spanish governments on the one hand and the Commission on the other. The British and French wanted to strengthen the role of the member states through beefing up the European Council and the Council of Ministers and getting rid of the six-month rotating presidencies of the EU. The UK favoured a semi-permanent president of the European Council elected by member states. The Commission, in a document published in May, set out its case for a stronger 'Community method' of running the Union. It said the system used for single market legislation of having the Commission propose legislation, which was then amended by the Council of Ministers and European Parliament using majority voting, should be greatly extended, with some modifications, to foreign and economic policy. The Commission also wanted Javier Solana's post of EU high representative or foreign policy supremo brought into the Commission itself.

These opposing views would not be discussed in the Convention for many months. But they were among Giscard's preoccupations as he engaged in the less visible part of his job – that of consulting with the heads of government who had appointed him.

4.7 GISCARD'S BILATERAL DIPLOMACY

Giscard's bilateral contacts with Union leaders started early in January 2002 when he met José Maria Aznar, the holder of the EU's rotating presidency. Before the Convention's opening ceremony, he visited Silvio Berlusconi in Rome, Gerhard Schröder and Joschka Fischer in Berlin, Tony Blair in London, Wim Kok in The Hague and Göran Persson and Swedish parliamentarians in Stockholm. By the time of the June 2002 Seville summit, there had been follow up visits to Blair, Schröder and Aznar and two meetings with Romano Prodi, the Commission president.

There was a general perception that Giscard preferred to deal with the big member states. This was not strictly true. In the early months, he also conferred with Wolfgang Schüssel, the Austrian chancellor, and regional leaders including Teufel and Edmund Stoiber, the Bavarian prime minister

and German opposition contender for the chancellorship in the 2002 national
elections. But it was only in June 2002 that Giscard met Belgium's Guy
Verhofstadt, when the two men put the animosities of Laeken to one side.
Paavo Lipponen, the Finnish prime minister who had proposed the
Convention before Nice, had to wait until September for a visit to Helsinki –
a delay that rankled with the Finns.

The Danish presidency took Giscard to Copenhagen in early July 2002 while
he met Greek premier Costas Simitis four times in the run up to the hand
over of the constitutional treaty at the Thessaloniki summit of June 2003. He
had an audience with the Pope in late October 2002 and visited Luxembourg,
Poland, the Netherlands, the Czech Republic and Ireland during the six
months to the end of March 2003. Meetings with French prime minister
Jean-Pierre Raffarin or his foreign minister Dominique de Villepin became
quite frequent after the French right won the National Assembly and
presidential elections of 2002. There were further meetings with Schröder,
Fischer, Blair, Verhofstadt, Schüssel, Persson, Berlusconi, Prodi and
German opposition leaders before the Convention's end.

While the proceedings of the Convention were open to all, Giscard's
bilateral meetings were not transparent. There was no schedule of his
forthcoming talks on the website and no comment after the meetings.
However, it was clear that potential problem countries, such as the UK or
Austria, were high on his list of priorities.

Giscard's travels to the member states were geared towards securing
consistency between the outcome of the Convention and the expectations of
the governments that would eventually pass judgement on its work in the
2004 IGC. Some visits – to Spain, Denmark and Greece – were because
these countries held the EU presidency at the time. But there was also a
strong pedagogic aspect to his travels that flowed in two directions.
Institutional reform was on the Convention's agenda and Giscard needed in
particular to know leaders' views about the future of the European Council
and the Council of Ministers. In the early months, there was a need to brief
heads of government about the unfamiliar creature they had created in
Brussels while towards the Convention's close Giscard himself was anxious
to discern any 'red lines' which would prevent his interlocutors accepting a
compromise. In some cases, where he deemed it necessary to establish a
rapport with a key figure, the meetings would be restricted in a small group
with key advisers. This was the pattern of his visits to Blair, which took
place in the flat above 10 Downing Street and where, on the first such
occasion, Giscard nearly tripped over baby Leo Blair's toys. In other cases,
such as his visits to Finland, Luxembourg, the Netherlands and Ireland, he
would travel to a capital and make a point of meeting not just the country's

leader, but ministers, parliamentarians and the country's conventionnels on their own turf.

4.8   GISCARD'S EARLY PERFORMANCE

Giscard's performance had been better than many expected or feared by the time the listening phase ended after the summer of 2002. He had the advantage of starting from a low base, after the damaging publicity over his demands for a salary and luxury accommodation in Brussels. But in the Convention's plenary sessions, he proved an alert, attentive and firm chairman, who was nonetheless willing to accept innovation.

The election of Peterle to the Praesidium and the provision of translation facilities for the candidate country representatives pointed to some flexibility. His introduction of a 'blue card' scheme, by which members of the Convention could catch his eye and make short responses or pose questions, injected more life into the proceedings, which otherwise would have been dominated by set piece statements, and showed a commitment to making the Convention work. It was not easy for the conventionnels to extract concessions from him and there was much muttering about his performance in the corridors. But very little dissent crystallised in the Convention chamber itself. In fact, a lot of steam was blown-off in the preparatory meetings before the sessions.

Giscard had established his authority. In part, this reflected an instinct for power, exemplified by his approach to the rules of procedure, and in part, his enormous knowledge and experience of the Union. Another factor was the relative feebleness of the Praesidium – a weakness which he did little to counter as he built up the secretariat with Sir John Kerr.

A third factor was the clear will of most of the conventionnels to move ahead and make the Convention work. By July, the listening phase was coming to an end. Giscard had agreed in May that working groups of Convention members should be set up to tackle issues in greater detail. It was time for the Convention to move up a gear.

CHAPTER 5
Working Groups and Constitutions

5.1   SETTING UP THE WORKING GROUPS

During the summer of 2002, the Convention was in full transition from the listening to the study phase. One sign of the shift to the second stage was the Praesidium's decision in May to set up six working groups. This 'first wave' got down to business in June with the aim of reporting during the autumn. Plans for four others to meet later in the year were announced in July before the summer break.

Each working group was chaired by a member of the Praesidium and had up to 30 members. Of the six early working groups, five focused on constitutional issues while the sixth, on economic governance, was policy related. Three of the four 'second wave' working groups were policy related, covering justice and internal security, the EU's external relations and defence. A working group on simplifying the Union's legislative procedures rounded off the constitutional agenda. The second wave groups were asked to report in late November or early December. In November, a reluctant Giscard agreed to set up an additional policy related working group, on Social Europe, to report early in 2003. The working groups with details of their tasks, chairpersons and reports are summarised in Table 1.

The topics of the working groups generally reflected the conclusions drawn by Giscard and the secretariat from the early months of the Convention. Although the set tasks of the first five groups looked dry, the answers they were seeking could go some way to bridging the gap between the EU and its citizens, which emerged as one of the key concerns in the Convention's early sessions.

Of greater potential significance for public opinion were the groups dealing with big substantive issues where the EU was felt not to be meeting its citizens' expectations. These centred on demands for a more effective common foreign and security policy and more EU engagement in justice and home affairs. Tackling organised crime and trafficking in drugs and human beings emerged as important issues for both existing and future member states in the listening phase debates, with candidate country conventionnels advocating more effective policing of the EU's borders.

The groups were instructed not to draft articles. Their aim was to look at legal and technical issues and not to reach political conclusions. However, the assumptions behind the groups were highly political. For example, Vitorino in drawing up the mandate for the group on the Charter simply assumed that 'the major political questions' of whether the Charter should be incorporated or whether there should be accession to the ECHR would 'meet with a positive political response' in the Convention.

The secretariat's enthusiasm for the subject matter varied. The group on economic governance was set up against the better judgement of the secretariat in response to the wishes of many Convention members. Giscard and Kerr then fought a long rearguard action before conceding a working group on social policy.

Table 1: The working groups: their tasks, chairs and reports

Task	Chair	Report
Subsidiarity, including its more efficient application and control	Inigo Méndez de Vigo	CONV 286/02, 23 September 2002
The EU's Charter of Fundamental Rights and its incorporation into the treaties, plus the issue of EU membership of the European Convention on Human Rights	Antonio Vitorino	CONV 354/02, 22 October 2002
The EU's legal personality and whether a single legal personality would contribute to simplifying the treaties	Giuliano Amato	CONV 305/02, 1 October 2002
The role of national parliaments in the EU architecture, including studying best practice among parliaments	Gisela Stuart	CONV 353/02, 22 October 2002
Complementary competences or areas where the Union would support actions at national or regional level	Henning Christophersen	CONV 375/1/02, 4 November 2002

Economic governance and increased cooperation in economic and financial matters following the introduction of the euro and a more social Europe	Klaus Hänsch	CONV 357/02, 21 October 2002
External action, including achieving better consistency of policies, investigating whether community methods can be applied, reviewing the role of the high representative and achieving better external representation of the EU	Jean-Luc Dehaene	CONV 459/02, 16 December 2002
Defence, including tasks, capabilities, speeding up decisions, exploring the possibility of enhanced cooperation and improving arms procurement and R&D	Michel Barnier	CONV 461/02, 16 December 2002
Simplification of legislative procedures, including reduction of procedures, extending QMV in step with codecision, simplifying the EU budget process and giving legal instruments clearer names	Giuliano Amato	CONV 424/02, 29 November 2002
Freedom, security and justice, including improvements needed to treaties and instruments, improving judicial cooperation on criminal matters and adjusting treaty wording on asylum and immigration	John Bruton	CONV 426/02, 2 December 2002
Social Europe, including the possible modification of Union competences and reduced resort to unanimity in decision making	George Katiforis	CONV 516/1/03, 4 February 2003

With the working groups getting down to business, the Praesidium began in July to consider the outlines of the eventual constitution. The activities of the working groups and the Praesidium were to be linked. Amato described the job of the working groups as 'preparing the building blocks for the final product' and the subjects investigated by the first five working groups, as well as that on simplification, went far to sorting out issues that needed clarification before embarking on the detailed drafting of the constitutional treaty. But only two groups – those on subsidiarity and the Union's legal personality – reported by the time Giscard unveiled the first 'skeleton' constitution on 28 October.

5.2   THE PRAESIDIUM PONDERS CONSTITUTIONAL OPTIONS

The Praesidium's decision to consider the content and structure of a constitutional text partly reflected pressure from Convention members. In June a group, organised by Maria Berger, an Austrian MEP and alternate, signed a motion demanding that the Praesidium ask the European Commission to prepare a draft constitutional treaty for discussion by the Convention at its meeting scheduled for end-October.[1] Although signed by only 18 conventionnels, the request was considered by the Praesidium which decided unanimously not to take up the proposal 'since it would imply that the Convention would shirk its own responsibilities'.[2]

But there was still great uncertainty inside the steering group over what the Convention should aim for. Discussions in the Convention left unclear whether it should ultimately produce a 'basic' treaty, which was one option in the Laeken declaration, a constitutional treaty, as mooted by Giscard at the opening ceremony, or a fully-fledged constitution.

An internal email that was released by accident in July to the member states' permanent representations pointed to a *chapeau* solution by which the Convention would agree new texts for a first, constitutional, part of a new treaty which would be superimposed on the existing Union treaties. The document, while causing a stir, turned out to have no official status.

Sir John Kerr at this time was inclined to opt for a short, basic treaty, which would include the most important 'constitutional' elements of the existing treaties. In his view, the Convention should then sum up the remaining, more mundane contents of the existing texts as a set of principles which would be

---

[1] CONV 181/02.
[2] Summary of Conclusions: Praesidium meeting of 10 July 2002, filed under Praesidium documents on the Convention website.

handed to the legal services of the Union's institutions to be turned into treaty language after the Convention had disbanded.

Meanwhile, Hervé Bribosia, a secretariat member who had previously worked for the European University Institute in Florence, had produced a draft paper which examined the complexities of simplifying and merging the existing treaties.

At the beginning of August, Kerr visited Giscard at his main country home north of Tours in France to discuss the contents of a refined version of Bribosia's paper before heading for a holiday on the Atlantic coast. Giscard in turn went to Paris for a lunch with Amato and Dehaene, to bring them up to speed on developments. Kerr began drafting a text by the seaside.

After six revisions, a paper based on Bribosia's work contained the outlines of a basic treaty. After a preamble, the treaty would address such classic constitutional issues as the nature, structure and values of the Union; citizenship and the rights of Union citizens; the Union's general objectives; its institutions and decision-making procedures; and the Union's policies before rounding off with the final provisions, which appear in all EU treaties, and deal with such issues as accession of new members and revision procedures.

But the paper also suggested making the basic treaty part of a broader reorganisation and simplification of the two main EU treaties: the treaty establishing the European Community (TEC) and the Treaty on European Union (TEU). Texts not included in the basic treaty would comprise 'part two' of the restructured product. This approach, the paper argued, was preferable to producing a new basic treaty and simply superimposing it on the existing treaties without adapting them. A *chapeau* treaty of this type, with the old and new systems coexisting, could pose a threat to legal certainty and 'might well prove a permanent source of conflict'.

The paper was destined for the Praesidium. But it was sent to all Convention members in September when an official clicked the wrong email icon. Its substance was eventually published by the secretariat on the website.[3]

Giscard too had been busy gathering his thoughts over the summer and had emerged with about a dozen detailed proposals which were presented to the Praesidium. All this activity left the Praesidium less than enthused. Some members felt 'bounced' by the developments and were wary of some of Giscard's enthusiasms.

---

[3] CONV 250/02.

But when the Convention met after the summer on 12–13 September, Giscard felt able to report some progress. The Praesidium would present the structure of a constitutional treaty to the Convention during its 28–29 October meeting. His own preference was for a single text containing a constitutional section and a section on policies (part two), possibly to be supplemented by protocols – in other words, a more ambitious project than envisaged by Kerr in July. Whatever the form, it was imperative that the Convention's work should be understandable to intelligent secondary school pupils.

By the time he dropped these hints, Giscard had been scooped. There were other constitutional drafts on the market. But instead of being official documents from the Praesidium or the Convention secretariat, they were the work of MEPs.

5.3   FREELANCE CONSTITUTIONS

Duff, Brok and Lamassoure were also busy during the summer. Duff produced an outline constitution, Brok a full draft, while Lamassoure published a paper weighing the pros and cons of four possible models for running the EU. While Duff's outline was just seven pages long, Brok's draft ran to more than 90.

Although the papers were not destined for discussion by the Convention, they enjoyed first mover advantage, contained some novel ideas and therefore influenced the Convention's work. Indeed, Duff, who published his draft treaty just before the September Convention meeting, received a fulsome compliment from Giscard at the start of that plenary session.[4] Duff's text, the president said, was 'a very remarkable contribution' and he urged all conventionnels to read it.

Duff's draft, entitled 'A model constitution for a federal Union of Europe', was no blue print of a final Convention text. Unashamedly federal in content, it was unlikely to win many friends in the UK. But the Duff text had some interesting points, not least its structure. After a pithy preamble stressing the determination of the states and citizens of the EU 'to live together in justice, freedom and peace; uphold democracy, fundamental rights and the rule of law; respect their diverse cultures and organise their relations together', it consisted of just 19 articles.

Duff's draft was also innovative. It included giving member states a right of secession with those dropping out able to become associate member states.

---

[4] CONV 234/02, CONTRIB 82.

He also proposed a new 'organic law' at the top of a hierarchy of legislative acts for quasi constitutional matters. His Union would have a right to levy taxes and duties. Among its institutions was a 'Congress' of national and euro-parliamentarians numbering 1,400 that would meet to elect or impeach the president of the Commission. Parliament would be dissolved if the Commission were dismissed. A voteless Commission president would chair sessions of the Council of Ministers. The Commission would be limited to the president, a vice-president for foreign, security and defence matters and 13 other members. One article allowed the EU to establish armed forces with 'the capacity to undertake security and defence operations' with a remit going well beyond the existing 'Petersberg' crisis management tasks. An EU mutual defence guarantee would be covered in a protocol that would not have to be adopted by all member states.

Clearly there were parts of the Duff plan that would not fly. It was difficult to imagine member states in the IGC accepting that organic laws should be passed by a three-quarters majority of member states in the Council and an absolute majority of MEPs. The Congress – an idea that echoed one of Giscard's pet ideas – was huge, and evoked the great hall of the people in China rather than any known democratic European forum. But Duff had shown a constitution need not be vast and daunting.

By contrast, Brok's contribution was just that and Giscard gave it only a passing mention at the September plenary. It was crafted with an eye to the European People's Party Congress in Estoril near Lisbon on 17–18 October. Due to meet under the motto of 'A Constitution for a Strong Europe', the EPP was having problems clarifying its thoughts about the ideal European constitution. As a political family, it now contained leaders such as Aznar and Berlusconi among its members and was markedly less federalist than the body once dominated by Helmut Kohl, Brok's mentor.

The Brok document was long, partly because it included the Charter in full as the constitution's first part. It contained no fewer than 29 articles on the court of justice and 13 on the budget. And following the 90 pages of the Constitution, there would be five protocols putting down the edited provisions of the existing treaties on the common market, economic and monetary union, the common foreign and security policy, police and judicial cooperation in criminal matters and nuclear safety.

It contained some interesting elements. One article gave strong encouragement to nuclear power. It also advocated raising revenue for the EU from 'a uniform direct tax'. Institutionally, the Council of Ministers would form a 'house of states'. The Commission would have one national of each member state. The Commission president would be elected by the

European Parliament. It proposed the Convention be reconstituted for future changes to the treaties.

But the overwhelming impression was one of German *Grundlichkeit* or thoroughness that was unlikely to meet Giscard's desire for a constitution that the average secondary school child could take to heart. That was part of Brok's plan. One of his main reasons for commissioning an EPP draft was to have a 'quarry' of positions, ready for when the Convention was required to pronounce upon, and submit amendments to draft articles prepared by the Praesidium. The draft was therefore revised several times to reflect changes in the EPP's position. Brok's strategy paid off in the very effective way the EPP would later marshal its troops behind specific positions in the detailed discussions on the draft articles for the constitutional treaty.

Most of the freelance constitutions produced at this phase of the Convention were noted and forgotten. Brok's text endured because of its party political relevance and the increasingly clear preponderance of integrationist opinion in the Convention. Indicative of this integrationist tilt in the Convention's mood was the way a constitutional draft, which Peter Hain forwarded to the Convention in mid-October, sank without trace. The draft[5], by Alan Dashwood, a Cambridge law professor and former director of the Council's legal service, was, Hain said, 'a constitution for a Union of sovereign states, not a blue print for a federal superstate.' The text provided for a president of Europe, eliminated the reference to an 'ever closer Europe' and included an exit clause to allow member states to leave the Union under certain conditions.

Providing a perspective in between those of Brok and Dashwood, Lamassoure produced an elegant and refreshingly short contribution analysing 'four possible models' for the EU.[6] It covered just 14 pages. Recalling the poor public reception of the treaties of Maastricht and Nice, the French MEP underlined that the Convention's texts must be clear, the procedures straightforward, and the proposed institutions democratic. 'The Union will be democratic, or it will not survive.'

Lamassoure's contribution found problems with all four models he examined. A confederation in which the EU would be 'a cooperative of states' – would meet neither the needs of today's Europe nor the aspirations of the Convention, where, he asserted, 'no one has suggested any reduction in the level of integration.' Public opinion would not sustain a federal model – 'a united states of Europe.' He looked at the possibility of combining the two – with the Commission having executive power in internal policies and the

---

[5] CONV 345/1/02, REV 1.
[6] CONV 235/02, CONTRIB 83.

Council the last word in external relations, security and defence. This would be 'quite an attractive compromise formula for those in the know'. But there would be disadvantages, including permanent competition between the two executives, lack of public control over foreign policy decisions, and the absence of an arbitrator in cases of conflict.

Another compromise might lie in developing the existing Community model, while making clear that constituent authority and basic power lay in the member states. The EU would have an executive but no individual head of state – that role would reside collectively in the European Council. Lamassoure's enhanced Community model was designed to counter criticisms that the Union was developing into a superstate. Thus his scheme included the right of secession; continuing with a very small EU budget; keeping all national languages as official languages of the EU; reducing the Community authorities to 'specific and limited' functions, and a judicial authority that was 'a constitutional court, for resolving conflicts of jurisdiction, but not a supreme court responsible for unifying civil, criminal and administrative law throughout the Union.'

Common to all four models were:

- legislative power shared between the People's chamber (the present European Parliament) and the chamber of states (the Council of Ministers);
- majority voting in the Council – unavoidable because of enlargement;
- a European executive to define the common interest, make proposals, coordinate and monitor their application;
- reform of the Commission;
  He suggested vesting democratic legitimacy in the Commission, (by the European Parliament, electing its president, for example) even though this would change its character. 'That is the price to be paid for allowing Europe to be taken over by its citizens: those who run it must be brought within the range of its ballot papers'.
- a changed European Council;
  With 30 members, it would be as big as the general assembly of the League of Nations in the 1920s, and while such a body could provide ideas and general guidelines, it could 'no longer claim to be at the helm of the ship'.

Lamassoure concluded that a Union of 500 million citizens must have a powerful engine: a 'European executive, provided that it enjoys genuine popular legitimacy.' His paper thus defined the overriding challenge facing the Convention. But he provided no clear definition of where this executive power should lie – and no wonder. As the Nice Treaty negotiations demonstrated, issues of power were hugely divisive in the Union. For this reason, Giscard wanted to keep them off the Convention agenda until its closing months, when it was in its third 'proposals phase'.

5.4   GISCARD'S IDEAS

The big issues that Giscard wanted to keep off the agenda were already pretty clear. They were what should replace the existing rotating presidency; what was the future of the Commission and who should do the Union's external relations. But he was determined the Convention should not rush ahead to tackle such questions for fear it would shatter under the strain.

His view was that the Convention's components – the MEPs, member states, national parliamentarians, Commission, existing and applicant countries and big and small countries – must achieve greater cohesion before defining answers. He found an excuse for delay. Only after the working group on legal personality completed its report, would he know whether it would be possible to merge the European Union and European Communities treaties and rationalise the Union's legal instruments, which currently were under different pillars. Although it soon became clear to Amato, the group's chairman, that it would opt for a single legal personality, the report was not due until early October.

In public statements and comments to the Convention's plenary sessions, Giscard did, however, give some indication of how his thoughts were developing. In an important speech to the College of Europe in Bruges on 2 October, he elaborated on his idea of achieving a synthesis of the Community and intergovernmental methods of running the EU.[7] Referring to Jean Monnet, the father of the Community method, he said it was necessary to 'update Monnet' because the EU had reached a major turning point in its history. Enlargement would soon bring in up to 10 new member states. The EU also needed to 'think, readjust and – in part – reinvent the system' because it had begun to organise itself to act in areas going beyond the initial ambitions and powers of the Rome Treaty.

Economic integration, culminating in euro notes and coins, marked the 'completion of the founding Europe'. By contrast, the new policies, defined in the Maastricht Treaty and relating to foreign and defence policy and justice and internal security policy, were at the 'very core of our concept of the state'. Europe therefore must build 'a broader, coherent system around

---

[7] Filed in the speeches section of the Convention website.

the *acquis* of European integration and the three European institutions – the Council, the Parliament and the Commission'. At the same time as enlarging, the system must allow the member states to act effectively where cooperation was currently only in the early stages.

His use of the word 'cooperation' was significant. This was a mild-sounding code word for intergovernmental action, and specifically designed to take the sting out of the quasi-religious dispute which wracked the EU between advocates of the intergovernmental and Community methods of government. Drawing on the Convention's debates, he stressed that no single blue print was applicable to the EU. The member states would not apply the Community method 'to the full range of the CFSP, let alone defence', while 'even die hard intergovernmentalists' would not abandon the Community method for external trade policy. 'We need the best of both methods: each has its part to play.' The new and better Union would, he said, be 'a Union of European States closely coordinating their policies and administering certain common competences, along federal lines.'

In an interview with the *Financial Times* a few days later, he elaborated on who would do what in his future vision of Europe.[8] 'The driving force depends on the subject. It's the Commission in the clearly *communautaire* subjects, but it's the Council for all the big changes in the Union and for defence and foreign affairs.'

After outlining his philosophy, Giscard used the Bruges speech to trail some other ideas in public in the confident expectation that they would stimulate debate in the Convention and national capitals. What, he asked, should the new and better Union be called? The European Community; European Union; United Europe and United States of Europe were the options, he suggested. He took the question no further in Bruges. But in the FT interview, he suggested a preference for United Europe.

Giscard was using a favourite technique of 'wondering aloud.' He deployed it to give some impetus to his idea of a 'Congress of the Peoples of Europe' which should bring together members of the European Parliament and a 'proportional' number of national parliamentarians to review the state of the Union from time to time. It would have no legislative powers, he told the students at Bruges. Two days later, having made no mention of the Congress during the 3–4 October plenary session, Giscard hinted at his post-Convention press conference that the Congress could debate how a future Commission president might be elected.

---

[8] *Financial Times,* 7 October 2002.

Giscard thus emerged as a man who let his thoughts mature under public scrutiny in the hope that this process could shape views in the Convention. It was a method of operation that irritated and alienated many Convention members. But it moved debate forward as well as ensuring a steady flow of headlines.

5.5   DRAFT CONSTITUTIONS: GISCARD'S SKELETON

On 28 October, eight months to the day after the start of the Convention, its members received their personally addressed copies of a 'preliminary draft Constitutional Treaty.'[9]

Advance briefing – notably by Amato – had aimed at scaling down expectations. The Praesidium's draft would be 'no more than a skeleton', comprising a list of contents only. It was 'sure to disappoint' the exaggerated expectations of the media. In the event, the skeleton turned out to be a rather more substantial document than the Praesidium's news management techniques implied. This positive surprise was one reason it was well received. Hailing the draft as a 'significant step', Giscard explained to a packed plenary session that the text built on the broad consensus reached in the early October plenary in favour of a single legal personality for the EU. This opened the way for a merger of the EU and EC treaties in a single text, which in turn marked a 'fundamental step' towards the simplification of the treaties demanded by public opinion.

The skeleton had some eye-catching features. It floated the idea of a strong executive for the Union in the form of a stable president of the European Council; signalled that the Charter would be incorporated and included, for the first time, the right of secession from the Union. It comprised three parts. The first laid down the EU's constitutional and institutional architecture while the second dealt with the Union's policies and action. The third would consist of general clauses, covering such issues as territorial application, language regime and rules for ratification and revision, as well as the provisions normally found in constitutional acts to ensure continuity with past treaties.

The first part, comprising 10 titles with 46 articles, was outlined in some detail. This, Giscard said, should be 'especially clear and incisive', should have 'some power and even some lyricism' and be 'comprehensible to all'. The aim of the text was to create a more ordered framework for the Convention's discussions. Some of the provisions, Giscard stressed, were

---

[9] CONV 369/02.

derived from previous plenary debates. Others were proposals for debate. Some ideas made their way into the draft simply because they were pet ideas of the president.

Other articles, including optional proposals for Council presidencies, touched on issues that had not been raised in the Convention. A note in italics at the top of the draft text said the inclusion, or non-inclusion, of some articles in the first part and the exact content of others would depend on the future course of the Convention. Their treatment in the text was not intended to prejudge the result of the discussions.

After a preamble, 'title I' of part one set down in four articles the definition and objectives of the Union, the values and goals that brought the member states together and recognised the Union's single legal personality. Title I got the draft off to a headline grabbing start – for Britain's eurosceptic press, at least. The first article didn't duck the 'f' word: the EU would be 'a Union of European States which, while retaining their national identities, closely coordinate their policies at the European level and administer certain common competences on a federal basis'.

It offended some Convention members by failing to refer to the EU as a union of peoples. It also opened up the possibility for a change of name by mentioning 'European Community', 'United States of Europe' and 'United Europe' as possible alternatives to 'European Union'. The mere possibility of a name change helped secure the skeleton treaty a good deal of publicity, especially after Giscard indicated his preference for 'United Europe'. This name translated 'simply and strongly' in the different languages of the EU, he claimed.

Title II established and defined Union citizenship, stipulating that every citizen would enjoy 'dual' European and national citizenship and be free to 'use' either. A second article in this title incorporated the Charter of Fundamental Rights, although leaving details to be fixed in the light of the conclusions of the Charter working group.

Title III covered the Union's competence and actions in seven articles. It established the principle that any competence not conferred on the Union by the Constitution rested with the member states. It also stated in black and white that Union law enjoyed primacy in the exercise of competences conferred on the Union. Title III set out the principles of subsidiarity and proportionality, promised rules for their effective monitoring, and indicated the areas of exclusive Union competence, shared competence with the member states, and areas where the Union supported or coordinated action by the member states.

Title IV on the institutions also stirred controversy. Its observation that the Union 'has a single institutional structure' signalled an end to the second and third pillars with their different rules for common foreign and security policy and justice and home affairs, created in the Maastricht Treaty of European Union. It broached the issue of separate presidencies for the European Council and Council of Ministers well in advance of the discussion on such potentially divisive matters in the Convention. Outside the Convention, Britain, France and Spain had already proposed having a long-term president of the European Council to give the EU strategic direction. As was to become clear in later months, this 'ABC' idea (propagated by prime ministers Aznar and Blair and President Chirac) was to establish a dividing line in the debate on the institutional future of Europe as the Commission and some small member states construed it as a move to concentrate power in a 'directory' of big member states.

Title IV (comprising 10 articles and three optional articles) would allow the European Parliament to introduce a motion of censure on the activities of the Commission and would detail 'the procedure and consequences' of such a motion. It also raised the possibility of a Congress of the Peoples of Europe even though this pet idea of Giscard's was given a consistently unenthusiastic reception in the Convention itself.

Title V, setting out how to organise implementation of EU action, listed the various instruments and procedures available to the Union's institutions for exercising their competences. The nine articles also would include implementing procedures for common foreign and security and defence policies and conditions for undertaking enhanced cooperation – that is allowing certain member states to move ahead of others on specific policies – within the framework of the treaty.

Introducing a new title compared with previous treaties, title VI set outlined in five articles the principles of the democratic life of the Union, with emphasis on equality and transparency. The EU's institutions were to ensure a high level of openness, allowing citizens' organisations to play a full life in the Union. The Parliament would be elected by a uniform procedure of direct universal suffrage in all member states. The debates in the Council, when legislating, would be public.

In three articles, title VII would detail the rules for the EU's finances, including the principles that the EU budget should be fully financed by own resources and in balance. Title VIII, in article 41, would set out who represents the Union in international relations, leaving scope for the Convention to define the future role of the high representative for CFSP.

Title IX, article 42 was to define a privileged relationship between the EU and its neighbouring states.

In four articles, title X would set out the terms for EU membership, including the procedures for suspension should a member state violate the EU's principles and values. Article 46 would mention for the first time the possibility of voluntary withdrawal of a member state from the Union and the institutional consequences of withdrawal. Giscard said it was logical to include a right of secession because the Constitutional treaty would probably have an unlimited life. This provision attracted considerable media attention, even though an exit clause had featured in other draft constitutions, including the 'Dashwood constitution' and Duff's outline constitutional treaty of September.

While part one was explained in some detail, parts two and three of the skeleton simply listed headlines. The draft explained that part two, detailing Union policies and their implementation, would contain the legal bases and in each area specify the type of competence (outlined in title III of part one) and the acts and procedures (title V of part one) to be applied.

As internal EU policies, part two listed the internal market (free movement of persons and services and goods); economic and monetary policy; policies in 'other specific areas' (nine ranging from competition policy to research and development); internal security; and areas where the Union might take supporting action (employment, health, industry, culture and education). External action formed a second cluster of policies, and group together commercial policy, development cooperation, external aspects of internal policies, CSFP and conclusion of international agreements. Defence formed a separate category of policy. So too did institutional, procedural and budgetary provisions grouped under a general heading of the functioning of the Union.

According to Giscard, some 205 of the 414 articles making up the existing treaties would remain unchanged; 136 would be altered slightly while 73 would have to be substantially rewritten or regrouped.

5.6   THE SKELETON: REACTIONS

The skeleton received a strong initial welcome from the conventionnels of the European Parliament. Klaus Hänsch, one of the Praesidium's two MEPs, hailed it as a document of 'courageous realism' that identified the most important elements of the future EU. Duff, while regretting the absence of a reference to the people in the first article, nonetheless pronounced it a 'splendid basis' for future work. 'It allows for a radical re-foundation of the EU along explicitly federal lines – entrenching the community system, clarifying objectives and strengthening parliamentary democracy at the European level.'

Seeing the draft more as 'spinal column' than a skeleton, Michel Barnier for the Commission hailed the courageous step of proposing to restructure all the treaties at the historic moment when the Europe would become reunified through enlargement.

But there were also some words of caution. Rytis Martikonis, the Lithuanian government representative, stressed the need to maintain the Union's present political and legal nature. 'I would ask for the assurance that none of our discussions or decisions give the impression that the present architecture, principles or institutions are unimportant or indeed obsolete. That is very important to my country.'

Calling for a more integrated Union, Gijs de Vries, who had recently been appointed the Dutch government's representative, urged a strengthening of each of the main existing institutions while maintaining the institutional balance. In remarks echoed by other representatives of small member states, he asked: 'Do we really need new institutions, such as a fixed Presidency of the European Council and a new Assembly?'

Joschka Fischer, Germany's foreign minister, who had just replaced Peter Glotz as the German government representative, highlighted the importance of strengthening the Commission and European Parliament in the institutional triangle, and stated as a German objective the election of the Commission president by the Parliament.

Britain's Peter Hain managed to sound both enthusiastic and sceptical. The text was a 'good start' and 'an important step towards settling our constitution for a generation or more'. However, the final treaty would need an 'inspirational preamble' and to be as short as possible for the EU to reconnect with its citizens. Hain also took issue with the idea of changing the Union's name. 'The European Union is a successful brand name, a name we are all proud of.' The United State of Europe and United Europe were unacceptable. 'United States of Europe implies a superstate. United Europe looks to me like a football team.'

Giscard, however, was in no mood to let United Europe drop. He claimed that a debate on the name was justified because merging the treaties would leave the present EU technically without a name. Europe could not be called the European Community-Union. The Convention should think of what people might want in 10 or 20 years. They should consult the citizens and then make their choice. Giscard also disclosed that he had been thinking about a mission statement or slogan for the Union and had come up with 'liberty, justice and solidarity'. However, the Praesidium told him to leave slogans to one side for the time being and come back to the matter later.

Publication of the skeleton gave a palpable boost to the Convention's proceedings and structured the subsequent discussions. It defined the form of the eventual constitutional treaty, although this was to have four rather than three parts after the Convention decided that the Charter should be included in full as its part II.

The skeleton was felicitously timed – and that was thanks to pressure from rank and file conventionnels. Kerr originally wanted to delay production of an outline treaty until the start of 2003. Had that been the case, the story of the Convention and its constitutional treaty could have been very different. Unknown to Giscard, Commission President Romano Prodi had in July commissioned a small group of officials to produce a full draft treaty. The Commission document – code-named Penelope – appeared in December, and because of a bungled launch, never had the influence that the Commission president hoped or the draft deserved. Had Penelope pre-empted the skeleton, she would have dominated the subsequent debate.

Part III

Issues and Working Groups

CHAPTER 6
Broad Constitutional Questions

The skeleton proved an important turning point for the Convention. It mapped out clearly the route it had to follow and threw the issues that had arisen during the eight months since the Convention's launch into sharp relief. Some of these – but not all – were clarified by the efforts of the working groups which, reporting during the autumn of 2002, added flesh to the skeleton's bones.

The issues, although often overlapping, can be categorised in five groups: broad constitutional issues; competences and their implementation; new or expanding policy areas; improving conditions for democracy in the Union, and the Union's institutions.

6.1   A CONSTITUTION OR A CONSTITUTIONAL TREATY?

The skeleton helped clarify one of the major uncertainties surrounding the Convention by making clear that its goal was to draft a constitutional treaty. Giscard had muddled the terms constitution and constitutional treaty in his speech at the Convention's opening ceremony. Consensus on a single recommendation would 'open the way towards a Constitution for Europe', he declared, only to add: 'In order to avoid any disagreement over semantics, let us agree now to call it a 'constitutional treaty for Europe'.

The two terms – constitution and constitutional treaty – were bandied about without clear distinction throughout the life of the Convention. But when Giscard introduced the skeleton, he was punctilious in calling it a project for a 'constitutional treaty'. The final text, submitted to Silvio Berlusconi in Rome on 18 July 2003[1] was similarly entitled a 'Draft Treaty establishing a Constitution for Europe', albeit with the words 'Constitution for Europe' printed bigger and in bold.

The distinction was important because it reflected on the nature of the Union. A constitution implied a structure with independent sovereignty in the form of a self-sufficient source of political power and was thus the goal of federalists and keen integrationists. A constitutional treaty was agreed and

---

[1] CONV 850/03.

ratified by the member states which conferred powers on the Union. It was
therefore a goal that could appeal to conventionnels more rooted in the
nation state.

Drawing the distinction was not easy, however, because of the Union's
unique hybrid nature.[2] The EU was clearly not a state, lacking such attributes
as a large budget, the resources to implement Community law and the
traditional means of coercion in the shape of an army or police. But the
treaties went far beyond the normal parameters of international treaties. They
provided for institutions with substantial powers and established a rule of
law with a Court of Justice, which had established the primacy of Union law
from an early stage.

The skeleton promised many of the attributes of a constitution. It outlined a
first part that would detail the Union's values and objectives, a bill of rights
in the shape of the Union's Charter of Fundamental Rights, powerful
institutions, the division of powers and political procedures including
elements of accountability and democracy. It left unclear key issues that
needed to be defined if the final draft was really to be a constitutional treaty
rather than a constitution.

One issue was the conferral of powers. The skeleton never mentioned that
the member states conferred power on the Union. Its definition of the EU,
although pithy, failed to resolve the conundrum.[3] Instead, the outline of
article 7 specified Union action 'must be carried out in accordance with the
provisions of the treaty, within the limits of the competences conferred by
the treaty.' Article 8 then muddied the waters by referring to 'the principle
that any competence not conferred on the Union *by the Constitution* rests
with the member states'.[4]

Others crunch issues were the procedures for ratification and revision of the
eventual draft. The skeleton gave no details of what it called part three[5] the
'general and final provisions', which would include these procedures.
Although the reference to a constitutional *treaty* indicated that the
Convention's eventual text would, like previous EU treaties, have to be
ratified by all member states and, therefore, be endorsed by national

---

[2] For a deeper discussion of these issues see Jean-Claude Piris, Does the European Union
have a constitution? Does it need one? Harvard Jean Monnet Working Paper No. 5/00,
http://www.jeanmonnetprogram.org/papers/00/00501.html.
[3] In article 1 of the skeleton: 'A Union of European states which, while retaining their national
identities, closely coordinate their policies at the European level, and administer certain
common competences on a federal basis.'
[4] Author's italics.
[5] Part IV in texts from May 2003.

parliaments or referendums, this was not explicit and would have to be clarified by the Convention.

Future amendments were another area of importance for distinguishing between a constitution and a constitutional treaty. A normal feature of constitutions with independent sovereignty was inclusion of the power of amendment among their political procedures. The position as regards future amendments in the skeleton was unexplained and remained unclear until the Convention's end.

There was insufficient time to achieve a consensus before the June 2003 European Council in Thessaloniki and no mandate afterwards to finish what by then had become part IV of the constitutional treaty.

However, the Laeken declaration had asked, when pondering a distinction between a basic treaty and other treaty provisions, whether this could 'lead to a distinction between the amendment and ratification procedures for the basic treaty and other treaty provisions?' The idea of a 'softer' amendment procedure for the non-constitutional parts of the treaty was taken up by the Convention because of concern that it would be impossible in an enlarged Union of 25 nations or more to obtain unanimous agreement and ratification for any amendment, no matter how minor.

In the Convention's final days, Amato, Duff and Brok drafted an amendment[6] on behalf of their three political families to introduce a five-sixths majority of member states for future amendments of part III provisions where no shift of competences would take place. The part I constitutional part of the final text and part II comprising the Charter of Fundamental Rights would stay subject to unanimous agreement and ratification by member states. At one point, Giscard promised to draw the IGC's attention to the draft amendment. But once it became clear that the Convention, after Thessaloniki, had no mandate to change the revision procedures, the matter was allowed to drop.

This meant the final text as presented to the Italian presidency took over existing treaty provisions[7] which stipulated unanimous agreement and ratification by all member states 'in accordance with their respective constitutional requirements.' This wording was consistent with the final text being a constitutional treaty.

---

[6] CONV 833/03.
[7] TEU article 48.

6.2   THE UNION'S VALUES AND OBJECTIVES

The Convention's first task in its listening phase was to debate what was expected of the European Union and the missions it should undertake. The Union's values and objectives were important questions. Its values would set standards for membership. Its objectives would justify its existence to exercise certain powers at the European level and would therefore shape its constitutional identity. In this respect, the Union differed from a nation state where a constitution would exist by virtue of the state's existence to describe how the state should function. The way the Union's values and objectives were defined was also important if the Convention were to stay true to the goal of producing a constitutional treaty which would be easy to understand and so help bridge the gap between the Union and its citizens.

In the skeleton, the outline of article 2 set out as Union values: human dignity, fundamental rights, democracy, the rule of law, tolerance and respect for obligations and for international law. Giscard was at pains to draw a distinction between the values in article 2, which were based on those in article 6 of the Treaty on European Union, and those in the Union's Charter of Fundamental Rights. This was because the values in article 2 could be used to initiate procedures for sanctioning member states for 'serious breach' of the Union's principles and values under article 45 of the skeleton.[8] For this reason, the article had to concentrate on core essentials – a point taken on board by the Praesidium when it set about turning the skeleton into the constitutional treaty's first draft articles early in 2003.

Article 3 of the skeleton outlined 'general objectives' and listed just eight. These were:

- protection of the common values, interests and independence of the Union,
- promotion of economic and social cohesion,
- strengthening of the internal market, and of economic and monetary union,
- promotion of a high level of employment and a high degree of social protection,
- a high level of environmental protection,
- encouragement for technological and scientific progress,
- creation of an area of liberty, security and justice,
- development of a common foreign and security policy, and a common defence policy, to defend and promote the Union's values in the wider world.

---

[8] Corresponding to article 7 of TEU.

The idea was that article 3 should give general objectives rather than a vast laundry list of all the Union's policies. The treaty's second part,[9] which was presented in the skeleton in headline terms only, would appear later and present the objectives and their legal bases in far more detail than most constitutions. But because, when introducing the skeleton, Giscard stressed the important role that the objectives had in defining the Union, the conventionnels proposed a mass of additional objectives after the Praesidium presented its first draft articles three months later.

6.3 RELIGION AND THE CONSTITUTION

The skeleton was silent on the role, if any, of God in the constitutional treaty. But the issue of religion had surfaced in the debates on the Union's missions and values and was to prove a contentious subplot in the life of the Convention.

There were heated exchanges in the previous Charter convention over proposals to include a reference to Europe's religious heritage in the Charter's preamble.[10] Various factors conspired to make religion a big issue in the discussions on the constitutional treaty. One was the participation of strongly Catholic Poland in the Convention. Convention members from the German Christian Democrat and Christian Social parties, like their predecessors in the Charter convention, also considered the issue of key importance. There was extensive lobbying of the Convention from religious groups, especially during the hearing of NGOs in June 2002. The lobbying went to the highest levels, as Giscard found when he met Pope John Paul II in Rome three days after the publication of the skeleton. Earlier that month, the Pope had underlined the importance of Europe's Christian roots and God's role as the author of life, human dignity and human rights.

On the other hand, there were strong arguments against. Europe was not just home to Christians. It was home to millions of Muslims and members of other faiths. Concentrated among the Socialist, Liberal and Green political families, the supporters of the secular tradition in European politics were equally vocal and determined that God should have no place in the constitution. Giscard gave an indication of his own position in his speech to the Convention's opening ceremony. He painted a picture of European history in which religion, and more specifically Christianity, was notable by

---

[9] Part III from May 2003.

[10] The issue of whether religion should be mentioned in a reference to Europe's 'spiritual and moral heritage' was only solved by a translating sleight of hand by which the word religious was dropped from the phrase in 10 of the EU's languages while the German text said 'spiritual-religious [geistig-religiösen] and moral heritage'.

its absence. 'Let us not forget that from the ancient world of Greece and Rome until the age of the enlightenment our continent has made the fundamental contributions to humanity: reason, humanism and freedom', he declared. These sentiments were echoed more than a year later when he wrote the first draft of the constitutional treaty's preamble – with the issue of God and the constitution still unresolved.

6.4   THE LEGAL PERSONALITY AND THE END OF THE PILLARS

There was no hedging in the skeleton, when it came to the Union's legal personality. Settling the issue once and for all, it said it would have 'explicit recognition'. The preliminary draft of 28 October was so clear because the working group on legal personality reported on 1 October[11] and came out in favour of a single legal personality for the Union in unambiguous terms.

One of the more pronounced oddities of the existing European treaty structure was that the Union had no explicit legal personality while the three communities that it encompassed (the European Communities, Euratom and the now defunct European Coal and Steel Community) did. This legacy of the Maastricht Treaty on Union meant the EU, unlike its three sub-units, could not represent Europe, sign treaties, go to or be summoned by a court, become a member of international organisations or accede to international conventions such as the ECHR.

In 1996, two proposals were made during negotiations on the Amsterdam Treaty to give the EU a legal personality. These failed although a new treaty provision[12] allowed the Union to negotiate international agreements. The Nice declaration half opened the issue of legal personality by naming 'simplification of the treaties' as one of the aims of the future IGC. The Laeken declaration went further. It suggested a review of the distinction between the Union and the Communities, and the consequent division of the EU's activities into three pillars, covering respectively the tasks developed through the Community method since the Treaty of Rome, the common foreign and security policy agreed at Maastricht and justice and home affairs.

The group on legal personality was chaired by Giuliano Amato. Working swiftly and effectively, it demonstrated how clever chairmanship could extract the most from a modest brief and expressed views which pointed to how the eventual constitutional treaty should look. The group was asked to examine the consequences of explicit recognition of an EU legal personality

---

[11] CONV 305/02.
[12] Article 24 TEU.

and its merger with that of the European Community and whether these moves would help simplify the treaties. Amato also asked what effect a single legal personality might have on the division of competences in the Union, whether the Union would act more effectively, and about the impact on its status in international organisations.

Amato's report concluded the EU should have its own explicit legal personality, with only William Abitbol, the French eurosceptic MEP, objecting. The single personality, the group argued, would boost the EU's effectiveness, create legal certainty and transparency, and a give the Union a higher profile vis-à-vis foreign states and its own citizens. The Union would become a 'subject of international law' and as such could engage in all types of international action.

Based on these findings, it foreshadowed the skeleton by expressing a preference for a new treaty that would combine the existing treaties into a 'single constitutional text'. This would be sub-divided into two parts – a basic part comprising constitutional provisions and a second part that would codify and reorganise all other operational and policy provisions in the existing Union and Community treaties. It also concluded that a single legal personality should mean abandoning the EU's pillar structure which would look anachronistic in the new circumstances. It entered the area of competences by suggesting amendments to strengthen the Union's international role.

Consideration of the EU's legal personality thus triggered quite wide ranging thought about the final shape of the constitutional treaty. Some of the group's findings clearly made Giscard nervous. Delivering a carefully calibrated rebuke during the 3 October plenary, Giscard mused that his deputy Amato could have exceeded his remit. It was left to the external action working group, chaired by Jean-Luc Dehaene, Giscard's other deputy, to determine the impact of a single legal personality on the common foreign and security policy.

6.5   THE CHARTER OF FUNDAMENTAL RIGHTS

A list of human rights is part of most constitutions but was missing from the EU treaties. Protecting fundamental rights, however, had gradually grown as an issue in Union affairs. Article 6 of the Treaty on European Union pledged that the Union would respect fundamental rights as guaranteed by the ECHR and as they resulted from the constitutional provisions of the member states. Since the 1970s, the Court of Justice had built up case law, deriving from the principle that fundamental rights formed an integral part of the general principles of EU law. During the same period, the European Parliament and Commission tried on several occasions to strengthen the protection of fundamental rights in the Union.

The Charter of Fundamental Rights was drawn up by the EU's only previous convention in 2000. Consisting of a preamble and 54 articles, it was presented to EU leaders at their informal European Council in Biarritz in October 2000 and solemnly proclaimed in Nice two months later. Both the Nice and Laeken declarations raised the question of incorporating the Charter in a new EU constitutional treaty. The Laeken declaration also urged consideration of whether the Union should accede to the European Convention on Human Rights. In the view of the secretariat the two initiatives were complementary and not alternatives.[13]

Incorporation of the Charter was an important goal for integrationists. Incorporation would supply the constitutional treaty with its bill of rights and give the Charter legal force. In addition, as the European Parliament pointed out, an enhanced status for the Charter would be more than welcome against the background of enlargement because it would help put fundamental rights at the heart of integrating the Union's old and new member states.[14]

Accession to the ECHR would reinforce the position of the Union as a community of human values. It had been debated for more than 20 years and while the secretariat study detailed plenty of technical issues there seemed to be nothing that political will could not overcome, especially with the issue of the Union's legal personality apparently resolved.

When Antonio Vitorino, the chairman of the working group on the Charter drew up its mandate at the end of May 2002, he focused on technical issues. The group, he said, should not be involved with 'the major political questions' of whether to incorporate the Charter or accede to the ECHR. These should be left to political debates in the plenary sessions 'on the assumption that the two questions will meet with a positive political response'.

However, the Convention had to overcome one big political issue: Britain's fears that the Charter, if incorporated, could be used by the Court of Justice or the Commission to extend Union competence to the UK's industrial and social legislation.

---

[13] CONV 116/02.
[14] CONV 368/02.

Despite its non-binding character, the Union's legal authorities had started to take account of the Charter following its proclamation at the Nice summit. There were several cases of an advocate general at the Court of Justice using the Charter to identify fundamental rights in the Union. The Court of First Instance had invoked articles of the Charter as confirmation of the constitutional traditions of member states. From March 2001, the Commission had decided to subject proposals for legislation to a Charter compatibility check.[15]

On the other hand, the Charter as proclaimed contained so-called 'horizontal clauses' (articles 51 and 52) intended to block it from being used to change laws in member states where the Union had no competence. Britain feared the horizontal clauses might not apply to several of the Charter articles, which dealt mainly with social and 'aspirational' issues and which were based neither on the EU treaties nor the ECHR. London wanted the horizontal clauses tightening.

Britain's reservations about the Charter had a bearing on discussions over how it might be incorporated in the constitutional treaty. The issue was left open in the October skeleton. The options ranged from simply 'attaching' it to the treaties as a solemn declaration; through making reference to the Charter, either indirectly or directly, in the new text or its preamble; to annexing it to the planned constitutional treaty as a protocol; to insertion in full of the Charter's 54 articles. Positioning was important because it would influence the Charter's legal value. According to the secretariat, a legally binding quality for the Charter could only be assured through direct reference to its text in the constitutional treaty text, annexation as a protocol or the Charter's full incorporation in the final treaty.

When Vitorino's group reported in late October, it decided that the Charter should be incorporated in the constitutional treaty and that the Union should be able to accede to the ECHR, while leaving the modalities unclear in both cases. [16] Vitorino stressed the group's decisions would give no new competences to the Union. There would be no change of substance to the Charter, save some editorial tweaking to make it fully compatible with the treaty. Even if the Charter were legally binding, the group said jurisdiction in action relating to it would lie principally in the courts of the member states.

The group recognised that it would be up to the Council of Ministers to decide unanimously on the separate issue of the EU acceding to the ECHR. But it gave the idea powerful backing by stating that accession would

---

[15] See footnotes page 4, CONV 116/02.
[16] CONV 354/02.

highlight the moral and ethical commitments of the EU and give citizens the same degree of protection of fundamental rights at EU level as they enjoy in their own countries.

In the subsequent plenary debate on 29 October, some Convention members said accession would also establish a proper relationship between the European Court of Justice in Luxembourg and the European Court of Human Rights in Strasbourg. But again, conscious of the need to appeal to Charter sceptics as well as Charter enthusiasts, Vitorino's report was at pains stress the limits to its decisions. Accession would, for example, only have an effect in relation to EU law. It would create no new competences. The Union would not become a member of the Council of Europe, as suggested during the summer by Council of Europe secretary general Walter Schwimmer. Nor would accession affect the individual positions of member states with respect to the ECHR.

The debate also left unclear how the Charter should be incorporated in the treaty: Whether it should be taken in lock stock and barrel or whether it should be mentioned and carried in full in a protocol. Some ambiguity also remained on the part of the UK government. The UK's Peter Hain appeared in the plenary to signal a shift towards supporting incorporation in the treaties when he announced 'we are ready to work towards incorporation'. But he stressed the UK wanted 'legal certainty' and underlined the importance of the horizontal clauses to preserve the status quo regarding UK courts and social provisions. This latter aspect assumed still greater importance for Hain after he returned to the UK following the Convention session and saw that his remarks were interpreted as accepting incorporation. He was later to deny this interpretation in an exchange of testy emails with Andrew Duff, the Liberal Democrat MEP and head of the Liberal caucus in the Convention.

The British position was summed up by UK prime minister Tony Blair in a speech on the future of Europe on 28 November in Cardiff, the capital of Wales.[17]

> Though we welcome, of course, a declaration of basic rights common to all European citizens and have ourselves incorporated the European Convention on Human Rights directly into British law, we cannot support a form of treaty incorporation that would enlarge EU competence over national legislation. There cannot be new legal rights given by such means, especially in areas such as industrial law where we have long and difficult memories of the battles fought to get British law in proper order.

---

[17] 'A clear course for Europe', filed under speeches on the Downing Street website http://www.number-10.gov.uk.

Although the UK eventually agreed to incorporation of the Charter, formal acceptance came late in the day and only after securing additional assurances.

The Charter was closely bound up with the issue of Union citizenship. As Lamberto Dini pointed out: 'The Nice Charter of Fundamental Rights and the citizenship of the Union complementing national citizenship are natural developments in a Community that embraces and protects individuals and not only the states participating in it'.[18]

However, when Dini wrote in June 2002, there was still work to do on defining Union citizenship. The skeleton referred ambiguously to 'dual' European and national citizenship where the individual would be 'free to use either, as he or she chooses, with the rights and duties attaching to each'. The option already in force and destined to be adopted by the Convention was the idea of Union citizenship as additional to national citizenship. Established in the Maastricht Treaty, Union citizenship conferred a series of rights: the right to move and reside freely within the territory of the member states; the right to vote and stand as a candidate in European Parliament and local elections in the citizen's state of residence; the right to the protection of any member state in third countries where a citizen's own country of nationality is not represented; the rights of petition to the European Parliament and access to the ombudsman, and the right to correspond with EU institutions and advisory bodies in any of the 11 official EU languages.

---

[18] CONV 123/02.

CHAPTER 7
Who Does What and How?
Competences and their Implementation

7.1 COMPETENCES: THE RESPECTIVE ROLES OF UNION AND MEMBER STATES

That there was a need for clarification of competences was clear. Citizens and politicians, as Giscard told the Convention, needed to know the responsibilities of the EU and the member states. They had to plough through hundreds of articles in two treaties to do this. No one did, resulting in misunderstandings and a weakening of the EU's credibility.

The issue of competences was put on the EU reform agenda, largely at German behest. Ahead of the December 2000 Nice summit, the German *Länder* had threatened to refuse to ratify the resulting treaty unless there was progress towards a definition or 'catalogue' of competences to curb what they considered unwarranted intrusion into their affairs by 'Brussels'. Although other governments, including the UK and France, supported Germany, it was mainly at the instigation of Gerhard Schröder, the German chancellor, that the Nice conclusions asked 'how to establish and monitor a more precise delimitation of powers between the European Union and the member states, reflecting the principle of subsidiarity'.

The Laeken declaration, a year later, asked the Convention to consider how the division of competences could be made more transparent, whether any reorganisation of competence was needed and how to avoid any new division of competences leading to a 'creeping expansion' of Union powers at the expense of the member states. The Laeken summit even raised the possibility of the Union restoring some powers to member states.

Competences were a big issue early in the Convention. An important stimulus was a European Parliament report drawn up by Alain Lamassoure, the French EPP MEP and Convention member, and agreed in April 2002. With the benefit of hindsight, the Lamassoure report [1] was a prescient document. Its suggestions included merging the treaties into a single text,

---

[1] 'Report on the division of competences between the European Union and the member states', European Parliament constitutional affairs committee. On the Parliament's website: ref's A5-0133/2002 and PE 304.276.

which would have two parts – one constitutional and the other relating to carrying out policies – and giving the Union a single legal personality. The Lamassoure report shied away from rigid lists. It pinpointed the competences shared between the Union and member states as the biggest difficulty and called for ground rules in this 'grey area' that would conform with the principles of subsidiarity and proportionality.[2]

The Lamassoure report spoke of 'powers' rather than competences and suggested clarity could be achieved by focusing on two broad categories: the powers of the Union and powers shared with member states. The shared powers were put in three groups: those complementing the single market where the Union laid down general rules; those where the Union could only intervene to complement action by member states; and a third area where the Union would coordinate policies which remained in the national sphere of competence.

A plenary discussion on competences in April appeared to put paid to the idea of a specific catalogue of competences. When Erwin Teufel, representing the German *Länder*, floated the idea of two catalogues which would clearly define the respective roles of the Union and the member states, it was rejected by representatives of several governments, including Germany, France and the UK. Britain's Peter Hain admitted that a catalogue had 'the advantage of clarity', but it would create 'a rigid, static, legalistic body of rules,' which would lack flexibility. Some weeks later, the government representatives of Germany, the UK, Poland, Ireland and France signed a joint paper saying the catalogue was not the right approach.[3]

In May 2002, a background paper from the secretariat acknowledged the existing treaties were 'complex and impenetrable' on the issue of competences.[4] It also highlighted criticisms that the Union had used articles 94, 95 and 308 of the European Communities Treaty to act in areas where it was not competent and so infringed the member states' powers.[5]

The October skeleton signalled a hybrid solution which would include both principles and detailed or indicative lists of different type of competence.[6]

---

[2] Subsidiarity will be discussed in detail later in this chapter. Proportionality meant that that the content and form of a given Union action should not exceed what was necessary to achieve the desired objective.

[3] CONV 88/02.

[4] CONV 47/02.

[5] Articles 94 and 95 detailed the rules for 'approximating' laws to achieve the internal market. Article 308 was the so-called 'flexibility clause' which allowed the Council, deciding unanimously, to take steps not specified in the Treaty to achieve an objective of the Union in the course of operating the 'common market'.

[6] See Chapter 5.

Article 7 set out the principles of Union action, stating that this must be carried out in accordance with the treaty, within the competences conferred by it, and in compliance with the principles of subsidiarity and proportionality. Article 8 outlined the rules following from the principles. These blended a federal tone[7] with a promise to involve national parliaments in the rules for 'effective monitoring of subsidiarity and proportionality'. The skeleton promised that article 9 would list the categories of Union competence; article 10 the areas of exclusive Union competence; article 11 the areas of competence shared between the Union and member states and article 12 the areas in which the Union supports or coordinates action by member states, but has no competence to legislate. Article 13 promised to deal with common policies subject to specific rules, such as the common defence and foreign and security policies and policy on police matters and crime.

It was shortly after publication of the skeleton that work on the competence issue hit trouble. The complementary competences working group chaired by Henning Christophersen produced a report which was very badly received. [8] It was and remains a confusing document. Admittedly, Christophersen faced problems. The focus of his group was difficult to define and seemed tangential to the 'grey area' of shared Union and member state competences identified by Lamassoure. There was initially no clear definition of complementary competences, although Christophersen filled this gap by describing them as covering 'areas in which intervention by the community is limited to supplementing, supporting or coordinating the action of member states' and where the power to adopt legislative rules remained in the hands of member states. That meant education, vocational training, youth, culture, health protection, industrial policy, employment policy, the supervision on national budgets, civil protection, tourism and sport.

But faced with what might have been a narrow brief, Christophersen chose to give his appointed task the widest possible interpretation. He saw the working group's job as clarifying the respective responsibilities of the member states and the Union. He then proceeded to tread on various toes. To some he appeared to be trying to reintroduce the catalogue of competences through the back door. His attempt to rechristen complementary competences 'supporting measures' provoked fury when it was explained that in normal circumstances, these would not be legally binding. Several conventionnels noted that such a position would have prevented the launch

---

[7] Thus 'any competence not conferred on the Union by the *Constitution* rests with the member states'. (Author's italics.)
[8] CONV 375/1/02, 4 November 2002.

of some very popular Union policies, such as the 'Erasmus' student exchange programme. Many federalist delegates were further angered that his group suggested a rewording of the expression 'an ever closer union' in article 1 of the Treaty on Union.

Speaking for the EPP members of the Convention, the normally mild and courteous Lamassoure brutally rejected the report and, to loud applause, said its conclusions were useless: 'They cannot be explained to the public and they are of no use to decision makers.' Klaus Hänsch, for the PES group in the European Parliament, said some of the conclusions would make the constitution more complex rather than simpler and would undermine the powers of the European Parliament. One of the few to back Christophersen was Lord Tomlinson of the British House of Lords. He cited as 'a most important recommendation' that 'which suggests and requires an explicit Treaty text stating that all powers not transferred to the Union by treaty remain with the member states'. However, this was hardly a novel idea – it was the first point of article 8 of the skeleton treaty.

At the end of a difficult plenary session a battered Christophersen retreated from the podium and it was announced that the Praesidium would return to the issue at some unspecified point in the future. To rub salt in the wounds, Dehaene told the press that the report's problems may have resulted from Christophersen's decision to leave its drafting to his own (Danish) assistant rather than entrust it to the Convention secretariat. The gulf that opened up between Christophersen and the Convention marked the most striking failure of the idea of delegating important preparatory work to working groups.

The discussion over competences took another twist towards the end of the study phase when the Commission, in its 'Penelope' text, took an entirely different approach.[9] Instead of classifying competences, the Commission's Penelope document of December highlighted various gradations of responsibility given to the Union. The Union's internal policies would thus be classified in terms of principal policies, flanking policies and complementary actions and so avoid any rigid classification of powers, which, as the Commission had explained in its May 2002 submission to the Convention 'would have the disadvantage of artificially straitjacketing the Union's capacity for action'.[10]

The result of all this confusion was to make the task of the Praesidium all the more difficult once it started drafting articles on competences.

---

[9] Working document at http://europa.eu.int/futurum/comm/documents/penelope_en.htm.
[10] COM 2002 247 final.

7.2   SUBSIDIARITY AND ITS MONITORING

As the Nice declaration and the skeleton made clear, subsidiarity was closely bound up with that of competences. The difficulties with competences did not stop the Convention from making good progress at clarifying the issues surrounding subsidiarity.

Subsidiarity was originally a principle of the Catholic church. It was introduced into Union law in the Maastricht Treaty which ruled that in areas outside the EU's exclusive competence, it should take action 'only if and insofar as the objectives of the proposed action cannot be sufficiently achieved by the member states and can therefore, by reason of the scale or effects of the proposed action, be better achieved by the Community.' Application of the subsidiarity principle was defined in a protocol attached to the Amsterdam Treaty which bound the Union's institutions to compliance. It said Community action should be as simple as possible and that the Community should legislate only to the extent necessary. The Commission was enjoined to consult widely before proposing legislation and justify the relevance of its proposals with regard to subsidiarity.

But the Laeken declaration clearly indicated something was amiss when it spoke of citizens not wanting 'European institutions inveigling their way into every nook and cranny of life'. One problem, as Jean-Claude Piris, the head of the Council's legal service, told the subsidiarity working group,[11] was the word 'better' in the Maastricht Treaty article, which meant subsidiarity was 'an essentially political and subjective principle'. The Court of Justice, which monitored compliance, had never annulled an act on the grounds of infringement of subsidiarity.

The working group, chaired by Inigo Méndez de Vigo, thus had to ask how subsidiarity could be monitored in the most effective manner possible, whether a monitoring mechanism or procedure should be established, and whether this should be of a political or legal nature.

The group, which was the first of the initial six working groups, completed its work around the middle of September and presented its findings to the 4 October plenary session.[12] It agreed what amounted to a module of a constitutional treaty in readiness for the skeleton that would come from the Praesidium later that month and demonstrated that the Convention could move swiftly and pragmatically to produce concise and easily understandable political results.

---

[11] Working group document WD 04 WG 1.
[12] CONV 286/02).

The group managed successfully to bring together the interests of the Convention's federalists and its national parliamentarians, the component which hitherto had proved difficult to integrate into the Convention's proceedings. That was largely thanks to Méndez de Vigo, who avoided a narrow partisan approach when chairing the group. He was criticised for this during the 4 October debate by fellow MEPs who thought his proposals were too generous to national parliaments, especially when they suggested national parliaments should have a right to challenge EU legislation on the basis of the subsidiarity principle in the European Court of Justice.

The working group concluded that subsidiarity could be both applied and monitored better. But it came out against the creation of any new monitoring body or the creation of a 'Mr or Mrs Subsidiarity' in the Commission. Instead it set out ways the Commission should take greater heed of subsidiarity in drafting legislation (including a 'subsidiarity sheet' in each draft law) and set in train steps to strengthen the protocol on subsidiarity.

More significant, it proposed the creation of an 'early warning system' allowing national parliaments to join in the monitoring of compliance with the principle of subsidiarity. Thus, the Commission would have to tell each national parliament (and each chamber in bicameral parliaments) of its legislative proposals at the same time as the Council and European Parliament. Using a football metaphor, national parliaments could then raise a yellow card within a six-week period and object to the presidents of the Commission, Parliament and Council if the proposal appeared to contravene the subsidiarity principle. Depending on how many parliaments raised objections, the Community legislator (the Council of Ministers and the European Parliament) would decide what to do. If the legislator received a 'significant number of opinions from one-third of parliaments', the Commission would re-examine its proposal and on the strength of the re-examination might decide to maintain, amend or withdraw it.

Should these political steps yield no results, the aggrieved parliament could refer the matter to the ECJ. In a move that would give new power to the hitherto obscure Committee of the Regions, the working group suggested that it too could turn to the court in certain cases. That would be when the Committee had been consulted and found that a piece of legislation was against the principle of subsidiarity and yet where the Council and Parliament had carried on regardless. The working group drew the line at giving similar rights to regions with legislative capacities, such as the German *Länder*.

The debate in the plenary and the concerns of MEPs were to prompt some further reflection in the Praesidium about aspects of the early warning scheme. The worries centred on the scale of national parliament involvement and whether one-third of national parliaments was sufficient to require the Commission to re-examine a proposal. Another concern was whether each chamber in bicameral national parliaments should be treated equally.

But broad support for the idea showed how different elements of the Convention – MEPs, member states, national parliaments and the Committee of the Regions (which attended the Convention as an observer) – could achieve a result with something for all and which avoided creating a new bureaucracy.

The subsidiarity group's final report hailed the early warning system as 'innovative and bold' and trumpeted it as 'the first time in the history of the European construction' that national parliaments would be involved in the EU legislative process. Although the criticisms of the MEPs took some of the shine off that hyperbole, the report's conclusions represented a useful step forward. It was wrong, however, to take the early warning idea – as some commentators did – as a sign the Convention was reallocating power to the member states. It was proving a body of mixed motives. The debate on legal personality, held on 3 October, and the draft constitutional treaties submitted by Duff and Brok had exposed strong integrationist tendencies among many of the Convention's members.

7.3   THE ROLE OF NATIONAL PARLIAMENTS

The role of national parliaments in EU affairs was a matter of concern for at least a decade and closely bound up with the debate about bringing the Union closer to the citizen. Much national legislation in the economic and social spheres resulted from Union directives, raising questions over whether national parliaments were consulted in an adequate and timely manner and whether they exercised sufficient scrutiny over developments in 'Brussels'. These issues became more pressing with the likelihood of the Union becoming increasingly involved in 'new' policy areas such as police and judicial cooperation, economic policy coordination and the common foreign and security policy.

The member states had annexed a declaration to the Maastricht Treaty on the role of national parliaments which called for a 'stepped up' exchange of information between the European Parliament and national parliaments. In it, governments promised to ensure that national parliaments received Commission proposals 'in good time' for information or examination. To enhance the opportunities for scrutiny, a protocol was attached to the Amsterdam Treaty which specified that a six week breathing space should elapse between the publication of legislative proposals and their being placed on the Council agenda for adoption as either an act or a common position of the Council.

But worries that national parliaments were insufficiently involved with the Union persisted. During 2000, Joschka Fischer in his Humboldt speech and Tony Blair[13] urged an enhanced EU role for national parliaments, in each case suggesting they send representatives to a second chamber in Brussels. One of the four major points of the Nice declaration was the 'the role of national parliaments in the European architecture'. More recently, both French president Jacques Chirac[14] and Spain's prime minister José Maria Aznar[15] had urged a greater role for national parliaments in EU affairs.

The Laeken declaration asked whether national parliaments should be represented in a new institution alongside the Council and the European Parliament, whether they should act in EU areas where the European Parliament had no competence, and whether they should engage in the issue of competences by preliminary checking of compliance with the subsidiarity principle.

In turn, the Convention's national parliaments working group was asked to look at their current role in the Union, the national arrangements that functioned best and whether any new mechanisms or procedures were required at national or European level. Chaired by Gisela Stuart, the German-born British Labour MP, the group proceeded to look at national scrutiny arrangements, to assess whether benchmarking or measuring best practice might do some good. It set out to examine if the Amsterdam protocol had improved information flows or whether an absence of transparency in the Council obstructed scrutiny by national parliaments of EU legislative procedures. Also on its agenda was the idea of a second chamber and whether this should focus on monitoring subsidiarity or even foreign policy and justice and home affairs, which were largely intergovernmental. It worked closely with the subsidiarity working group.

Stuart was unlucky in that the important issue of subsidiarity had been already successfully handled by the working group chaired by Méndez de Vigo. Her group, moreover, soon became the battle ground between supporters of an additional parliamentary chamber and MEPs who were

---

[13] At the Polish Stock Exchange, Warsaw, 6 October 2000. Filed under speeches on the Downing Street website, http://www.number-10.gov.uk.

[14] Election address in Strasbourg, 6 March 2002, filed in the speeches section of http://www.elysee.fr.

[15] Speech at St Anthony's College, Oxford, 20 May 2002, available among the Council of Ministers contributions on http://www.europa.eu.int/futurum.

determined – successfully as it turned out – to protect the legislative prerogatives of the European Parliament. When the group finally reported,[16] it was difficult to avoid a sense of anti-climax. Thinly disguised criticism came from the highest level – Giscard – when he summed up the 28 October plenary debate on Stuart's report. Hinting at a lack of ambition in the group, the president twice warned the Convention needed to be imaginative and must go beyond simply improving existing treaties.

Stuart's report reinforced the main findings of the subsidiarity working group by underlining that national parliaments should play a key role in monitoring the principle of subsidiarity. It added its voice to calls for the Council to enact all legislation in public and other activities 'with open doors as much as possible'. It recommended that the Amsterdam protocol be strengthened. The idea of possibly incorporating the Convention method in the planned treaty for preparing future amendments was innovative. The suggestion that COSAC – the Conference of Community Affairs Bodies of the parliaments of the European Community – could become a forum for exchanging ideas of best practice in monitoring EU policies was modest but sensible, and would give greater purpose to a little known talking shop.

But its broad conclusions that national parliaments should be better informed and more involved in EU affairs, inter alia by acknowledging their role in the constitutional treaty, were worthy rather than gripping. Some of the group's ideas – such as organising 'European weeks' involving national parliaments and European institutions – were thin. While rejecting any new institution, the group's suggestion that the Convention should examine the desirability of periodic meetings of national parliaments and the European Parliament to debate important and strategic issues helped keep alive Giscard's unpopular idea of a Congress of European and national legislators. For that the president was grateful.

7.4   THE EXERCISE OF POWER

The question 'who does what?' usually invites the supplementary queries 'and how?' and 'with what effect?'. It was therefore inevitable that attempts to clarify competences and subsidiarity should lead to questions about the way the Union exercised its powers.

But other factors made a thorough examination of the Union's instruments of power imperative. The Laeken declaration put the highly political issue of extending qualified majority voting (QMV) in the Council of Ministers at the

---

[16] CONV 353/02.

expense of unanimity on the Convention's agenda. For many conventionnels, the Union's prospective enlargement to 25 or more member states spelled blockage unless the QMV issue was reopened less than two years after heads of government agreed a limited extension of majority voting at the acrimonious Nice summit.

In pondering how to increase the democratic legitimacy and transparency of the Union's institutions, the Laeken declaration asked whether the EU should extend 'codecision', the procedure which gives the European Parliament equal powers in legislating with the Council of Ministers, and which had been extended in the Amsterdam and Nice treaties. Another issue was whether the codecision procedures could be simplified and speeded up.

Enlargement also prompted questions over what to do when small groups of member states wanted to move ahead with policies for greater integration which not all Union members could accept. The history of the Union was full of expedients for dealing with such cases, such as the British opt-out from the single currency. The Amsterdam and Nice summits had first created and then improved a mechanism known as 'enhanced cooperation' by which groups of countries would be permitted to move ahead without destroying the Union's spirit of solidarity. But enhanced cooperation was fearsomely complicated and remained untried throughout the life of the Convention. One of the tasks of the Convention was to make enhanced cooperation more user friendly.

The inventiveness of past Union policy makers added to the challenges facing the Convention. What should be done with new policy instruments which were not properly embedded in the treaties? One such instrument was the 'open method of coordination', adopted with gusto at the March 2000 Lisbon summit as the way to boost the Union's economic performance and based on the principle of member states tailoring their policies in response to a system of benchmarking and policy targets.

The Nice declaration merely nibbled at these problems, listing as one of its four points: 'A simplification of the treaties with a view to making them clearer and better understood without changing their meaning.' Reflecting Verhofstadt's interest in simplification, the Laeken declaration was less circumspect. After noting that 'successive amendments to the treaty have on each occasion resulted in a proliferation of instruments', it concluded that 'the key question is therefore whether the Union's various instruments should not be better defined and whether their number should not be reduced.'

The dreadful complexity of the Union's legal instruments was exposed in a detailed note from the Praesidium, published in June 2002.[17] This recalled that the Council, the Parliament and the Commission could 'make regulations and issue directives, take decisions, make recommendations or deliver opinions'.[18] Of these, the two most important instruments were regulations, which were uniform laws applied with binding force throughout the Union, and directives, which were also binding, but where it was left to the member state to decide the form and methods necessary to achieve the desired result.

However, this relatively simple categorisation of policy instruments had long been supplemented by 'specific instruments of diverse scope and nature, the legal effects of which are often difficult to pin down'. These specific instruments included 'guidelines', 'framework programmes' and (more) 'decisions'. One of the more bizarre qualities of the EU treaties was that policy instruments would share the same name but have different characteristics. In some cases, they would be in different parts of the treaties, in other cases not. Thus in the TEC, there were 'decisions' governed by article 249, which were directed to a specific entity or person as with administrative acts for appointing a senior official, and other 'decisions' which would be very different and anchored in other articles. Some 'Decisions' with a capital D were very big policy decisions indeed, such as the Decisions on Own Resources which defined the sources of the EU's revenue in 1970 and 1988 after protracted negotiations.

A further complication was that the European Union treaty (TEU) included instruments specific to the areas of foreign policy and justice and home affairs which also had their own names and characteristics. In implementing foreign policy the EU would resort to 'principles' and 'guidelines', 'common strategies', 'joint actions', 'common positions' or such mouthfuls as 'enhancing systematic cooperation'. The justice and home affairs field could boast 'common positions', 'framework decisions', (yet more) 'decisions' and 'conventions'. Like the TEC, the TEU included instruments with the same name but different characteristics. Thus, a common position in foreign policy would define the Union's approach to a particular matter and member states would have to comply with it in their national policies or diplomacy. In justice and home affairs, common positions also defined the Union's approach to a particular matter but there was no mention of binding force. Little wonder that the Praesidium note asked: 'Is this increase in the number of instruments a factor of legal uncertainty, and one of the reasons for the opacity of which the Union stands accused?'

---

[17] CONV 162/02.
[18] According to article 249 of the European Communities treaty (TEC).

That was not all, however: there was no clear system of assigning powers to the various Union institutions. Oddly, in a Union so influenced by France, the EU treaties had escaped the influence of Montesquieu, the 18th century French political philosopher, who first enunciated the principles of the separation of powers which came to be incorporated in much constitutional law. 'Legislative power is not defined by the treaties; they merely define, on a case by case basis, the respective roles of the institutions involved,' the Praesidium observed. As a result, these roles were exercised 'via a very large number of procedures'. There were, for example, nine different ways in which the Council and Parliament, acting together as the Community legislator, could pass legislation.[19] A later paper from the Praesidium, which took account of the involvement of other institutions, found more than 22 different decision-making procedures in the TEC for adopting legislative acts.[20]

Inconsistencies abounded, often as a result of political compromises aimed at circumventing or mitigating blockages created by unanimous decision making. As a general rule, codecision meant QMV in the Council but articles 42, 47 and 151 of the TEC specified codecision with unanimity.[21] In some articles, such as article 18 on freedom of movement, some provisions required QMV and others unanimity. Other articles contained 'bridges' or *passerelles* which allowed issues to move from unanimity to QMV at a point in the future.[22] Although one of the Convention's goals was to simplify procedures, it would resort to new *passerelles* for several issues as a way of loosening the stranglehold of unanimity over future policy actions.

A further problem was that the treaties made no distinction between legislative and executive acts, leaving the whole area of secondary legislation in limbo. There were also questions about the quality of EU legislation. Because political compromises often made matters very complicated, legislation sometimes took years to pass, leaving the Union ill placed to adapt to a complex and fast changing world, especially in the economic sphere. Once again, the Praesidium felt obliged to pose a rhetorical question: 'Is this lack of a coherent system of decision-making

---

[19] Qualified majority with codecision; qualified majority with cooperation; qualified majority with assent; qualified majority and straight opinion; qualified majority without involvement by the Parliament; unanimity with codecision; unanimity with assent; unanimity with a straight opinion and unanimity without participation by the Parliament.

[20] CONV 216/02.

[21] Article 42 covered social security for migrant workers; article 47 the implementation of directives coordinating professional qualifications and article 151 incentive measures for encouraging cultural cooperation.

[22] For example, article 67 on visa, asylum and immigration.

procedures and their great diversity an additional cause of complexity and opacity?'

The October skeleton at least held out the promise of coherence with its plan to group nine articles covering the instruments and procedures to implement Union action in title V of the planned constitutional treaty.

The working group on simplification was chaired by Giuliano Amato, who had earlier successfully sorted out the Union's legal personality. As he took control, he commented: 'Nothing is more complicated than simplification.' Amato was not resigned, however. He believed simplification was vital for encouraging democracy and faith in EU institutions. If citizens could not understand the system, how could they 'identify its problems, criticise it and ultimately control it'.

His working group came up with proposals that simplified both legislative procedures and instruments and significantly fleshed out the constitutional skeleton.[23] Giscard described them at the Copenhagen summit as 'audacious but reasonable'. In the 5 December plenary debate on simplification, Alain Lamassoure said Amato had 'earned the stripes of a founding father of Europe'.

On procedures, it produced two profoundly important recommendations:

- Codecision, by which the Council of Ministers and Parliament are equals in legislating, 'should become the general rule for the adoption of legislative acts'. There would be exceptions, as in cases of great political sensitivity for the member states. But to underline the significance of codecision, it should be known as the 'legislative procedure' in the constitutional treaty.

- QMV in the Council and codecision should automatically go hand in hand. This recommendation transformed the debate over the group's reports from the technical to the political and drew the plenary into discussion over whether the EU should retain unanimity at all. Britain, Ireland and Sweden were swift to insist on its retention for tax policies. Speaking for France, Dominique de Villepin insisted codecision should not apply to farm policy.

To reduce confusion, the group recommended that codecision should replace the cooperation procedure, which would be scrapped. Once important but now barely used, the cooperation procedure gave the Council the last word

---

[23] CONV 424/02.

in legislating and was limited to just four articles in the economic and monetary area. The assent procedure, under which Parliament must deliver a positive opinion for an act to be adopted, should be used solely for ratifying international agreements. In consequence, legislation covered by the assent procedure – including article 161 setting down the rules for spreading money to weaker regions through the Union's structural and cohesion funds – should be handled by codecision.

Amato's group took the bewildering array of EU legal instruments – which he put at 15 – and proposed cutting them to *six*, giving them more understandable names in the process. There would in future be two key, binding legislative instruments: *European laws*, which would correspond to existing regulations and therefore be acts of general application, binding in their entirety and directly applicable in all member states. And *EU framework laws*, equivalent to existing directives, which bind member states as regards the results to be achieved but leave the choice of form and implementation to national authorities. In addition, there would be binding, non-legislative acts, to be known as *decisions*. These might be directed at specific addressees as in the case of appointments or state aid decisions. The EU would also have two acts of non-binding force: *recommendations* and *opinions*. The new names would apply to the instruments of the common foreign and security policy as well as the classic community instruments, although foreign policy decisions, for example, would be known as *CFSP decisions*.

Notwithstanding this simplification, there would still be scope for so-called non-standard acts, such as resolutions, conclusions and declarations. These are not covered by treaty, are technically non-binding, and yet, as the example of European Council conclusions shows, can still be extremely important. Most of Amato's renamed instruments found an enthusiastic consensus in the Convention. Problems arose, however, in connection with a sixth type of instrument he suggested. These would be delegated acts, which, the report suggested, could in future be known as *regulations*.

Delegated acts would kill two birds with one stone. First, they would play an important part in clarifying the boundary between matters falling to the legislative and executive arms of the EU institutions and tackle the EU's failure to live up to Montesquieu's precepts for a proper division of powers. Introduction of delegated acts would solve a second problem: the absence of any provision in the EU's treaties for secondary legislation in the EU.

To deal with the division of powers, Amato's group proposed a clearer 'hierarchy of legislation' in which laws and framework laws would be categorised as legislative acts. These would be adopted on the basis of the treaty and generally adopted by codecision of the Council of Ministers and the Parliament. The delegated acts or regulations would form a second category of acts and normally be adopted by the Commission to flesh out or amend legislative acts in line with rules set by the Council and Parliament in their joint capacity as legislator. A third category would be implementing acts, which would put into force legislative or delegated acts. Implementing acts would normally be enacted by member states although the group mooted the possibility of giving regulatory authorities the right to adopt some implementing acts.

That there was a need for secondary legislation became clear in 2000 and 2001 when the EU's ambitious 'action plan' to complete the single market in financial services was falling badly behind schedule, in part because of the extremely technical nature of the material which was beyond the ken of most Euro-parliamentarians. The absence of rules for secondary legislation forced the EU to fall back on a complex committee-based process of accelerated decision making, devised by a group of 'wise men' chaired by Alexandre Lamfalussy, a former Belgian central banker and one of the fathers of the euro. This was eventually introduced in 2002 after a year-long delay caused by an institutional tussle involving the Commission, the Council of Ministers and the European Parliament at the heart of which lay parliamentary concerns over the ceding of democratic control to executive institutions.

Amato's group suggested control mechanisms, such as a parliamentary 'call back' to bring delegated acts back into the power of the legislator or 'sunset' clauses to force a review of the acts' operations if necessary. But, in a rerun of the controversy that prompted Parliament to hold up the Lamfalussy method of passing financial services legislation, the plenary debate revealed some concern that delegated acts might represent a shift in the EU's institutional balance. As a result, Giscard called for more detailed proposals covering delegated acts to be submitted to the Convention at a later date.

The 'open method of coordination' also proved controversial, even though it had been adopted in large measure at the March 2000 Lisbon summit. The group said the open coordination method should be given constitutional status – an approach backed by the economic governance and Social Europe working groups. But some MEPs – notably the UK Liberal Andrew Duff and the Austrian Green Johannes Voggenhuber – opposed the idea. Duff said non-standard acts and open coordination should be 'outlawed' where legislative procedures were allowed under the treaties. Voggenhuber warned that open coordination could bring intergovernmental practices 'by the back door'.

Amato's report contained some other important recommendations. It said EU institutions must sit in public when legislating. It touched on the need for better quality legislation, raising the issue of improved consultation at all stages of the process. Poor consultation has been a serious impediment to drawing up financial services legislation.

Stimulated by Amato's fertile mind, the group considered some issues outside its mandate, which were listed in an annex to its report. Two are worthy of note here because they foreshadowed important issues to be tackled by the Convention in 2003. A 'large number' of group members proposed that the existence of a qualified majority in the Council should be determined by a double majority system – which would reflect a majority of states and a majority of populations – rather than the complex voting weights negotiated at Nice and liable to revision with each addition or subtraction of a member state. The report also referred to Duff's idea of an 'organic law', suggesting it might be used for 'lightening' the procedure for revising that part of the future constitutional treaty dealing with policies[24] instead of the cumbersome existing method of unanimity in the Council and ratification by member states.

7.5   THE UNION'S FINANCES

The Union's budget had been the cause of epic struggles among the member states in the 1980s, when Britain's Margaret Thatcher battled to reduce the UK's net contributions and vowed never to accept 'half a loaf'. The power of the European Parliament to sign off on the Union's budget provided the constitutional lever for Parliament to force the mass resignation of the Commission in 1999.

But, in general, the Union's budget had dropped out of the headlines through the 1990s. Agreements between the main institutions on budget discipline and the introduction of multi-year financial perspective had taken much political heat out of the annual setting of the Union's revenues and expenditure, which in global terms were tiny at a fraction above one per cent of the Union's gross domestic product. Although there were ongoing problems of fraud against the Union – highlighted each year by highly critical reports from the Union's Court of Auditors – these were not really constitutional issues.

The problems surrounding the Union's finances that faced the Convention were far more prosaic and boiled down to improving procedures for agreeing the budget which were baroque in their complexity and bewildering to all

---

[24] The skeleton's part two and part III from May 2003.

but the most dedicated of experts. An allied issue was to determine the proper role of the democratically elected European Parliament, which had no control over revenues and control over only half the Union's spending. This limited power over spending reflected a distinction between obligatory spending (on farm guarantees) over which Parliament had no control and non-obligatory spending, which covered such outlays as the structural and regional funds, where Parliament had the main say.

Amato's group on simplification urged a streamlining of the annual EU budget process, so that setting expenditure would be a similar procedure to codecision between the Parliament and Council. The Commission would submit a preliminary draft budget to the Parliament and Council. Amato's group proposed the Council would decide by a qualified majority while Parliament would have the last word, or special provisions to prevent a stalemate.

In a move that would increase Parliament's influence, Amato's group called for an end to the distinction between compulsory and non-compulsory spending. It recommended that the Union's various budgetary principles, such as the need for a balance between revenue and spending, should be grouped in one article rather than dotted around in separate articles as in the existing treaties. A further useful proposal was that the multi-annual financial perspective should be included in the constitutional treaty to give it more weight.

The revenue side of the budget was potentially more controversial because of pressure from some conventionnels, notably the Commission and Belgium, for the Union to be able to raise its own taxes in place of other funds known as 'own resources' that financed the budget. There were four categories of own resources. Two of these, agricultural levies and duties from the common customs tariff, were relatively transparent but of structurally declining importance. The other two categories, a percentage of notional value added tax revenues and a levy linked to GDP, were impenetrable once the Union's methods of calculation had been applied.

The advocates of the Community tax claimed not to want a source of higher revenues but instead a revenue stream that would be transparent and allow Europe's citizens to know how they were contributing to the Union. Taxes have never been popular. But through the centuries they have done wonders for creating political awareness. A Union tax or a system by which the Union might take a share of national taxes could help promote a European *demos*. For this reason, it was a step too far for the traditionally less integrationist governments such as the UK, Sweden and Denmark.

The plenary discussion on Amato's report revealed consensus on the need to list the main budgetary principles of the Union but discord on other issues. Giscard concluded that the group's ideas for reform of procedure needed more study with the result that the EU's finances remained unresolved until fairly late in the Convention.

CHAPTER 8
New or Expanding Policy Areas

The Convention met to consider more than just the constitutional aspects of Europe's future. It was also a response to the perception that the EU was punching below its weight in a very complex and dangerous world, made all the more perilous by the September 11 terrorist attacks on the US. Opinion polls showed strong support across the Union for a more effective European foreign policy and action to combat what Chris Patten, the European external affairs commissioner, called the 'dark side' of globalisation: organised crime, terrorism and trafficking in drugs and human beings. The successful introduction of euro notes and coins on 1 January 2002 in the 12 member countries of the eurozone gave heart to those who wanted more integrated economic and social policies to balance the very lopsided construction of Europe's economic and monetary union with its federal monetary policy and decentralised fiscal policies. Discussion of the new and expanding policy areas of foreign and defence policy, economic and social policy and justice and home affairs crystallised differences between conventionnels over how far the constitutional treaty should promote greater integration. In particular, the process highlighted the UK's special position. Justice and home affairs apart, the conclusions of the working groups in these areas contrasted with the UK's predominantly intergovernmental approach and pointed to fundamental differences between the Blair government's vision of Europe and the strong integrationist group of conventionnels.

8.1   COMMON FOREIGN AND SECURITY POLICY

The European Council in Laeken made sure that Europe's global role was one of the main issues on the Convention's agenda. Among the three main challenges it identified was 'how to develop the Union into a stabilising factor and a model in the new, multi-polar world.' Europe's citizens, the Laeken declaration noted, wanted to see Europe more involved in foreign affairs, security and defence.[1] These were new areas of policy compared with trade and development where the Union was long established as a powerful global operator.

---

[1] An assertion backed by opinion polls. Eurobarometer 58, conducted in autumn 2002, reported that 67 per cent polled were for 'one common foreign policy among member states' and 73 per cent for 'a common defence and security policy'.

But while there was general agreement that Europe should be more effective on the world stage, there was a profound disagreement about how best to go about it. On the one hand, the Commission and integration minded member states such as Belgium, favoured an extension of the Community method into foreign policy. For the more sovereign minded countries, which at Maastricht had negotiated that foreign and security policy should be intergovernmental, it was anathema to consider giving the Commission the right of initiative and using qualified majority voting in the Council. As was to become all too clear when the member states split over Iraq, the Union was also liable to deep divisions on the substance of specific policies.

The Union's external relations covered a very broad front indeed, with strikingly different responsibilities and policy instruments.

- The European Community always had responsibility for trade and development cooperation. It had grown to become the world's largest trading bloc and its largest provider of development aid, giving the Commission (and the commissioners for external relations, trade and development assistance) a very important say in external affairs.
- The Community and member states had a shared responsibility where internal Union policies had international ramifications. Thus the Commission, Council and member states would share the management of the external aspects of monetary policy, research, the environment and where international agreements were needed to achieve internal Union objectives.
- Since the Maastricht Treaty, the common foreign and security policy (CFSP) existed to safeguard the Union's interests and values, strengthen peace and security and promote international cooperation, democracy, the rule of law and human rights. This 'second pillar' of the Maastricht Treaty on European Union was the preserve of the member states and had its own intergovernmental procedures and policy instruments. To increase the effectiveness of CFSP, the member states agreed in the Amsterdam Treaty negotiation to create a high representative for foreign and security policy to assist the Council. Javier Solana, the first incumbent, began operating in 1999.

As Solana pointed out, a common foreign policy was not a single policy. The Union did not aspire to replace 15 national foreign ministries and 15 sovereign policies with a single policy run from Brussels.[2] The aim was to identify common ambitions and ways of pursuing shared aims that gave 'real added value'.

---

[2] Solana speech in Stockholm, 25 April 2002, filed as S0078/02 in the Secretary General's archived speeches on the Council website, http://www.ue.eu.int.

The common foreign and security policy was, therefore, what the member states chose to make of it. As the Praesidium observed, within CFSP 'there are no limits to the potential scope and intensity of foreign policy.[3] The decision whether and how far to use the existing options provided for in the treaty depends entirely on the political will of the different actors involved.' The rub was that common political will implied consensus and was therefore extremely difficult to achieve.

The important actors in CFSP were very different to those in the Community method of decision making. The European Council decided principles and general guidelines while the Council of Ministers (in its General Affairs and External Relations formation) developed common policies on the basis of the guidelines. There was the high representative, often deployed in trouble-shooter role, and the member state holding the six-month rotating presidency. The Commission was accorded only a minor role in CFSP although it had responsibility for managing the CFSP budget, which at €30 million to €40 million a year was very small. It amounted to less than 1 per cent of the Union's €6 billion external relations budget and was insignificant compared with the €70 billion spent annually on external action by the member states.[4]

The Laeken declaration had great expectations for the Union in the world. It couched its future role in high moral tones. With its citizens 'living in a globalised, yet also highly fragmented world', Europe needed 'to shoulder its responsibilities in the governance of globalisation.' Europe would be 'a power resolutely doing battle against all violence, all terror and all fanaticism, but which also does not turn a blind eye to the world's heartrending injustices.' Europe wanted to change the course of world affairs to benefit the poorest as well as the rich countries. It was 'a power seeking to set globalisation within a moral framework, in other words to anchor it in solidarity and sustainable development.'

But Laeken provided only a few detailed ideas on the approach the Convention should take on external affairs. The declaration twice asked how to develop a 'more coherent' common foreign policy and wondered whether the 'Petersberg' tasks,[5] which defined the Union's commitments in crisis management, should be updated. In the section on institutions, it asked how to strengthen the synergy between the posts of high representative for foreign and security policy, held by Javier Solana, and the external affairs

---

[3] In a background paper CONV 161/02.
[4] According to Pierre de Boissieu in a hearing organised by the working group on external action on 15 October 2002.
[5] Listed in article 17.2 of the TEU and named after the German government guesthouse and conference centre outside Bonn where they were agreed.

commissioner, Chris Patten, and whether to extend the EU's external representation 'in international fora'.

The end-October skeleton also made only a few references to the Union's external role. Article 3 listed among the objectives of the Union 'development of a common foreign and security policy, and a common defence policy, to defend and promote the Union's values in the wider world.' In title V on the implementation of Union action, there was a promise that articles 29 and 30 would set out the respective implementing procedures for the common foreign and security and the common defence policies but no details.

Near the end of the skeleton were two other provisions. Entitled 'Union action in the world', title VIII consisting of article 41 would deal with whoever represented the Union in international relations and define the role and future rank of the high representative, while taking account of competences already exercised by the Community. Dubbed 'the Union and its immediate environment', title IX, consisting of article 42, 'could contain' provisions to define a privileged relationship between the Union and its neighbouring states, should a decision be made to create such a relationship. Eight months later, Solana succinctly defined the goal of a possible neighbourhood policy as 'to promote a ring of well governed countries to the east of the European Union and on the borders of the Mediterranean with whom we can enjoy close and cooperative relations'.[6]

It was the job of Jean-Luc Dehaene, the former Belgian prime minister and vice-president of the Convention, to put flesh on these bones as chairman of the external relations working group. He set out to answer five very practical questions:

- How should the interests of the Union be defined and formulated?
- How should the consistency of Union activities be ensured, taking into account all the instruments at its disposal (including trade policy and development aid)?
- What should be done to speed decision making, giving attention to the possible extension of the Community method or easing unanimity?
- What were the lessons from creating the Solana post?
- What changes in the Union's external representation would boost its international influence?

---

[6] 'A secure Europe in a better world' presented to the Thessaloniki European Council, June 2003.

Dehaene came to the Convention in the plenary session of 20 December with a substantial report on external affairs.[7] It was a skilfully drafted work that glossed over divisions inside the group. The report was studded with references to 'large consensus', 'high degree of support', 'significant numbers in favour of' and 'a large trend' that spoke of less than full consensus. But as the power of the written word tended to outweigh protests in the plenary, this technique allowed ideas to go forward to the Convention and influence later discussions.

The group started from a general acknowledgement that the EU needed to be a strong and effective player on the world stage in political as well as economic terms. 'The central question,' the report stated, 'was therefore not whether the Union had a role to play but how it should organise itself in order effectively and coherently to promote fundamental values, defend common interests and contribute to the overall objective of global peace, security and sustainable development.'

Dehaene stressed the inclusive nature of his work. The group, he said, focused on 'how to coordinate and consolidate' the two different channels of EU decision making – the community and the intergovernmental. It was not changing competences or powers, but trying to improve the coordination of policies to ensure the Union's common action was truly common.

CFSP, he added, would stay 'intergovernmental in character'. It would remain the job of the European Council to define EU strategic objectives and interests and establish parameters to guide EU and member states' action. But there were areas where the EU's internal policies, determined by the Community method, impacted on the world stage. Here the working group suggested that the eventual constitutional treaty make explicit the competence of the EU to conclude external agreements on issues which lay in its internal competence and for the Council to use qualified majority voting (QMV) in such cases.

Some of the group's recommendations were relatively uncontroversial. There was no serious objection to grouping in one section of the new treaty all the existing articles that covered the different aspects of EU external policy or to keeping different instruments for different policy areas. Similarly there was agreement on a text defining 'principles and objectives' of external action.[8]

---

[7] CONV 459/02.
[8] Later adopted with minor changes only as article III-193, paragraphs 1 and 2.

The group reported 'a high degree of support' for separating a distinct External Action Council from the General Affairs and External Relations Council, with a 'significant number of members' wanting the high representative to chair the External Action Council, while not having a right to vote. There was also strong support for a 'focal point', possibly a vice-president, within the Commission to coordinate all external issues. The group went on to consider ways of linking the posts of high representative and external affairs commissioner and set in motion ideas that would result in a proposal for a European foreign minister.[9]

One of the distinctive features of Dehaene's report was the support it gave to more QMV in foreign policy. Later in the life of the Convention, there would be wide differences between a large majority of integrationists wanting more QMV in CFSP against the wishes of intergovernmentalists, among whom the UK government was a notable supporter of unanimity.

Advancing an idea that would surface in the draft articles on external action, Dehaene's report suggested creating 'joint initiatives' of the high representative and Commission. Several group members suggested these should be approved by QMV in the Council because, by definition, they would represent 'a common EU interest'. In a passage that would resonate in the Convention's final days, Dehaene reported 'a high degree of support' in the working group for QMV in all areas of commercial policy, including services and intellectual property.

Dehaene's report agreed that 'maximum use' should be made of the existing, very limited provisions for QMV in foreign policy and recommended that the treaty should allow the European Council to extend (on the basis of unanimity) the use of QMV in CFSP. This was the first mention in the Convention of bridge or *passerelle* articles designed to eliminate the need for future treaty changes (with the attendant problems of ratification by all member states) for specific cases of moving from unanimity to QMV.

In the plenary session of 20 December, the UK's Peter Hain disclosed that he, as a member of the group, had proposed the bridging clause 'to facilitate flexibility and the evolution of a stronger foreign policy'. At the same time, however, Hain appeared to be having second thoughts about QMV in foreign policy. He claimed it could expose internal fault lines in the EU's decision making to the outside world and he ruled out majority voting for operations under ESDP, the European security and defence policy. 'I do not think we should go any further on QMV at the moment,' Hain declared.

---

[9] Described in Chapter 10.

It was not the message that a majority of conventionnels wanted to hear, least of all Joschka Fischer. In the plenary, Fischer called for a 'bold fundamental decision' that all decisions in external affairs, apart from those on security and defence, should be taken by QMV. He argued that QMV was a way of achieving consensus rather than an instrument for voting down individual member states. 'We are not facing a decision in the enlarged Union between QMV and unanimity but between QMV and total lack of importance.'

Hain, however, bluntly ruled out 'communitarisation' of foreign policy and warned against reducing external representation to one EU seat in international bodies from 15, as suggested in the report. His remarks, together with other sceptical comments about the defence document, were a warning that broad agreement or consensus in working group or Convention did not exclude stiff opposition from powerful member states.

While Hain appeared to be drawing lines in the sand against communitarisation, others felt Dehaene did not go far enough. Typical was Alain Lamassoure, the French centre-right MEP and former aide to Giscard. Dehaene, he noted, had single-handedly achieved as much as an intergovernmental conference. But the documents lacked ambition: 'We have advances of 100 metres when we should be covering a kilometre.'

Lamassoure's downbeat assessment underestimated how influential the Dehaene working group would be. The report's significance lay in the way it maximised partial agreement in the working group to push an integrationist agenda. Its conclusions were a synthesis between the community and intergovernmental methods of running an area of policy where, in the previous ten years, considerations of national sovereignty had meant little movement away from the system agreed at Maastricht. As such, it was an important pointer to future developments in the Convention.

It also showed that Dehaene was a class act. Occupied in the dialogue with civil society in the Convention's early months, he had hitherto been rather a backroom figure. His achievement pointed to a more prominent role once the Convention negotiated draft treaty texts. A convinced federalist but also a pragmatist, Dehaene knew not to allow ideological considerations get in the way of a compromise that could appeal to a broad cross section of the Convention's 105 members and 102 alternates.

8.2   DEFENCE

Defence was supposed to be one of the first European projects, following the agreement of the European Coal and Steel Community in the early 1950s.

But a treaty on a European Defence Community, negotiated among the original six member states, foundered after its ratification was rejected by the French National Assembly in 1954.

The issue slipped into the background, as the EEC and later the European Communities and the EU integrated along economic lines. However the Maastricht Treaty provisions on the common foreign and security policy (CFSP) said it 'shall include all questions related to the security of the Union, including the eventual framing of a common defence policy, which might in time lead to a common defence.'

The Amsterdam Treaty gave the European Council the right to decide on the adoption of a common defence and made provision for cooperation on armaments 'as member states consider appropriate'. It also incorporated the so called Petersberg tasks – agreed at a conference outside Bonn some years before. These, it said, 'shall include humanitarian and rescue tasks, peacekeeping tasks and tasks of combat forces in crisis management, including peace making.'

A key development came unexpectedly in December 1998 when the EU's two most powerful military nations – Britain and France – agreed in St Malo that the Union 'needs to be in a position to play its full role on the international stage'. This meant 'making a reality of the Treaty of Amsterdam', with full and rapid implementation of its provisions on CFSP, including 'the responsibility of the European Council to decide on the progressive framing of a common defence policy in the framework of CFSP.' To achieve this, the Union must be given better structures and capacity for military analysis, intelligence and strategic planning, as well as strengthened armed forces, able to react rapidly to new risks and backed by a strong and effective defence industry and technology.

Defence moved rapidly up the agenda thereafter, with the European Councils of Cologne and Helsinki in June and December 1999 agreeing on the principles and modalities of a rapid reaction force. Nice in December 2000 created decision-taking bodies: a political and security committee to provide political oversight and strategic direction of crisis management operations; a military committee to direct military activities and a military staff, which would supply the necessary expertise. The Laeken Council decided the EU was 'now able to conduct some crisis management operations' and would be in a position to take on more demanding operations as its assets and capabilities developed.

But there was no clear guidance to the Convention on defence from the Nice or Laeken declarations or from the skeleton. It was left to the working group chaired by Michel Barnier to fill in the gaps. As a commissioner, Barnier was in many respects an unexpected choice to chair the defence group. Kerr had floated the idea of putting Lamberto Dini in charge, until it was pointed out that this could provoke ructions among other conventionnels outside the Praesidium who had fancied themselves as working group chairs. But Barnier, perhaps, because the Commission has no realistic aspirations to get involved in defence policy, managed to produce a report that won widespread approval from the pre-Christmas plenary session and even attracted some kindly words from Giscard, who was no friend of the French centre-right politician.

If anything, Barnier faced an even more difficult task than Jean-Luc Dehaene. Defence was a recent arrival in the panoply of EU policies and as his working group's report noted, a 'special policy' at both national and European level. [10] 'By nature it belongs to the most sensitive areas of sovereignty and calls upon essentially national resources.' It was for this reason that a defence working group separate from that on external relations was set up.

There was no denying the complexities posed by the very different commitments, capabilities and constitutional provisions covering member states' and applicant countries' defence policies. As the report noted, 11 member states were NATO members and 10 of these were also members of the Western European Union (WEU), and so bound by collective defence clauses. Four member states were neutral while special opt-out provisions applied to NATO member and non-WEU member Denmark. The applicants included NATO members, NATO candidates, WEU associates and aspirants and, in the cases of Malta and Cyprus, two non-aligned countries.

But while committing forces (and, by implication, taking responsibility for casualties) should remain a matter for national governments and parliaments, the report staked out a claim for greater EU involvement following the events of 11 September 2001. The European Security and Defence Policy (ESDP) now had to cope with global insecurity and new risks including international terrorist organisations and weapons of mass destruction. 'A purely national framework is no longer enough. At the same time, public opinion is calling more than ever for security and protection and appears to be very much in favour of European defence.'

Barnier decided to make a virtue out of necessity and not seek to produce a truly consensual report. The main recommendations, he said, 'received large support ... A fully consensual report could only have reflected a minimalist

---

[10] CONV 461/02.

agreement'. This approach at least enabled him to ask some important questions. Going to the heart of divisions over EU policies on defence, he asked:

> Should or should not an enlarged Union with some 30 member states allow certain member states to cooperate more closely? Is it acceptable for all the member states to have to align themselves with the least committed states? Must the Union abandon some policy aspirations, which are not shared by everybody?

His report proposed a two pronged approach in response this problem. The EU should 'go as far as possible down the road travelled since Maastricht and Amsterdam of commitment by everybody to common goals'. In practice, this would mean expanding the existing Petersberg tasks of crisis management and peace enforcement with additional tasks such as conflict prevention; joint disarmament operations; post conflict stabilisation and support for third countries combating terrorism, should they request it – an idea that was strongly supported in the 20 December plenary debate on defence.

To cope with the diversity of views and capacities among member states in an enlarged Union, some members of the working group suggested greater flexibility in decision making and action. This could mean a form of 'enhanced cooperation', sometimes described as a eurogroup for defence', which would enable member states that so desired and had credible enough forces to cooperate more closely. If the willing states were brought into the orbit of 'enhanced cooperation' along the lines set out in the Treaty of Nice, they could operate within the institutional structures of the Union rather than outside. Conversely, countries which did not want to join a mission would be encouraged not to oppose it in a unanimous vote but to abstain under a procedure known as 'constructive abstention' and thereafter not participate in decisions relating to the execution of the mission.

Barnier's report also spoke of the need to boost the role of the high representative, although with a somewhat different emphasis to the discussion in the Dehaene report. The HR would have 'a right of initiative in crisis management matters' and be empowered in urgent cases to take decisions. But he or she would be very clearly reporting under the authority of the Council and in permanent contact with member states' representatives in the political and security committee (PSC). The report spoke of 'majority support' for a fund to cover costs in the early stages of a crisis management operation.

The plenary debate revealed widespread support for the idea of a collective defence clause in the treaty, which would provide for the mobilisation of both civil and military means to help member states deal with the new threat of terrorist attacks within the EU. There were sharp divisions, however, on extending such solidarity to a general collective defence clause. This idea was opposed in the working group by conventionnels from neutral states and advocates of collective defence as a matter for the NATO alliance, such as the UK.

However, there was strong support for an armaments and strategic research agency to be set up on an intergovernmental basis. Industrial policy was partly behind this idea, which had Giscard's backing. Barnier pointed out that the EU invested €10 billion in military research each year against €53 billion in the US, with the gap increasing rather than falling. 'This has important consequences not only on the military industry but also quite clearly on the civilian sector,' he said. 'In the medium term, thousands of jobs in the civilian sector will be threatened by the under-investment in leading-edge technologies which would never be developed for purely commercial civilian purposes.'

The agency might also spur member states towards meeting their obligations to supply capabilities for the 60,000 strong rapid reaction force pledged at the December 1999 Helsinki summit. The working group report listed several 'critical shortcomings' in meeting the Helsinki goal, notably in the areas of command, control and communications; strategic intelligence and the surveillance of troops in the field; strategic transport by air and sea and effective engagement capacity.

It is easy to be cynical about the armaments agency idea, given the past failure of EU member states to achieve much in the way of rationalising procurement despite cooperative arrangements (known as OCCAR and LoI) covering production of 90 per cent of EU military equipment. But Barnier clearly believed it had potential: he summed up the debate by comparing it to the European Coal and Steel Community in the early 1950s which was the forerunner of the EU.

Barnier's report said 'most' working group members wanted to move from unanimity to other decision-making procedures in defence 'relying more on consent and a culture of solidarity among member states.' One Convention member who did not was Peter Hain of the UK. Speaking for one of only two EU members with a rising defence equipment budget and for the country with arguably the most effective and mobile military forces in Europe, he reminded the Convention that 'only national governments have the right to commit their armed forces where they might risk their lives'.

The discussion on defence was 'at the limits of our ambition,' Hain warned. It was dealing with national sovereignty in a situation where only a few governments committed soldiers. Speaking for the UK, he added: 'We are only going to do that if we have a decisive say'. He urged the Convention to realise the 'realities of power', that 'foreign policy has to be serious' and could not be based on European Parliament resolutions that could not be implemented. Hain was signalling there were limits to what the UK would accept. Three weeks before, in a speech in Cardiff, Tony Blair had also pointed to difficulties ahead. 'To achieve a unified European foreign policy, we need to decide what we are unifying around. In matters of defence and security, they are so fundamental to a nation's sense of itself, there is no institutional fix that can overcome a genuine difference of view.'

8.3   THE AREA OF FREEDOM, SECURITY AND JUSTICE

The collapse of the Soviet Union, the bloody break up of Yugoslavia, the failure of states in Africa and Asia and the globalisation of crime posed new challenges to Europe's internal security in the 1990s, with which the Union had difficulty keeping pace.

Justice and home affairs (JHA) made a first appearance in the Maastricht Treaty in the form of intergovernmental cooperation to deal with 'matters of common interest'. These were listed as policies on asylum, border controls, immigration, combating drug addiction and international fraud, judicial cooperation in civil and criminal matters, customs cooperation and police cooperation to prevent and combat terrorism, drug trafficking and international crime. The new area of activity was covered by rules different to those applied in the European Community and the common foreign and security policy. In its original form, this 'third pillar' of the European Union was to prove largely ineffective because of its reliance of unanimity, with the result that it was subject to a major overhaul in the Amsterdam Treaty.

The Amsterdam Treaty cut back the third pillar by 'communitarising' the policies on immigration, asylum, border controls, visas and judicial cooperation in civil matters and transferring these to the 'first' community pillar. But again, progress proved disappointing, largely because the treaty stipulated that unanimity must apply for five years, after which the Union might move to qualified majority voting – provided all member states agreed. There was thus remarkably little effective follow through to the October 1999 European Council in Tampere, Finland, which agreed an ambitious programme to breathe life into the Union's 'area of freedom, security and justice'. However, in the judicial field, the shock of the September 11 attacks, backed by pressure from the European Council, provided the necessary impetus for justice and home affairs ministers to agree a European arrest warrant and a framework decision on combating terrorism.

The Laeken declaration noted 'frequent public calls for a greater EU role in justice and security, action against cross-border crime, control of migration flows and reception of asylum seekers and refugees from far-flung war zones'. Opinion polls suggested public support for Union involvement in securing greater internal security was greater even than that for heightened involvement in foreign and defence policy. [11] Article 3 of the skeleton included 'creation of an area of liberty, security and justice' among the Union's objectives while it was promised that article 31 would set out implementing procedures for policies on police matters and against crime.

It was therefore natural that the Tampere summit programme should be taken up by the Convention and, in the light of the slow progress achieved towards meeting the Tampere goals, that a working group should be set up to see how best to improve matters. Chaired by John Bruton, the plain speaking, former Irish prime minister who was one of the representatives of the Irish parliament in the Convention, the group concluded that the battle against crime was 'an area in which the EU can demonstrate its relevance to its citizens in the most visible way'. [12]

'We are dealing here with crimes that affect people directly, such as threats of terrorism, illegal immigration, organised crime, drug trafficking, trafficking in human beings, crime using and abusing the Internet and the laundering of money and the associated international fraud,' Bruton told the plenary session of 6 December. 'These are issues that need a response at European level.'

Bruton's group proposed sweeping changes, which – should the Convention's proposals ever be adopted – will be those that the average citizen is most likely to notice. But as well as coming up with many practical suggestions to make the Union more effective in the area of freedom, security and justice, his working group also reinforced the drive for simplification of the treaties by proposing a common general legal framework which would group all JHA provisions under a single title of the treaty and end the special 'third pillar' provisions for EU policies on justice and home affairs [13].

---

[11] Eurobarometer in April 2002 found nine out of ten of a representative sample of EU citizens thought fighting organised crime and drug trafficking should be policy priorities for the Union.

[12] CONV 426/02.

[13] Not that a single legal and institutional framework would mean identical procedures. In a rather wordy manner, the report said its proposals 'would combine elements of the

Bruton's group gave a push to existing plans for a common European asylum system by recommending that qualified majority voting and codecision be applied in the treaty to legislation on asylum, refugees and displaced persons. It urged that a common policy on immigration be enshrined in the constitutional treaty and that the Union be allowed to provide incentive and support measures to integrate legally resident nationals of third countries, with QMV and codecision in these areas. QMV and codecision should also be applied to all measures needed for a common visa policy.

Turning to the third pillar, the group said the principle of mutual recognition of judicial decisions, where the judgements of one member state are recognised by the authorities of another, should be enshrined in the treaty. This was one of the main Tampere recommendations. To make this possible, it urged measures to 'approximate' certain areas of the member states' criminal law where there was a cross-border dimension. There should be minimum rules, defining the constituent elements of crimes and penalties in particularly serious cases[14] or where the crime was committed against an EU policy (such as counterfeiting the euro). There would also have to be approximation of some elements of criminal procedure and of rules organising police and judicial cooperation between the authorities of member states.[15]

The group reached a 'broad consensus' that subjecting cooperation in criminal matters to unanimity could not survive enlargement. As a result a majority of the group's members called for QMV and codecision for legislation fixing the minimum rules for dealing with very serious cross-border crimes and those against common Union policies. As a balance to mutual recognition, QMV and codecision should also apply for setting common minimum standards to protect the rights of individuals in criminal procedure and for some common rules on aspects of criminal procedure, such as admissibility of evidence throughout the Union. In civil law, the group called for the principle of mutual recognition of judicial decisions to be enshrined in the treaty and covered by QMV and codecision.

---

community method with mechanisms allowing in some cases for reinforced coordination of operational collaboration at Union level and the involvement of national Parliaments, in order to take into account the specific features of the area of police and criminal law.' But the specific third pillar procedures of conventions, framework decisions and decisions would be replaced by laws and framework laws, as recommended by the Amato simplification working group.

[14] Tampere mentioned among others, drug trafficking, trafficking in humans and the sexual exploitation of children.

[15] For example, in the area of arrest warrants.

These far reaching steps in the direction of the Community method were hedged somewhat. The group proposed continued unanimity for pooling certain core functions of member states, such as the creation of Union bodies with operational powers (Europol and Eurojust, for example). To the annoyance of Commissioner Vitorino, the group suggested the Commission should share its right of initiative in what were 'third pillar' issues with member states, so that a quorum of one quarter of states could take an initiative.

The group also sought greater involvement of national parliaments in JHA issues, particularly in the definition of strategic guidelines by EU heads of state. It came out in favour of more operational powers for Europol, the nascent EU police body, and Eurojust, the cooperation forum for public prosecutors, but was divided over whether to back the creation of a European public prosecutor. This hotly debated issue was a policy goal strongly supported by backers of a more federal Europe and the Commission.

Bruton's report received broad based support in the plenary debate, prompting Giscard to hail its findings as 'important and visible progress' towards a homogenous European justice system which would be more simple, clear and efficient. The president observed that suppression of the third pillar might appear banal after nine months of the Convention, but few had considered such a development would be so easy at the start of its deliberations. Giscard noted that there had been many detailed objections to the group's report. Moreover, the concern of some candidate countries about the shift to QMV and codecision must be taken into consideration. However, there was little sense that the problems raised in connection with the freedom, security and justice agenda could become deal breakers in the further negotiations on the constitutional treaty.

8.4   ECONOMIC GOVERNANCE

Developments in the EU economy at the time of the Convention's launch were justification enough for it to take a hard look at the Union's economic governance. The successful launch of euro notes and coins – the culmination of more than 10 years planning and preparation – coincided with growing strains in the single currency zone. In the two months between the Laeken summit and the Convention's launch, the Commission had called Germany and Portugal to account for threatening to breach the excessive deficit rules of the eurozone's stability and growth pact which limited national budget deficits to three per cent of gross domestic product. Although a fudged settlement solved the German and Portuguese problems with the stability pact for the time being, the episode focused attention on economic policy coordination in the Union. The question posed by the Laeken declaration: 'How can economic policy coordination be stepped up?' was taken up by conventionnels during the listening phase. It was pressure from the Convention, supported by Giuliano Amato and Klaus Hänsch in the Praesidium that led to the creation of an economic governance working group. Hänsch's reward was to be given the chair.

The Convention was straying into a difficult area, however. Economic and monetary policy was in the hands of well entrenched forces. While the European Commission was always keen to boost its coordinating role, neither the European Central Bank nor the member states' finance ministers were inclined to change the status quo.

Hänsch set his group a number of questions.

- Did the introduction of the euro justify transferring competence for some aspects of economic policy to the Community?
- Was the stability and growth pact operating effectively?
- Should there be additional measures to help strengthen economic policy coordination?
- Should social and employment policies be considered of 'common concern' and require coordination in the same way as economic policy?
- Did the euro's introduction affect arguments for or against fiscal harmonisation and should some procedures for deciding tax issues be changed?
- Were responsibilities properly shared out in managing the euro?
- Should the informal 'eurogroup' of finance ministers from the eurozone be given a formal status, to take account of enlargement, when the number of eurozone countries would fall from a big majority to less than half of Union members?
- Should the euro be better represented in international fora, and if so how?

He ran into trouble. The working group was soon badly split between left and right on a host of issues. Some were very familiar, such as an impasse over whether decisions on taxation should be taken unanimously or by qualified majority voting. Others centred on the wish of many Convention members (about a fifth) to inject a greater social component into EU economic policy making. Hänsch had hoped to finish the group's deliberations in September 2002. Instead, his final draft (replete with plenty of square brackets indicating discord) attracted comments from group members running to 66 pages. The discussion on the report[16] in the plenary did not take place until 7 November.

On the big issue of competences, the group backed the status quo, leaving the monetary policy of the euro to be exercised by the ECB as a competence of the Union and economic policy the responsibility of member states.

It put its weight behind maintaining the eurogroup and called for stronger eurozone representation in international organisations. The eurogroup received even greater support during the plenary discussion when more than a dozen conventionnels said it should have a stronger institutional position in the Union. Pierre Moscovici, the soon to be replaced French government representative, presciently proposed that it should be mentioned in the eventual treaty (possibly in an annex) with the eurogroup president being appointed for an extended period of two years.

But the group split several ways over how to improve economic policy coordination, although some of its ideas garnered sufficient support to resurface later in the life of the Convention. There was strong but not unanimous support for strengthening the role of the Commission in policing the EU's broad economic policy guidelines (BEPG), which constituted one of the main tools of economic policy coordination, and the stability and growth pact. In the event of non-compliance with the BEPG or an excessive deficit, the group was 'inclined to propose' that the Commission should be able to issue warnings directly to the member state concerned. Given that Commission president Romano Prodi had recently denounced the stability pact as 'stupid', the group's inclinations were quite an endorsement for the Commission's Ecfin directorate general and its Commissioner Pedro Solbes.[17]

There were predictable divisions in the group and the plenary over tax harmonisation, with the UK leading the Convention members who rejected more qualified majority voting in this area. Britain's Peter Hain was supported by government representatives, Lena Hjelm-Wallen of Sweden, Dick Roche of Ireland and Henrik Hololei of Estonia.

However, in a rerun of the debates before the Nice summit of December 2000, there was widespread support in the working group for QMV for tax measures that would further the single market. Again this idea met fierce

---

[16] CONV 357/02.

[17] Shortly after President Prodi's remarks, his predecessor Jacques Santer, Luxembourg's representative in the Convention, observed during the 7 November plenary session that: 'The arrangements of the pact are not always as stupid as those who read it.'

resistance from the UK. But Giscard in his account of the Convention to December's Copenhagen European Council said it was 'nevertheless gaining ground'. Poland, for example, generally supported unanimity in tax matters but was prepared to accept QMV for single market measures. The idea was wholeheartedly endorsed in a joint Franco-German paper on economic governance published just before Christmas.

The economic governance group also divided along party lines between right and left on whether the treaty should take more account of 'Social Europe'. After protests by more than 40 conventionnels and alternates, a reluctant Giscard accepted the creation of a new working group on Social Europe to take this debate further and report by early February. At the end of the debate, Giscard noted various majority positions but decided these fell short of consensus. 'Consensus does not mean unanimity. But it does mean more than a majority', he declared.

8.5   SOCIAL EUROPE

If proof were needed that the Convention had a mind of its own, it came with the insistence of a vocal group of more than 40 Convention members and alternates for thorough discussion about the place social policy should have in the planned constitutional treaty.

For its many advocates, 'Social Europe' was an essential part of European integration. They could point to the European Community Treaty's article 2 on the EU's tasks, which mentioned promoting 'a high level of employment and social protection' and 'economic and social cohesion' among the member states. Social policy was in the treaties from the beginning in 1957 while the first regulations covering the coordination of social security of workers had been adopted by the Council in 1958. The Union's involvement in what was a shared competence grew substantially in the intervening years with social policy being given a prominent place in the Treaty of Amsterdam. The Laeken declaration asserted that 'citizens want results in the fields of employment and combating poverty and social exclusion' and asked how the EU could intensify cooperation in the field of social inclusion.

Yet it rapidly became clear that Giscard had little time for social policy. He turned a deaf ear to calls for a working group on the issue during the early months of the Convention's listening phase. The fear in the Convention secretariat was that, as a single issue topic, Social Europe would trigger a left-right split in the Convention and also spawn demands for other working groups (on the regions or agriculture, for example) that would absorb scant resources and deflect the Convention from its core constitutional preoccupations.

However, neither Giscard nor Sir John Kerr had reckoned on the stubbornness of the social policy supporters, who ranged behind Anne Van Lancker, a Belgian socialist MEP. With two other MEPs – Johannes Voggenhuber, the Austrian Green and Sylvia-Yvonne Kaufmann of Germany's former Communist PDS party – Van Lancker gathered 45 signatures in September 2002 to demand a debate and a working group on 'Social Europe'. During the 3–4 October plenary session, more than 40 members and alternates spoke up in support of these demands. Of the 20 or so speakers who rose to debate the matter on 3 October, only Lamassoure opposed the idea, arguing that the Convention should confine itself to constitutional rather than policy issues.

After some back stage negotiations between Kerr and Van Lancker, the dissidents settled for coverage of social issues in the Hänsch working group and a debate on social matters in the November plenary discussion on the report. It proved only a temporary respite, however. Following the debate on 7 November, Giscard gave way and preparations were made for a 'Social Europe' working group. The group was to be chaired by George Katiforis, the Greek government representative and Praesidium member. Cynics interpreted its large size, with 60 members or twice the level of the previous groups, as a ploy by Kerr to limit its effectiveness.

The mandate for the working group harked back in part to the skeleton, and asked whether article 2 on the values of the Union and article 3 setting out its objectives properly reflected Social Europe.[18] Among other points, it asked whether competences in social matters should be modified and how far QMV and codecision should replace unanimity.[19]

By the time the group reported to the plenary on 6 February 2003, activity in the Convention was picking up.[20] The first draft articles, including full versions of articles 2 and 3, were published on the same day. Not

---

[18] CONV 421/02.

[19] The debate in the working group on moving from unanimity to QMV focused on areas that were the subject of difficult negotiations in Nice: notably TEC article 13 to combat discrimination, article 42 on social security for migrant workers and the Union's supporting measures in article 137 paragraph 1 clauses c, d, f and g covering social security and social protection of workers, protection of workers where their employment contract is terminated, representation and collective defence of workers and employers interests, and conditions for employment of third country nationals legally resident in the Union. A bridge or *passerelle* clause already existed for clauses d, f and g to allow the council to move to QMV on a unanimous decision.

[20] CONV516/03 and CONV516/1/03 REV 1 COR 1.

surprisingly, draft article 2 failed to include the additional social values agreed by the group while draft article 3 only imperfectly reflected its long list of 14 social objectives. But the Convention's social policy enthusiasts at least had an arsenal of proposals to help them submit amendments.

Strong opposition from a minority of group members representing member states stood in the way of agreement on any further move to QMV in social policy. In the following plenary session, Peter Hain for the UK was adamant the UK 'cannot accept any more QMV here'. However, there was consensus that TEC article 152 on public health should be strengthened to give the Union greater scope to deal with cross-border epidemics and the threat of bio-terrorism. The group also agreed the Convention should consider facilitating EU legislation on 'services of general interest' – EU jargon for public services – as these were perceived by many group members as an important part of Europe's 'social model'. All agreed the constitutional treaty should recognise the role of the social partners – the organised lobbies of employers' and trade unions – in Europe's social dialogue.

Katiforis admitted that the achievements of the group looked modest. But the ensuing debate showed that very many conventionnels wanted to replace unanimity by QMV in the social sphere, with some suggesting a 'superqualified' majority voting system to overcome the blockages. Majority voting in social policy was, as Giscard noted, a difficult issue – and under the watchful eye of Anne Van Lancker it would stay on the Convention agenda until the very end.

8.6 THE LEGACY OF THE WORKING GROUPS

The working groups drew mixed reviews during and immediately after the Convention's study phase. Hindsight has been kinder.

Those that functioned well produced consensus on issues that had eluded successive intergovernmental conferences, including:

- agreement on a single personality for the Union, which was an important preliminary to completing the skeleton and elimination of the pillars;
- consensus on creating the 'early warning system' for national parliaments to police subsidiarity;
- an understanding that the Charter of Fundamental Rights should be included in the treaty;
- accord on reducing and reforming the bewildering array of legal instruments currently used by the Union to legislate;

- an understanding to extend the Community method and qualified majority voting to important areas of internal security, including asylum and immigration.

Although there were important areas of discord, notably in foreign affairs, defence policy, taxation and economic policy and social policy, some of these yielded partial agreement or generated momentum towards solving problems when the Convention turned to drafting the articles of the constitutional treaty. The preference – expressed in the external action working group and the Convention itself – for merging the Solana job of high representative for foreign and security policy with the Patten post of external affairs Commissioner was one example. Another was Jean-Luc Dehaene's proposal to the external action working group for bridging or *passerelle* clauses that would allow the Union to move some day from unanimity to qualified majority voting on specific issues without the palaver of renegotiating the treaty and obtaining ratification from 25 or more member states.

In the view of Giuliano Amato, the working groups allowed much freer discussion than the plenary debates and this in turn helped positions to change. The participants in the working groups found they had to explain their positions – a task rarely necessary in the plenary where contributions were generally limited to three minutes in length and virtually unknown in an intergovernmental conference. A 'sovereign no' in an IGC was just that – a rejection with no obligation to explain. The dynamics of the successful working groups were very different. There the government representative would be obliged to debate and explain or risk losing credibility and influence in the peer group.

The working groups also helped bring the Convention together and accelerate the process of creating an esprit de corps among its members. Amid the pressures of work, the distinction between full Convention members and alternates, which had been such a preoccupation of Giscard in the early weeks, disappeared.

The groups allowed a determined participant to influence the consensus. By investing a great deal of effort in the Social Europe working group, Britain's Peter Hain ensured no real progress was made towards more qualified majority voting in social policy. The groups relied on the good will of their participants to function. At times this came close to breaking down, as when the MEPs in the national parliaments group turned against their chair, Gisela Stuart, over her support for an additional chamber of national parliamentarians in Brussels.

The working groups were no panacea. They were never used for the Convention's biggest challenge – resolving the institutional questions – because the governments made clear they would not surrender their bottom lines in such fora where parliamentarians usually formed a majority of active members. For this reason, Giscard, Kerr, Amato and Dehaene never wanted a working group to deal with institutions.

A general problem was that the groups could be unrepresentative of the Convention or the Union as a whole. This, according to Jean-Luc Dehaene, was the case with the complementary competences working group, which failed badly. The groups were self-selected bodies, where there was no guarantee of balance and where not all members had the stamina or capacity to attend all meetings. Some were very poorly attended.

Imbalance, for example, was evident in the defence working group, chaired by Michel Barnier. Just over a quarter (11 out of 40) of its members came from neutral or non-aligned countries while one of its members Sylvia-Yvonne Kaufmann, the east German former Communist, waged a determined campaign for the group to be recast as the working group for peace policies. Barnier was therefore obliged to be quite cavalier in the editing of its final report.

Amato's working group on simplification contained only one EU government representative (Ireland's Dick Roche) from a membership of 38 despite it dealing with important issues of legislation and procedures and suggesting that codecision, with qualified majority voting in the Council of Ministers, should become the normal procedure for the Union.

Skilful drafting could paper over cracks within a working group. But the resulting report then ran the risk of being given a rough ride in the broader context of the Convention's plenary session. This was apparent in the plenary treatment of the group on subsidiarity, although broad consensus on its findings survived. On the other hand, turning internal conflict into an uncontroversial report, as was the case with the group on national parliaments, proved an unsatisfactory option because it did little to advance the debate.

CHAPTER 9
Managing Democracy in the Union

9.1 A MORE DEMOCRATIC UNION?

The Union had a directly elected Parliament since 1979. Greater involvement of national parliaments was an obvious priority following the Nice and Laeken declarations and was being tackled by the Convention's working groups on subsidiarity and national parliaments. And yet, there was a strong sense that more must be done to increase the democratic legitimacy and transparency of the institutions.

The Laeken declaration reflected this unease. It said the Union and its institutions must be brought closer to its citizens. It spoke of people who 'undoubtedly support the Union's broad aims, but they do not always see a connection between these goals and the Union's everyday action'. Citizens wanted institutions to be 'less unwieldy and rigid and, above all, more efficient and open.' They worried that 'deals are all too often cut out of their sight and they want better democratic scrutiny'.

Despite its continually growing powers and importance, only 49 per cent of Europe's electorate turned out to vote in the European Parliament elections of 1999. Turnout in Britain was just 24 per cent and only 30 per cent in the Netherlands and Finland. Where people did vote, it was often to make a point on local rather than European issues. Equally there was little awareness of European affairs in national polls. Giscard observed that they barely figured in the French and German national elections of 2002.

So how to change this state of affairs? One answer, strongly supported by civil society lobbyists[1] and Scandinavian conventionnels, was for the Union to provide more information to citizens. Another option, strongly supported in the Convention, was to strengthen transparency by opening the Council of Ministers' meetings to public scrutiny when legislating. This was taken up in the October skeleton which proposed a title on 'the democratic life of the Union'. Title VI was an innovation compared with previous treaties and included two new articles: one to establish the principle of democratic

---

[1] For example: Information for the European Citizen, a June 2002 report by Richard Upson for the Euro Citizen Action Service, which proposed a new article giving citizens a right to information about the EU.

equality of citizens vis-à-vis the Union's institutions and another setting out the principle of participatory democracy, which would allow 'citizens' organisations of all kinds to play a full part in the Union's affairs'. But the skeleton draft was far from comprehensive: it made no direct mention of European political parties and omitted all reference to the European Ombudsman.

There was also a general problem in trying to enhance the Union's democratic life that could be summed up in the old adage: 'You can lead a horse to water but you cannot make it drink.' As Jean-Luc Dehaene pointed out: 'you cannot have a democracy without information ... but the availability of information does not automatically entail a higher degree of interest.'[2]

Many issues in the debate over the Union's democratic life were not really constitutional. Presentation, although important, was one such matter. Here Dehaene offered some sage advice: 'At the EU level there must be a much greater effort to communicate with the citizen: the Brussels institutions must not become ivory towers, where insiders conduct impassioned debate in terms which are wholly unintelligible to the outside world.'

9.2　PRESSURE FOR A REFERENDUM ON EUROPE

The idea of a Europe-wide referendum to approve the constitutional treaty was a more radical solution to the problem of connecting Europe with its citizens and which gathered support as the Convention progressed.

The case was made by 15 full Convention members and 20 alternates in a submission to Sir John Kerr at the end of March 2003.[3] The signatories argued that referendums on the constitutional treaty should be held on the same day as the European Parliament elections in June 2004. A Europe wide referendum on European election day would focus the voter's attention on the merits or otherwise of the constitutional treaty rather than other issues. It would give the constitutional treaty 'real democratic legitimacy' and send a signal that Europe was 'about the people' and not governing elites.

> While it is the case that a 'European People' does not exist, it is equally clear that a Europe-wide referendum would create a common political space. It would be a means of bringing the peoples of Europe closer politically; it would ensure that the people were more engaged with and had a greater knowledge of the project.

---

[2] At a Friends of Europe conference: 'Understanding Europe: the citizens right to know,' 3 April 2003.
[3] CONV 658/03.

The attractive idea behind a Europe-wide referendum was that it would force the supporters of the constitutional treaty to get out and sell their product to Europe's voters. If accepted, the Union could no longer stand accused of being a top-down elitist venture. But referendums had a habit of being hijacked by domestic issues – and who was to say that would not happen even in a Europe-wide poll. What would happen if the referendum failed in several countries? Would the constitutional treaty have to be dropped altogether? Given the limited voter appeal of Union issues, a Europe wide referendum would be a high-risk strategy.

A glance at the signatories suggested some might have mixed motives. They came from a broad cross section of the Convention and included the constitutional expert Alain Lamassoure, eurosceptics, Jens-Peter Bonde and David Heathcoat-Amory, as well as such keen integrationists as Olivier Duhamel and Jürgen Meyer.

There were, it was acknowledged, legal difficulties. In cases where countries had no constitutional provisions for referendums, it was suggested they should at least hold 'consultative referenda'. After proposing that a majority of citizens and a majority of states would be necessary to secure ratification, the submission admitted that there would be problems if the constitutional treaty was rejected in a member state. The member state could try again, or seek bilaterally to regulate its relations with the Union. But there would also have to be a clause in the constitutional treaty permitting a member state to withdraw. This was envisaged from the October skeleton onwards.

The campaign was taken up by the European Referendum Campaign, a pressure group backed by direct democracy NGOs. By the time the Convention ended, 97 conventionnels had signed the ERC petition for a Europe wide referendum. At least seven member states were committed to holding a referendum.

9.3 A EUROPE OF THE REGIONS?

The discussion over bridging the gap between Europe and its citizens brought other actors into the frame and notably the Union's regions. While it was convenient shorthand to describe the EU as a Union of states and peoples, the 1980s and 1990s were a period of decentralisation and regionalisation in Europe that in some ways formed the political flip-side of economic globalisation. Historic nations within long established states, such as Catalonia in Spain and more recently Scotland and Wales in the UK, sought and won greater control over their affairs. Belgium became the most federal of all EU member states. According to the Lamassoure report on competences, 70 to 80 per cent of Community programmes were managed by local and regional authorities in the member states, suggesting that their role as partners of the Union should have greater recognition. These developments called into question the role the regions should have in a constitutional treaty. And, as Sir Neil MacCormick, the Scottish Nationalist MEP and alternate, pointed out, [4] the regional issue would grow in importance with enlargement because many of the nation states joining the Union would be smaller, but far better represented in Union institutions, than regions such as Scotland, Catalonia or Flanders.[5]

The Treaty of Maastricht recognised an increased role for the regions in the Union by allowing member states to be represented in the Council of Ministers by a regional minister if they so chose and by setting up the Committee of the Regions as an advisory body. But the committee, which had observer status in the Convention and which wanted to increase its powers, was an imperfect reflection of Europe's regional diversity. It also failed to reflect the demographic realities of the member states, so that a Luxembourg committee member would represent 71,500 citizens while a German colleague, from the other side of the national border, would represent 3.42 millions.[6]

The regions were also very diverse in their size, powers and responsibilities, ruling out a 'one size fits all' approach. There was also little appetite for creating new institutions. After toying with setting up a working group on the regions,[7] the Praesidium decided the role of local and regional authorities should be the subject of a plenary debate on 7 February 2003. This reached general consensus that the regions should be recognised in the opening articles of the constitutional treaty but revealed divisions over whether regions should have direct recourse to the European Court of Justice in cases where they considered the principle of subsidiarity was infringed. The plenary was similarly divided over the future role and composition of the Committee of the Regions.

9.4   EURATOM AND THE GREENS

The future of the Euratom, the European Atomic Energy Community, came on to the Convention agenda at the insistence of environmental activists and proved to be an issue with regional and referendum ramifications.

---

[4] 'Stateless nations and the Convention's debate on regions' CONV 525/03.

[5] Among the anomalies, Slovakia with a population of about 5 million and no coastline, would have direct representation in the fisheries council while Scotland, with about the same population and a very important fishing industry, would not.

[6] Praesidium paper on the regional and local dimension in Europe: CONV 518/03.

[7] Giscard floated the idea of a regional working group in the Praesidium of 13 June 2002.

Euratom was a blast from the past. It was agreed in 1957, when the peaceful use of nuclear energy appeared to be a clean, safe and secure route to prosperity. By the 21st century, opinion had moved decisively against nuclear power and several member states planned to phase it out. To the Greens and other environmental activists, Euratom – with its provisions for financial support of the nuclear industry – was 'completely anachronistic and obsolete' and should be scrapped. In parts of the Union, nuclear power was a source of tension among present and future member states. Thus Austria was deeply concerned about nuclear power generation in the neighbouring Czech Republic. Ireland accused Britain of contaminating its eastern coast, the home of Dublin Bay prawns, with water borne nuclear discharges from the UK's Sellafield nuclear processing plant in north-west England.

But what, if anything, should the Convention do about Euratom? The otherwise so comprehensive Laeken declaration was silent on the issue. The Praesidium had neither the appetite nor the resources to steer the Convention towards a substantial amendment of the treaty. And yet a vocal group of conventionnels wanted action and made the point clear during the autumn of 2002.

Initially, there were calls to tame Euratom. In October Hannes Farnleitner and two other Austrian conventionnels suggested Euratom should be merged into the Union's new single legal personality and subjected to greater democratic control. [8] Four months later and invoking the Laeken declaration's call to bring Europe's institutions closer to the citizen, John Bruton urged that Euratom be refocused to concentrate on safety and, with an eye on Sellafield, turned into an instrument for closing down unsafe nuclear plants.

However, the mood changed before the end of the Convention with the realisation that a referendum on the eventual constitutional treaty was likely in Austria and certain in Ireland. Johannes Voggenhuber, the Austrian Green, and John Gormley of Ireland warned that inclusion of Euratom in the treaty would 'put a bomb' under the constitutional treaty. Their argument was that the complexities of the constitutional treaty would be reduced to the simple question, 'are you for or against nuclear energy?' with voters choosing to vote 'no'. In these circumstances, keeping Euratom's separate legal personality became an attractive option because it would prevent the nuclear issue contaminating the new constitutional treaty. The Greens also believed the old and unloved Euratom would also be easier to abolish or amend as a separate treaty.

---

[8] CONV 358/02.

CHAPTER 10
The Institutions

At the end of their bad tempered summit in Nice in December 2000, the European Union's leaders declared they had 'completed the institutional changes necessary for the accession of new Member States'. Less than two years later, institutions were back on the Union's agenda.

They were, however, being kept out of the mainstream of the Convention's discussions. This was not what the conventionnels wanted. But Giscard and Sir John Kerr had decided that the power questions facing the Convention – the 'who does what?' of EU politics – could only be solved if they were left towards its end. Thus, with one or two exceptions such as the discussion over the Union's foreign minister or the idea of a legislative council, the institutional issues that would have to be resolved in the constitutional treaty swirled around the periphery of the Convention sessions for the whole of 2002.

National leaders raised important issues in speeches and in the margins of European Councils. Giscard, in the course of his bilateral diplomacy, met these leaders and discussed their concerns. But none of these contacts informed the Convention's discussions. The Praesidium fell in with the wishes of Giscard and Kerr. It agreed on 28 October there would be no working groups to discuss institutional questions. Instead, the institutions would be discussed by the Convention in plenary sessions. Although the skeleton constitutional treaty of October 2002 outlined no fewer than 13 articles on the institutions, the Praesidium was in no mood to hurry the discussions. The first plenary debate on the institutions was scheduled for January 2003, nearly 11 months after the Convention's launch and barely six months before it was due to end.

The reasons for this reticence were not difficult to discern. Institutional questions had caused an ugly split in the Union between big and small countries at the Biarritz and Nice European Councils in 2000 and again in Seville in June 2002. Their capacity to polarise was undiminished. And yet the big and small country issue was one that Giscard felt the Convention must solve if the Union were to fulfil the Laeken summit objective of becoming more efficient, while expanding to 25 or more member states.

10.1   BIG AND SMALL

It became a constant refrain of Giscard that the agreements reached at Nice may have opened the way to enlargement but had failed to consider in sufficient depth the political and institutional consequences that would follow from the change of the size and composition of the Union and its greater cultural diversity.[1]

This concern was accentuated by his perception that the Union of 25 would, because of the differing size of its members, be like no other. Its most populated state would have more people than the most populous state in the US, while its least populated would have fewer inhabitants than the least populated state in America.[2]

In a Union of 25 with 452 million inhabitants, the population of the six most populous states with more than 40 million inhabitants each would be 336 million people, or 74 per cent of the total. They would account for 77 per cent of the Union's economic output as measured by gross domestic product. A middle group of eight countries, with between eight million and 16 million people each, would have a total population of 85 million (just three million more than Germany, the Union's biggest state). These would account for 19 per cent of the Union's population and 17 per cent of its GDP. Eleven Union members, with populations between 400,000 and five million each, would have a total population of 30.5 million (less than Poland, the smallest of the six biggest states) and account for just seven per cent of Union population and six per cent of GDP.

The European Union of 25, with the large states in a minority of six, would thus be radically different from the European Economic Community of the 1950s when the founding six member states were evenly split between three big and three medium and small countries. It would be substantially different from the EU of 15, divided between five big members, six medium sized and four small. Yet the emergence of a Union in which the majority of states would have fewer than 10 million persons each[3] had been accompanied by an enhanced insistence among the medium and small countries on equality of states' rights.

---

[1] See Giscard's remarks to the European Parliament Constitutional Affairs Committee 10 October 2001. Available in the archives section of the future of Europe page on the Parliament's website.

[2] Giscard – The Henry Kissinger Lecture, Washington 11 February 2003, filed under speeches on the Convention website.

[3] 13 countries in a Union of 25 ranging upwards from Malta with 400,000 people to Sweden with 8.9 million. The 12 states with populations above 10 million each ranged from Hungary with 10.2 million to Germany with 82.4 million.

In Giscard's mind, the difference in member states' size raised fundamental issues for the Union's institutional architecture. How would it be possible to find the right balance between the demands for equality between the Union's citizens and demands for equality of rights between member states, when the latter were so different in size? Was this balance fairly reflected in the institutional structure made up of the triangle of the Council of Ministers, Commission and European Parliament? This was a particularly apposite question to put with regard to the Commission, which was charged with defining the common European interest and yet after the European Parliament elections of 2004 would be formed of one member per member state, irrespective of size. And what should be the role of the European Council, the gathering of the EU's leaders which he had initiated back in 1974, and its president?

10.2   A PRESIDENT FOR THE UNION?

The European Council was also exercising the minds of European leaders. The regular meetings of the EU leaders in the European Council were the Union's principle agenda setter. But the Union's six-month rotating presidencies were variable in performance, depending on the quality of national leaders, their government machines and their domestic political situations. They were frequently hijacked by the specific enthusiasms of the country leader holding the post of president or bogged down by trying to settle problems unresolved by member states in the Council of Ministers. The Laeken declaration put a question mark next to the Union's six-month rotating presidencies. Drawing on his experience of the Belgian presidency, Louis Michel, the Belgian foreign minister, said after Laeken that the system must change. Looking ahead to enlargement, it was easy to see why.

When the European Council first met in Dublin in 1975 the European Communities had just nine member states. With a six-month rotating presidency, each Union leader could expect to arrange its agenda and chair its regular summit meetings every four and a half years. The growing prospect of a 'big bang' enlargement raised two issues. It meant member states would soon be facing a turn in the driving seat only once every 12 and a half years with no prospect of maintaining any institutional memory between outings. Moreover, the already challenging task of keeping in touch with the fellow leaders in a Union of 15 member states to secure consensus would become much more difficult with 25 or more.

There were, of course, ways around the problem. The Seville European Council in June 2002 instituted some useful reforms to make the European

Council summits run more effectively.[4] But by this time, the idea of a stable chair for the European Council was firmly in the public domain. It had become known as the 'ABC agenda' after José Maria Aznar of Spain, Tony Blair of Britain and France's Jacques Chirac.

The week before the Convention began, Britain's foreign secretary Jack Straw mentioned the possibility of having longer term chairs of perhaps two and half years for the Union's sectoral Councils and added: 'whether the European Council chose to operate on a similar basis or to maintain the existing six-monthly rotation is a matter for discussion.'[5]

A week after the Convention's launch, Jacques Chirac publicly floated the idea of a 'president for the European Union.' While campaigning for the French presidency in Strasbourg, Chirac said it was his priority to give more political leadership to Europe.[6] The existing system of rotating presidencies would no longer be viable in the enlarged Union so he envisaged leadership resting with the European Council, which consisted of the EU leaders and the president of the Commission. They should elect at their head a person who would hold office for a 'sufficient' period, would represent Europe in the eyes of the world, give the Union the necessary institutional structure to be strong, and 'lean on' a more transparent, better coordinated Council of Ministers which would take decisions by qualified majority voting.

In May, Aznar put his own gloss on the idea in a speech in Oxford.[7] Just over four months of Spain's presidency convinced him that the rotating presidencies would no longer be viable and that a president of the European Council with a longer mandate of five or two and a half years would be a good way of ensuring that the Union's institutions were more effective. He proposed the president should not hold national office, should probably be a former head of state or government and could be helped by a 'presidential team' of five or six heads of state or government on a rotation system. The European Council would continue to be 'the political apex' of the Union and could have some extra powers – such as the capacity to dissolve Parliament on an initiative of the Commission.

Tony Blair's support for the idea was broadcast less clearly. But in his first speech to the Convention in March 2002, Peter Hain said Britain wanted stronger political leadership for the EU 'through a radically reformed

---

[4] Ludlow, *The Seville Council*, EuroComment, Brussels, 2002.
[5] Speech in The Hague 21 February 2002, filed under speeches on the British Foreign Office website http://www.fco.gov.uk.
[6] Speech of 6 March 2002. Available at http://www.elysee.fr.
[7] At St Anthony's College 20 May 2002. Available at http://europa.eu.int/futurum.

European Council giving strategic directions'. By May, the British were briefing that the UK too wanted a full-time elected president of the European Council below whom would operate a reduced number of sectoral Councils run by team presidencies. The twin ideas of a 'fixed chair' of the European Council and team presidencies were taken further by Blair in November 2002 in a speech on the future of Europe in which the prime minister was sharply critical of the system of rotating presidencies.[8] It had 'reached its limits'. It stood in the way of Europe being taken seriously at international summits and hindered the development of the common foreign and security policy. It was also difficult for the European Council to follow up initiatives such as the Lisbon agenda for modernising the EU economy 'across a wide range of sectoral Councils, each with their own hobby horses and vested interests'.

By early 2003, the UK was informally circulating ideas that would make for a very powerful European Council president. He or she should:

- prepare and preside over at least four European Council meetings a year;
- undertake a 'tour of the capitals' around all 25 member states at least four times a year;
- cooperate with the Commission president in preparing the Union's multiannual strategic agenda;
- chair the General Affairs Council;
- supervise the work of sectoral Councils;
- represent the Council in inter-institutional meetings with the Commission and European Parliament;
- supervise the high representative's work and coordinate foreign policy discussion at European Council level;
- oversee the Union's relations with the major world powers;
- attend Group of Eight meetings and work with the Commission president on issues including international financial matters, immigration counter terrorism;
- play a 'particular role' in crisis management and defence.

This ultra ambitious job description implied a very powerful figure indeed and was symptomatic of how far discussion on a stable European Council chair had developed outside the confines of the Convention. This was despite strong opposition from small member states, the Commission and federally inclined members of the European Parliament, who feared he or she would be the democratically unaccountable representative of a 'directory' of big nations and would fatally undermine the position of

---

[8] In Cardiff, 28 November 2002.

Commission president, as the guardian of the European general interest and reduce the Commission to the role of a depoliticised secretariat. To counter the arguments of the ABC group, opponents of the long-term presidency pointed out that some of the most effective of the recent rotating presidencies were run by small member states (Finland in 1999 and Portugal in the first half of 2000) while the French presidency in the second half of 2000 was an acrimonious shambles. Moreover, the rotating presidencies helped bring the Union to the citizens of the member states. All this was to no avail: the long-term European Council chair was mooted in the skeleton as a possibility.

The issue was finally debated in the Convention after being put forward as one of the main features of joint institutional proposals from France and Germany in January 2003.[9] By this time certain conventionnels, led by Lamberto Dini and Pierre Lequiller of the Italian and French parliaments and the Liberal caucus leader Andrew Duff, were suggesting the Union should aim for a single president, who would unify the positions of president of the European Council and Commission. Although mooted for the distant future, the idea proved too bold to be adopted by the Convention.

10.3   THE FOREIGN MINISTER

The idea that the Union should have a more effective foreign and security policy, commensurate with its status as one of the world's great economic and trading powers, was strongly embedded in the Convention from its first day. So too was the realisation that the division of labour between a high representative for foreign and security policy, who reported to the Council, and an external affairs commissioner, who was a member of the Commission's college, was far from ideal. The incumbents, Javier Solana as high representative, and Chris Patten, the external affairs commissioner, had in general cooperated well since the high representative's post was created in 1999. But the structure was inherently unstable. There was a risk of turf wars and large disparities in culture and financial resources between the low-budget, fast moving operation of the high representative and the very well endowed but lumbering Commission external affairs directorate. The Laeken declaration asked whether synergy between the two office holders could be reinforced. When the Convention discussed foreign and security policy in July 2002, the question was echoed by many conventionnels.

However, any proposals to change the relationship between the two office holders risked upsetting a delicate institutional balance. The future of the

---

[9] See Chapter 12.

high representative and commissioner for external affairs became a battlefield. On the one hand were the advocates of an enhanced Community method for the Union, who wanted to see external affairs become a responsibility of the Commission. On the other, were the intergovernmentalists who wished to see the high representative reinforced, perhaps by his being able to draw on the diplomatic services of the Commission, but not at the cost of his role being 'communitarised' and thus brought under the Commission's wing.

The Commission fired an early shot in this controversy in its May 2002 paper to the Convention. Arguing that the Community method could make foreign and security policy more effective, it proposed that the high representative should be gradually integrated into the Commission and operate under the responsibility of the Commission president. The Convention debate on foreign policy on 11 July highlighted other, different approaches to the issue. Elmar Brok of the EPP suggested merging the high representative's post into that of external affairs commissioner, but giving the office holder a special relationship with the Council because not all issues in foreign and security policy could be decided by the Community method. The UK's Peter Hain called for the high representative to have a formal right of initiative on common foreign and security policy matters and the right to attend Commission meetings on external policy. But for Hain, foreign policy would remain 'essentially an intergovernmental matter' and talk of it being communitarised was neither realistic nor deliverable. The July debate also saw the first proposals for a 'double-hatted' individual who would carry out the duties of Solana and Patten and yet not be part of the Community method of decision making. Hain was unenthused. 'To which body would that individual answer and be accountable: the Council or the Commission? Who is the master? That is the question. Can you have two bosses?' he asked.

The future of the high representative and the external affairs commissioner was taken up by the external action working group chaired by Jean-Luc Dehaene. In its final report, it outlined four options:[10]

- Keep the roles of high representative and external affairs commissioner separate while proposing practical measures to strengthen the HR's role and increase synergies between the two jobs.
- A full merger of the HR's functions into the Commission. This radical, federal approach would apply the Community method to external relations and greatly increase the Commission's powers by making it responsible for policy initiation, implementation and external

---

[10] CONV 459/02.

representation in all areas of EU external action. Dehaene found that even its advocates accepted that the idea would not fly because there was no consensus supporting it among member states.

- A compromise proposal for a 'European external representative' who would be a member of the Commission, preferably with the rank of vice-president, but who would have a separate mandate from, and be accountable to, the Council for the common foreign and security policy (CFSP). This 'double-hatted' individual would be appointed by a qualified majority of heads of state and government, with approval of the president of the Commission and endorsement of the European Parliament. There would be various provisions to prevent the two roles getting confused: for example, when the external representative used his or her right of initiative on CFSP in the Council, the Commission should abstain from a competing initiative. In the Commission, the representative would, as head of external relations, be able to make proposals, which would be decided in the college as now by majority voting. This double-hatted person would represent the EU and be given a number of deputies to be able to carry out what by any standards would be a huge job.

- An 'EU minister of foreign affairs' who would combine the functions of the HR and external relations commissioner under the direct authority of the European Council. Under this option – pushed by the French government – she or he would chair the External Relations Council.

The group reported 'a large trend' in favour of the third, double-hatted option. Dehaene described it as an attempt to 'bridge' the gap between the intergovernmental and Community methods. But, pointing to a potential weakness, he admitted the Union would have to make sure the individual did not come into conflict with himself.

It was this aspect that drew the scorn of Peter Hain during the subsequent 20 December plenary session. Citing doubts about double-hatting voiced by none other than Solana, Hain said no one had answered the question who would mediate in a dispute between Council and Commission. Also who would chair the external part of the External Relations Council if the HR were double-hatted with a Commission college role? And how could a full member of the Commission college chair a discussion of defence issues? It would be 'folly – actually gesture politics' to take such an important institutional step without convincing answers to these questions, he warned. Double-hatting should be a matter for discussion in the 'end game' – the final difficult negotiations in the Convention – when the issue of the long-term presidency of the EU would be addressed.

Nor was Hain alone. De Villepin of France, while backing the idea of a foreign minister, opposed double-hatting, as did Lena Hjelm Wallen, the Swedish government conventionnel. Alfonso Dastis, the increasingly active deputy to Ana Palacio, the Spanish government representative, warned that a dual function for a single person 'might create all sorts of institutional difficulties'. However, the double-hatted solution was enthusiastically supported by Joschka Fischer, recently installed as German government conventionnel. Shortly afterwards, the Dehaene working group's third option would surface as the basis for proposals from France and Germany for a Union foreign minister.

10.4 THE COUNCIL OF MINISTERS AND QUALIFIED MAJORITIES

Reform of the Council of Ministers was ongoing Union business when the Convention first met. There were two broad difficulties: one arising from the past and one looming in the future. The problem arising from the past was that the institution which was intended to represent the member states' interests in the Union's institutional triangle was no longer functioning well. Giscard liked to observe that inside the Brussels ring road, people spoke of the EU as if it had only two institutions, the European Parliament and the Commission. They neglected the Council even though it was a key decision-making body, in which the member states defended their interests and reached common positions to be negotiated with the Commission and Parliament. The problem in the future was enlargement. Germany's foreign minister Joschka Fischer pithily highlighted the potential nightmare of Council of Ministers' meetings after enlargement in his Humboldt University speech. 'How long will Council meetings actually last?' he asked. 'Days, maybe even weeks?'

The Council's malaise reflected years of growing complexity in the tasks it faced. There had been the emergence and proliferation of sectoral Councils which were difficult to coordinate and control. Some of these, such as the Ecofin Council of finance ministers, became extremely powerful and jealous of their prerogatives. Others, such as the JHA Council of justice and home affairs ministers, commanded issues of rapidly growing importance for the Union and yet were prone to the 'hobby horses and vested interests' of which Tony Blair complained. The Seville European Council took the axe to the Council formations, reducing their number from 16 to nine.

The Council of Ministers was still beset by a lack of democratic accountability and untouched by Montesquieu's ideas for a separation of powers between the legislative and executive. It was, as Brussels wags observed, the only legislative body apart from those of North Korea and

Cuba to pass laws away from the public gaze. For this reason alone, there was a strong intellectual head of steam behind the idea of a separate 'Legislative Council' which would be equivalent to a second chamber of the European Parliament, representing the states.

There was the special problem of the General Affairs and External Relations Council (GAERC), as the General Affairs Council was known after the Seville summit. The General Affairs Council was in a particularly sorry state because the foreign ministers who took part showed a marked lack of commitment to the nitty-gritty of running the Union while glorying in the televisual media opportunities offered by its discussions on foreign affairs. Because of bad feelings between the big and small members of the Union, the Seville summit failed to institute a planned reform of the Spanish presidency to separate general affairs from external relations. Although functions were separated within the Council, the GAERC still held responsibility for the management of the Union (general affairs) and for its foreign policy, its nascent defence policy, development policy and trade (external relations). The growing importance that the Convention expected to accrue to Union foreign and defence policies combined with the growing support for the idea of a Union foreign minister – apparent in the discussions of the external affairs working group – strengthened the arguments for a separate Council of external relations. Meanwhile the Union needed a more effective General Affairs Council to improve its management.

The challenges that enlargement posed for the six-month rotating presidency of the European Council applied also to the various Council formations and threw up a host of questions. Should they have longer term chairpersons and if so who? Should this be taken as an opportunity to spread responsibilities for running the Union among member states through team presidencies, and in so doing ease the tensions between big and small, north and south, new and old? Also, should there be special provisions for very important Council formations? If the choice were made to have an External Relations Council and a foreign minister, would it not make sense for the foreign minister to chair that formation of the Council? And who should chair the General Affairs Council?

The voting methods of the Council were a further issue. The question of whether or not to adopt more qualified majority voting as a way of facilitating decision making after enlargement was discussed under the heading of 'simplification' with Giuliano Amato's working group recommending it should be adopted as a general rule in the Union. But the modalities of qualified majority voting found their way into the debate on institutions.

This issue was supposed to be resolved at Nice, and it was, but through a compromise that most agreed made voting in the Council more complex. Member states are not equal in the Council. They have different voting weights depending on their size. Part of the Nice negotiations concerned the 'reweighting' of member states' votes in the Council better to reflect their populations. Because the negotiations generated more heat than light, the final outcome owed more to negotiating styles than logic with the toughest negotiators securing the biggest prizes. Thus Germany would have 29 votes from 2005, the same as France, the UK and Italy even though Germany was more than one-third bigger than each of the three. Poland and Spain would each have 27 votes even though these had less than half Germany's population. The Netherlands with 16 million people had 13 votes, only one more than the 12 votes each of Greece, Portugal, Belgium, the Czech Republic and Hungary with around 10 million inhabitants apiece.

True, Germany was compensated by having more MEPs than any other member state. Germany also secured a clause in the Nice Treaty by which a member state could halt a qualified majority decision if states representing fewer than 62 per cent of the total population of the Union had approved it. But this just increased the complexity of an already complex system. From 2005, a decision by QMV in a Union of 25 would thus have to go through the following hoops. It would need at least 232 votes in the Council from a total of 321: a pass rate of 72.27 per cent. It would have to be approved by a majority of member states, if it was based on a proposal of the Commission – otherwise the threshold would be two-thirds. It could then be blocked by the 62 per cent population rule.

An alternative, supported by the Commission and considered by the Amato group on simplification, was for a system of double majorities by which a qualified majority would represent a majority of member states and a majority (to be defined) of the Union's population. This would be easy to understand for the citizen and not require renegotiation with future enlargements. But acceptance of the double majority would require some states, notably Spain and Poland, to give up privileged positions secured in the bear garden that was Nice.

10.5 THE COMMISSION

The Commission represented the common European interest in the institutional triangle. In the Convention, it stirred national passions among some member states when its future was considered in the context of the 'numbers questions' posed by enlargement.

The paradox was rooted in a disconnect that had grown between the role of the Commission as depicted in the Union's treaties and the perception of its role in many (mainly small) member and accession states. The Commission was conceived as a collegiate body to be the guardian of the treaties and safeguard the European spirit as well as exercise considerable powers through its right of initiative and administrative duties. To this end, the treaty speaks of a body made up of individuals chosen on merit and 'whose independence is beyond doubt' and who in the performance of their duties 'shall neither seek nor take instructions from any government or from any other body'.[11] Yet during the 1990s, as enlargement to the east developed from possibility to near inevitability, this vision of the platonic, non-national, pan-European commissioner took a knock. The perception took hold among many present and future member states that each must have *equal* representation in the Commission through their own commissioner to safeguard their national interests.

This was new and would have profound implications. In the original European Community of six nations, there were nine commissioners, comprising two each for the big countries and one for each of the smaller member states, giving the big countries an automatic preponderance which went some way towards recognising their increased weight in the Union. In the Union of 15, the five big countries retained two commissioners against one each for the 10 smaller members, resulting in an even division between big and small in a college of 20.

The problems experienced by the Santer Commission, which was forced to resign *en masse* in 1999, and the Prodi Commission persuaded many that a large Commission of 20 or more was a weak Commission. However, in the Union of 25, there would be 25 commissioners from 2004 because under the Nice Treaty settlement, each member state would have one commissioner until the Union included 27 member states. At that point, the Nice Treaty specified there should be fewer commissioners than member states, with the members of the Commission chosen according to the principle of equal rotation. The Council would work out the details of the system by a unanimous decision at the appropriate time. In the meantime, thoughts tended to concentrate on a two or multi-tiered Commission with senior commissioners, who would vote in the college, and junior commissioners, who would not. Romano Prodi appeared to favour such a solution, when in the summer of 2002 he floated plans to create an inner cabinet of senior commissioners.[12]

---

[11] TEC article 213.

[12] *Financial Times,* 3 July 2002.

Although the outline of a future reduction was set at Nice, the issue of the Commission's composition shot up the Convention agenda, partly because of the impending unprecedented 'big bang' enlargement and partly because Nice niggled with Giscard. The Commission was a particularly high profile institution for the accession countries because it was their partner in the enlargement negotiations. They argued, with some justification, that each must have a commissioner as the most effective way of learning how to operate in the Union and to persuade sceptical voters that they were appropriately represented in Brussels.

For Giscard, there was first the problem of whether a Commission of 25 or more could possibly be collegiate and whether there would be sufficient proper jobs in the college for it to operate efficiently in Europe's best interest. But he was also concerned by the political problem of so many small countries making up a body that could vote decisions by a simple majority and also by the eventual implications of equal rotation on the presence of the large member states in the Commission. What legitimacy would the Commission have in the eyes of citizens of the larger member states if their interests could be outvoted by countries with a total population of fewer than 50 million in a Union of 450 million? And would a France or a Germany willingly obey a Commission instruction if, once the Union had more than 27 members, it were excluded from the decision-making college of commissioners?

The end October skeleton referred to the numbers question in a brief description of the proposed article 18. Depending on the future deliberations of the Convention, this 'would envisage the Commission either as small college or a larger body'. The skeleton was unforthcoming on the other big issue concerning the Commission. This was whether or not to elect the Commission president, and if so how.

It is standard journalistic practice (at least in Britain) to insert the word 'unelected' in front of the word 'Commission'. In fact, the Commission president is selected by a tenuously democratic process in that the (democratically elected) members of the European Council nominate a candidate for president of the Commission by qualified majority voting who is then approved by a simple majority of the European Parliament. However, the final say on the appointment of the president and the commissioners rests with the European Council.

For its advocates, election of the Commission president by the European Parliament would kill several birds with one stone. It would increase the democratic legitimacy of the Commission and so, it was argued, strengthen it as an institution. Election by the Parliament would enhance its own role, and could generate some positive spin-off in terms of greater voter interest in the European Parliament elections. As a properly elected office holder, the Commission president should also enjoy more clout in the European Council, where he (and it has always been 'he' so far) is the only non-elected leader.[13] All three consequences would be good news for integrationists. It was thus unsurprising that election of the Commission president was strongly supported by most MEPs and representatives of smaller governments and by Germany, the most federally inclined of the big member states.

The Commission itself favoured election, despite some reservations from Antonio Vitorino. It proposed in its December submission to the Convention on institutional architecture[14] that the existing procedure should be reversed and the Parliament should elect the Commission president (thus ensuring the results of the European elections would be taken into account) before he or she was confirmed by the European Council. There were more radical ideas abroad. John Bruton, for example, suggested direct election by universal suffrage of the Commission president on the grounds this would help create a European *demos*, or political identity, and conform to Montesquieu's separation of powers. The Irish government suggested an electoral college of national and European parliamentarians should do the job.

Others, notably Britain and Spain, needed persuading. There were fears of a politicisation of the Commission that could undermine its regulatory functions, notably in the field of competition policy. Questions were raised over whether Parliament would choose a Commission president of the right calibre and what safeguards should be built into the process of nominating candidates for the post. As a compromise, the centre-right European People's Party at its October 2002 congress in Estoril decided the heads of state and government should nominate the president in the light of the European election results with Parliament having the power to endorse or reject the nominee.

The question of how to appoint the other Commission members depended largely on the answers to the questions over the number of commissioners and the process of choosing its president. If the Convention decided to strengthen the Commission president by making him or her elected, it would be logical to give the president-elect a greater say in choosing the college. But the exact size of the college and the pool of talent on which to draw would depend on the choices made in answer to the numbers question as

---

[13] As is the case for all members of the European Council 'club' the personality and ability of the Commission president would also be crucial to his acquiring influence as opposed to mere acceptance.

[14] CONV 448/02 and COM (2002) 728 final entitled 'Peace, Freedom, Solidarity.'

well as specific issues such as the location of the foreign minister in the institutional structure.

10.6   THE EUROPEAN PARLIAMENT

While numbers stirred passions over their institutional implications in the Council and the Commission, their impact on the European Parliament tended to be less controversial. The directly elected Parliament operated with a manifest inequality of representation – to the disadvantage of the big member states. But it was ever thus. The system, known as degressive proportionality, meant a member for Luxembourg represented 72,000 citizens while a German MEP represented 829,000. The numbers were renegotiated at Nice but the disparity remained. From 2004 the Parliament, with a maximum of 732 seats, would include 99 MEPs from Germany and six from Luxembourg.

However, there were stirrings to adjust this situation. Before Nice, the Parliament itself had proposed that the MEPs per member state should be determined 'on the basis of populations under a proportional allocation system', adjusted to give states a minimum of four seats and with a maximum of 700 seats in the assembly. The argument in favour of such a system was that the number of MEPs could adjust more or less automatically in line with future enlargements rather than be subject to difficult negotiations as at Nice.

A bigger worry concerning the Parliament was its democratic legitimacy – or the widely perceived lack of it. Despite successive revisions of the EU treaties which had increased its powers, fewer than 50 per cent of citizens in the EU bothered to vote in the 1999 European Parliament elections. The simplification working group promised to boost Parliament's relevance by recommending that codecision, by which the Council of Ministers and Parliament are equals in legislating, 'should become the general rule for the adoption of legislative acts'. The Laeken declaration asked whether there should be a review of the way MEPs were elected. In particular, it asked whether there should be a 'European electoral constituency' or whether constituencies should continue to be determined nationally. The European Communities treaty, as modified in Nice, set the stage for elections by direct universal suffrage 'in accordance with a uniform procedure in all member states or in accordance with principles common to all member states'. This idea was echoed in article 35 of the skeleton which promised to 'refer to a protocol containing provisions for elections to the European Parliament by a uniform procedure in all member states'. But this was later dropped from the Convention's agenda.

10.7   THE CONGRESS

The 'Congress of the Peoples of Europe' was one of Giscard's pet ideas and surfaced on the margins of the Convention during its listening phase, much to the irritation of many conventionnels. Giscard's idea was to bring together members of the European Parliament and members of national parliaments from time to time to review the state of the Union. The Congress would have no legislative power, but in his 2 October speech to the College of Europe in Bruges, Giscard suggested that it 'would be consulted' on the Union's development and possible future enlargement. As well as hearing reports from the president of the European Council and the Commission president, it 'could make, or confirm, appointments to certain high political offices in the Union'.

Thus on the one hand, it could be seen as innocuous – a sort of bridge to overcome the obvious gaps in understanding between national and European politicians. On the other hand, Giscard was not averse to giving it some powers. In this he was not alone. Andrew Duff in his 'model constitution for a federal Union of Europe' proposed a Congress of MEPs and national parliamentarians 'to elect or to impeach' the Commission president.[15] Article 19 of the skeleton mentioned the possibility of a Congress without providing any details. Most conventionnels were hostile, however. Debating the skeleton, Poland's Danuta Hübner said it was unnecessary to create new institutions when the existing ones needed improvement. Elmar Brok for the EPP denounced the Congress as a Franco-British inspired ruse to weaken both the European Parliament and national parliaments – the latter by giving their members tasks far away from their national capitals.

10.8   THE COURT OF JUSTICE AND OTHER INSTITUTIONS

The issues concerning the Court of Justice were less politically charged than those relating to the Union's policy-making institutions but they were difficult nonetheless. A special 'discussion circle', chaired by Antonio Vitorino, met early in 2003. Among its concerns, it considered the procedures for appointing judges, whether to change the titles of the Court of Justice and the Court of First Instance (CFI), whether to shift some laws governing the court from unanimity to qualified majority voting, whether to extend judicial review to the acts of Union 'agencies and bodies' and whether to make the penalties for noncompliance with Court judgements more effective. Several conventionnels also raised the issue of whether individuals should have better access to the CFI because case law in certain

---

[15] CONV 234/02.

cases could make this impossible. A difficult political issue that crept on to the group's agenda was whether the Court of Justice should have jurisdiction against acts of the common foreign and security policy (CFSP).

As solving these problems turned into a largely separate process from achieving consensus over the main political issues facing the Convention, the results can be summarised here. The Convention ultimately opted for reforms, largely in line with the Vitorino group's recommendations. It was agreed to set up an advisory panel to help member states select the correct candidates to be judges. It renamed the CFI the 'High Court' to reflect the fact the Union was planning to set up further specialised courts, including a patent court, which would also deal with issues 'at first instance'. The creation of the specialised courts, the extension of the Court's jurisdiction to patents and changes to most of the Court's statute were made the subject of laws to be passed by QMV, rather than unanimity. In an important change, the Convention decided the Court should be able to review the legality of acts of agencies and bodies.[16] It adopted simplified wording to help give individuals access to the High Court in carefully defined circumstances. On foreign policy, it stipulated that the Court would have no jurisdiction over foreign and defence policy although it would be able to rule on the legality of sanctions imposed by the Union.

The Convention included the European Central Bank among the Union's institutions for the first time, albeit outside the constitutional treaty's main institutional framework.[17] The Convention ignored the efforts of a small minority of left wing members to have the ECB take account of economic conditions such as growth or employment alongside its 'primary objective' of price stability when setting monetary policy. One change of potential interest to the financial sector opened the way for the ECB to be given tasks related to the prudential supervision of banks and other financial institutions, excluding insurance companies, by QMV and codecision rather than unanimity in the Council with Parliament's assent.

Existing rules governing the Court of Auditors were unchanged by the Convention, which took no account of a call from the UK's Peter Hain and other government representatives for a shake up in the court's structure. The Nice summit agreed the court should consist of one national per member state. Hain, who was following up suggestions from the British House of Lords, sought put the court under the management of a nine member board of 'auditors general', who would come from the member states on the basis of strict rotation, and rename it the European Union Audit Office. The UK

---

[16] Article III-270.
[17] Article I-29.

argued that the Nice arrangements threatened to make the court unwieldy and ineffective.

10.9   GISCARD AND THE INSTITUTIONAL DEBATE

The institutional debate in the Convention was fraught with hazard. It was so easy to view the institutions individually and as protagonists in a turf war. Yet for the Union to thrive in the 21st century, all three sides of the institutional triangle needed to be strengthened.

This point was made by Giscard. But in the eyes of many conventionnels, he suffered from a credibility problem. He was after all, the man who had invented the European Council and he made no secret of his view that President Prodi's vision of the Commission forming the 'government' of the Union was based on a misunderstanding of history. When Giscard met the European Parliament's constitutional affairs committee in October 2001, he observed that the Union's founding fathers had indeed envisaged that the Commission would develop into a European government. But things had changed with the creation of the European Council. That was when Jean Monnet had told Giscard, 'You are right, the future European executive will be the European Council'.

After that, Giscard modified his rhetoric somewhat. At a later meeting of the constitutional affairs committee, a month after the Convention started, Olivier Duhamel, the French Socialist MEP, asked Giscard whether he was a 'Council man' or a 'Communitarian'. Giscard replied that he was a communitarian at the time of the Treaty of Rome but then became a Council man. He now believed Europe needed a new form of cooperation between the two as well as an identifiable executive. For his listeners, it marked a change of viewpoint, but hardly a conversion.

Giscard faced another problem. He was generally perceived as a 'big country' man – an impression he did nothing to dispel while chairing the plenary. While it was clear that he paid attention when Peter Hain or Joschka Fischer spoke, he would often be seen chatting to Sir John Kerr or Amato during the interventions from small member states. Such behaviour rankled and helped exacerbate ill feeling among the 'smalls' as the Convention progressed.

Part IV

Changing Dynamics:
From Skeleton to Early Draft Articles

CHAPTER 11
The Member States Awake
and the Commission Confuses

The dynamics of the Convention underwent a radical change during the final months of 2002 and early 2003. As the working groups laboured to put flesh on Giscard's skeleton, the member states' governments woke up to the Convention's importance. Germany and France in particular upgraded their input, drafting in their foreign ministers as government representatives and simultaneously beefing up support staff. By contrast, and through no fault of the two commissioners in the Convention, the European Commission saw its influence erode because of disunity in the college and tactical errors. At the start of the Convention, the Commission had encapsulated the hopes of integrationists and was seen as the natural guardian of the interests of the small countries. Self-inflicted wounds were to render it largely irrelevant in the final forging of consensus.

11.1 THE INVASION OF FOREIGN MINISTERS

Spain's decision in July 2002 to promote its conventionnel, the MEP Ana Palacio, to foreign minister and keep her in the Convention and its Praesidium appeared an eccentric move at the time. But it set a trend that transformed the Convention. During autumn, first Germany and then France appointed their foreign ministers to the Convention. Joschka Fischer and Dominique de Villepin were joined later by the foreign ministers of Slovenia and Latvia and in 2003 by George Papandreou, the Greek foreign minister, who represented Greece in the Praesidium during the Greek EU presidency.

The upgrading of the German and French representations partly reflected the outcome of the two countries' general elections. Pre-election uncertainty – compounded in the French case by the stultifying effects of cohabitation between Lionel Jospin's socialist-led government and Jacques Chirac's right wing presidency – meant both countries had little to say in the Convention's early months. Germany's Peter Glotz, it is true, produced several interesting interventions, but he lacked the clout of ministerial office. France's Pierre Moscovici, the minister for Europe in Jospin's left wing government, lost both office and power base once cohabitation was swept away and the centre-right Raffarin administration took over in Paris. Moscovici was a semi-detached figure during the autumn of 2002, especially following France's decision during the summer to appoint a new alternate: Pascale Andréani, a precise and petite, bespectacled brunette who was a trusted adviser of President Chirac.

Fischer's appointment, announced in October, also reflected the increased strength of his Green party following a good election performance which gave Germany's red-green coalition an unexpected further four years in power. Joining him as Germany's alternate and Gerhard Schröder's eyes and ears in the Convention was Hans Martin Bury, a Social Democrat minister of state at the German foreign ministry.

Fischer was Germany's most popular politician and its best known Green. He was a one time radical firebrand, who as environment minister in his home state of Hessen in the 1980s caused a stir by wearing sneakers in the Wiesbaden legislature. He had become the epitome of silken suited probity since taking over the Auswärtiges Amt after Schröder's first election victory in 1998. When he joined the Convention, Fischer was one of Europe's most respected foreign ministers and one of few who could claim to be an original thinker. He was a passionate European whose idealism was leavened by pragmatism. During Germany's EU presidency in 1999 he played a key part in launching the convention for the Charter of Fundamental Rights and developing Europe's security and defence initiative. His Humboldt lecture in May 2000 was the catalyst that led to the calling of the Convention and his decision to take part in its sessions gave it a palpable boost. Aged 54 when he joined the Convention, Fischer was a brilliant speaker who became one of a select band (including Vitorino, Lamassoure and Duff) who was guaranteed an attentive audience on taking the floor. But Fischer was also rather an elusive character, having, like his boss Schröder, re-invented himself several times in a long political career. He was not clubbable. He liked to fix issues behind the scenes and saw his trips to Brussels as occasions for bi-lateral wheeling and dealing rather than open discourse. A true conventionnel he was not.

If Fischer was elusive, de Villepin was showy. He joined the Convention around his 49th birthday, an impressive sight with a slender, tanned alert face and a shock of wavy grey hair. De Villepin cut a dashing figure and he knew it. He was also very cultured and let others know that. His first major speech on Europe[1] was a rhetorical *tour de force* that took his audience in its three opening paragraphs on a whirlwind tour of the continent's culture and history, from its ancient glories to the horrors of Guernica and Auschwitz which were still in living memory. De Villepin swept through a pantheon of

---

[1] 2 December 2002 in Marseilles.

continent's cultural icons and inspirational politicians, invoking poets from Byron to Villon, holy men from St Bernard to Bonhöffer, radicals from Victor Hugo to Mazzini, and Europe's founding fathers of Adenauer, Gasperi, Monnet and Schuman to whom he added General de Gaulle, who had known 'to combine the essential: Europe's ambitions with respect for its nation states'. De Villepin had joined the French foreign service in the 1980s, been posted as a diplomat to Washington in the 1980s and was a specialist in Asia, Africa and Madagascar before he became Chirac's secretary general in the Elysée in May 1995, a post he held for seven years. He was no expert on Europe when he took over as foreign minister in May 2002. He didn't need to be, with the diligent and efficient Pascale Andréani as his alternate and Pierre Vimont, Andréani's predecessor as alternate and a distinguished former permanent representative in Brussels, at the Quai d'Orsay.

Fischer lost no time in telling the Convention what he expected. In his first appearance on 28 October, he called for a European constitution, without options which could be adopted without detailed negotiations in the subsequent intergovernmental conference. The Charter of Fundamental Rights would be included as a justiciable part of the text. He also wanted greater democratic legitimacy for the Union, a clear separation of powers at Union level, maintenance of the institutional triangle so that any strengthening of the Council would only be acceptable if the Commission and Parliament were also strengthened, and more integration to strengthen the Union's ability to act after enlargement. The latter point, he stressed, meant no reversal of policies determined by the Community method in favour of intergovernmental decision making. The Union's democratic legitimacy could best be served by having the European Parliament elect the Commission president.

De Villepin was similarly forward looking when he made his debut in a plenary session on 5 December. He too spoke of a better balance of forces in the institutional triangle, but with a rather different emphasis. De Villepin found it odd that the Commission should only be accountable to the European Parliament and without any reciprocal obligation. He therefore suggested that the Commission should also be accountable to the European Council, which would be able to dissolve the Parliament on a proposal from the Commission. Whereas Fischer stressed the importance of strengthening all sides of the institutional triangle, the European Council bulked large in de Villepin's vision of Europe. It would have the responsibility for setting the strategic guidelines in all areas of Union action. The Council of Ministers' job would be to adopt decisions marked out by the Union's leaders. The Commission would 'imagine, propose and implement'. The Parliament would control, legislate with the Council, vote the budget and 'perhaps one day, a community tax'. At first sight, Germany and France seemed to have little in common on the institutional front.

It was partly the inertia of Germany and France that had allowed Britain's Peter Hain to shine so much in the early months. Fischer was determined to change this. Hain recalls how at their first meeting in Brussels, Fischer greeted him with the words: 'I hear you Brits are running the Convention, that's why I'm here.' Ironically, the appointment of such heavyweights from the founding members of the original European Community came as Hain was promoted from being minister for Europe to secretary of state for Wales – a cabinet position in the UK, whereas minister for Europe was not.

Hain, one of the most assiduous of government representatives at the Convention, stayed as Britain's representative and was as busy as ever. But his promotion left the UK Foreign Office with no direct representation in the Convention. Baroness Scotland, the UK government alternate, was a junior minister in the Lord Chancellor's office – the legal part of the UK government machine.

Hain's retention was a sign that Britain's Prime Minister, Tony Blair, was taking a keen personal interest in the Convention. But the broader personnel changes in the Convention came at an awkward time for Britain. As the Convention turned to tackle detailed issues, there were ever more questions where the UK had problems being part of a consensus. The working group discussions saw the UK in a minority on aspects of foreign, defence and tax policy while the UK had difficulties accepting the incorporation of the Charter of Fundamental Rights in the eventual constitutional treaty. As far as Hain was concerned, the Convention's high profile meant he had to be doubly sure that the great departments of state in the UK – the Treasury, the Home Office and the Foreign Office – understood what he was doing and would not work against him. Hain could work a room in Brussels but was in no position to overrule his colleagues in Whitehall.

There were also new faces representing the Netherlands, Portugal, Ireland, and Turkey. The appointment of Gijs de Vries, a former MEP, for the Netherlands in place of Hans van Mierlo brought a more active and thoughtful contributor to the Convention floor. The appointment of Dick Roche, the Irish minister for Europe, provided the small countries with a fluent and rugged advocate.

The invasion of the foreign ministers killed off for good the *canard* that the Convention was a just a talking shop. Its profile, as measured by the number of television teams covering its meetings, rose appreciably. Officials noted how the quality of support staff rose in those delegations represented by high ranking ministers. The foreign ministers, and ministers of cabinet rank such as Hain or Fini, could negotiate and cut deals in the expectation that they would be supported by their governments and parliaments. This was less certain for those countries represented by non-politicians, be they officials or academics. It is interesting that Finland, which chose not to be represented in the Convention by a politician, was among the more disappointed member states at its close. Rank was also an important consideration for Giscard. Quite apart from his natural elitism, Giscard was more inclined to take note of a powerful minister representing a country because he or she would be better able to help determine the final consensus and bind their government to it.

There was an immediate inflation of expectations as pundits forecast that the appointments of Fischer and de Villepin would turn the Convention into the locus for negotiations and deal making that would reduce the subsequent IGC into little more than a rubber-stamping operation.[2] This appeared to be Fischer's view in the plenary session of 8 November, when he warned that: 'Anything that is not settled within the Convention will not be settled elsewhere.'

But the appointment of foreign ministers to the Convention was not without risk. They were very busy people with many other claims on their time. Ana Palacio, one of the Convention stars in its early months, was far less in evidence after her promotion in July and in the late autumn was frequently absent from Praesidium meetings. Louis Michel, Belgium's foreign minister and a Convention representative from the start, hardly shone. Papandreou turned out to be a very spasmodic attendee, which was hardly surprising given the pressures of the Greek presidency in the first half of 2003. Fischer raised eyebrows on his first appearance at the Convention, when he appeared, delivered a speech and left shortly afterwards. In the final plenary session of 2002, which dealt with the important issues of foreign and defence policy, Fischer arrived near the end of the meeting, having been held up by a crucial parliamentary vote in Berlin. De Villepin was not much better, appearing after lunch for the second half of the all day session. The time pressures on the two ministers grew dramatically during 2003 as war loomed in Iraq and Germany started a two-year stint in the UN Security Council. Absenteeism and perfunctory appearances did not go down well with the other conventionnels.

---

[2] A trend that Giscard was determined to resist on the grounds that the Convention would lose its democratic legitimacy. See Giscard's article in *Le Monde* 14 January 2003: La Convention européenne à mi-parcours.

11.2 THE FRANCO-GERMAN MOTOR STARTS TO TURN

The upgrading of the French and German representations was followed by a revival of the Franco-German partnership inside and outside the Convention room.

As early as March 2002, President Chirac had called for a 'new founding pact between France and Germany' in January 2003 to mark the 40th anniversary of the Elysée Treaty of reconciliation between the two countries.[3] As the anniversary approached, it became clear that this would also be the occasion for substantial thoughts about the future of Europe. Before the anniversary, however, the two foreign ministers submitted three joint contributions to the Convention. Their proposals on defence policy, justice and internal security and economic policy demonstrated shared ambitions for greater integration.

The paper on defence was best timed to influence the debate in the Convention.[4] It was published on 22 November, a month before the plenary discussion on the report of the defence working group which mirrored many of its ideas. The Franco-German defence paper struck a decisively European (as opposed to NATO) note with a call for a 'solidarity clause' to bind member states in the new Treaty against terrorism and other risks. Its advocacy of reinforced cooperation in defence policy was also reminiscent of long past Franco-German aspirations to form an *avant-garde* in Europe. But the laudable and heavy stress placed on the need to build up military capabilities, strengthen military research and development, and create a European defence procurement market rang rather hollow in the light of Germany's shrinking military budget and its failure fully to support projects such as the urgently needed Airbus A400 heavy lift transport aircraft.

The second joint paper on freedom, justice and security, produced at the end of November, was a strongly integrationist document that went beyond the ideas already drafted for the final paper of John Bruton's working group.[5] It urged a step-by-step transformation of Eurojust into a European public prosecutors' office; powers for Europol to carry out investigations, and rules for member state police forces to operate on the territory of other Union members in certain circumstances. It talked of 'harmonising' rather than approximating criminal law, urged 'effective controls' of asylum and immigration at the Union's borders and called for a target date in the

---

[3] 6 March 2002 in Strasbourg, available in the speeches section of the French presidents website http://www.elysee.fr.
[4] CONV 422/02.
[5] CONV 435/02.

constitutional treaty for creating a European border police. The third pillar would disappear. Qualified majority voting would be introduced after a transitional period for all except coercive measures in the area of police cooperation and for most areas of judicial cooperation. Like Bruton, Fischer and de Villepin suggested that both the Commission and member states should have the power of initiative in policing issues. France and Germany also advocated reinforced cooperation, even when fewer than eight member states supported a given measure in Council. The two countries differed on one detail: the best way of defining minimum standards when harmonising criminal law.

Joint proposals for strengthening the Eurogroup and improving economic policy coordination, published just before Christmas, came too late to influence discussions in the working group on economic governance.[6] But, again, the two countries threw their weight behind integrationist proposals that went beyond the working group's conclusions. Germany shifted its position, which had hitherto stressed the importance of keeping the 15 nation 'Ecofin' Council of EU finance ministers as the forum for economic policy decisions, to backing a 'Euro-Ecofin' Council in which the eurogroup members could take their own economic policy decisions for the single currency zone. The paper called for recognition of the eurogroup in a protocol to the constitutional treaty, appointment of its chair for two years and its single representation in international fora such as the International Monetary Fund. The paper also backed QMV for a number of key tax issues, including taxes as they affected the single market and some harmonisation of turnover and consumer taxes, thus posing a significant challenge to the UK, Sweden and Ireland.

11.3   THE COMMISSION AND PENELOPE

As the member state governments were raising their profile in the Convention, the European Commission was having problems. The Commission embarked on the Convention in a sprit of optimism and buoyed by a fund of goodwill, especially from the applicant countries and smaller member states. In addition to having two commissioners in the Praesidium, a large majority of the other Praesidium members could be counted as natural allies of the institution that represented the European interest and sought to preserve and enhance the Community method of decision making in the Union. The three government representatives, Henning Christophersen, a former commissioner, George Katiforis, an MEP, and Ana Palacio, an MEP until July 2002, knew the ways of Brussels and therefore to appreciate the

---

[6] CONV 470/02.

Commission's role. The same applied to the two representatives of the MEPs, Inigo Méndez de Vigo and Klaus Hänsch. Among the national parliamentarians in the Praesidium, the two from small countries, John Bruton from Ireland and Alojz Peterle of Slovenia, could be expected to sympathise with the Commission's goals. Jean-Luc Dehaene, one of Giscard's two deputies, had been an adviser to Romano Prodi, the Commission president, in the months before the Nice European Council. The Commission set up its own task force in its Breydel headquarters building who would spread its message through briefing notes and background information to inexperienced or sympathetic conventionnels. As an institution, it seemed particularly well placed to reach out to Convention members from national parliaments and accession countries while in the Praesidium and plenaries, Michel Barnier and Antonio Vitorino, could draw on the resources of the 'house' to shine.

Words of goodwill came from the unlikeliest of sources. Peter Hain spoke of Britain's desire for a stronger Commission in his first speech to the Convention in March 2002. His sentiments were echoed some months later by Tony Blair in his keynote speech on the EU delivered in Cardiff on 28 November. Yet by early 2003, the Commission had lost much influence in the Convention. Instead of the Commission leading the debate, the Convention's secretariat had established an unchallenged monopoly of initiative.

The root cause was discord in the college on how to play the Convention. The problems started early in 2002 when the Commission was working on a paper to put to the Convention. The document, expected first for April and then early May, failed to appear. Instead there were reports in April of the college holding an acrimonious seminar in Val Duchesse, the historic house in the Brussels suburbs where the Commission and the Belgian government held their 'away days'. When the document finally appeared on 22 May, it was worthy rather than gripping: a Chinese meal of a paper that left the consumer still hungry for more.[7] Those conventionnels who expected it to structure the debate in the Convention were disappointed. Although entitled 'A Project for the European Union' it was far from comprehensive. It touched only on a few key aspects of the Convention's work: economic policy, CFSP, freedom, security and justice. Its passages on the constitutional treaty and the Union's institutions were discursive and circumspect.

The pattern repeated itself in the following months. The Commission was expected to produce a follow up document shortly after the summer break. It

---

[7] COM(2002) 247 final.

failed to appear amid reports and rumours of strains in the college. Only at the beginning of December, did the Commission publish its long awaited second contribution to the Convention, which contained its ideas on the EU's future institutional architecture under the title 'Peace, Freedom, Solidarity'.[8]

It was a campaigning document rather than one which aimed to bridge the already obvious gap between 'communitarians' and 'intergovernmentalists'. At the heart of the Commission's plan to 'consolidate and develop the integration of Europe' lay an enhanced Community method of agreeing and implementing policy. Intergovernmental cooperation was disqualified as a 'source of inefficiency' while allowing the EU's future to be directed by just a few member states was 'a potential source for tension and dispute'. Unfortunately, hopes that this document might give a boost to the integrationist/small country camp as the Convention moved from the study to the negotiation phase were frustrated by the Commission's inept handling of its launch.

The first December week saw the release of not just one but two Commission documents. In addition to the formal communication, which was approved after much difficulty by the college, there emerged a more radically federalist, full draft treaty for an enlarged EU in which almost all decisions would be taken by majority votes. Codenamed Penelope and variously described as a feasibility study or working document, this text was produced at Romano Prodi's request by a small group of Commission officials headed by Francois Lamoureux, a close former aide to Jacques Delors. The furore that surrounded Penelope's appearance overshadowed the official text.

Persons unknown[9] contrived to have Penelope leaked to the French daily *Le Monde* and leading newspapers in Italy, Spain and Germany. The reports about it appeared on the streets of Paris just as the Convention Praesidium was meeting in Brussels on the afternoon of Wednesday, 4 December for the first of its December meetings. This was just hours before the college of commissioners was due to give final approval to the official document and on the eve of presentations of the formal communication by Prodi to the European Parliament, the press and the Convention.

In the Praesidium, Michel Barnier and Antonio Vitorino found themselves on the spot. They had come prepared to discuss the official document but instead were quizzed about Penelope. Later denials notwithstanding, a

---

[8] COM (2002) 728 final.
[9] Generally thought to be in the Prodi cabinet.

reliable source reported that the two disowned any knowledge of Penelope in the Praesidium. It later transpired the two commissioners were aware of the project but were not privy to its imminent, unorthodox disclosure. Giscard was especially peeved, probably because he did not know what to believe. He had obtained a copy of the Penelope text in unusual circumstances. The Convention president was at the Gare du Nord in Paris boarding the train to travel to the Praesidium meeting in Brussels when the individual sent by the Commission to Paris to brief *Le Monde* about the document gave Giscard his copy. It seems that Giscard was under the impression that this was the official Commission document.

The Wednesday night meeting of the Commission was long and stormy with Neil Kinnock, one of Prodi's vice-presidents, cutting Prodi's opening remarks off in mid-flow and demanding to know what was going on. Mario Monti, the Italian competition commissioner and normally a supporter of Prodi's, denounced the leak as unacceptable. According to one official, only four Commissioners (Pascal Lamy, Philippe Busquin, Michaele Schreyer and Anna Diamantopoulou) supported the Penelope draft.

The following day, 5 December, Prodi presented the official Commission document to the Parliament, the press and the Convention. He glossed over Penelope, saying this was 'simply a mock up, a feasibility study, a technical working tool'. It was 'neither discussed by the college nor submitted for its approval'. The college had 'no political responsibility for its content'. Although Prodi said he, Barnier and Vitorino had commissioned it from the group of experts, the pained expressions and uncomfortable body language of the two Commission members of the Convention when the three appeared before the press lent credence to reports that they had agreed to have their names associated with Penelope after its unofficial disclosure as a face saving exercise only.

The confusion did nothing to enhance Prodi's credibility. 'I don't think you have done any political favours with this text,' Méndez de Vigo told Prodi after his morning appearance in the Parliament. 'Everyone is now talking about Penelope rather than the good document that you put forward.' As soon as Prodi finished presenting the Commission's formal document to the Convention in the afternoon, Giscard prevented any opportunity for questioning by immediately steering him through the door at the back of the podium. The snub delivered, conventionnels sitting just below the dais were amused to see Giscard return to his seat with a slight smile on his face and rubbing his hands together as if in satisfaction at a job well done.

Giscard's condemnation of the Commission's official contribution and Penelope came the following day. 'One might have thought there would be some emotion' in reaction to the Commission document, 'but no', he said. He fastened on Penelope's preamble, which took over the text of the European Coal and Steel Community treaty with minor amendments, to deliver the *coup de grace*. Penelope, Giscard sniffed, was 'not current' and had 'an introduction that is 50 years old'. The message was clear. She could hardly serve as a constitution that should last 50 years into the 21st century.

But Giscard was being unfair to a damsel in distress. Penelope, as a full draft treaty, was of considerable technical importance and as the Convention's work unfolded it became a handy source of reference throughout Brussels, not least for Giscard himself.

11.4   THE OFFICIAL COMMISSION DOCUMENT

The underlying message of the official Commission Contribution[10] was that the EU must consolidate and develop its integration with a modernised Community method and develop so as to 'exercise the responsibilities of a world power'. An important aspect of the Commission's paper was its call for the creation of an EU foreign minister who would be 'secretary of the EU, as a vice-president of the Commission with a special status' and who would report to both the European Council and the president of the Commission. Although the Commission paper took some account of the sensibilities of the more intergovernmental member states, it rejected the idea of a long-term president of either the European Council or the General Affairs Council. It recommended maintaining six-month rotation for the presidency of the European Council, the General Affairs Council and Coreper.

Warning that a long-term presidency of the European Council 'would open a rift in our institutional structure', Prodi asked 'Who would elect the President of the Union? Who would he or she be accountable to?' and echoing a recent speech by Guy Verhofstadt, the Belgian prime minister, he added: 'And above all, what would this president be doing for the other 360 days of the year when the [European] Council is not meeting and George Bush is not calling?'

Prodi declared that tomorrow's EU must have a third basis of legitimacy as well as being 'a Union of peoples and states'. The Union would be there 'to defend the common interest' and become 'the world's first true supranational democracy'. The Commission's paper made much of maintaining the EU's institutional balance. But the process of reform that it advocated would inevitably enhance the Commission's role.

---

[10] COM (2002) 728 final and CONV 448/02.

The document was unashamedly federal in tone. The Commission's right of initiative should extend to the whole legislative field and, military matters apart, to areas where policies are coordinated, including the economy, employment, police cooperation and – eventually – foreign and security policy. The Commission would have a stronger role coordinating the eurozone economy and represent it in international organisations.

Codecision should be applied without exception to the adoption of all European laws. This would also apply to the EU budget, in the process ending the distinction between compulsory and non-compulsory expenditure. Qualified majority voting should be made the general rule in the Council, and determined by a simple dual majority of member states representing a majority of the total EU population rather than the complex arrangements agreed at the Nice summit. Unanimity would therefore go. But the Council could take special decisions by 'enhanced majorities' reflecting three-quarters of governments and two-thirds of the total EU population.

Prodi put abolishing unanimity as the first priority among the Commission's demands for improving the functioning of the Union. 'That rule has marked the bleakest periods in the Union's recent history,' he told Parliament. 'If the veto has brought paralysis with 15 member states, think what would happen with 25 or more.'

In return for its increased role, the Commission would be more clearly accountable to both the Parliament and the European Council. The Commission president would be elected by the Parliament, by at least two-thirds of the votes in a secret ballot. The European Council, after confirming the Parliament's choice, would then designate the other Commission members 'by common accord with him or her'. The Parliament would then approve the whole Commission.

The paper opened the door cautiously to a smaller college. It noted that the next Commission would comprise one commissioner per member state. But if the new Commission were to perform its executive functions efficiently, it would 'need to be restructured, as soon as the new member states enter, around the Union's core tasks'.

The election of the Commission president by the Parliament and confirmation by the European Council would reverse the present procedure. But in another innovation, the Commission proposed dual accountability to both the Parliament and the European Council by giving both institutions the right to pass a motion of censure on the Commission.

In proposing the post of Secretary of the EU, the Commission took further thoughts first expounded in its 22 May communication to the Convention in which it recommended merging the functions of the high representative and external affairs commissioner.

The passage of the Commission paper dealing with the secretary is dense even by EU standards. Fortunately a background note issued on the same day was more explicit. 'What the Commission proposes is to integrate the HR into the Commission, i.e. where most of the Union's instruments and resources of external action are already located', it said. In short, CFSP would be put on the same basis as trade or development policy. According to Prodi, this would give the EU 'a single voice in international politics'.

Arriving at this point would be a step-by-step process, however. The secretary would be appointed by common accord of the European Council and the Commission president designate, would report to both and could be fired by both. Only after an unspecified transitional period, would he or she 'autonomously exercise the Commission's right of initiative in terms of foreign and security policy' in line with Council guidelines. She or he would represent the Union vis-à-vis non-member countries and international bodies and be responsible for implementing common decisions.

The Commission's paper was debated, by the European Parliament, immediately after its presentation in the morning of 5 December and before the Convention session that afternoon. MEPs had hardly any time to scrutinise the text. It received a generally warmer reception from the centre-right than the centre-left. Senior socialist MEPs, including Enrique Baron Crespo and Klaus Hänsch, criticised giving the European Council a right of censure over the Commission as did Elmar Brok of the centre-right EPP. In Hänsch's view the text was not a solution to the EU's institutional problems and created more rather than less confusion in certain areas. 'What happens if the Parliament is for you and the European Council against? Do you stay or go?' he asked.

Both Hänsch and Brok criticised the proposal that the Commission president would need support of two-thirds of MEPs. Hänsch, the representative of the socialist MEPs in the Praesidium, warned that the Commission president would always be elected by a grand coalition of left and right and so could not represent the will of the electorate in European elections. Declaring that the paper 'doesn't set out to win over the people of Europe', Johannes Voggenhuber, the outspoken Austrian Green, criticised a lack of 'sparks' and 'great visions' and its failure to address social policy. Dual accountability would turn the Commission into a weak ally of the Parliament, he warned. That evening, long after Prodi had left the Parliament building and the Convention chamber, Peter Hain put the boot in, referring to 'a very disappointing report from the Commission and President Prodi this afternoon'.

And no doubt it was for the UK's man in the Convention. However, Hain appeared to overlook some important political points in the Commission's paper. It was crafted to reach out even to the UK government, and the two-thirds voting rule found favour with officials close to Downing Street. They pointed to Blair's 28 November Cardiff speech in which the prime minister spoke of the need to strengthen the Commission, favouring 'more effective scrutiny and the fullest democratic transparency' for the institution. Blair seemed to shift towards accepting the election of the Commission president when he warned 'at all costs' against 'turning the election of its president into a partisan wrangle, or allowing the Commission to become a prisoner of the parliamentary majority'. The two-thirds voting rule would circumvent this problem.

Similarly, dual accountability appealed to the UK. It emphasised the unique, hybrid nature of the EU with its balance of supra-nationalism and intergovernmentalism. In Cardiff, Blair had said 'we cannot simply see the Commission as an executive accountable to the Parliament. The Commission also has a crucial partnership with the Council which we must not weaken.' Dual accountability was part of this partnership. More, it was a guarantee that the Commission would never become the government of Europe.

11.5 PENELOPE UNVEILED

Penelope[11] on the other hand, was all about turning the Commission into a European government. While the Commission's official text hid radical proposals in circumlocution, Penelope and the explanatory texts for the 145 page document were a typical Lamoureux product: intellectually rigorous and blunt to the point of brutality.

After the hours of haggling that resulted in careful compromises secreted in the Commission's official text, the more radical Penelope draft treaty came as a shock to most of Prodi's colleagues in the college of Commissioners. The preamble, adapted from that in the 50-year-old ECSC, spoke of practical achievements leading to 'development of the European model of society'. The Constitution would be 'the foundations of an ever closer union' in a Europe 'whose vocation is to exercise the responsibilities of a world power'.

---

[11] Available on the EU's 'futurum' website http://europa.eu.int/futurum/index_en.htm.

The idea of the long-term European Council presidency was quickly despatched. 'Given the general set of proposals made in the Constitution… the function of Council President will be confined substantially to organising and chairing Council meetings. There is therefore no need to provide for a President of the Union or any other special status for the Council Presidency', a covering note said.

There was no question of the treaty including the possibility of intergovernmental action within the Union. The Commission's tasks, on the other hand, were 'presented more fully than in the current treaties'. The Commission was to be given a new function of directly recording treaty infringements committed by member states. The EU would also have a Supreme Court.

As in the official text, qualified majority voting would be the rule. 'The unanimity requirement is dropped in all cases, even for the revision of the Constitution, except for the admission of new members.' Penelope's rigorous approach to QMV led its authors into radical proposals for the ratification of the Constitution that would entail booting out countries that failed to ratify, for example through a 'no' vote in a referendum. As the authors noted, this was 'a thorny problem' that all other proposals – including the official Commission text and Giscard's skeleton – 'have shied away from'.

The curious outcome was that this particular draft constitutional treaty meant, above all, to enable the EU to cope with enlargement, was preceded by a detailed agreement which gave in laborious detail a quasi-automatic procedure for the Union to shed existing recalcitrant members. Penelope did a service by making clear that the treaty changes in prospect would necessitate ratification by all member and applicant states. But in pursuing the implications of this insight, Prodi's Praetorian Guard quickly turned the right of secession in Giscard's skeleton into a formula for cleansing the Union of awkward member states.

The simultaneous appearance of the two documents damaged the Commission's standing inside and outside the Convention. The two commissioners in the Convention were perceived as not having had the full trust of the Commission president. The creation and leaking of Penelope, moreover, reeked of the sort of backroom skulduggery that the Convention method was supposed to have replaced. Most worrying, the obvious disarray of the college of commissioners over Europe's constitutional future pointed to an institution that could at best only follow the Convention and was in no position to lead.

11.6 BENELUX DEFENDS THE COMMUNITY METHOD

The confusion surrounding the two Commission documents was a setback for those small country representatives who had become fearful that the largely intergovernmental 'ABC' group of Aznar, Blair and Chirac was having its own way in the drive to equip the EU with a powerful president and that the Community method was in danger of being sidelined in the institutional debates surrounding the Convention.

The integrationists were therefore lucky that the Benelux countries were able to agree a memorandum early in December which addressed the institutional framework of 'an enlarged, more effective and more transparent Union'.[12] This stated that: 'The Union must have strong common institutions, must favour and extend the Community method and must strengthen those institutional elements which can best further the common interest.' It came out against new institutions, such as the Congress, arguing that the challenge was to make existing institutions more effective.

The Benelux also favoured keeping rotation for the European Council and specialised Councils. Putting down a marker of sorts, the memo said: 'the Benelux will in any case never accept a President elected from outside Council'.

The memo called for a stronger Commission. Its president should be elected by the European Parliament with a three-fifths majority of members and then confirmed by a qualified majority of leaders in the European Council. Louis Michel, Belgium's foreign minister and representative in the Convention, said this voting system would ensure that the post could not be monopolised by the large countries. The text also provided for censure and dismissal of the Commission, while leaving details vague. The Commission would be 'responsible before the two institutions involved in its appointment and subject to dismissal through censure by one of those institutions'.

It called for sharper legislative procedures with more QMV and the extension of the Community method to the fight against crime and legislation on asylum and migration and judicial cooperation. The Council should meet in public when legislating. Codecision must be extended and the Parliament given equal powers with the Council on spending the EU budget. In the process the distinction between compulsory and non-compulsory spending would go.

---

[12] CONV 457/02.

The executive should be improved by giving the Commission clearer powers to adopt secondary legislation, a stronger role in the monitoring of the stability pact and the extension of the Community decision making to eurozone economic policy in a special eurozone Council.

The Benelux countries made one unorthodox proposal intended to enhance the power of the Commission president: that he or she should chair the General Affairs Council. The Commission should also chair the External Relations Councils through the offices of a 'double-hatted' Commission vice-president combining the roles of high representative and external relations commissioner. The Commission should represent externally other policies of the Union in the same way that it represented the EU at the World Trade Organisation.

The Benelux paper served as a signal that the big countries would not be able to ride rough shod over the Convention. Gijs de Vries, the Netherlands government conventionnel, reported that the Benelux could count on the support of Ireland, Finland, Portugal, Greece, Denmark, Austria, the Czech Republic and Slovenia in calling for the retention of the rotating presidency, which was a principle that guaranteed the equality of member states.

The list of Benelux supporters was a first public reference to a group of government conventionnels from small and medium sized countries that had begun to organise to protect their interests. The group met first in October 2002 in the house of Gregor Woschnagg, the Austrian permanent representative to the EU, and subsequently over dinner during two-day plenary sessions in the Brussels Dorint Hotel. Spurred on by Austria's Hannes Farnleitner and Ireland's Dick Roche, the representatives called themselves the 'Friends of the Community Method'. The group would grow to 16 countries and hold the Convention in thrall in the spring of 2003.

11.7 CONCERN OVER THE TIMETABLE

Muscle flexing by the smalls was in the future when the conventionnels returned to Brussels after the Christmas break. A more pressing concern was the tight timetable for completing their work. Tempers were frayed when Giscard refused to present a complete draft text of the constitutional treaty by February despite a request, submitted in the final plenary of 2002, from four MEPs (Alain Lamassoure and Hanja Maij-Weggen of the EPP and Anne Van Lancker and Carlos Carnero Gonzalez of the PES) which was backed by 53 other signatories.

Instead, the president announced plans to present the first draft treaty articles to the Convention in January for discussion in February. These would cover titles I, II and III of the skeleton treaty on the definition and objectives of the Union; citizenship and fundamental rights and the contentious matter of Union competences and actions. The second set, due in February, would cover titles V, VII and IX, on the implementation of Union action; the Union finances and the relations between the Union and neighbouring states. The really difficult institutional questions would be tackled in the third set of draft articles due in March/April. Titles IV, VI, VIII and X would cover respectively the Union institutions (including the mooted presidencies of the Council and European Council and the Congress); the democratic life of the Union (including voting rules of Union institutions); Union action in the world (and especially the role and status of the high representative) and Union membership (including the issue of withdrawal from the Union).

A general debate on the EU's institutional architecture was scheduled for the January plenary session. But Giscard did little to dispel the conventionnels' fears about lack of urgency: two or three further meetings might be needed before drawing up draft articles, he said. Easter was the target date for the Convention to have a complete draft of the first part of the treaty. The draft articles of part three of the treaty, detailing general and final provisions, would be circulated in April.

Meanwhile, the Convention would begin work on the second, policy-related part of the Treaty covering Union policies and their implementation. The Praesidium promised an analysis of existing treaty articles by the end of January, which would specify those needing replacement in the first and second parts of the treaty and those needing only technical amendment. The Praesidium would prepare articles that needed major amendment, while work on the others would be delegated to the Convention secretariat and experts from the legal services of the Council, Commission and Parliament.

The handling of the draft articles would depend on the plenary discussions. If drafts were broadly accepted in plenary, members of the Convention would be able to submit detailed points in writing. If big differences emerged, the Convention would set up 'discussion circles' with specific mandates and tight deadlines to sort out the problems. The circles would be small but comprise representatives from all the Convention's groups – governments, national parliaments, the European Parliament and the Commission – and so avoid the distortions caused by the self selecting nature of the working groups.

Would it work or would it all end in tears? Giscard's message to the final session of the Convention in 2002 smacked of caution as well as optimism. He was not sure the Convention had grasped the implications of the 'big bang' enlargement agreed at December's Copenhagen European Council. 'The perception of this enlargement, which is now a reality, has suddenly made me aware of the huge and extraordinarily difficult job we have before us,' he said.

On the other hand, he insisted his working methods were the best guarantee of the Convention reaching as large a consensus as possible by the summer. The final product, he added, should be 'precise and lyrical with a certain poetry and strength of expression'. By any standards, there was an enormous amount of work ahead, particularly as the leaders in Copenhagen made absolutely clear that the Convention must complete its work in time for June's summit in Thessaloniki. There was very little margin for error if the Convention were to meet Giscard's goal of drafting a constitution for an enlarged EU that would be good for 50 years.

CHAPTER 12
Divisions Among the Member States

In the early months of 2003, the Convention began to run on two tracks, both of which were overshadowed by the build up to war in Iraq. The split between big and small member states, which had poisoned the Union since the French presidency in the second half of 2000, spread to the Convention and encompassed the accession countries alongside the established member states. At the same time, the Convention's Praesidium embarked on the difficult task of writing the first draft articles of the constitutional treaty. Although it never generated a split in the Convention as such, the division among member states over the conflict in Iraq cast a pall over the proceedings and contributed to delays. These various currents were to come together in April and May when draft articles on the Union's institutions were presented and debated in the plenary. This chapter looks at the tensions between big and small member states and the effects of the Iraq crisis. The next will follow the Convention as the Praesidium drafts the treaty texts.

12.1 FRANCO-GERMAN PROPOSALS ON INSTITUTIONS

The revival of the Franco-German partnership in the final two months of 2002 was welcomed by many conventionnels. Historically, the two countries had functioned as a motor for the Union and it was known that they were working on a significant joint position to mark the 40th anniversary of the Elysée treaty in January 2003.

When the joint Franco-German proposals on the Union's institutions appeared in January they had a huge impact. They greatly advanced the debate on institutions, albeit in the direction of the 'ABC' suggestions of prime ministers Aznar and Blair and president Chirac. This was at the cost of deepening the emerging split between the big and small countries in the Convention.

The first three joint papers, while signalling close cooperation on major policies, had followed rather than led the debate in the Convention. By contrast, the joint Franco-German proposals on the institutions were to prove a key turning point in the life of the Convention. They were published on 15 January 2003, the day after Chancellor Schröder and President Chirac met over a working dinner in the Elysée with their two foreign ministers.[1] The text set the tone of the institutional debate for the rest of the Convention.

As so often in Franco-German relations, a pragmatic deal lay at the heart of the proposals. Chirac was one of the earliest advocates of a stable presidency of the European Council in place of the system of rotating every six months, while Germany, as a federal state and a traditional champion of the smaller member states, backed a stronger Commission with a president elected by the European Parliament. The 15 January compromise papered over these differences by meeting both aims, with plans for a long-term president of the European Council and an elected Commission president. The two countries also proposed a 'double-hatted' foreign minister for the Union, more QMV and codecision, and a restructuring of the formations of the Council of Ministers to cope with increased executive responsibilities in the fields of justice and home affairs and the common foreign and security policy.

The two countries proposed a full-time president for the European Council of the enlarged Union who would be elected by Council members using QMV for five years or for two and a half years with the possibility of re-election. The European Council would determine the basic political and strategic guidelines of the Union in cooperation with the Commission, and set ground rules and guidelines for CFSP and defence policy. Its president would prepare and chair the meetings of the Union's leaders in the European Council and supervise the implementation of its decisions. He or she would have an external role, representing the Union at meetings of heads of state or government. But the text stressed that the president must not upset the competences of the Commission and its president and must be aware that the Union's foreign minister would carry out the operational tasks involved in CFSP.

The European foreign minister would be created from the Solana and Patten jobs to boost the coherence and credibility of Union foreign policy. The minister would be appointed by the European Council by QMV with the approval of the Commission president. He or she would have a formal right of initiative on CFSP issues and would take part in Commission meetings both *ex-officio* and as a special member of the Commission. CFSP matters would not be decided in the college of commissioners. But fulfilling a long cherished German goal – and a striking novelty for France – the two countries agreed CFSP issues would generally be agreed by qualified majority voting among member states, except for military and defence matters which would be decided unanimously. The foreign minister would be supported by a European diplomatic service, which would include the

---

[1] CONV 489/03.

Commission's external affairs directorate, the foreign section of the Council Secretariat and diplomats seconded from the member states and the Commission. The Commission's delegations abroad would become delegations of the Union. The Franco-German plan laid down rules in case a member state could not accept a foreign policy decision for reasons of national interest. It would first be the job of the foreign minister to seek a compromise solution. If the minister failed, the chair of the European Council would try. Failing that, the European Council would decide by QMV.

The two countries said the constitutional treaty must strengthen[2] the role of the Commission 'as motor of the European construction, guardian of the treaties and embodiment of the common European interest'. Claiming their proposals would improve the Commission's legitimacy without endangering its independence, the joint text proposed the nomination of the Commission and its president after the European elections. This would be followed by the election of the president by a qualified majority of MEPs and confirmation by the European Council, also by QMV. The president would appoint the college of commissioners, taking account of geographical and demographic factors and would be able to make a distinction between commissioners with sectoral, functional or special responsibilities on the basis of equal rotation. After approval by the European Parliament, the European Council would appoint the commissioners by QMV. The Commission president would provide political leadership in the Commission, which as an institution would be accountable to both the European Parliament and European Council.

The Franco-German paper proposed greater Commission powers in economic policy, notably the right to determine that an excessive deficit existed under the stability pact. In addition, the Commission must have sufficient powers to execute EU laws and supervise their implementation by the member states. In connection with this, the paper proposed a radical simplification of the Union's complex network of committees.

The European Parliament's powers of codecision would be extended automatically in line with each extension of QMV in the Council. The Parliament might also be given powers over Union revenues in a much simplified budgetary system.

The text acknowledged that national parliaments had a role in the Union. It backed the 'early warning system' devised by the subsidiarity working group

---

[2] With some nuanced differences: the German text said 'muss … stärken' or 'must strengthen'; the French text 'doit confirmer' or 'must confirm.'

and said national parliaments should take part in future conventions to revise the treaty. Without creating any new institution, it suggested they take part in a dialogue with the European Parliament, which would include a joint annual debate on 'the state of the Union' in the framework of a 'Congress' to be held in Strasbourg and chaired by the European Parliament president.

The Council of Ministers should in future concentrate on essentials, leaving the Commission and member states more responsibility in the execution of decisions. The paper proposed separating the Council's executive and legislative functions, with legislative discussions held in the public domain. Council decisions should as a rule be taken by QMV.

There would be a shake up of chairs of the various Councils, with General Affairs being chaired by the Council secretary general; foreign and defence affairs by the Union foreign minister and Ecofin, the eurogroup and justice and home affairs each selecting their own chair for two year periods. The other Council chairs would be arranged to give member states as much participation as possible on the basis of equal rotation.

The two countries proclaimed their goal was greater clarity, legitimacy and efficiency through a balanced strengthening of the Union's institutional triangle and its external representation. Their vision was of Europe as a Union of states, peoples and citizens with its institutions operating in a federation of nation states.

While the Franco-German paper covered the waterfront, it lacked coherence in crucial parts. On detailed issues, the text bore the hallmarks of a fudge – which it was. It was not all clear, for example, who should nominate the candidates to be the commissioners or the Commission president or whether there should be more than one candidate for Commission president. The paper appeared to hint at a two or three tier structure for the Commission, but again was not clear.

It addressed the problem of a member state being unable to accept a common foreign policy position in the Union, but had nothing to say about potential conflicts of interest between the presidents of the European Council and the Commission and the Union foreign minister. The lines of command and influence between the European Council president and the sectoral Councils, which were established through the machinery of national governments in the EU's rotating presidency system, appeared not to exist in the Franco-German plan.

The paper was very much a Schröder-Chirac agreement and testified to a strengthening working relationship between two pragmatic, if not opportunist, leaders who were not natural soul mates. It was a relationship in which Jacques Chirac seemed to have the upper hand. The two men had reached an agreement on agricultural policy in the autumn of 2002 that was good for France and bad for the cause of reform of the common agricultural policy that Germany notionally espoused. For Schröder acceptance of the long-term European Council president was not such a radical step: he had already signalled movement towards supporting the idea, provided the post would not undermine the Commission, and had passed this message to Prodi over dinner at La Truffe Noire restaurant in Brussels in October.[3]

For Fischer the plan was a setback. He made clear his lack of enthusiasm for the European Council president on the day the text was published, commenting that it was 'about the art of the possible'. It transpired that he had proposed combining the roles of Commission president and Council president, but this was rejected by Chirac and Schröder as too complex. Fischer's stance verged on the disloyal in the days following disclosure of the Franco-German plan. When asked in a *Frankfurter Allgemeine Zeitung* interview,[4] what the twin presidents of the Commission and European Council would achieve for the EU, Fischer ignored the question and stressed how he had wanted more, and that the agreement was the only way of bridging the difference between France's intergovernmental and Germany's integrationist approach to the EU.

Andrew Duff was quick to describe the agreement as 'more a barter deal than a genuine compromise'. The creation of two executive presidents was 'a recipe for internal conflict and external cacophony' and 'potentially disastrous'. Hans-Gert Pöttering, floor leader of the EPP in the European Parliament, warned it could lead to a shift of the institutional balance in favour of the national governments. Although the plan for an elected Commission president fulfilled a long held goal of the Parliament, Pöttering warned of a weakening of the Community method and a slide into intergovernmentalism. As if to confirm Pöttering's fears, Denis MacShane, Britain's minister for Europe, described the agreement as a 'good result for Europe and British policy'.[5]

In one special sense, the Franco-German initiative proved counter productive for Berlin. Since the spectacular row between big and small states at the special European Council in Biarritz in autumn 2000, any coalition of large countries tended to produce an allergic reaction among the smaller EU countries. The strong support of other small countries for the Benelux

---

[3] *Financial Times,* 11 October 2002.
[4] *FAZ,* 17 January 2003.
[5] *Financial Times,* 16 January 2003.

THE CONVENTION MEETS
The first plenary session in the European Parliament
Source: European Convention

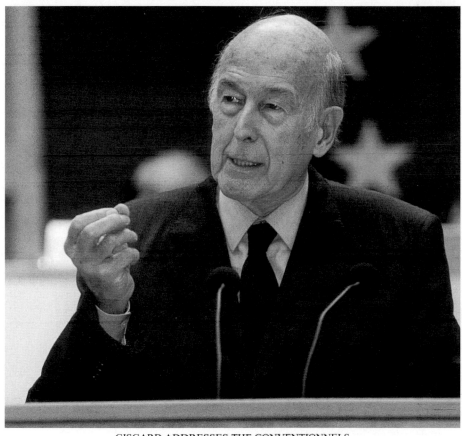

GISCARD ADDRESSES THE CONVENTIONNELS
At the Parliament's 'lectern of honour' during the 13 June 2003 plenary
Source: European Parliament

THE TRIUMVIRATE
From left to right - Amato, Giscard and Dehaene on the Convention's opening day
Source: European Convention

GISCARD AND SIR JOHN KERR
Absorbing reactions to the first draft articles on 6 February 2003
Source: European Parliament

GISCARD GREETS SPAIN'S NEW FOREIGN MINISTER
A warm welcome for Ana Palacio during the July 2002 plenary as Andrew Duff looks on
Source: European Convention

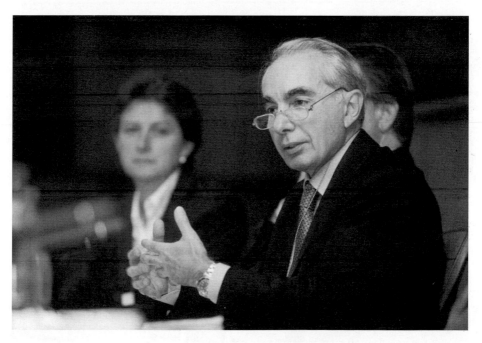

AMATO MAKES A POINT
As Gisela Stuart (background) reports on the National Parliaments working group
Source: European Parliament

ELMAR BROK
Denouncing the Praesidium at an EPP press conference, 27 May 2003
Source: EPP-ED

INIGO MÉNDEZ DE VIGO
Praesidium member, 'Pope of subsidiarity' and Brok's rival in the EPP
Source: EPP-ED

NEW KID ON THE BLOCK
Joschka Fischer (left) catches up with Klaus Hänsch on Fischer's first day at the Convention
Source: European Parliament

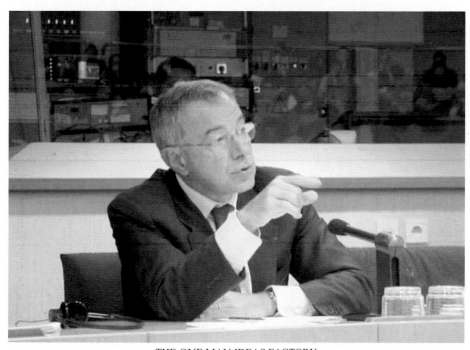

THE ONE MAN IDEAS FACTORY
Alain Lamassoure assesses the Franco-German deal on institutions, January 2003
Source: EPP-ED

10 JULY: COMMISSIONER VITORINO SIGNS THE FINAL TEXT
As fellow Praesidium member Henning Christophersen (right) looks on
Source: European Parliament

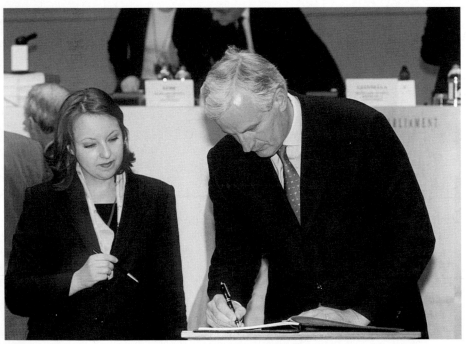

COMMISSIONER BARNIER
Adding his signature to the constitutional treaty
Source: European Parliament

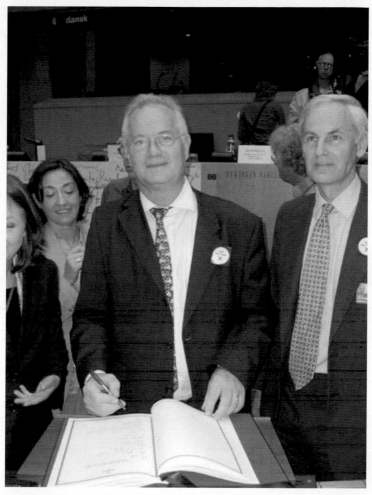

EUROSCEPTICS GRIT THEIR TEETH AND SIGN
Jens-Peter Bonde and David Heathcoat-Amory (right) add the words 'minority report'
Source: Bonde.com

PICADOR AND BLOGGER
Olivier Duhamel during the plenary of
4 July 2003
Source: Ambroise Perrin, GPES

TIRELESS BATTLER FOR
'SOCIAL EUROPE'
Anne Van Lancker finds time to relax in
the 4 July 2003 plenary
Source: Ambroise Perrin, GPES

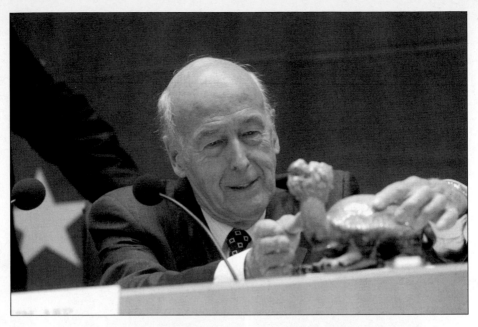

A FOUR LEGGED FRIEND NEVER LETS YOU DOWN
Giscard tends to the needs of his mascot Wui Kei
Source: European Convention

THE BUSY NETWORKER
Britain's conventionnel Peter Hain (right) meets Pat Cox, European Parliament president
Source: European Parliament

memorandum in December was one symptom of this trend. Aware of this, Elmar Brok, the German Christian Democrat Euro parliamentarian and leader of the centre-right EPP caucus in the Convention, had suggested that Germany be a champion of the smaller states. But Brok was a Christian Democrat appealing to a government of Social Democrats and Greens that was under pressure from Chirac to agree the institutional accord before the celebrations of the 40th anniversary of the Elysée Treaty on 22 January. The German government agreed to the Franco-German institutional proposals without consulting its smaller Union partners. That was a mistake as the following meeting of the Convention showed.

12.2 THE SMALLS REVOLT

The Franco-German paper on the institutional architecture of Europe was meant by the two countries to give new impulses to the Convention as it embarked on the difficult task of addressing power questions in the EU. It did. But in ways that took its authors by surprise.

The paper dominated the proceedings when the Convention met on the afternoon of 20 January for its first discussion of the EU institutions. The tone was set by the first speaker to follow Giscard's introductory remarks. Gijs de Vries, the Netherlands government representative, condemned the paper, focusing on its proposal for twin presidents. His arguments were echoed by many speakers who followed. The full-time European Council president would encroach on the powers of the Commission president, encouraging acrimony and stalemate. She or he would unbalance the position of the high representative or foreign minister. The plan would not bring the EU closer to its citizens. An EU of 25 needed a stronger not a weaker Commission. The rotating presidency was essential for the smaller countries. In fact, all four institutions needed strengthening and not just the Council.

To applause, speaker after speaker, from the smaller member states, applicant countries and the European Parliament joined the refrain. Duff returned to the attack to condemn the paper as a 'cut and paste' exercise that accentuated the differences between the presidential and parliamentary Europe. Brok thought there was a risk of two separate European Unions with the Commission subordinated to the Council and confined to managing the internal market while the European Council focused on foreign and security policy. This could not function in the long term. Dick Roche, the Irish government conventionnel, warned against an 'institutional coup d'etat'. Johannes Voggenhuber the outspoken Austrian Green observed sarcastically that 'an evening meal was no system for framing a constitution' adding that 'the desire of Europeans for a Napoleon IV was limited'. Another prominent rejectionist was Louis Michel, Belgium's Convention member and foreign minister.

Among the rank and file Convention members, the French and Germans were less outspoken in their opposition. But only Hubert Haenel, the right of centre French senator, was enthusiastic. Predictably, another enthusiast for the long-term presidency was Peter Hain, the UK representative. Outside the Convention hall, he claimed a 'critical mass' of governments (the UK, France, Germany, Spain, Sweden and possibly Denmark) supported an elected president.

When the French and German foreign ministers took their places in the Convention on the morning of Tuesday, 21 January (having been at the UN in New York the afternoon before) Joschka Fischer gave a singularly lacklustre performance in its support. In the margins of the Convention, Fischer was heard apologising to Brok for having failed to prevent the two countries' leaders agreeing the text.

By the end of the meeting at lunchtime on 21 January, the Dutch Christian Democrat MEP Hanja Maij-Weggen announced she had listened to 91 speakers of whom only 12 were for the long-term European Council presidency; 15 had serious reservations and 64 were against.

The revolt appeared to deal the Franco-German paper a serious blow. But the joint proposals were to be the template for all future discussions on the institutional settlement. Ironically, the paper was also the last significant joint contribution from Paris and Berlin as the two foreign ministries became increasingly preoccupied by events in Iraq.

The episode contained some lessons for Paris, Berlin and other governments. *First*, it showed that the Convention was not yet an Intergovernmental Conference, despite the influx of foreign ministers since Spain's decision in July 2002 to promote Ana Palacio to foreign minister and keep her in the Convention. Although Peter Hain claimed a critical mass of member state governments supported the long-term presidency and that many national parliamentarians in the Convention agreed with the idea, the strong opposition in the Conventional hall suggested otherwise.

Second, the mass condemnation of the proposal for a European Council president showed how well organised certain groups of conventionnels had become. The main political families – the EPP, PES and Liberals – met before the session on Monday to coordinate their members' interventions. It was around this time that Giuliano Amato, as head of the PES conventionnels as well as one of the two Convention vice-presidents, established close ties with Brok, the head of the EPP caucus, which were to be of considerable significance when the time came to broker compromises.

Ad hoc groups also played an important role: a 'federalist' breakfast on the morning of the Tuesday, for example, bore fruit in coordinated 'blue card' interventions in support of the rotating presidency and Community method late in Tuesday's session. The conventionnels were learning the advantages of solidarity and numbers. Away from the excitement of the 20–21 January Convention session, there had been several cases of Convention members forming lists in support of various propositions. An early example during the autumn was the rallying of about 40 conventionnels and alternates in support of a 'Social Europe' by the Belgian Socialist MEP Anne Van Lancker, that helped overcome Giscard's resistance first to having a debate on the issue and second to a special Social Europe working group.

By early 2003, any Convention member worth his or her salt seemed to be rushing around garnering support for one proposition or another. Examples included Andrew Duff, who gathered signatures from 20 Convention members and 11 alternates (from ELDR, PES and EPP) for 25 proposals on institutional reform; Joachim Würmeling, a Bavarian Christian Social MEP and alternate, who mustered 19 signatories in favour of a reference to God in the constitutional treaty and Gisela Stuart, the UK House of Commons Convention member and member of the Praesidium, who was active with Haenel of France in assembling names to ensure national parliaments were not left behind as the institutional debate gathered pace.

12.3   POINTS OF ATTRACTION

While the noisy condemnation of the Franco-German paper dominated the Convention's debate on the institutions on 20–21 January, there were signs of a narrowing of differences in other areas. These were highlighted after the plenary by Giscard and the European Parliament's two Praesidium members: Klaus Hänsch and Inigo Méndez de Vigo.

According to Giscard, the debate had shown 'extremely broad' support for maintaining the institutional balance between Commission, Council and Parliament and for the EU's federal/confederal mix. He claimed consensus was reached on extending codecision, making more use of qualified majority voting, setting up a legislative Council and the election of the Commission president by the European Parliament. However, he also noted that the details remained in dispute, not least in the case of electing the Commission president by the Parliament. If QMV were adopted (such as the two-thirds vote suggested by the Commission or the Benelux idea of a three-fifths majority) what would happen if no candidate gained the necessary majority? Would the vote go to several rounds and end on a simple majority?

In Méndez de Vigo's view the Convention was working well, with a very positive atmosphere. Hänsch was even more upbeat, declaring that a 'breakthrough' had been achieved. He repeated Giscard's summary of consensus points and added the enhancement of the Parliament's budgetary powers and the creation of a European foreign minister. Hänsch even made some positive noises about the European Council presidency, provided it met certain conditions. These were that the president should have a clear job description with a strict definition of competences vis-à-vis the Commission president; no own administration; the reversion of the European Council to its original role so that it would not be a repair body for other Council formations; and the retention of rotation, with some changes, for other Council formations.

There were other signs of attempts to bridge the gap over the European Council presidency. Britain's Peter Hain went out of his way to call for a strong Commission in the plenary. 'We do not want a president of Europe', he insisted. Instead, circulating a job description to Convention members, he used the neutral term 'chair of the European Council' rather than president.

Giuliano Amato moved further along this line. In the plenary, Amato, who enjoyed kudos as one of the Convention's most accomplished problem solvers, underlined the desirability of more continuity in the presidency of the European Council to cope with the 'revolution of numbers': the expansion of the EU from the original six to 25 members. Amato believed the president should be seen less as the EU's leader as the chairman of the European Council, which itself was collective head of the Union. In such a role, a long-term president might help form consensus inside the European Council.

UK-Spanish paper

Although Franco-German support for the long-term president was criticised by a large majority of conventionnels in the January plenary and later rejected by the small countries, the big countries continued to view the paper as the basis for an eventual compromise on institutional issues. Despite growing differences over Iraq between France and Germany, which opposed war and Britain and Spain, which supported the US, many of the Franco-German ideas on institutions were echoed in a UK-Spanish paper, published on the last day of February.[6]

---

[6] CONV 591/03.

Both papers called for a long-term presidency of the European Council and gave roughly similar job descriptions. Both wanted an EU foreign minister cum high representative although the Franco-German paper opted for the double-hatting of the Patten and Solana jobs while the UK and Spain wanted him or her based firmly in the Council. Both claimed to want a strong Commission president, although the election procedures differed. France and Germany wanted election by qualified majority voting in the European Parliament. Spain and the UK proposed QMV in the European Council followed by approval by the Parliament.

Certain details of the big country positions remained unclear, not least concerning the election of the Commission president, should this be entrusted to the European Parliament. But while differences on institutions among the big member states were at the level of detail, those between the big and the small states were fundamental.

12.4   THE SMALLS ORGANISE

The Franco-German paper on institutional reform shocked the small and medium sized member states into more action to find common ground against the threat of a *directoire* of big member states. The components of a bandwagon were in place. Calling themselves variously the 'like minded group' or the 'friends of the Community method', representatives of small countries built on ties forged the previous autumn.

At the end of March 2003, 16 government representatives submitted a paper to the Convention entitled 'Reforming the institutions: principles and premises.'[7] First among the paper's 'key general principles' was maintaining and reinforcing the Community method. It went on to insist on preserving the Union's institutional balance, rejecting the idea of new institutions, stressing as a core principle the equality of member states and demanding the principle of one commissioner per member state 'provided there is full equality'. The group was not completely at one on the issue of the long-term presidency because Sweden and Denmark had by this time accepted the idea. But while admitting 'a number of varying views on the detail of possible models' relating to the presidency, the paper saw retention of rotation 'as the predominant aspect of a new system', particularly for the European Council, General Affairs Council and Coreper, the important committee of ambassadors to the EU in Brussels.

---

[7] CONV 646/03.

The paper acknowledged its affinity to the Benelux contribution of December with its vision of a strengthened Community method, retention of the principle of rotation and hostility to a long-term European Council president.[8] It was not signed by the Benelux states. Instead, the government representatives of Austria, Portugal, Ireland and Finland signed, as did those of Sweden and Denmark – the latter expressing reservations about the passages on the rotating European Council presidency. It was also signed by 10 accession and applicant states: Cyprus, Hungary, Latvia, the Czech Republic, Slovakia, Bulgaria, Lithuania, Estonia, Slovenia and Malta – Poland being the notable absentee.

On 1 April, prime ministers and foreign ministers from Austria, Finland, Ireland and Portugal joined their Benelux colleagues in Luxembourg at the invitation of Jean-Claude Juncker, the Luxembourg prime minister and holder of the presidency of the Benelux group, to discuss institutional reform. The group was immediately dubbed the 'seven dwarfs'. After their discussions, Juncker attacked the proposals of the big countries for a long-term European Council president. The plans, he warned, could make the EU slide towards the intergovernmental method and could 'create a second Commission', reducing the Commission president to being the secretary or assistant of the president of the European Council. The Commission, he said, should keep 'all its rights and all its potential'.

The bandwagon continued to roll through April. On the eve of the Athens European Council on 16 April, when the leaders heard from Giscard about the Convention's progress, the leaders of 18 smaller countries gathered in the ballroom of the Athens Inter Continental hotel for a 'Benelux breakfast'. Among points agreed were a call for equality among member states, institutional balance and a refusal to create a new president of the European Council. The seven dwarfs were there from the member states as were nine of the accession countries (Poland being absent) and Romania and Bulgaria, which are candidates for membership, possibly in 2007. Greece, as holder of the presidency, stayed away to maintain neutrality but it was no secret that its sympathies lay with the 18.

The division between big and small worried many – notably Jean-Luc Dehaene, one of Giscard's two deputies. It appeared also to pose a threat to Giscard's ability to manage the Convention in its final, hectic phase because of his ill-disguised preference for the big country positions. But the unity among the small and medium sized countries proved fragile. There were differences inside the Benelux and difficulties coordinating its activities

---

[8] CONV 457/02.

because of the volatile state of Dutch politics.[9] As early as February 2003, Guy Verhofstadt, the Belgian prime minister, was privately not at all convinced that a rotating European Council president was tenable and doubted whether there were sufficient proper jobs for a Commission of 25 or more. Furthermore, strong though the group of small countries appeared on institutional issues, there were differences among big and small over Iraq.

12.5   THE IMPACT OF THE IRAQ CRISIS

The Iraq crisis overshadowed the Convention but came nowhere near destroying it. To some extent, the Convention became a haven for the government appointed conventionnels from either side of the old-new Europe divide diagnosed by US defence secretary Donald Rumsfeld. During Convention sessions, the foreign ministers of France and Germany would go out of their way to chat civilly with their fellow Convention members from Spain and Britain, both within and beyond the range of lurking television cameras. 'I was really struck how little to negligible the impact was that Iraq had on the person to person negotiations, the meetings in the Convention and the outcome for the UK,' Hain said later.

There were few direct references to the split in the debates. The conventionnels instead pressed on with their task of criticising and trying to modify a steadily increasing flow of draft articles from the Praesidium from the beginning of February. A casual observer would have had little sense of the pall cast by Iraq other than to note how Giscard would preface each plenary session from 27 February onwards with a doleful diagnosis of disarray in the continent he was seeking to reform.

The Iraq crisis did have an impact, however. It exposed the weakness of the common foreign and security policy, which, according to the Treaty on Union, obliged the member states to 'work together to enhance and develop their mutual political solidarity'. There was no working together or mutual solidarity in January when France and Germany publicly criticised the US for the Rumsfeld remarks without consulting their partners. There was still less when the leaders of Spain, the UK, Italy, Poland, Hungary, the Czech Republic, Denmark and Portugal signed a letter to the *Wall Street Journal Europe* calling for unity with the US in its policy to rid Iraq of weapons of mass destruction without contacting Paris or Berlin.[10] As Giscard noted, the

---

[9] There were two general elections in the Netherlands during the Convention: on 15 May 2002 and 23 January 2003.
[10] *WSJ-E*, 30 January 2003.

Union seemed to be backsliding from commitments made at Maastricht ten years before.

The split silenced Javier Solana and Chris Patten. In the absence of a common political will, they had nothing to say over Iraq, raising the question of whether a double-hatted Union foreign minister would do much better. However, supporters of a long-term elected president of the European Council argued that such an individual would surely have brought the issue to the notice of EU leaders whereas the existing rotating presidencies had left Iraq off the agenda of successive Union summits.

The Iraq crisis gave new impetus to an idea that had barely surfaced in the Convention's previous discussions – that of 'enhanced cooperation' by which a small number of member states might push ahead of others with policies of greater integration. The interest in enhanced cooperation and by extension the possible emergence of a core Europe sprang from the total failure of the EU to hold a common position over Iraq.

For some, the failure of EU foreign policy over Iraq had a positive side. 'In the long-term the crisis could become an opportunity for the common foreign and security policy,' Elmar Brok told the German newspaper *Die Welt* on 3 March. Others considered that progress would depend on just a few countries taking the initiative. This idea was taken up by Belgium's prime minister Guy Verhofstadt in the course of the European Council of 20–21 March when he proposed an 'avant-garde' of Belgium , Germany and France to develop a common defence and security policy. This would become the 'defence mini summit' of Belgium, France, Germany and Luxembourg in Brussels on 29 April.

While Germany's chancellor Gerhard Schröder spoke of the desirability of Britain, the EU's most effective military power, being involved in any defence initiative, his foreign minister Joschka Fischer was equally clear that countries which wanted to push ahead of the rest had a right to do so. 'Europeans must agree greater integration within the EU treaties,' he said.[11] 'But if that doesn't work out, then a group of countries must press ahead, if necessary outside the treaties as in the case of Schengen. Whatever they decide can later be moved across into the treaties. There is an old rule in the EU: 'Nobody has to wish for something; but those that wish, must also be enabled to act'.

The plans for the four nation defence meeting split the Benelux and kept alive the divisions exposed by the letter of the eight in January. Early in

---

[11] In *Handelsblatt*, 2 April 2003.

April, the Dutch prime minister Jan Peter Balkenende was quoted as saying European defence without the UK was 'unthinkable'. Manuel Durao Barroso, the Portuguese prime minister said any European defence identity must 'not go against our Euro-Atlantic alliance'. On 29 April, the leaders of the four mini-summit countries met and announced plans for a military planning centre in the Brussels suburb of Tervuren, which would be independent of NATO. In so doing, they challenged one of the central planks of British policy on European defence, which was to maintain close links between the EU and NATO. The meeting of the four hardened, in the short term, the UK's determination to resist enhanced cooperation in the foreign policy and defence sectors.[12]

But the extreme tensions surrounding the defence mini-summit proved not to be lasting. The four insisted that their initiative was open to all and not directed against the Atlantic alliance. This position appeared to be accepted by Union foreign ministers when they met for an informal 'Gymnich'[13] meeting on a luxury yacht in the Aegean Sea a week later. By September the UK was in discussions with Germany and France to find common ground. Meanwhile, the communiqué issued by the four leaders after their 29 April meeting gave wholehearted support to the proposals on security and defence policy before the Convention[14] and so strengthened the position of those conventionnels calling for enhanced or structured cooperation in the defence field.

The Iraq crisis had other consequences for the Convention. The crisis – or rather French president Jacques Chirac's verbal assault in February on those accession countries that had the temerity to side with the Anglo-American coalition – worked wonders for the accession countries' sense of self-awareness. Partly because of Chirac's strictures that some of the former Communist countries had been 'very rude and rather reckless' in signing a letter of support for the US and partly because of the liberating effect of having agreed the terms of enlargement at the December Copenhagen European Council, the conventionnels from the accession and applicant countries at last began to play a more prominent role in its discussions.

Less happily, Iraq made it difficult for the foreign ministers who had joined the Convention in the autumn of 2002 to keep up their attendance. Fischer and de Villepin would sometimes miss plenaries because of other commitments, including the United Nations' Security Council. Their

---

[12] See Chapter 14.6.
[13] Named after Schloss Gymnich between Bonn and Cologne, where the first such meeting was held in 1974.
[14] See Chapter 4.4.

appearances at the Convention would be brief, limited to a few minutes either side of their pre-planned interventions: it was behaviour hardly calculated to win the affection of ordinary conventionnels. George Papandreou, the Greek foreign minister appointed to the Praesidium and Convention after the start of the Greek presidency, was a notable absentee. Spain, which started the fashion for drafting foreign ministers into the Convention drew a sensible conclusion. Early in 2003, foreign minister Ana Palacio became Spain's alternate while her former deputy, Alfonso Dastis, succeeded her as Spain's member in Convention and Praesidium. The promotion of Dastis provided much needed backbone for the government representatives in the Praesidium and brought to the fore a formidable negotiator and operator on Spain's behalf.

The crisis added to the time pressure of the final months because the writing, publication and discussion of the draft articles on the Union's external action were postponed. The texts on the common foreign and security policy and defence were missing when, at the end of February, the Praesidium published draft articles 24 to 33 of the first – constitutional – part of the treaty. The two articles, which were foreshadowed in the skeleton, and the detailed provisions relating to the two policies in the second part of the treaty, were instead published in the first plenary after Easter.

Iraq held up the spring review of the Convention's progress by the European Council. The detailed discussion of the Convention, originally scheduled for the spring European Council in Brussels on 20–21 March, was held over to coincide with the signing in Athens on 16 April of the accession treaties for the 10 new members that were due to join the Union on 1 May 2004. That in turn helped delay discussion in the Praesidium and presentation to the plenary of the all important draft articles on the Union's institutions.

CHAPTER 13
The Praesidium Produces

The Praesidium started writing the first draft articles of the constitutional treaty in January 2003. The exercise proved more difficult than expected and put the 13 strong steering group on a steep learning curve.

Whereas the working groups were phased to achieve some early 'easy wins' and give the Convention momentum into autumn 2002, the secretariat and Praesidium decided to tackle some of the most challenging issues in the planned constitutional treaty first. The Praesidium began with competences, which were tricky to define and where the working group had got nowhere. Although Praesidium members were allowed a specialist legal adviser in the meetings, there were whispered complaints from Commission officials about the legal soundness and technical quality of the drafting. As the Convention plenary started on 20 January, Giscard disclosed that two Praesidium meetings reached agreement on no more than three or four articles. Amato admitted that the work was taking longer than expected and that the 'rhythm was not adequate'.

13.1 THE DRAFT ARTICLES: AN OVERVIEW

When Giscard unveiled the first 16 articles in draft form on 6 February he announced that the texts, defining the Union, its values, objectives and competences, would give Europe's citizens the ability 'immediately and simply to grasp the essential characteristics of the Union, why it had been created, what it does and what it seeks to achieve'.[1]

The new texts fleshed out the first three titles of the skeleton draft constitutional treaty, published at the end of October.[2] Giscard explained that the Praesidium had tried to draw up the first seven articles in language that was at once 'simple, forceful and solemn'. Four articles made up the first title, 'the definition and objectives of the Union'. As in the skeleton, they covered respectively: the establishment of the Union; the Union's values; the Union's objectives and its legal personality. The second title, the 'fundamental rights and citizenship of the Union', now comprised three

---

[1] CONV 528/03.
[2] CONV 369/02.

rather than the two articles indicated previously. Reference to the Charter of Fundamental Rights was brought forward to article 5. Article 6, a last minute insertion, barred any discrimination on the grounds of nationality. Article 7 (formerly article 5), defined Union citizenship.

Articles 8 to 16 in title III, 'the Union's competences', sought to bring clarity to a complex area in line with requests raised at the summits of Nice and Laeken. Following the outline of the skeleton, article 8 defined the fundamental principles governing the limits and use of Union competence. Article 9 laid out the rules for their application. Article 10 listed the different categories of competence. Articles 11 and 12 set out to define respectively the Union's exclusive competences and those shared with member states. Articles 13 and 14, a novelty compared with the skeleton, sought to define respectively the coordination of member states' economic policies and their obligations in exercising the common foreign and security policy. One of the few reminders of the Christophersen working group was article 15, which outlined areas where the Union might help member states with 'coordinating, complementary or supporting action'. Responding to a strong consensus in the Convention, article 16, the so-called 'flexibility clause', updated the existing article 308 of the European Community treaty and gave the Union the capacity to achieve objectives set in the constitutional treaty in cases where it lacked the necessary powers.

The Praesidium's early efforts proved highly controversial. The 16 articles attracted 1,187 amendments, of which 435 referred to the first three articles alone. They were debated in the plenary session of 27–28 February and required extra one day meetings of the Convention on 5 and 26 March after which many issues remained unresolved.

In a cover note, the Praesidium paid tribute to the reports of the working groups on legal personality, the Charter, economic governance, complementary competences, subsidiarity and external action, as well as guidelines that emerged during the convention's plenary debates. But in many ways the activity over the preceding 10 months was less than helpful for the Praesidium. There had been no working group to clarify the issues in the first three articles. Only articles 4, 5 and 7 were based on the conclusions of successful working groups: those on legal personality[3] and the Charter.[4] Articles 8 to 16 on competences were prefigured by Henning Christophersen's group on complementary competences, which was the least successful and most contentious of all the working groups.

---

[3] Reported in CONV 305/02.
[4] Reported in CONV 354/02.

This lack of clarification in advance, combined with the constitutional significance of the first two titles plus the sheer technical difficulty involved in dealing with competences, helped explain the problems the Convention faced in dealing with the articles. Another problem was that the draft articles had to be taken on trust to some extent. As Giuliano Amato, the Convention vice-president, pointed out, the initial 16 articles had to be judged in the light of later articles fleshing out the EU's policies, which only appeared at the end of May. The absence of satisfactory background references to the as-yet unwritten policy section the draft constitution may have added to the large number of amendments.

The first 16 draft articles were followed by others at each plenary session before Easter. Draft articles 24 to 33 of title V,[5] 'the exercise of Union competence', were unveiled during the plenary of 27–28 February. They dealt with the instruments required to exercise the Union's competences, although details of articles 29 to 31 on common foreign and security policy, defence and police and criminal justice were left for later.

Title VII,[6] 'the finances of the Union', comprised articles 38 to 40 and was released on 17 March. So too was the delayed article 31 of part one and 23 articles of part two,[7] laying out the details of the area of freedom, security and justice.

On 4 April, the Praesidium published draft articles 33 to 37 of title VI,[8] 'the democratic life of the Union', and articles 43 to 46 of title X[9] on 'Union membership' including, for the first time, an exit clause giving the rules for voluntary withdrawal. Another novelty, foreshadowed in the Skeleton and published on 4 April, was article 42 making up title IX[10] which covered 'the Union and its immediate environment' and defined future relations between the Union and its neighbouring states. The Praesidium also published nine articles of what was provisionally called draft part three of the constitutional treaty.[11] These were the 'general and final provisions', which are found in all Union treaties. They defined such issues as legal continuity with past treaties, the geographical scope of the Constitution and, importantly, provisions for its revision, adoption and ratification. The articles on the institutions as well as the delayed articles dealing with foreign and defence policy appeared on

---

[5] CONV 571/03.
[6] CONV 602/03.
[7] CONV 614/03.
[8] CONV 650/03.
[9] CONV 648/03.
[10] CONV 649/03.
[11] CONV 647/03.

24 April, after Easter and less than two months before the deadline for producing the constitutional draft.

In other respects, the first four months of 2003 brought some changes of style to the Convention. As it tackled successive articles, its discussions became more interactive. Those chaired by Giuliano Amato, the former Italian prime minister and one of Giscard's two deputies, often appeared like university seminars.

13.2   DIFFICULTIES WITH FEDERALISM AND GOD

The very first sentence of article 1 [1][12] on the 'establishment of the Union' ensured a stormy launch for the draft articles and drove a wedge between the Convention's integrationists and intergovernmentalists. 'Reflecting the will of the peoples and the States of Europe to build a common future, this Constitution establishes a Union [entitled ...], within which the policies of the member states shall be coordinated, and which shall administer certain common competences on a federal basis,' it said.

Mention of the peoples as well as the states of Europe was an important modification compared with the skeleton, and in Giscard's words, placed the will of the people 'at the centre of the European construction'. The decision to leave the Union's proper title to be settled later was pure Giscard and bore witness to his hankering after 'United Europe'. But the storm broke over the 'f-word' (federal). Even though it had appeared in the skeleton, it prompted hostile criticism and amendments from a sizeable minority of accession country representatives as well as the UK's Peter Hain and the eurosceptics. It was no recompense that draft article 1 also emphasised that the Union

---

[12] Because the evolution of the articles is integral to understanding the eventual constitutional treaty and the frantic bargaining of the Convention's final phase, this chapter and Chapter 15 deal with the draft articles in some detail. The articles are introduced with the numbers they were given at the stage of the drafting process being discussed. Because the numbers sometimes changed as new articles were created and others deleted, references to the individual articles in this chapter are accompanied at the first appropriate point in the text with the number of the article in the final treaty text in square brackets. The part I articles and selected articles from elsewhere in the treaty are reproduced with some notes in a Documentary Annex to this book. Until the 16 April Athens European Council, the Convention worked on the assumption that part I of the final text would be the constitutional part, part II would detail policies and legal bases and part III the general and final provisions. This order was modified after the Athens meeting so that the first complete draft on 26 May designated the Charter of Fundamental Rights as part II of the constitutional treaty, moving the policies and legal bases to part III and the general and final provisions to part IV. The constitutional text stayed as part I.

'shall respect the national identities of its member states'. The f-word was still generating heat during the special session of 26 March.

By contrast, de Villepin and Fischer, the French and German foreign ministers, were among a broad cross section of integrationists who wanted a reference to 'ever closer union', which was part of the EU canon but missing from the Praesidium text. Several parliamentarians, notably from France and the Party of European Socialists, wanted mention of the symbols of the Union, such as its flag, money, holiday and anthem. Many conventionnels suggested a reference to citizens rather than peoples. Others wanted a reference to the regions.

The Union's values were dealt with in article 2 [2]. It was to be 'founded on the values of respect for human dignity, liberty, democracy, the rule of law and respect for human rights.' This article, Giscard explained, concentrated on the essential values at the very heart of society and was brief so the values could serve as a base for action and sanctions against a delinquent member state if necessary. The later draft articles 43 [57] and 45 [58], detailing the eligibility criteria for Union membership and the rules for suspension of membership rights, made specific reference to the values in article 2.

Missing was any mention of spiritual values or God in the article, despite heavy lobbying from the Catholic church and its supporters in the Convention. The pros and cons of the religious question bulked large in the amendments to the first articles and was the subject of heated debate in plenaries up to and including the special meeting on 26 March. Conventionnels from the EPP called for a reference to God on the lines of the Polish constitution.[13] Others fiercely contested the place of God in such a text and sought help from outside. In late February, the Spanish socialist Parliamentarian Josep Borrell submitted a resolution signed by 163 MEPs, of whom 80 were from the PES and only nine from the EPP, asking the Convention to assure that 'no direct or indirect reference to any specific religion or belief is included' in the future constitution. Instead it called for promotion of the right of freedom of religion and the principle of 'separation and independence between church and state'. The Praesidium's view was that the best place for a spiritual reference was in the (as yet unwritten) preamble. When presenting the draft articles of title VI, the democratic life of the Union, in the early April plenary session, the Praesidium also included, as draft article 37 [51], a statement respecting the status of churches and

---

[13] 'The Union's values include the values of those who believe in God as the source of truth, justice, good and beauty as well as those who do not share such a belief but respect these universal values arising from other sources.'

religious associations as well as philosophical and non-confessional organisations.

Article 3 [3] detailing the Union's objectives was less pithy, having expanded in length during the Praesidium's deliberations. A brief opening paragraph, which defined the Union's aim as 'to promote peace, its values and the well-being of its peoples', was followed by a long list of economic, social and technological objectives including full employment, high levels of competitiveness, equality between men and women and even 'the discovery of space'. The various objectives sought to embrace interests as varied as free marketers and social welfare adherents. Later paragraphs bundled together the Union as an 'area of freedom, security and justice' with respect of cultural diversity. A passage projecting the Union's objectives in the wider world pledged contributions to another eclectic list including sustainable development, eradication of poverty and protection of children's rights.

Giscard said the text sought not to produce a bewildering full list of EU policies which would soon lose the attention of the average citizen, but to define objectives in a more forceful and political way. Inevitably the approach triggered opposition. Many conventionnels sought to add more objectives. Some, including representatives of 10 governments, wanted a reference to improving the environment. A broad cross section of the centre-left demanded mention of the 'social market economy' and explicit support for public services. Only in the case of the discovery of space, Giscard's symbol of modernity, were there significant calls to reverse this 'Christmas tree' approach and drop an objective.

The influence of an effective working group was clear in article 4 [6]. The single line, 'The Union shall have legal personality', reflected the conclusion of Giuliano Amato's first working group aimed at consolidating the EU and TEC treaties and ending the EU's pillar structure. This, the least controversial of the first articles, stayed unamended throughout.

Article 5 [7] said the Charter 'shall be an integral part of the Constitution' and therefore mirrored the conclusion of Antonio Vitorino's working group. Pending clarification of UK objections, it left open whether it should be in the treaty text or a protocol. Article 6 [4] barred discrimination on the grounds of nationality and was separated from the following article 7 on the grounds that it would also apply to non-EU citizens. Article 7 [8] on Union citizenship, said every national of a member state would also be a citizen of the Union, and as such equal before the law. The article repeated rights already defined in the Charter and the current citizenship part of the European Communities treaty.

13.3   MAKING SENSE OF COMPETENCES

The Praesidium's draft articles on competences were a blend of the fundamental and the specific and the result of difficult internal negotiations. Drafting treaty texts proved a difficult technical exercise even though Giscard had grudgingly allowed each Praesidium member to bring a specialist assistant to the meetings. Parliament's Lamassoure report, the deliberations of the Christophersen working group and the Commission's 'Penelope' draft constitution all offered different approaches to the problem. Consequently, the Praesidium found the going heavy and it took four meetings in January to complete the articles on competences.

The Praesidium started work on a secretariat draft which was concise and relatively simple and owed a lot to Lamassoure's pioneering work. It immediately upset the Commission and some members of the European Parliament. Reflecting the determination of Commission president Romano Prodi to promote the Penelope document, Michel Barnier tabled an alternative draft, based on the Penelope principles[14] and sought to mobilise the Commission's allies in the Praesidium.

The conflicting philosophies of the secretariat draft and Penelope made for protracted and tense discussions. Barnier and Vitorino were under instructions not to negotiate on the basis of the secretariat's draft articles on competences. The upshot was three days of angry debate in the Praesidium which cost time and caused Dehaene and Amato to reconsider their support for the Commission. When it became clear that Barnier's initiative was failing to win sufficient backing, the way was clear for the Praesidium, helped by commissioner Vitorino one of the Convention's key problem solvers, to clarify the principles and the categories. The result was a 'first', according to Giscard. He told the Convention that the articles presented the entirety of competences attributed to the Union and the fundamental principles underpinning their application 'in just four pages' without falling into the trap of a rigid catalogue of competences.

Unfortunately, the articles were also confusing in parts. The Praesidium, in embellishing the simpler secretariat text, had allowed some errors to creep in. Hence the text included the four freedoms as an exclusive competence in article 11, against the advice of the secretariat, while also listing the internal market as a shared competence in article 12. But these were mere quibbles compared with the anger stirred among intergovernmentalists and eurosceptics by the Praesidium's use of language and the surprise that

---

[14] See Chapter 7.

simply spelling out the powers of the Union provoked among many conventionnels and commentators.

Article 8 [9] stated that the limits and use of Union competences were governed by 'the principles of conferral, subsidiarity, proportionality and loyal cooperation', the first three points of which should have offered comfort to non-federalists. But in attempting to pin down how powers were conferred on the Union, it stirred a hornets' nest when it said: 'In accordance with the principle of conferral, the Union shall act within the limits of the competences conferred upon it *by the Constitution* to attain the objectives the Constitution sets out. Competences not conferred upon the Union by the Constitution remain within the member states.'[15]

The idea that member states confer powers on the Union was missing. Article 9 [much truncated as 10] defined the application of the fundamental principles in the previous article and was drafted in a similar manner. Moreover, it put down in treaty language for the first time the idea that Union law had primacy over national law. It said: 'The Constitution, and law adopted by Union institutions in exercising competences conferred on it by the Constitution, shall have primacy over the law of member states.' Although long established in EU case law, the principle came as a shock to many, including Britain's eurosceptic media. The balancing item that the Union's institutions would apply the rules of subsidiarity and proportionality as detailed in a separate protocol when exercising non-exclusive competences went unnoticed.

Article 10 [11] contained more surprises for those not steeped in the ways of Brussels when it spelled out the broad categories of competence and the consequences for member states of the Union's exercise of its competences. Leaving no doubt of the significance of exclusive competences, it said: 'When the Constitution confers on the Union exclusive competence in a specific area, only the Union may legislate and adopt legally binding acts, the member states being able to do so themselves only if empowered by the Union.' A bigger surprise came with the definition of competences shared between the Union and member states. Here it said, 'the Union and the member state shall have the power to legislate and adopt legally binding acts in this area' but member states would exercise their competence 'only if and to the extent that the Union has not exercised its'.

Using phrases that would stir the wrath of the UK and the eurosceptics, article 10 stated baldly that 'the Union shall have competence to coordinate the economic policies of member states' and equally 'the Union shall have

---

[15] Author's italics.

competence to define and implement a common foreign and security policy, including the progressive framing of a common defence policy'. Again, there was no mention of competences being conferred by member states.

Article 11 [12] ambitiously gave the Union exclusive competence over the four freedoms 'to ensure the free movement of persons, goods, services and capital, and establish competition rules, within the internal market'. It also specified exclusive powers for the Union over the customs union, monetary policy for euro zone members, the conservation of marine biological resources under the common fisheries policy as well as the 'common commercial policy'. The blanket reference to the common commercial policy as an exclusive competence was controversial to the very end of the Convention. It threatened a compromise in the Treaty of Nice that left national governments with a veto over the negotiation and conclusion of trade agreements covering cultural and audio-visual services. Known as the 'cultural exception', this was a fiercely defended French national interest.

Article 12 [13] on shared competences provided an illustrative list of 11 policy areas ranging from the internal market (duplicating the reference in article 11), through agriculture and social policy to consumer protection and included energy, which would require a new legal base in the policies part of the Constitution.

The coordination of economic policies and the common foreign and security policy were given their own articles – 13 and 14 – because of their political importance and because they did not involve legislation. Again the texts stirred opposition. Article 13 [14] appeared to give the Union greater powers when it said 'the Union shall coordinate the economic policies of the member states'. Using words from the Maastricht Treaty, which were unfamiliar to several government representatives, article 14 [15] said 'member states shall actively and unreservedly support the Union's common foreign and security policy'.

Article 15 [16] listed employment, industry, education and youth, culture, sport and protection against disasters as areas for supporting action with the important qualification that legally binding acts in these areas could not lead to harmonisation of member states' laws.

Unlike most of the articles on competences, the flexibility clause, article 16 [17], was relatively uncontroversial despite increasing its scope to all the policies that would be detailed later in the treaty, while the existing article 308 of the TEC applied only to the 'common market'. The flexibility clause allows the Union to act in cases where it has not been given specific powers. To prevent the article becoming an engine for integration, it diverged from the general principle that acts should be taken on the basis of qualified majority voting and codecision between the Council of Ministers and the European Parliament, instead specifying unanimity in the Council on a proposal from the Commission after winning the assent of Parliament. In an important safeguard, member states' national parliaments would be alerted to a flexibility clause proposal.

The articles on competences prompted a large number of proposed amendments although when debated in the 28 February plenary session, they won broad support from MEPS Hänsch (representing the PES) and Lamassoure (EPP). Many conventionnels objected to the lists chosen to augment the articles, with several proposing deletion of the illustrative list of shared competences. Duff for the Liberals thought the classification too rigid while, as champion of Penelope, commissioner Barnier sniffed that he would have 'preferred a more political classification more in line with what the EU represents'. Predictably, de Villepin and the French parliamentarians sought to maintain the Nice compromise on commercial policy.

The UK's Hain was especially insistent that articles 1, 8, 9 and 10 make clear member states had conferred powers on the Union. Nor was he alone. Dick Roche, the Irish representative, submitted amendments to make clear the member states conferred powers on the Union. Like Hain, de Villepin of France, Fischer of Germany and Lena Hjelm-Wallen of Sweden sought to change draft article 13 so that the member states, and not the Union, would coordinate economic policies. However, there appeared to be a significant difference in Hain's body language to that of most other conventionnels. Clearly angry on the day of the articles were released, he appeared at times to be more in harmony with the Convention's small group of eurosceptics than the representative of a government that sought to be at the centre of Europe.

13.4   THE UK: STRUGGLING TO KEEP WITH THE MAINSTREAM

The UK had approached the Convention in a positive mood. Hain later recalled that when Tony Blair appointed him to the Convention 'he said it was more important than Iraq'.[16] While other EU leaders treated the Convention as a peripheral talking shop, Hain was active from the first morning, when he hosted a breakfast for conventionnels from the applicant countries. Hain would usually fit in seven or eight meetings in the margins of each plenary to 'do business' with other Convention members and Patricia Scotland, the UK alternate, perhaps three or four. These were generally

---

[16] Interview with *The Times*, 9 September 2003.

carefully prepared, with speaking notes and specific objectives. In addition, the UK took the working groups seriously, with Hain particularly active in both the external affairs and social policy groups.

But conditions for the UK proved increasingly difficult from the final quarter of 2002. As the various working groups reported, Hain sounded increasingly like a minority voice and had difficulty making his rhetoric sound conciliatory while voicing frank concern over a succession of integrationist issues. These ranged from how the Charter should be incorporated in the treaty, through 'double-hatting' the high representative and external affairs Commissioner, to 'communitarisation' of foreign and defence policy and QMV on taxation and social security provisions.

The Praesidium's first draft articles on 6 February threw this growing estrangement into still sharper relief. Although there was no formal debate on the 16 articles, Hain was swiftly on his feet, using the 'blue card' procedure to complain that the Praesidium had gone far beyond the findings of the working groups when drawing up its drafts. He complained that working group compromises reached on the Charter, competences, economic and social policy and CFSP were not reflected in the draft Praesidium texts.

Hain strongly objected to the word 'federal' in the first paragraph of article 1, even though this was included in the end-October skeleton treaty. He was also exercised about the text on CFSP in draft article 14 by which member states would pledge 'actively and unreservedly' to support CFSP, even though this echoed the language of the Maastricht Treaty. When the time came to submit amendments, Hain put forward changes or observations relating to 15 of the 16 draft articles.

Hain's objections were notable for their tone as much as their content. His rejection of 'federal' in article 1 was eventually shared by many other conventionnels. His call to revise article 10 and similar passages to make clear that member states, and not the constitution, conferred competence on the Union was supported by Giscard. But he stood out in the stridency of his reaction to what he perceived as creeping federalism, especially in the fields of foreign, economic and social policy. His dislike of draft article 14 was such that he proposed a complete rewrite, deleting the Maastricht Treaty text and inserting references supportive of NATO. Hain stood almost alone in objecting to article 5 'as it stands' with its assertion that the Charter of Fundamental Rights was an integral part of the constitution. Underlying this was the UK government's long-standing concern that its incorporation in an eventual constitution could undermine UK social legislation at great cost to the state, unless circumscribed by sufficiently strong 'horizontal articles'.

The Convention was not accustomed to such frankness. Nor was Hain alone. Gisela Stuart, the British parliamentarian and Praesidium member, was also sounding the alarm although less publicly. She was concerned that Tony Blair's office in London was taking too soft a line. She met Blair four days after the draft articles appeared and warned that the dynamics of the Convention were changing, and not in Britain's favour. She submitted a report to Blair in February which depicted the Convention as an increasingly integrationist body and which urged the government to make clear 'red lines,' marking out policies that would be unacceptable.

Hain's tough, outspoken approach gave the small group of eurosceptics some satisfaction. Jens-Peter Bonde, the Danish MEP, claimed that the draft articles had presented Hain with plans for a unitary state and compromises reached by Blair with Giscard had been overruled. Bonde's fellow eurosceptic, David Heathcoat-Amory, the UK House of Commons Conservative, said the new texts went far beyond the previous draft: they pointed towards an EU state which would be 'more powerful, more remote and less democratic'. Hain and the UK government were 'paying the price for being too nice, too early. He should have been tough early on'.

At times during the 6–7 February debates on social and regional policy, Hain appeared to be singing from the same hymn sheet as the eurosceptics. He intervened on successive days to stress that he was 'strongly' opposed to more QMV in social policy, mainly because of the links in the UK between tax and social policies. Later in the special 6 March plenary, he was embroiled in a spat with Antonio Vitorino over the primacy of EU law, before backing down. Such behaviour did not go down well with the bulk of the conventionnels. Hain's rhetoric and Gisela Stuart's letter also caused alarm in Downing Street, where there was no wish to stir anti-EU sentiment in the UK. Blair's advisers felt that the prime minister and Giscard had established a good relationship and that Giscard was looking after the interests of the large member states.

But Hain's reactions to the early articles were important. They were a signal to Giscard and the secretariat that the UK government had 'red lines' which would cause trouble for consensus at the Convention and at the subsequent IGC if not accommodated. The point, which Giscard accepted, about the competences of the Union being conferred by the member states was also a warning to the secretariat and Praesidium that they should take greater care in drafting future texts. By setting out his stall so clearly, Hain made clear to the more integrationist Convention members that a final consensus that included the UK would necessarily mean they would have to trim their ambitions. In return, the UK was prepared to compromise, as it did when it finally accepted the Charter of Fundamental Rights in the constitutional treaty. In a curious way, Hain's outburst made the mood in the Convention harder to judge as it moved through the negotiating phase. The UK would often appear isolated in its resistance to integration whereas it was providing cover for other countries with reservations.

Hain became less strident as Easter approached. After publication of the draft internal security and budget articles at the beginning of April, which Hain welcomed, British spin doctors were claiming he was 'in the mainstream' and 'right at the centre' of the Convention. However, such positioning was not immediately apparent from his testimony to the House of Commons foreign affairs committee on 1 April when Hain played down the significance of the Convention to a remarkable degree. At one point, he said the Maastricht Treaty 'was arguably far, far more wide-reaching and deep in its impact than this one is likely to be, which after all is likely to be a tidying up exercise.' Such comments caused concern in the Convention's secretariat.

Hain's assessment of the Convention's role was partly motivated by his insistence that the UK should not have a referendum after the IGC. It may also have reflected his conviction – as expressed to the committee – that he was winning an argument. 'There is not a cat in hell's chance of a federal superstate being agreed by this Convention,' he said.

> It is not just a question that we will not agree it. Spain will not agree it, France will not agree it, Italy will not agree it, Poland will not agree it, and that is just for starters. So whatever the ambitions of some European parliamentarians, and maybe some members of the Commission, and maybe some of the smaller existing member states, there is no chance of that happening at all.

13.5 THE PRAESIDIUM UNDER PRESSURE

It is debatable whether Hain, and occasionally other government representatives, would have needed to be so robust in plenary sessions had the government representatives in the Praesidium not been so weak in the first months of 2003. The less integrationist governments had to use the plenary to claw back points conceded in the Praesidium, adding to an atmosphere of rancour. The drafting of the first 16 articles was the first real test of the Praesidium as a body. Its first attempts were painfully slow. As the Praesidium's work speeded up – overshooting its self-appointed end-January deadline by a week – it emerged as a more integrationist body than the Convention itself.

This reflected a tendency of Praesidium members to revert to instinctive reactions when under pressure. More than half the members were integrationist by vocation or instinct, including the two commissioners, the two MEPs' representatives and Giscard's deputies, Amato and Dehaene. As the drafting work progressed, the commissioners could call on extra resources from the Commission, which provided 12 officials to help them out.

The three national government representatives were either unable or unwilling to form a strong countervailing force. Ana Palacio, the Spanish government representative and an MEP until being promoted to foreign minister, was absent from many sessions from November. Her deputy Alfonso Dastis, when attending, was not allowed to speak until formally promoted to take her place in March 2003. George Katiforis, until March the Greek representative, was also an MEP and was absent from several sessions after a road accident early in 2003. Henning Christophersen, the Danish government representative, was often alone in putting a nation state viewpoint.

The three national parliamentarians – Gisela Stuart of the UK, John Bruton of Ireland and Alojz Peterle of Slovenia – also punched below their numerical weight. The national parliamentarians were numerically the biggest group in the Convention but less cohesive than others. The three therefore tended to represent only themselves. They also had the additional disadvantage of no great Brussels experience – although Bruton, as a former Irish prime minister was a former European Council member.

In January, Gisela Stuart was heard to complain of being 'outnumbered and outgunned' as the dynamics in the Praesidium ran in a federal direction. A first draft from the Convention secretariat might be broadly acceptable in her terms. But then a 'mass of amendments' would be presented by the federalist members of the Praesidium and 'the goalposts move'. When reporting to a joint standing committee on the Convention of the two houses of the UK parliament, [17] Stuart contrasted the cohesion of most European parliamentarians with the divisions among national parliamentarians. The debate in the Convention was affected by the ability of the European parliamentarians to overcome their political differences, she claimed.

However, there was an alternative view that the problem lay with Stuart and Bruton, who were handicapped by not being able credibly to represent the disparate bunch of national parliamentarians in the Convention as a whole. Thus when Stuart spoke up for a more stringent 'red card' or veto control over subsidiarity by national parliaments, she was seen as representing Downing Street's interest rather than the views of the biggest group in the

---

[17] On 12 February 2003.

Convention. Similarly, when Bruton put forward his idea of a directly elected Commission president, it was viewed as a personal enthusiasm, shared perhaps by two or three other conventionnels.

13.6 THE UNION'S INSTRUMENTS

The Praesidium put up a better show when it presented its second batch of draft articles on 28 February. Having dealt with the *who* and the *what* of competences earlier in the month, draft title V, comprising articles 24 to 33[18] was concerned with *how* the Union would carry out its tasks.

The Laeken declaration stressed the importance of simplifying the many and varied policy instruments available to the Union's institutions. The Praesidium, in turn, was well prepared after two plenary debates and Amato's successful simplification working group.[19] The result was a low harvest of amendments of just 237 by the time the Convention debated the articles on 17 March.

The Praesidium built on a broad consensus in Amato's working group to reduce sharply the legal instruments from 15 to six, give them more readily understandable names and, in the process, introduce a hierarchy of legislation in the Constitution. Article 24 [32] therefore adopted the names and definitions of the Amato working group, prescribing 'European laws, European framework laws, European regulations, European decisions, recommendations and opinions' and also made provision for some non-standard acts such as resolutions, declarations and conclusions not provided for in the Constitution.[20]

Taking over some of Amato's most important recommendations, article 25 [33] said laws and framework laws would be adopted by codecision, which was renamed 'the legislative procedure'. This meant qualified majority voting in the Council of Ministers. It added that the Council of Ministers and Parliament should meet in public 'when acting under any procedure' for the adoption of laws or framework laws. It made clear, however, that special rules would apply to the common foreign and security policy and former third pillar legislation in the area of freedom, security and justice.

Despite qualms in earlier plenary discussions, the Praesidium tackled the problem arising from the lack of any procedure for secondary legislation in

---

[18] CONV 571/03.
[19] On 23–24 May and 12–13 September 2002.
[20] See Chapter 7.

the EU. In article 27 [35], it proposed a new type of act – 'the delegated regulation' – by which laws or framework laws could delegate to the Commission the power to enact delegated regulations. Only non-essential, technical elements of legislation would be delegated and strict conditions would apply. These would include 'call back' provisions for the EU legislators, the Parliament and the Council, or 'sunset' clauses in the legislation itself. The delegated act, inspired largely by the difficulties of pushing complex financial market legislation through the institutions, would encourage Parliament and Council to focus on essentials and avoid excessively complex legislation in future.

The plenary discussions on the new articles raised few negative passions. Indeed among the MEPs, Klaus Hänsch for the PES and Alain Lamassoure, speaking for the EPP, were enthusiastic. Hänsch described articles 24 to 33 as 'a major qualitative leap forward' while Lamassoure said the presentation was 'simpler and clearer, reflecting a political and legal hierarchy in line with our vision of the EU'. The eurosceptics were less enthused, with David Heathcoat-Amory warning that non-legislative instruments, mentioned in article 26 [34], could lead to 'rule by decree'.

On detailed issues, Andrew Duff MEP made a renewed pitch for the creation of 'organic laws', which would allow constitutional change with super-qualified majorities. There was strong opposition among MEPs to the idea, in article 25, that the Council could make laws without reference to Parliament, although Bobby McDonagh, the Irish government alternate, pointed out that it had been agreed that merging the pillars would not rule out different procedures. By contrast, the idea of delegated acts was given a warm reception, although, several MEPs and commissioner Vitorino urged that Parliament and Council should be able to use call back powers independent of each other.

13.7 PROTOCOLS CLARIFY SUBSIDIARITY AND THE ROLE OF NATIONAL PARLIAMENTS

On 27 February the Praesidium presented a pair of draft protocols, on applying the principles of subsidiarity and proportionality and the role of national parliaments, to the Convention.[21]

The draft protocol on subsidiarity was important, although not as important as suggested by Inigo Méndez de Vigo, the chairman of the subsidiarity working group. Méndez de Vigo, whom Giscard dubbed 'the pope of

---

[21] CONV 579/03.

subsidiarity', told the 18 March plenary that 'nothing of such proportions has been achieved in 50 years'. The protocol detailed how EU institutions would respect the principles of subsidiarity and proportionality and built on the clear proposals of an effective working group.[22] It described a 'yellow card' early warning system by which a national parliament could object to a legislative proposal on the grounds that it failed to comply with subsidiarity and set out the procedures for informing national parliaments of Commission proposals at the same time as the Council and the European Parliament.

The yellow card rules said:

- Each national parliament could activate the early warning system. They would be responsible internally for sorting out which chamber did what, where there were bicameral parliaments or regional parliaments with legislative powers.
- One-third of national parliaments could force the Commission to review its proposal.
- The Court of Justice should be able to rule on infringement actions brought by member states at the behest of national parliaments and regional parliaments and by the Committee of the Regions, in cases where it was consulted.

Of less constitutional significance, the draft protocol on the role of national parliaments laid down the rules for information on legislation and other documents to flow from the Commission and other institutions. It also promised that the European Parliament and national parliaments would examine how to promote inter-parliamentary cooperation in the EU.

The protocols on subsidiarity and national parliaments were given a fairly smooth ride, although in the March plenary session conventionnels were divided over whether parliaments and regional assemblies should have direct access to the court. To enable both unicameral and bicameral parliaments to work the one-third yellow card threshold, several conventionnels proposed that each parliament should have two votes that could be retained by a unicameral parliament and shared between the bicameral bodies.

Gisela Stuart proposed having a 'red card', by which two-thirds of parliamentary votes would force the Commission to withdraw a proposal.[23] But this was trounced, with many conventionnels using unusually forthright language. Providing a foretaste of later divisions between these two leading members of the national parliamentarians group, Lamberto Dini, the Italian senator and former prime minister, poured scorn on Stuart's idea, declaring it

---

[22] See Chapter 7 and CONV 286/02.
[23] Footnote: CONV 340/03.

unthinkable that any Commission proposal would attract opposition from two-thirds of parliaments because to do so 'would mean the Commission was out of its mind'. Dini demanded the red card idea be dropped because 'it means giving national parliaments the power of veto over the initiative of the Commission and that we should not do'.

A relatively low key discussion on national parliaments was notable only because it allowed Giscard, when summing up, to keep alive his idea for a European Congress of MEPs and national parliamentarians. The Convention was consistently unenthused by this pet scheme of Giscard's but, undeterred, he signalled it would be on the agenda when the Convention finally turned to institutional questions.

13.8   THE AREA OF FREEDOM, SECURITY AND JUSTICE

The articles on 'the area of freedom, security and justice' gave conventionnels a first chance to see how a draft article in the first constitutional part of the treaty would dovetail with the detailed policy provisions of what then was called part two and was to be part III. Comprising draft article 31 [41] of part one and no fewer than 23 articles in part two, the new articles were also important because for the first time the Convention could see the practical consequences of doing away with the third 'justice and home affairs' pillar of the Maastricht Treaty.

Presented to the plenary on 17 March, the articles followed closely the conclusions of John Bruton's working group.[24] Article 31 outlined three types of Union action in the area of freedom, security and justice. These 'specificities' prompted a flurry of amendments and much debate in the plenary session of 3 April. The 23 detailed articles showed that the Community method would extend far into areas of government, which until the September 11 terrorist attacks in the US had strongly resisted EU influences. Adoption of legislative procedure under the Community method was widespread and would result in a switch to qualified majority voting in several articles. Unanimity was retained where new competences would be added.

Article 31 envisaged:

- Community action – 'laws and framework laws' – particularly to approximate national laws in areas such as asylum, immigration and border controls, detailed in part two.

---

[24] See Chapter 8 and CONV 426/02.

- Promotion of mutual confidence between member states authorities 'in particular on the basis of mutual recognition of judicial and extrajudicial decisions'.
- Operational cooperation between all competent authorities of member states for internal security.

It charted special roles for national parliaments in evaluating JHA policy as a whole and monitoring the activities of Europol, the EU's fledgling police authority. These were detailed in part two in articles 3 [III-160], 4 [III-161] and 22 [III-177]. In a provision unique to this section of the constitutional treaty, article 31 also awarded member states a right of initiative in police and judicial cooperation in criminal matters alongside the Commission's right of initiative. Article 8 of part two [III-165] stated that this could be triggered by a quarter of member states.

Of the 23 detailed articles, nine in part two [later eight from III-158 to III-165] defined the area of freedom security and justice, its institutional framework and operations. Four articles [later five from III-166 to III-169] then detailed the policies on border checks, asylum and immigration, specifying in nearly all cases that codecision, now named the 'legislative procedure', would apply to law making. One article [III-170], laid down the Union's policy of judicial cooperation in civil matters, specifying that generally the legislative procedure would apply for adopting measures to approximate national laws. Unanimity would apply to most aspects of family law, however.

Six articles [later five from III-171 to III-175] dealt with judicial cooperation in criminal matters, stipulating the legislative procedure for the approximation of laws and setting of minimum standards in areas such as criminal procedure and crime prevention. Article 17 [III-172] on substantive criminal law included a list of especially serious cross-border crimes, such as terrorism, trafficking in humans, drugs and arms, sexual exploitation of women and children, money laundering, counterfeiting and computer and organised crime, where minimum rules could be set by the legislative procedure. The Council of Ministers would also have the right to add crimes to the list on the basis of unanimity.

In this section, article 19 [III-174] specified the role of Eurojust, the mechanism by which national prosecutors can cooperate in combating cross-border crime. It stated that the European Parliament and Council 'shall' determine its structure, workings, scope of action and tasks by legislative procedure. Controversially, article 20 [III-175] gave the Council of Ministers the option ('may adopt a European law'), acting by unanimity, of setting up a European Public Prosecutor's office within Eurojust to bring to book 'the perpetrators, and their accomplices, of serious crimes affecting several member states and of offences against the Union's financial interests'.

Three further articles [III-176 – III-178], covered police cooperation and specified the legislative procedure for laws relating to information collection, processing and analysis and exchange of staff and equipment. But laws covering 'operational cooperation' among internal security authorities would be subject to unanimity. In the case of Europol, the EU's fledgling police authority, codecision would be the norm for setting laws on its structure, operation, field of action and tasks, while operational action would require agreement of the member states whose territory was involved.

The result highlighted the hybrid community and intergovernmental nature of this part of the Union's activities and inevitably exposed the gap between the strong group of integrationists in the Convention and those of a more intergovernmental bent. This divergence was reflected in the relatively large total of 733 amendments.

Many federalists called for article 31 to be deleted on the grounds that it perpetuated the pillar structure. Elmar Brok gathered 31 signatures from the EPP group and sympathisers for deletion, Olivier Duhamel of the PES 10, and Andrew Duff, of the Liberals 20. The Liberals complained that the drafting displayed 'a lack of self-confidence on behalf of the Praesidium in following the logic of the in-principle decision to merge the third pillar with the first.'

Even more Convention members urged deletion of the second of the part two articles, which stated that the European Council 'shall define the guidelines for legislative and operational action within the area of freedom, justice and security'. Brok, probably influenced by the use of the German word *Richtlinie,* which implies some directive power, for guideline, thundered that was 'not acceptable' for the European Council to issue non-negotiable guidelines to the legislator.

On the other hand, eurosceptics warned that dispensing with the third pillar would lead to excessive centralisation and increase the gap between the EU and its citizens. Jens-Peter Bonde, the Danish MEP, warned that 'policemen and bureaucrats would take decisions instead of elected national representatives' while David Heathcoat-Amory, the UK Conservative MP, said the proposals were 'the very opposite of what we were asked to do in Laeken'.

The general debate on the articles exposed a gulf between most MEPs and the two commissioners on the one hand and government representatives and some national parliamentarians on the other. Sweden's Lena Hjelm-Wallen argued that the main responsibility for public security should remain with the member states while Hubert Haenel of the French parliament warned: 'We cannot communitarise the entire third pillar and we cannot communitarise criminal law.'

But even the most wary of governments were prepared to move ahead with the Community method in some areas. Speaking for the UK, Hain said his government 'strongly believed in effective action' on justice and home affairs and 'fully supported' QMV for asylum and immigration. Accession country representatives, including Danuta Hübner of Poland and Neli Kutskova of Bulgaria, enthused about a provision in article 10 [III-166] that opened the way for European laws or framework laws enacting 'any measure necessary for the gradual establishment of a common integrated management system for external borders'.

As Joschka Fischer noted, the Praesidium's draft articles were 'a step towards integration that would have been unimaginable at the beginning of the Convention'. However, in one important area Germany itself balked at more integration. To the dismay of many, Germany insisted on minimum rules only to cover asylum and immigration that would leave member states controlling access to national labour markets.

The divergence between those in favour of Community method versus national rights was most pronounced over the proposal to create a public prosecutor's office. Integrationist MEPs rallied strongly to the idea, reflecting recent support from Parliament for a Commission consultative document recommending such a post. The idea was also backed by de Villepin of France and Jürgen Meyer, the German SPD parliamentarian, who pointed out that fraud affecting the Community budget ran at €1 billion a year. However, the public prosecutor was strongly opposed by the UK's Hain and both representatives of the British House of Commons, as well as the representatives of the Irish, Netherlands and Swedish governments.

Such opposition should have killed the idea. But Henning Christophersen for Denmark argued successfully that it would do no harm to put the option into the constitutional treaty, particularly as the Convention was creating a treaty that should last, and no one knew how conditions might change after enlargement. Recalling that only a small number of offences against the Union were effectively prosecuted, John Bruton suggested that the issue of the public prosecutor would be far less controversial in five to 10 years time and it would be right to create a legal base for creating such a post.

13.9 UNION FINANCES

The Praesidium had only limited guidance from the working groups when it came to tackle the Union's finances.[25] It therefore retreated from its previous practice of trying to draft 'ready to use' articles and instead raised questions where it could provide no answers. It set up two discussion circles – one on budgetary procedures and another on own resources – to fill in the gaps for future consideration by the Convention. That the Union's finances were a minority taste was shown by the small catch of 69 amendments which covered a wide range of issues.

In draft form, article 38 [53] on the Union's resources simply reproduced existing article 269 of the European Community treaty (TEC). It stated that the Union's budget 'shall be financed wholly from own resources' and that it was the Council's job, acting unanimously on a proposal from the Commission and after consulting the Parliament, to lay down provisions for a system of own resources which it would recommend to member states. However, in accompanying comments the Praesidium wondered whether unanimity would work in an enlarged Union and whether, as some Convention members had suggested, the categories of own resources should not be changed to include a European tax or participation in national taxes.

Article 39 [52] detailed the budgetary and financial principles of the Union, drawing on preparatory work by Giuliano Amato's simplification working group. By weaving together elements of articles 268, 270, 271, 274 and 280 of the TEC with article 36 of the May 1999 Inter-institutional Agreement on budgetary discipline the seven paragraphs provide a blue print for financial rectitude. Article 39 enshrined ideas such as having revenue and expenditure in balance and implementing the budget 'in accordance with the principle of sound financial management' and was generally well received.

The Praesidium observed bluntly that its draft article 40 [55] on the Union's budgetary procedure reflected 'the lowest common denominator of the opinions expressed by the Convention members'. These had favoured a simpler annual procedure for setting the budget and for incorporating the EU's multi-annual financial perspective, with its limits on spending, in the Constitution.

The draft article stated that the Parliament and Council shall, on a proposal from the Commission, jointly adopt the Union's annual budget, which shall be established in compliance with the multiannual financial perspective. The perspective, which is agreed by the European Council and sealed in the

---

[25] CONV 602/03.

aforementioned Inter-institutional agreement, currently runs for seven years and is the main instrument for ensuring budget discipline in the EU.

After scrutinising the amendments, the secretariat concluded that there was 'a broad consensus' for formally establishing the financial perspective in the Constitution as a binding framework for the annual budget but that there were deep divisions over how it should be adopted. Similarly, there were divisions over whether Parliament or the Council should take the lead in setting the annual EU budget.

Many of these divisions were still apparent when the plenary on 4 April debated the Union's finances and the discussion circle on budgetary procedure, chaired by Henning Christophersen, concluded its discussions the same day.

Incorporation of the financial perspective yielded the greatest agreement. The discussion circle called for a new article [54] in part one to incorporate the renamed 'multiannual financial framework' in the treaty as a binding framework for the annual budget to keep spending under control. A majority of the circle thought EU leaders, probably meeting in the European Council, should adopt the framework, which would then be given Parliament's assent. Most discussion circle members wanted unanimity among the member states replaced by a super-qualified majority, to be fixed by the Convention.

Details of the financial framework would be set in part two. These would include its duration, with the group suggesting five instead of seven years; scope to amend the framework in the event of exceptional circumstances and provisions to deal with any failure to adopt a new framework and to ensure the Union could meet its legal obligations. The last point would be important if the Convention decided to scrap the distinction between compulsory and non-compulsory expenditure in the annual budget procedure, as the discussion group suggested.

This idea was one of several elements intended to simplify the annual budget procedure which brought new difficulties in its train. It ran into problems with France, which wanted existing rules to continue on farm spending.

Christophersen's group also proposed that the Commission should present the draft budget and a simplified codecision procedure for Council and Parliament to turn it into law. The existing rules gave Parliament and Council two readings each on the budget, with the Council having the last word on compulsory spending and Parliament the final word on non-compulsory spending. Getting rid of the distinction between the two types of spending raised the question of which institution would in future have the last word on the budget overall. Because the discussion group was unable to agree, it put forward two options – one beginning with the Parliament and the other with the Council.

A diversity of views on budget procedure was clear in the plenary session on 4 April. A majority, led by the MEPs, called for an end to unanimity in the Council and equal participation of the European Parliament. A bigger role for the Parliament was supported by several government representatives including Ms Hübner of Poland. However, Peter Hain said he could only accept codecision on the budget if there were mandatory ceilings, which would be set by the European Council.

Big differences also emerged on the issue of the Union's own taxes to replace or augment the present system of own resources. The French, Belgian and Austrian government representatives and a number of MEPs and national parliamentarians filed amendments proposing the authorising of European taxes, while in the plenary of 4 April Pierre Lequiller, the French parliamentarian, was one of several conventionnels to suggest 'real' EU taxes would boost the Union's legitimacy and be a new 'conceptual jump' following the euro. However, others including several Scandinavian members expressed strong opposition to the idea in the plenary.

13.10 THE DEMOCRATIC LIFE OF THE UNION

At the plenary session of 4 April, the Praesidium put forward a *pot pourri* of articles. Appropriately, Jean-Luc Dehaene presented them as many, especially those concerning the democratic life of the Union, were of particular interest to the non-government organisations grouped under the general heading of civil society for whom Dehaene had been the point of contact since the Convention started.

As Dehaene concluded his introductory remarks, the drafts, which also covered Union membership, relations with nearby countries and part three – the general and final provisions of the Constitution – won high praise from an unlikely source. 'Unusually for me,' announced the UK's Peter Hain, 'I can say all the articles are excellent.'

Boosting the democratic legitimacy and transparency of the EU's institutions was a key element of the Laeken declaration. The seven articles of title VI, numbered from 33 to 37, were intended to show citizens that they could contribute towards framing Union decisions and could follow, and therefore evaluate, the Union's decision-making process.[26]

Articles 33 and 34 were both new. Article 33 [44], stating 'the principle of democratic equality', established that citizens were equal before the Union's institutions. Article 34 [45], on 'the principle of participatory democracy' pledged the Union to a dialogue with citizens which, the Praesidium claimed, was 'largely already in place between the institutions and civil society' through means such as Internet chats.

The remaining articles reproduced existing articles in the treaties but with substantial amendments. Article 35 [48] described the role of the European Ombudsman, making good in the process an omission from the original skeleton Constitution of 28 October. Article 35a [45] briefly described the role of political parties at a European level.

Article 36 [49], on 'the transparency of the proceedings of the Union's institutions' echoed article 1 of the present Union treaty when it said 'the Union institutions shall conduct their work as openly as possible.' Not only should the European Parliament meet in public, but so should 'the Council when it is discussing a legislative proposal'. An accompanying note said the reference to such openness was intended to cover discussion of legislation in its entirety from the first discussion of a draft in the Council to its adoption. The rest of the article set out citizens' right of access to documents. Article 36a [50] said 'everyone has the right to the protection of personal data concerning him or her' and set out the legal base (legislative procedure) for ensuring data protection by EU institutions.

Draft article 37 [51] reproduced the declaration annexed to the Amsterdam Treaty on the status of churches and non-confessional organisations and committed the Union to a regular dialogue, much as it was committed – in article 34 [47] – to dialogue with civil society and representative NGOs.

However, departing from the October skeleton, the Praesidium held back planned articles on the voting rules of the Union's institutions, which would have defined qualified majorities and the possibility of constructive abstention and a uniform procedure of voting for the European Parliament. It also dropped plans for an article to give constitutional status to the 'open method of coordination' (OMC), the process of benchmarking immortalised in the Lisbon agenda for turning the Union into the world's most competitive economic area by 2010.

---

[26] CONV 650/03.

The decision on the open method of coordination was a surprise and worried supporters of the Lisbon agenda, who feared that it would lose some of its validity if not backed in the constitutional treaty. But according to Amato, the OMC needed to be flexible and there was a 'very high risk of creating rigidity' if it were included. The Praesidium, after much mulling, decided it was covered by article 15 on supporting action. The decision to drop the article was supported by a curious coalition of integrationists who feared OMC was a way of undermining the Community method and those of a more intergovernmental persuasion, worried that an article could open the backdoor to meddling in the way it operated by the European Parliament and Commission.

The proposals on the Union's democratic life attracted 235 amendments[27] and one swift protest: from Emilio Gabaglio, secretary general of the European Trade Union Confederation (ETUC) and an observer to the Convention. Complaining that the Praesidium had given 'birth to a mouse', he objected to the absence of any reference to the social partners and the enhanced social dialogue, urged by both trade union and employers' representatives among the Convention's observers. Gabaglio's views found a ready echo among conventionnels who put forward amendments to add a reference or a paragraph on the social partners and the social dialogue to article 34. Thus Elmar Brok gathered 34 EPP signatories and Andrew Duff 22 Liberals for an additional paragraph acknowledging and promoting the involvement of the social partners in the Union's social and economic governance. Anne Van Lancker, the vigorous Belgian socialist MEP, rallied 11 PES backers for a separate article on the subject.

These group amendments highlighted the growing organisational capacity of the big 'political families' in the Convention's life. Apart from occasional amendments from the Swedish and Lithuanian conventionnels, there was no comparable grouping of conventionnels in national blocks.

Several amendments sought to delete draft article 33 on the grounds that it was covered by the Charter. Another, signed by the three key small state representatives from Austria, Finland and Slovenia, wanted the principle of equality to include member states. Draft article 35 on the Ombudsman prompted massed ranks of MEPs to file or sign amendments specifying that he or she should be appointed by the European Parliament. Many amendments sought to flesh out article 35a on European political parties or substitute the existing article 191 of the TEC to recognise the parties' importance for integration in the Union. Other amendments proposed deleting article 37 on the status of churches and non-confessional

---

[27] CONV 670/03.

organisations, arguing instead for keeping these points in a declaration as with the Amsterdam Treaty.

13.11 UNION MEMBERSHIP

The headline grabbing novelty among the four articles of title X on Union membership was draft article 46 [59] laying down the rules for a voluntary withdrawal from the Union.[28] The 'exit clause', article 46 was mooted in the October skeleton. The Praesidium decided to put it forward largely to meet the demands of eurosceptics and the less integrationist Convention members.

The procedure chosen drew on the Vienna Convention on the Law of Treaties. A member state wanting to withdraw would notify the Council after which the Union would negotiate and conclude an agreement for withdrawal and the state's future relationship with the Union. The article specified that the Council would act by QMV after obtaining the Parliament's consent. The constitutional treaty would cease to apply to the member state withdrawing once the agreement took effect, or, failing that, two years after the notification of the Council.

The articles attracted 90 amendments of which 35 related to the exit clause.[29] Nine amendments, signed by 41 conventionnels, wanted the article deleted. Duff, backed by 20 Convention members, proposed a new article to create the status of 'associate member' for Union members that leave or countries that have not joined.

Most other amendments sought to toughen the Praesidium draft by limiting the possibility of voluntary withdrawal or make its consequences more severe for the departing state. It was suggested the right of withdrawal be limited to exceptional situations such as a change in the constitution; that a state be unable to withdraw automatically; that the Council should decide by unanimity, giving other states a veto over withdrawal, and that a waiting period (suggestions ranged from five to 20 years) be imposed before a withdrawing state could request to rejoin the Union. Only three conventionnels – the eurosceptics, David Heathcoat-Amory and Jens-Peter Bonde and the Hungarian PES parliamentarian Pal Vastagh – called for a softening of the exit terms by reducing to one year the time before withdrawal would automatically take effect.

---

[28] CONV 648/03.
[29] CONV 672/03.

Article 43 [57], giving the eligibility criteria for Union membership, was also new. Opening the Union to all European states whose peoples shared and respected the values of article 2, it incorporated the Copenhagen criteria for enlargement into the constitutional treaty. Some conventionnels sought the deletion of article 43 on the grounds that it duplicated article 1. Twelve amendments, signed by 56 conventionnels including eurosceptics, the representatives of Sweden, Germany and the UK and Elmar Brok heading a phalanx of 34 EPP-aligned signatories, said the article should state that only European states, and not their peoples, must share and respect the Union's values. This was the line that prevailed in the final text.

Article 44 [merged into 57] covered how to apply for Union membership and gave a boost to elected representatives by saying the European Parliament and national parliaments should be informed as soon as an application was made. Article 45 [58] detailed the procedure for the suspension of membership rights and made no change in substance to existing rules.

13.12 THE UNION AND NEIGHBOURING COUNTRIES

Title IX,[30] consisting of draft article 42 [56], was another departure from the status quo, although it was foreshadowed in the October skeleton. The objective, as Jean-Luc Dehaene explained, was to establish a neighbourhood policy with near-by as well as adjoining countries. The Union should 'develop a special relationship with its neighbouring states, aiming to establish an area of prosperity and good neighbourliness characterised by close and peaceful relations based on cooperation'. It would be able to conclude specific agreements with the countries concerned, which could contain reciprocal rights and obligations. The Praesidium's covering note said the text would provide for a 'loose but coherent framework' bringing together existing arrangements and create no new obligations.

The article attracted around 30 amendments.[31] Several, including a well supported amendment from Brok, suggested the EU make full use of the Strasbourg-based Council of Europe in its neighbourhood policy. With countries such as Belarus in mind, other amendments, including one signed by 10 PES conventionnels, urged that any special relationship respect basic values, such as human rights, the rule of law and democracy. This proposal, couched in terms of the Union's values, was included in the final text.

---

[30] CONV 649/03.
[31] CONV 671/03.

13.13 GENERAL AND FINAL PROVISIONS

Nine draft articles, comprising part three or the general and final provisions of the constitutional treaty were also published on 4 April.[32] To a great extent these articles, now part IV, were not contentious, dealing as they did with the necessary business of repealing earlier treaties, establishing legal continuity, defining the geographical scope of the constitution, permitting regional unions such as Benelux and the Belgo-Luxembourg economic union, defining the treaty languages and stating that the protocols to be annexed to the constitutional treaty would be an integral part of it.

However, two articles were significant. In article F [IV-7] spelling out how to revise the new constitutional treaty, the Praesidium retained the existing procedure of the Intergovernmental Conference for treaty changes. But, in accompanying notes, it suggested that IGCs be preceded in future by more preparatory Conventions.

It also raised the very important issue of how to amend the constitutional treaty. Should this be by the Council or a special conference of member states; by unanimity or QMV and what roles should be played by the Commission, European Parliament, national parliaments and even a Congress, should such a body be created? Another tantalising question was what to do if a member state failed to ratify a revision to the constitutional treaty.

Article G [IV-8] on the adoption, ratification and entry into force of the constitutional treaty repeated the existing provisions, by which a treaty cannot enter force unless ratified by all member states which sign it. One member state failing to ratify would mean the constitutional treaty could not take effect and the existing treaties would continue to apply.

With such deadlock in mind, the Praesidium added a paragraph calling on the European Council to take up the issue if two years after the signing of the treaty four-fifths of member states had ratified it and one or more member states were having difficulties. In the accompanying notes, the Praesidium recalled that some contributions to the Convention, such as the Penelope document, had suggested the constitutional treaty should take effect once a certain threshold of member states had ratified it, while noting that such a course would pose the question of what should happen to the existing treaties. Despite the support of all major party groups, this idea was not included in the final text because the Convention's mandate to finalise part IV ended before its work on the issue was completed.

---

[32] CONV 647/03.

Of 147 amendments relating to the nine articles, 46 were concerned with article F on revising the treaty and 27 with article G on its ratification.[33]

On article F, Brok and Duff tabled an amendment signed by 48 conventionnels that proposed the European Parliament should have the same right as the Council and Commission to propose amendments to the constitutional treaty: altogether 71 Convention members supported the idea, including some non-MEPs of whom the most prominent was Joschka Fischer. Many other amendments supported having a Convention prepare future IGCs and several the idea that IGCs should confirm the results of Convention.

Duff and 21 supporters proposed that in future the consensus needed to amend the constitutional treaty should be five-sixths of member states, or 21 out of 25 countries, with the European Parliament giving assent by a two-thirds majority. Others suggested four-fifths or three-quarters of member states.

Discussion on article G revealed a growing interest in referenda as a route to ratification. Earlier, at the end of March, 15 Convention members and 20 alternates of all political persuasions called for Europe wide referendums to endorse the new constitutional treaty in June 2004 to coincide with the next European Parliament elections.[34] Four amendments to article G mentioned national referenda for ratification and three the idea of a European referendum in May or June 2004.

13.14 UNION LEADERS DECIDE AGAINST DELAY

After a shaky start the Praesidium and the Convention had achieved a great deal by Easter 2003. As Giscard explained to the special European Council with the accession countries in Athens on 16 April, it had provided answers to the four questions posed by the Nice summit. Thus competences had been clarified with due regard to subsidiarity. The Charter would be incorporated as the second part of the constitutional treaty.[35] The Convention had agreed a radical simplification of the Union's policy instruments. And national parliaments would be more actively involved in the life of the Union, notably through controlling subsidiarity.

---

[33] CONV 673/03.

[34] CONV 658/03.

[35] Giscard's announcement meant the section of the constitutional treaty dealing with policies and legal bases would become part III in future drafts and the 'General and final provisions' part IV.

He also claimed success on four elements of the Laeken mandate. Thus the Union would have a single legal personality. The Treaties of Union and the European Community would be replaced by a single text. The Union would have a single institutional structure. And the Convention had defined the methods and means for creating a true area of freedom, justice and security.

Some might dispute elements of his summary. Peter Hain, for example, was not yet willing to accept constitutional status for the Charter. It was also legitimate to question whether the 733 amendments to the articles on the area of justice, freedom and security amounted to no more than 'sorting out various editorial matters' as Giscard claimed.[36] Moreover, the Praesidium had not provided a complete draft of the first part of the constitutional treaty by Easter as envisaged late in 2002.

But this was not just because of the delays caused by its difficulties with the early drafts and the Iraq conflict. Giscard and Kerr were determined not to unveil any drafts dealing with controversial institutional issues before meeting the Union's leaders in the European Council. When Giscard finally met the leaders in April he sought answers to five questions which would dominate the Convention in its penultimate stage before drawing up the draft constitutional treaty.

Giscard's questions concerned the Union's institutional architecture and were:

- How to guarantee the greatest possible continuity in the work of the European Council and other Council formations.
- The future size and composition of the Commission after enlargement to 27 members, when according to the Treaty of Nice, the Commission was due to change from having one commissioner per member state to less than the number of member states.
- The means of appointment and the powers of the Commission president.
- The means of appointment and the powers of a foreign minister for the Union.
- And (keeping alive a pet project) the eventual role of a body, call it a Convention or a Congress, to be composed of representatives of national parliaments and the European Parliament.

On one issue, the Union's leaders made progress. After the meeting Giscard announced 'virtual unanimity' on the appointment of a foreign minister for

---

[36] Giscard's oral report to the European Council of 16 April, available in the speeches section of the Convention website.

the EU, who would combine the roles of Solana and Patten.[37] The difficult issues, Giscard admitted, were whether to retain the six-month rotating presidency of the European Council or move to a more permanent arrangement and the composition of the Commission. The Commission, he pointed out, started as a 'very small collegiate body' but had grown and become less collegiate with successive enlargements.

Giscard gave some clues as to how he hoped to resolve these difficulties. He harked back to the numbers problem and its implications.[38] He stressed first the importance of equality of rights of citizens in the constitution – a principle 'which is perhaps less spoken of in Europe but which is equally important' to that of the equality of states. This meant that when considering institutional issues such as the long-term presidency or the composition of the Commission it was necessary to take the size of populations of member states into account. 'The number of people who want one solution or another, that number is important,' he said. 'And at the moment, there is quite a broad majority of the population which is represented and which is in favour of a somewhat more stable presidency.'

But Athens also dealt Giscard a harsh blow. He had been dropping hints for weeks that the Convention might have to run into July or even past the summer break to finalise a polished text and went to the summit hoping for an extension. The evening before Giscard gave his progress report to the 25 leaders of the member states and accession countries, the Greek prime minister Costas Simitis told him the Union's leaders wanted the final product at their summit in Thessaloniki on 20 June at the latest. Already running late, the Convention was given just two months to complete its task of producing a draft constitutional treaty for the European Union.

---

[37] Text of presidency press conference, 16 April 2003 on http://www.eu2003.gr.
[38] See Chapter 10.1.

Part V

The End Game

CHAPTER 14
Institutional Imbroglio

Giscard was not happy with the decision of the European Council in Athens. To his aides, he seemed depressed in the days afterwards, worried about squeezing so much work into so little time before the Thessaloniki summit. His first priority was to push ahead with the draft articles on the institutions that had been promised for the plenary of 24 April. And it was here he had a surprise up his sleeve.

He had been working on a text for six to eight weeks, helped primarily by Sir John Kerr and two collaborators. The work mainly took place in Giscard's study in his house in Paris, well away from the Convention secretariat offices.

When the Praesidium met late in the afternoon of 22 April to start discussions, it was Giscard, the stickler for correct procedure and confidentiality in the steering body, who unashamedly broke the rules. While unveiling his 15 draft articles – printed on paper bearing the imprint of the Convention secretariat – to the 12 other members of the Praesidium, he had his spokesman Nikolaus Meyer-Landrut brief the press about them. The impact was immediate. No sooner was the briefing underway, than the mobile phones of Praesidium members began to ring as journalists sought reactions to the unfolding story.

Praesidium members were flabbergasted and furious. They felt betrayed. There was an understanding the previous autumn that the Convention method of debate, working groups and more debate would be an unsuitable procedure for preparing the institutional drafts, not least for fear that the Brussels insiders would dominate the process. The idea then was that the Praesidium itself would act as a working group and develop a comprehensive approach. Instead, it had been cut out of the loop and presented with a *fait accompli*. Months later, Praesidium members would shake their heads at the events of that afternoon. Giscard's motives remained unclear, although some speculated that he had come back to Brussels from Athens so convinced that the Convention would fail that he wanted to get his vision of Europe's institutional architecture on record and into the history books. Adding insult to injury, the drafts Giscard and Kerr unveiled were very intergovernmental and appeared extreme and divisive.

14.1   GISCARD'S ARTICLES[1]

Giscard's articles looked like a blueprint for a *directoire* of large member states to run the Union. The European Council, the body he founded in the 1970s, would be the 'highest authority of the Union'. Newly categorised as an institution, it would be in a position to take formal decisions. The system of rotation for its president would go. The European Council would have a long-term chair, elected by the members by qualified majority voting for two and a half years, renewable once. He or she would 'prepare, chair and drive' its work to ensure continuity, would report annually on the state of the Union to a Congress of representatives of the European Parliament and national parliaments. The president would ensure the Union was effectively represented in the wider world.

The president or chair would be supported by a board. Sometimes called the bureau, this would consist of its president, vice-president, two European Council members 'chosen in equal rotation', the foreign minister (in his capacity as president of the foreign affairs Council) plus the presidents of the economic and financial affairs Council and the Council on justice and security.[2] The impression of a powerful cabinet was boosted by the provision that this board 'may' (not shall) meet with the Presidents of the European Parliament and the Commission to ensure consistency in the Union's activities, implying that it could barrel ahead in making policy without bothering to consult the heads of the other institutions in the triangle. The president or chair would have at least two years' experience as a European Council member. Neither the president nor vice-president would be members of another European institution. Neither the European Council president nor the Commission president, an ex-officio member of the European Council, would vote in it.

The foreign minister would conduct the Union's common foreign and security policy and be a double-hatted figure. This official would be appointed by the European Council by qualified majority after consulting the Commission president, and would remain very much a Council person. She or he would make proposals for development of common foreign and security and defence policies 'which he shall carry out as mandated by the Council'. The minister would also be a Commission vice-president and 'responsible for handling external relations and for co-ordinating the different aspects of the Union's external action'. As Commission vice-president, the minister would be bound by Commission procedures 'in this capacity, and for these aspects alone.'

---

[1] See articles in Documentary Annex.
[2] The vice-president was a complete novelty in the institutional debate thus far.

Giscard proposed amending important parts of the hard fought Treaty of Nice. His most provocative article revised the rules for qualified majority votes in the European Council and the Council of Ministers and thus threatened the privileged positions of Spain and Poland, which had emerged from Nice with good deals. Giscard sought to overturn the complicated Nice settlement of weighted votes for each member state by reviving the much simpler concept of the dual majority. QMV was to consist of the majority of member states, representing a relatively high proportion of at least two-thirds of the population of the Union. QMV in the Council of Ministers would be the rule 'except where the Constitution provides otherwise'.

He also proposed to overturn the difficult Nice compromise on Parliament's composition. The number of MEPs should not exceed 700 (against 732 at Nice) and representation of European citizens would be proportional, with a minimum threshold of four members per member state. The word 'proportional' spelled danger for the smalls. The Nice compromise, which was the result of late night horse trading rather than any mathematical or demographic formula, gave greater weighting to smaller member states.

Also to the alarm of the smalls, his draft article on the Commission envisaged a body much reduced from the present 20 member college or that of one member per member state agreed in the Treaty of Nice until the Union consists of 27 countries. 'The Commission shall consist of a president, two vice-presidents and up to ten other members,' it said. Creating a subsidiary breed of second rank commissioners, it added: 'It may call on the help of Commission Counsellors'. There was no mention of the important safeguard of a 'rotation system based on the principle of equality' as specified in the Treaty of Nice for the time after Union membership reached 27 and when there would be fewer commissioners than states.

The text on the European Commission also provoked a storm of protest among the Commission's many supporters in the Convention because of its limp definition of the Commission's role compared with the existing article 211 of the European Communities Treaty (TEC). The Commission was merely 'called on to give voice to the general European interest' and 'monitor the application of the Constitution and steps taken by the institutions under the Constitution.' The article enshrined the Commission's right of initiative 'except where the Constitution provides otherwise' and confirmed the Commission would be completely independent in carrying out its responsibilities but made no mention of the Commission's functions as a coordinator or executive.

Another article gave Parliament power to elect the Commission president by a majority of three-fifths. But the European Council, consisting of national leaders, would decide the candidate by qualified majority following the European elections. If the candidate failed to gain the requisite support, the European Council would choose another candidate within a month.

The Commission, as a body, would be responsible to the European Council and the European Parliament, *both* of which could pass a motion of censure on the Commission. If the censure motion were passed, all Commission members must resign.

Choice of commissioners would be a shared task of the member states and the president-elect of the Commission. Each member state would submit a list of three people of suitable competence, European commitment and independence, of whom (in a typical Giscardian touch) at least one must be a woman. From these, the Commission president elect would choose up to 11 persons, taking into account political and geographical balance. The president and the commissioners would be approved as a body by the Parliament. The Commission president would decide on its internal organisation, ensuring it would act consistently, efficiently, and on a collegiate basis, and be able to appoint Commission counsellors on the same criteria as full members. The president would appoint one of the two vice-presidents of the Commission, but not the other, who would be the foreign minister.

Articles on the Parliament and the Council of Ministers made clear that codecision – in future to be known as the legislative procedure – would be the general form of enacting legislation in the Union. The Council of Ministers would also 'carry out executive and coordinating functions, as laid down in the Constitution'. It would consist of a representative of each member state at ministerial level who alone 'may commit the member state in question and cast its vote'.

There would be only five distinct Council formations, down from 9 as agreed in Seville and 16 previously. The article created a Legislative Council 'to consider and jointly, with the European Parliament, enact European laws and European framework laws'. Each member state's minister in this nascent chamber of states (roughly equivalent to the German Bundesrat) could be assisted by a specialist minister, reflecting the Council agenda.

Taking up an issue hotly contested in June 2002 Seville European Council, Giscard sought to split off the General Affairs Council (GAC) from the current General Affairs and External Relations Council (GAERC) and give it the coordinating role that it is accorded in the European Communities treaty. Under the Seville reforms, the two configurations of the GAERC hold separate meetings with separate agendas. Giscard's text proposed that the

GAC 'shall ensure consistency in the work of the Council of Ministers' and be chaired by the European Council vice-president.

The foreign affairs Council would 'flesh out' the Union's external policies on the basis of strategic guidelines laid down by the European Council and be chaired by the Union's foreign minister. There would be only two other Council formations – economic and financial affairs and justice and security – although the General Affairs Council would have the power to decide on further formations.

In line with the Seville conclusions, the European Council would meet quarterly, rather than 'at least twice a year' as in the Treaty on Union. It would be 'convened by its president'. Depending on the agenda and in line with the Seville decision for delegations to be limited to just two seats, its members could decide to be assisted by a minister and in the case of the Commission president a commissioner. The European Council president was empowered to call additional meetings when the international situation required.

As in the TEU, Giscard's text said the European Council 'shall provide the Union with the necessary impetus for its development'. But using more precise language it added that it 'shall determine' (rather than define) the Union's 'general political directions' (with directions replacing guidelines). Going into detail absent from the Union treaty, the European Council would 'set out principles and strategic guidelines' for external action and 'give guidance for action, legislative and operational' in the area of freedom, security and justice. 'It shall maintain oversight of the unity, consistency and efficiency of Union action'. Except where provided otherwise, its decisions would be taken by consensus.

The European Council was a monument to Giscard's past achievements as an architect of Europe. The proposed Congress of the Peoples of Europe was his contribution to the present and he envisaged a far greater role for it than anticipated. Starting innocuously, his draft article proposed the Congress should meet at least once a year to provide a 'forum for contact and consultation in European political life'. It would be chaired by the president of the European Parliament, be limited to 700 members and comprise two-thirds national parliamentarians and only one-third MEPs.

The Congress would not intervene in the Council's legislative procedure. But it might be consulted by the President of the European Council or called on by the European Council to 'work up proposals for amendments' to the Constitution. Moreover, if the European Council so chose, it could, by unanimity, turn the Congress into an electoral college to elect the European

Council's president and vice-president. The Congress in turn would decide the appointments by a majority of its members.

14.2 SHOCKED REACTIONS

Giscard's proposals for the European Council mirrored the most ambitious ideas of the 'ABC' group of Spanish, British and French leaders and, combined with his dismissive approach to the Commission, appeared a deliberate snub to the small member states and the Commission. 'As a courtesy' he sent copies of his articles to the Danish, Greek and Italian governments, as holders of the past, present and future six-month EU presidencies and to Romano Prodi, Commission president. If the latter move were to ensure the greatest possible publicity for his ideas, he was not to be disappointed.

The Commission discussed the articles at its meeting early on Wednesday morning and almost immediately published an angry statement in response. By leaving copies of Giscard's articles lying around in its Breydel building, the Commission also ensured they reached a wider public. Giscard's spokesman, when briefing the press the previous evening, had not released the text.

Providing an interesting reflection of its priorities, the Commission chose first to criticise the breach of procedure and the release of the news to the press. On substance, the Commission complained that Giscard's proposals ran counter to the 'orientations of the debate in the Convention and its working groups' and failed to reflect the discussions of the 16 April European Council in Athens where 18 smaller EU countries and accession states rejected the long-term European Council president, calling instead for institutional balance and equality among member states.

The Commission directed much of its fire against Giscard's proposal for a seven strong board, or bureau. This 'intergovernmental bureau' would, it charged, 'undermine the checks and balances in place between the EU institutions'. It could lead to unequal treatment of member states, jeopardising trust between them, and would undermine accountability, effectiveness and the Community method, the Union's 50-year-old success story. It would duplicate bureaucracy rather than simplify the Union's executive powers.

The Commission acknowledged the Union needed a clearly defined and accountable executive but argued that Giscard's proposals would fall short of this goal and add to institutional fragmentation. It grumbled that no mention was made of the Commission's own executive function, its duties of external representation or its responsibility for executing the EU budget. Privately, Commission officials were apoplectic. According to one in-house analysis, Giscard proposed a completely new institutional structure, based on intergovernmentalism that would leave the enlarged Union dysfunctional. The articles would make the European Council the *de facto* government of the EU. The revised provisions for representation in the European Parliament plus the new QMV rules would make population the dominant criterion of power in the Parliament and Council of Ministers to the detriment of the small and medium sized states.

The reaction of European parliamentarians was equally vituperative. Elmar Brok described Giscard's move as 'autistic' and 'unacceptable'. Pervenche Beres and Olivier Duhamel, French members of the Party of European Socialists, denounced Giscard as a *'grand provocateur'*, who had abandoned consensus and produced articles which insulted the small states, the Franco-German contribution to the Convention, the European Parliament, the Commission and its president and the Convention itself.

The anger continued after the Praesidium had substantially modified the text. When Giscard gave details of the revised articles to the Convention there were loud guffaws in that normally deferential body as he remarked that he had been listening carefully to the conventionnels' contributions for a year. Bringing some light relief to a fraught session, Kimmo Kiljunen, a Socialist member of the Finnish parliament, chided Giscard for 'trying to copy a president from the United States, a Peoples' Congress from China and a Politburo from the Soviet Union'. Issuing a 'personal vote of no confidence' in Giscard, Johannes Voggenhuber, the outspoken Austrian Green, declared that 'the bitter irony of this Convention is that, if it fails it will be because of its president and if it succeeds, it will be despite him'.

14.3   THE PRAESIDIUM REVISIONS

Giscard's articles survived in their entirety for less than 24 hours. The Praesidium met on the evening of Tuesday, 22 April and on Wednesday, 23 April from 9.30am until after midnight, as usual behind closed doors but this time without the members' assistants present. The revised texts of title IV on the institutions were broadly complete by late Wednesday afternoon. The subsequent hours were spent arguing about the Congress and drafting a cover note that made clear there was not unanimous agreement on all issues. The debate was described as heated but not angry. One participant was later to sum up the day as. 'Eighteen hours without a shower – disgusting'.

The most obvious changes in the Praesidium's articles[3] were the removal of the reference to the European Council being the Union's 'highest authority', its demotion to number two in the institutional ranking, the disappearance of the European Council vice-president, the radical slimming down of its board or bureau and deletion of all reference to the Congress becoming an electoral college. Although Giscard's spokesman said all points in the Praesidium draft were supported by strong majorities, the cover note was candid about the disagreements which focused on plans to rewrite the Treaty of Nice.

'On several major points,' it observed, 'two approaches were available: to keep to the provisions of the Treaty of Nice or go beyond them. Following the discussions of the Praesidium on the full range of issues, the proposals put forward concerning the representation of the European Parliament, the definition of qualified majority and the composition of the Commission reflect solutions which go beyond the Nice Treaty. It will be for the Convention to reach a view on this choice.'

Two Praesidium members from small countries – the Irishman John Bruton and the Slovene Alojz Peterle – objected to the slimmed down Commission. Alfonso Dastis and Inigo Méndez de Vigo, both Spaniards, objected strongly to the proposed changes to the method for calculating a qualified majority in the Council and the composition of the European Parliament.

The voting arrangements in the Council gave Spain (and Poland) weight almost equal to the Union's four big powers, a deal which Madrid regarded as fair exchange for the loss of a commissioner when the Commission moves to one member per member state after 2004. The Nice decision, amended by the October 2002 Brussels European Council to take account of 10 new member states in May 2004, gave Spain and Poland 27 Council votes each from 1 January 2005 compared with 29 each for the big four. Spain, with a population of 40.4 million, thus would have a voting weight of 8.41 per cent against weightings of 9.03 per cent for Germany, with a population of 82 million, and France, the UK and Italy with between 59 million and 56 million people each.

At first sight, the proposed redefinition of QMV to reflect population size appeared to favour Spain as its population is 8.94 per cent of the 452 million inhabitants of the soon to be enlarged Union and thus higher in percentage terms than the share of the votes decided at Nice. But in addition to issues of prestige, the change would upset the ability of Spain (and Poland) to block unwelcome legislation by giving extra voting power to the four biggest member states and leaving a multitude of small states each with very little

---

[3] CONV 691/03.

voting weight. Acts passed by QMV under the Nice rules in a Union of 25 would require the support of at least 232 votes, or 72.27 per cent of the total, putting Spain with its 27 votes in a good position to marshal a blocking minority behind its interests. In an enlarged Union with greatly increased recourse to QMV, this would be a valuable asset, especially for a country which never was shy of standing up for its rights.

Although the opposition to revising the Nice Treaty was serious, Giscard appeared more concerned in the Praesidium meeting about the reaction of Jean-Luc Dehaene. The avowedly federalist former Belgian prime minister was furious that Giscard had leaked his articles before he had seen them. Dehaene was also unwilling to accept the permanent president of the European Council. He feared the post would upset the Union's institutional triangle of Council of Ministers, Commission and European Parliament and that, with a permanent president, the European Council could be formalised even more as the appellate body for the other Councils and so end up taking all key decisions in the Union. Giscard's ability to overcome Dehaene's reservations prevented a split in the triumvirate and kept the idea of a long-term European Council president in the Praesidium text. That achievement may have been one reason why the president seemed serene when he appeared before the Convention on Thursday afternoon.

He presented the Praesidium's draft articles as proposals to strengthen all sides of the institutional triangle that were sufficiently flexible to last for the long term – possibly 50 years – in the face of widely different expectations of the future of Europe. They respected three principles that might sometimes seem mutually inconsistent, namely equality before the law of citizens and member states; maintaining the three main Union institutions, and respect for the Community method. He had a word of warning for the Convention. Citizens, he opined, were not too bothered about institutions. They wanted results.

As Giscard outlined the revised texts, it became clear that he had given up a lot.

Article 14 [18][4] of the Praesidium text continued to regard the European Council as an institution of the Union, but took it down a peg, positioning it below the European Parliament. The article also stated that the Union 'shall be served by a single institutional framework' which 'shall aim to' advance its objectives, promote its values and service the interests of the Union, its

---

[4] As in Chapter 13, article numbers of the final draft treaty (CONV 850/03) follow in square brackets.

citizens and member states. Giscard said this innovation compared with his own text reflected the disappearance of the pillars.

Reflecting the changed institutional hierarchy of article 14, the European Parliament was covered by article 15 [19] in the Praesidium draft instead of article 16 in Giscard's text. This repositioning, Giscard said, was to 'underline the democratic legitimacy of the system'. The Parliament's mission statement was fuller. In addition to legislating jointly with the Council, it would 'exercise functions of political control and consultation'. The article was explicit in stating: 'It shall elect the president of the European Commission'. The most notable change compared with Giscard's draft concerned the rules for apportioning members. The new draft said representation of European citizens 'shall be degressively proportional' with a minimum threshold of four members per member state. The concept of degressivity was pushed by Bruton to protect smaller states which stood to lose most from the 'proportional' representation of Giscard's draft.

Article 16 [20] curtailed the European Council's mission statement as well as cutting out mention of it being the Union's highest authority and the reference to the vice-president. The European Council would still meet quarterly. But the specific Giscardian tasks in relation to external affairs and freedom, justice and security were cut as was reference to maintaining oversight of Union actions. Giscard explained the absence of national foreign ministers from the future European Council as a response to the 'numbers problem' of the greatly enlarged Union.

Article 16a [21] on the European Council Chair kept the idea of a full-time, elected president, who would be a former European Council member and hold the job for two and half years, renewable once. It added that the European Council would be able to end the mandate by the same procedure of QMV 'in cases of serious malpractice'. The job description was similar to that of Giscard's text, retaining the duty of representation in the wider world and adding, by way of more detail, that she or he 'shall endeavour to facilitate cohesion and consensus within the European Council'. However, the president's position was weakened. He or she would report to the European Parliament after each meeting rather than just give an annual report to the Congress. The reference to Congress being able to elect the president and vice-president went. The board became optional ('The European Council may decide by consensus to create a board'). It no longer contained other Council presidents and would be smaller. An important change, which partly reclaimed the principle of rotation, specified it would consist of three European Council members 'chosen according to a system of equitable rotation'.

As revised, articles 16 and 16a significantly trimmed Giscard's ambitions and his presentation to the Convention was correspondingly disingenuous. He pointed to the linguistic difficulties caused by the words 'chairman' in English and 'president' in French. The two words were interchangeable but their meanings were not. The president of the European Council would be a chairman 'and it is in this capacity that he presides and coordinates the meetings of the European Council for which he ensures the preparation and, at the end of the day, presents a report to Parliament'. The president/chairman would not be an executive and potential rival to the Commission president. As for the board, 'many motives have been impugned', he observed. But a large European Council of 25 would need a board. Indeed, town councils needed boards or bureaus.

The Praesidium made few changes to article 17 [22] on the Council of Ministers. It would carry out policy-making rather than executive functions. In response to the complaints of parliamentarians in the Convention that member states were often represented by unelected officials in the Council, the article specified that they would be represented at ministerial level 'for each of its formations'.

As before, article 17a [23] named only five Council formations – General Affairs, Legislative, Foreign Affairs, Economic and Financial and Justice and Security – although it continued to give the General Affairs Council power to decide more. The General Affairs Council would still ensure consistency in the overall work of the Council, although the disappearance of the vice-president left open who would chair it. A new sentence, stating, 'With the participation of the Commission, it shall prepare meetings of the European Council', gave both the Commission and the General Affairs Council some say in the European Council agenda. Another new sentence gave the European Council power, by consensus, to give the presidency of a Council formation, other than foreign affairs, to a member state for at least a year 'taking into account European political and geographical balance and the diversity of all member states.'

Giscard said the latter provision was one way of ensuring equal treatment of member states in the absence of a rotating presidency. The aim would be to balance the interests of northern and southern, big and small and old and new members in a non-mechanistic way. He also explained the Legislative Council 'as a kind of second chamber' whose meetings would be public.

In article 17b [24] on qualified majority, Giscard's original draft was modified so that QMV in the European Council and Council of Ministers would reflect a majority of member states and three-fifths (rather than two-thirds) of the Union's population. This, he deemed 'equitable and fair' although he noted that some members wished to retain the Nice Treaty rules.

Article 18 [25] on the European Commission retained Giscard's wording on the right of initiative, set the maximum size at 15 members, including the president, and gave it a much fuller mission statement. The Commission, it said, 'shall safeguard the general European interest. It shall ensure the application of the Constitution, and steps taken by the institutions under the Constitution. It shall also exercise coordinating, executive and management functions as laid down in the Constitution.'

Article 18a [26] on the Commission president increased the role of the European Parliament in electing the head of the Commission and holding the Commission to account. While Giscard's wording said the European Council would put forward its candidate for Commission president 'following the European elections', the new text gave the process more political significance by obliging it to take notice of the election results. It also stipulated the Commission president would be elected by a majority of Parliament's members rather than three-fifths as in Giscard's draft. The new article retained the procedure of member states submitting lists of three potential commissioners but gave the Commission president-elect the right to select up to 13 Commission members, up from 11. As in the Giscard text, the Commission president and commissioners would be approved as a body by the European Parliament. However, the Commission as a body would be responsible only to the European Parliament, which could censure the Commission, and not to the European Council and Parliament as proposed by Giscard.

The Commission president was given power to appoint vice-presidents (in the plural, rather than just one in Giscard's text) from among the Commission members and 'associate commissioners'. The associate commissioners would not be part of the college of commissioners and would have no voting powers.

Viewed together, the revised articles significantly curtailed the power the European Council president compared with Giscard's vision. The changes in article 18 and 18a also amounted to a significant enhancement of Parliament's role in life of the Commission president compared with the Giscard text and reflected the effectiveness of Méndez de Vigo and Hänsch, the two MEPs in the Praesidium. The European Council's ability to determine the candidate for Commission president was subtly reduced and could decline further if European political parties were to get their act together in future European Parliament elections and put forward persons of Commission president material.

Article 19 [27] on the foreign minister contained one notable modification compared with the Giscard text. The minister would still be appointed by the European Council using QMV, but would need the 'agreement' of the Commission president: the Giscard text spoke of a decision 'after consulting' the head of the Commission. As before, the foreign minister would carry out the common foreign and security and defence policies 'as mandated by the Council' and also be one of the Commission vice-presidents and 'responsible there for handling external relations and for co-ordinating other aspects of the Union's external action'. She or he would be bound by Commission procedures 'only for these responsibilities' in the Commission.

The Praesidium took an axe to the proposals on the Congress of the Peoples of Europe, deleting three paragraphs which would have given the Congress the possibility of preparing amendments to the Constitution and functioning as an electoral college for the president of the European Council.

Both Giscard's text and that of the Praesidium mapped out the responsibilities and, where appropriate, the membership of the Court of Justice, the European Central Bank and the Union's advisory bodies (the Committee of the Regions and the Economic and Social Committee), without triggering controversy.

14.4 FOREIGN AFFAIRS AND DEFENCE

Giscard's presentation of the institutional articles on 24 April overshadowed the introduction by Jean-Luc Dehaene of the Praesidium's draft texts on the Union's external action immediately afterwards.[5] This was a pity because the external action provisions were a meaty part of the draft constitutional treaty and quite radical. They consisted of three articles in part I and 37 articles in the policies section, which, since the Athens summit, was known as part III.[6] The part I texts as published in April gave the provisional numbers 29 to the article on the implementation of the common foreign and security policy (CFSP) and 30 for the common security and defence policy (CSDP) while an article detailing a solidarity clause against terrorism was unnumbered. In the final text submitted to the president of the European Council in Rome on 18 July, the three part I articles were numbered 39, 40 and 42 respectively, while the detailed articles on external action made up title V of part III and ran from article III-193 to III-231 inclusive. The draft articles drew heavily

---

[5] CONV 685/03.
[6] From this point, the Praesidium began to use Roman numerals to distinguish between the parts of the constitutional treaty.

on the work of the external action and defence working groups, chaired respectively by Dehaene and Michel Barnier, and gave more details of the planned Union foreign minister.

The April drafts were drawn up in the shadow of the splits among EU and accession countries over the conflict in Iraq, and yet amid evidence that voters wanted common foreign and defence policies for the Union. Article 29 [39] of part I therefore took the view that developing CFSP was a process to be achieved by encouraging convergence and mutual solidarity among member states. One aim of the constitutional treaty was to provide more effective institutional mechanisms to assist this process. Dehaene was cautious when presenting the texts. 'We are not proposing a miracle solution but are trying to devise procedures and structures which permit more joint action on the part of the Union,' he said.

Opinion poll evidence encouraged the Praesidium in this approach. A Eurobarometer poll, commissioned at Giscard's request and carried out between mid-February and mid-March, found 63 per cent of EU citizens favoured a common foreign policy (with 22 per cent against) and 71 per cent backed a common defence policy (with 17 per cent against). The poll, published at the end of April, showed a slight flagging of support compared with the previous survey. There was also a divergence in enthusiasm between countries such as Luxembourg, Greece and Italy, which were strongly in favour of common policies in both areas, and the traditionally neutral countries like Finland, Sweden, Austria and Ireland, where support was significantly below the Union average. But only in Britain did more people oppose a common foreign policy than support it.

Article 29 on the common foreign and security policy made clear the European Council was to 'identify the Union's strategic interests and determine the objectives' of CFSP while the Council of Ministers framed the policy. Both bodies would adopt the necessary decisions while the foreign minister and the member states would put the policy into effect, using Union and national resources.

The member states were to consult in the Council or European Council 'on any foreign and security policy issue which is of general interest in order to determine a common approach' and also before taking international action or making any commitment which could affect the Union's interests. Using language that alarmed UK eurosceptics, but was already in article 11 of the TEU, article 3 [III-195] in the policies section of the treaty underlined the duty of member states to support CFSP 'actively and unreservedly in a spirit of loyalty and mutual solidarity'. They were also to 'refrain from any action which is contrary to the interests of the Union or likely to impair its effectiveness as a cohesive force in international relations'.

The minister would carry out tasks formerly done by the high representative, the presidency and the Commission and have a right of initiative. The creation of this 'double-hatted' post and the minister's proposed right of initiative were responsible for most of the changes in existing CFSP articles. The April texts assumed the minister would help draw up and be in charge of implementing the Union's foreign and defence policies on a mandate from the Council of Ministers and not be subject to Commission collegiality in this area. But he or she would also be a member of the Commission and the rules of the college would apply for external relations issues dealing with traditional Community responsibilities. The minister could seek the Commission's support on CFSP and put forward joint proposals with the Commission. There could be extraordinary meetings of the European Council in case of international crises.

Member states were expected to boost the minister's role: those in the United Nations Security Council were told they should give the foreign minister the right to speak in support of Union positions. Provision was made to provide urgent financing, especially for operations under the CSDP.

Although article 29 stated a general rule that decisions relating to CFSP would be unanimous in the European Council and Council of Ministers, it gave the European Council the power to decide by unanimity to extend QMV to policies that were subject to the national veto. This bridge or *passerelle* clause in draft article 9 [III-201] of the policy section of the treaty was in addition to a controversial provision for QMV in the event of the foreign minister and the Commission producing a joint initiative.

Based on existing article 23 of the TEU, draft article 9 included rules for abstention, including qualified abstention, which would exempt a country from applying a CFSP decision, although it would have to accept the decision would commit the Union and undertake not to obstruct it. However, if member states representing more than one-third of the weighted votes in the Council qualified their abstentions, the decision would not be adopted.

Draft article 30 [40] described the common security and defence policy (CSDP) as 'an integral part' of CFSP to 'provide the Union with an operational capability' making use of military and civilian means. These, it added, may be deployed 'on tasks outside the Union to preserve peace and strengthen international security in accordance with the principles of the UN Charter.'

The tasks, defined more closely in draft article 17 [III-210] of the policies part of the treaty were an expanded version of the 'Petersberg' tasks. To the existing humanitarian and rescue, peacekeeping, crisis management and peace making tasks would be added disarmament operations, military advice and assistance, conflict prevention, support in combating terrorism at the request of a third country and post-conflict stabilisation. These duties had been recommended by the defence working group.

The high ambitions set for CSDP became clearer in paragraph two which declared: 'The common security and defence policy shall include the progressive framing of a common defence policy for the Union. This will lead to a common defence when the European Council, acting unanimously, so decides.' But the text then attempted to ease the concerns of those countries, among both existing and future member states, which saw their security anchored in the Atlantic alliance. Reiterating article 17 (1) of the TEU, it said the Union's policy 'shall not prejudice the specific character of the security and defence policy of certain member states and shall respect the obligations of certain member states, which see their common defence realised in NATO ... and be compatible with the common security and defence policy established within that framework'.

The article went on to underline how CSDP depended for its capabilities on member states' military and civilian resources and, picking up on defence working group recommendations, urged them 'progressively to improve their military capabilities'. It made provision for a 'European Armaments, and Strategic Research Agency' to help strengthening the defence industry and helping define a European capabilities and armaments policy. Article 30 also said member states establishing multinational forces could make them available to CSDP.

In taking decisions, the Council would unanimously adopt measures proposed by the foreign minister or a member state. The Commission would have no right of initiative in defence.

In one important area, article 30 on defence broke new ground. Largely because of UK objections, the Nice negotiations rejected enhanced cooperation in defence. The draft article, by contrast, broached various forms of 'flexibility' or enhanced cooperation to cope with cases where not all member states would engage in military action together. Thus under paragraph five, the Council would be able to entrust a crisis management task to a group of Union members that would be both willing and able to carry out the task. The Council decision would be unanimous. The nations involved would then agree management of the task among themselves but would have to refer back to the Council if completing the task entailed a new objective or conditions.

Paragraph six envisaged member states with stronger military capabilities establishing 'structured cooperation' and taking on more demanding tasks. The details, including the states involved, would be set out in a declaration attached to the constitution. The states would be able to use Union structures such as the political and security committee (PSC) and the military committee but their operations would not be Union operations. The foreign minister would attend meetings on such cooperation and inform the other member states of what was going on.

Most controversial of all, paragraph seven would allow member states to give mutual defence guarantees in case of armed aggression against any one of them. The aim here was to reproduce the mutual defence commitment of article 5 of the Brussels Treaty of the Western European Union which binds 10 current member states and allow them to use Union structures. The article would be a transitional provision until the creation of the 'common defence' envisaged in paragraph two. It fuelled fears that the Union's defence policy could undermine NATO.

The articles incorporated important changes in other parts of the constitutional treaty. They took into account the disappearance of the CFSP 'pillar', which followed acceptance by the Convention of a single legal personality for the Union, and the simplification of its instruments and procedures. The external action articles struck a blow for clarity by bringing the Union's many external activities together into a coherent whole for the first time. The 37 draft articles in part III were concentrated in eight chapters under a single title. The first chapter comprised two 'horizontal' articles, the first setting out the principles and objectives of the Union's external policies and the second summarising how the European Council, the Council and Union foreign minister would use the external action instruments at their disposal [III-193 and III-194 of the 18 July text]. The articles to implement CFSP, including defence, formed the next chapter [III-195 to III-215]. They were followed by a further six chapters covering the common commercial policy; cooperation with third countries (including development cooperation, economic, financial and technical cooperation and humanitarian assistance); restrictive measures (Brussels jargon for giving the Union a legal base to impose sanctions); international agreements; relations with international organisations and third countries; and provisions to implement the solidarity clause [III-216 to III-231].

Draft article 24 [III-217] on the common commercial policy contained an important change to bring it into line with article 11 on competences. It categorised trade in cultural and audiovisual services, educational services and social and human health services as an exclusive competence of the Union, and thus subject to QMV and codecision. In article 133 of the TEC these activities, known as the 'cultural exception' and of huge political importance in France, counted as a shared competence and so were subject to national vetoes.

Dehaene underlined that the grouping of the articles – like the elimination of the pillars – did not mean the harmonisation of procedures or instruments. These, and the roles of the actors involved, would vary according to policy. The Praesidium also made clear that CFSP was not covered by the Court of Justice.

14.5   A BASIS FOR FURTHER WORK?

Despite the sometimes savage changes to his own articles on the institutions, Giscard was in fine spirits when he presented the Praesidium's articles to the Convention plenary on the afternoon of Thursday, 24 April. Elsewhere, the revised texts prompted a good deal of crowing at Giscard's expense. For Hänsch, Giscard's vision now looked like 'a plucked Gallic cockerel' and 'we have the rare case that a plucked foul looks better than one with feathers.' Méndez de Vigo said the Praesidium deserved credit for producing a text that was 'radically different' from Giscard's draft.

Some of Giscard's critics had calmed down somewhat. Brok, for example, said the new text was 'negotiable' although he still criticised the institution of a long-term European Council president for being unaccountable to any Parliament. While welcoming the weakening of the board, the long-term presidency was a recipe for power struggles with the Commission and the new Union foreign minister. The slimming of the Commission could lead to small countries turning against the Union in future referendums, he warned. Duff adopted a nuanced approach, welcoming the separation in the Council of Ministers of executive and legislative roles but warning that institutional rivalry between the Commission and European Council would only be overcome by eventually integrating their presidencies.

But ominously, Katiforis, who chaired the government representatives' meetings during the Greek presidency in the absence of George Papandreou, reported 'great unease' at their meeting on the morning of 24 April because the opinions of the 18 small to medium sized states that met in Athens the week before were not reflected in Giscard's proposals. These countries feared Giscard's definition of consensus in the Convention 'could be a demographic definition made up by three or four bigger states of the Union'.

The unease was expressed most forcefully by Hannes Farnleitner, the Austrian government *conventionnel*. Farnleitner was by now emerging as one of the most forceful of the small country spokespersons. A former economics minister, Farnleitner shared with his boss, chancellor Schüssel, a fondness for brinkmanship in negotiation that he put to good use as the Convention progressed. Like his fellow Austrian Voggenhuber, he enjoyed controversy. But whereas Voggenhuber's message would sometimes get tangled in florid, classical metaphors, Farnleitner's style oscillated between the folksy and the frank. On this day, he chose to be brutally frank. He told Giscard that the views of 21 government representatives ranged from 'rejection to very sceptical'. Only two countries in the meeting supported the Praesidium, while two others could not comment because of the absence of their foreign ministers. Farnleitner warned Giscard that the mood among governments had shifted towards drawing up options rather than a single text for the IGC. The threat made, Farnleitner urged Giscard to listen more in future.

In Giscard's defence, Germany's Joschka Fischer, who was absent from the morning meeting, said the Praesidium text was a 'good basis for discussion'. But the government *conventionnels* of the three Benelux countries sent a stiff note to Giscard rejecting those articles which 'undermined the Community project and the fundamental equilibrium between institutions and member states'. They pledged they would, with others, draw up alternative proposals.

The events of 22–24 April put the Convention under considerable stress with some members vowing never to trust Giscard again. However, Giscard emerged from the imbroglio with some gains. He secured the Praesidium's backing for the long-term presidency of the European Council while only minor changes were made to his plans for a slimmed down Commission. He brought forward the debate on the most difficult part of the remaining work of the Convention by a good three weeks, which was important given the pressure at the Athens European Council for the Convention to complete its work by 20 June. Giscard and the Convention were also back on the front pages of Europe's newspapers and in the evening television news bulletins.

Some Convention members later spoke of a sense of catharsis that week. Choices were on the table. Time was short. The gloves were off. There were deals to be done. Even as the Benelux representatives were firing off their note to Giscard, there were rumours that Belgium was working towards a compromise. The president, Giscard's aides reported, was happy with the Praesidium's deliberations and was prepared to defend the outcome.

At the end of the week, some conventionnels were prepared to credit Giscard with a tactical success. His easy acceptance of the Praesidium's changes lent credibility to reports that he had loaded his draft articles with dispensable bargaining chips, such as the deputy president of the European Council, and was pleasantly surprised that so much of his original text survived. It was suggested that by setting his sights high in his initial proposals and drawing opprobrium onto himself, he had bamboozled hostile critics into accepting the Praesidium text as the basis for further work. Giuliano Amato, one of Giscard's two deputies, went so far as to describe the Praesidium proposals as 'a sort of mainstream'.

14.6   ENHANCED COOPERATION AMID CONTINUED DISCORD

For once, Amato's judgement appeared wide of the mark. The Praesidium articles on the institutions attracted 650 amendments and those on foreign policy and defence nearly 850. As the conventionnels gathered in Brussels on 15 May for two solid days of debate on the articles on institutions and external action, it appeared as if the Praesidium's efforts had merely magnified existing divisions in the Convention.

True, there was broad acceptance of the new foreign minister when more than 70 speakers took the floor to debate external affairs on 16 May, although many saw a need to clarify aspects of his double-hatted role in Council and Commission. But on practically all other issues there were divisions.

A wide gulf opened between the keen integrationists, concentrated among members of the European Parliament with the support of Germany and France, who sought far more QMV in foreign policy and a cohort of government representatives, of whom the most outspoken, the UK's Peter Hain, wanted CFSP 'ring-fenced' to maintain its intergovernmental nature and general use of unanimity.

The proposals for various forms of enhanced cooperation in article 30 on defence, and especially that covering mutual defence, revived the split between 'new' and 'old' Europe. While de Villepin for France and Bury of Germany spoke in praise of the recent defence mini summit and the idea of an *avant garde* of more integrationist member states, Hain, said bluntly that Britain would not agree to an EU common defence because London supported the NATO guarantee provided to 19 of the soon to be 25 member states. From the accession countries, Poland's Danuta Hübner warned a defence guarantee rivalling NATO would risk unnecessary duplication of structures and capabilities. Her concerns were echoed by government representatives from Lithuania, Latvia and the Czech Republic.

The divergence over *avant garde* proposals for foreign policy and defence continued to grow. When at the end of May, the plenary discussed a separate article 32b [I-43] setting down the rules for implementing 'enhanced cooperation', Hain, backed by Lena Hjelm-Wallen of Sweden and Rytis Martikonis of Lithuania, rejected outright its extension to defence.[7] Hain remained impervious in the face of a passionate intervention from Lamberto Dini, the former Italian prime minister and foreign minister, that enhanced cooperation was necessary if the UK insisted on continuing restrictions to more QMV in the Union.

Gaining acceptance of enhanced cooperation in the constitutional treaty thus became an important goal of the integrationist conventionnels. Although mainly a technical adaptation of existing provisions, draft article 32b, published in the middle of May, envisaged a significant easing of the restrictions on enhanced cooperation in the enlarged Union by stipulating a minimum threshold of one-third of member states for countries to participate, compared with eight out of 15 member states under the Treaty of Nice. The Praesidium's view was that enhanced cooperation was a 'last resort' mechanism which would promote integration by encouraging groups of states to cooperate inside rather than outside the Union. Although hitherto never used, it was thought that it could be useful in the long term in the context of a much bigger and more diverse EU.

When the Convention debated the institutions on 15 May, there was strong opposition to the long-term European Council president, especially from the smaller member states and followers of the centre-right EPP. Many Convention members rejected the idea of the European Council being included among the Union's institutions. Greece, Benelux and the EPP tabled amendments to strengthen the executive role of the Commission. The candidate country Convention members, with strong support from their Irish and Nordic colleagues, pressed for a collegiate Commission with equality of commissioners. There were few backers of the Praesidium draft on the Commission's composition. Indeed, most amendments urged one commissioner per member state.

The UK, Spanish and Polish governments, backed in this case by Ireland, rejected the idea of a Legislative Council. In the debate on 15 May, Hain spoke out so strongly against the legislative Council that it seemed to join the other 'red line' issues such as tax harmonisation and QMV in foreign

---

[7] CONV 723/03. The draft articles on enhanced cooperation were published in mid-May and the plenary debate on them two weeks later was a rather curious interlude in a Convention otherwise preoccupied by splits over institutional issues and the first full draft of the constitutional treaty.

policy which Britain had pledged to resist at all costs. Some amendments, notably from the Benelux countries, explicitly called for retention of the six-month rotating presidency. Reacting to the Praesidium proposal on MEPs' numbers, some small state conventionnels countered by demanding higher minimum thresholds of five or even six MEPs per country. The idea of 'degressive proportionality' in allocating European Parliament seats brought the Spanish and Polish government representatives, as prime beneficiaries of the Nice settlement, onto the same side as many 'smalls'.

The amendments highlighted Spain's outright opposition to changing the Nice decision on votes in the Council. 'My country cannot accept', wrote Ana Palacio, the Spanish foreign minister, about the Praesidium's proposals on QMV. Her preference for the Nice formula was shared by government representatives from the UK, Sweden, Denmark, Cyprus, Poland and Slovakia and many national parliamentarians. Some governments, including several from the accession countries, backed the Nice arrangements but were prepared to consider a simple double majority should the Convention decide to reopen Nice.

The articles on the institutions prompted the conventionnels from the small member states to confer and rally their forces behind the Community method. Just before the Convention was due to discuss foreign and defence policy on 16 May, Henrik Hololei, the energetic alternate for the Estonian government, spoke on behalf of the 16 old and new smaller states that at the end of March had signed a paper on 'principles and premises' for reforming the Union's institutions.[8]

Rattling through his text to pack as many words as possible into his allotted three minutes, Hololei laid out the group's case. 'The Union should in the future be a Union of equal member states, cooperating efficiently on the basis of the Community method ... The imminent enlargement of the Union does not necessarily constitute a good excuse for a radical reform of what has been, so far, well-served decision-making'. Nice should be given a 'fair chance'. The Councils and the European Council should have rotating presidencies. The Commission should have one commissioner per member state, on a basis of full equality. Success for the Convention lay in maintaining and reinforcing the Community method. Hololei closed the lid of his lap top to the sound of loud applause from his fellow smalls.

But the small and medium sized countries were not as solid as the 'friends of the Community method' liked to claim. While they could agree on joint statements, they were never able to draw up draft articles together. Moreover,

---

[8] CONV 646/03.

the Benelux countries were no longer aligned with the 16. Early in May, Belgium, the Netherlands and Luxembourg produced amendments to the Praesidium articles which backed away from one commissioner per member state and moved towards the Praesidium line with a proposal for a college of up to 15 commissioners, supported by an equivalent number of assistant commissioners who would not vote. Their plan, however, included the important qualification that the slimmed down Commission would be appointed on an equal and rotating basis.[9]

There were hints of possible compromise elsewhere. Hain took time out from the 15 May plenary to try and persuade sceptical British journalists that a 'historic compromise' was in the offing, based on the Franco-German deal of January. Inside the plenary, he sought to reassure the Convention that Britain, in pushing the long-term presidency of the European Council, was 'not talking about a super-president who is going to be either a rival of, competing with, or dominating the president of the Commission ... We just want an effective chairman of the Council to carry out the existing functions, remit or duties far more effectively.'

Duff, Dini and Pierre Lequiller, a French parliamentarian, began seeking signatures for an updated version of their idea, first unveiled in January, for a single presidency of the European Council and Commission.[10] This project, which they wanted inserting in the constitutional treaty as a proposition for the distant future through enabling legislation, was supported by Michel Barnier, one of the two commissioners in the Convention. Thinking even more 'out of the box', George Papandreou, the Greek foreign minister and Praesidium member, suggested a European Council president chosen by direct elections.[11]

Despite all the fury about Giscard's handling of the institutional debate, by mid-May positions were beginning to shift. For practical reasons such as printing and translation, the 20 June deadline for handing over the text to the Union's leaders in Thessaloniki meant the work had to be completed by 13 June, less than a month away. Amato sensed the changing currents, noting: 'Some members of the Convention are realising that if they want to be founding fathers, they will have to move. Otherwise, they will be founding failures.'

---

[9] CONV 732/03.

[10] CONV 746/03.

[11] When he managed to find time for the Convention, Papandreou proved a source of imaginative proposals. It was his idea that the Praesidium should take to a cruise ship in Greek waters for the arduous task of drawing up the complete draft constitutional treaty before the end of May – a proposal killed by Sir John Kerr.

CHAPTER 15
The Revised Draft Constitution

The same choice of being a founding father or a founding failure faced the members of the Praesidium when they met on 21 May for a three day session to finish the first complete draft of the constitutional treaty. They had to fulfil a promise by Giscard, made in a letter of 8 May, that the Convention's members would be able to debate the complete treaty during the plenary scheduled for 30–31 May.

The intensity of the Praesidium's work had already increased compared with the second half of 2002 when there were never more than three meetings a month and few lasted longer than half a day. The steering body agreed on 19 December that from 9 January its meetings would last all day and be more frequent. It met respectively on four days in January, February and March, five days in April and eight in May. The three-day session starting on 21 May came after four two-day sessions since early March. The days were long with one session continuing until 2.30 in the morning.

As well as producing new draft articles, the Praesidium had to consider the amendments and feed back in the plenaries to articles it had produced. It also had to keep track of work delegated to a team of six legal experts from the Council, the Commission and the European Parliament who were charged with bringing the policy related articles and legal bases of the existing treaties into the single text that would become part III of the final draft. Although the experts covered a prodigious amount of ground, they were not mandated to take political decisions. Controversial areas of drafting – such as the part III articles on justice and home affairs and foreign and economic policy – were left for the Praesidium and the Convention to resolve.

The amendments posed a huge challenge to the Praesidium and the secretariat. Nearly 3,000 were submitted to the draft articles published between February and mid-May. These had to be collated and analysed by the secretariat. When Convention members arrived at plenary sessions, they would find all the amendments piled on their desks and bound with thick rubber bands. Sir John Kerr and his officials would then try to monitor the interventions to see which of the many amendments submitted by a conventionnel really mattered to the individual. If time allowed, or diplomacy dictated, eye contact would be made with the speaker if only to suggest to the conventionnels that their points were being taken seriously.

Creating this feel good factor was important because the amendments put forward often reflected political priorities at home. A Convention member who felt well treated in the hall would be able to tell constituents that they were being heard and should be less likely to cause trouble. The secretariat papers analysing the amendments and grouping them into categories were an important public relations tool, because they helped conventionnels to feel that their own amendments were influencing the Convention.

Few really did. Many amendments were of an editorial nature and so politically insignificant and easy to deal with. More controversially, the Secretariat disregarded many on the grounds that they were cancelled out by other contrary amendments. The secretariat paid more attention to amendments that carried a lot of signatures, such as those submitted by the party groups, or which carried special weight, such as those from key governments. Although the European parliamentarians would claim that the Convention method meant all conventionnels were equal and should count as such in drawing up the final draft, processing the amendments showed this was not the case.

Giscard's activities outside the Convention turned to massaging important special interests. He stepped up his bilateral diplomacy over a three-week period from 30 April in which he saw Pierre Raffarin, the French prime minister, with de Villepin; German opposition leaders including Erwin Teufel; Joschka Fischer; Gianfranco Fini, the Italian deputy prime minister and government conventionnel, with Lamberto Dini and Marco Folini, the two Italian parliamentarians in the Convention; Britain's prime minister Tony Blair and Romano Prodi, the Commission president. This was while the revised draft articles were being drawn up in the Praesidium. It was a time of concern that the Convention could be derailed. Britain appeared insistent that the Convention should not cross its 'red lines'. Rejecting the Praesidium's articles on the institutions, Prodi had thrown his weight behind one Commissioner per member state. The German opposition was pushing hard for a reference to God or Christianity in the constitutional treaty. An important element in these meetings was to tease out the 'bottom lines' which key Convention participants required or could not accept as part of a final consensus.

15.1 THE END-MAY TEXTS

Monday, 26 May was an important milestone in the life of the Convention.

Fifteen months after they started work, the conventionnels were sent the revised text of part I of the draft constitution.[1] Volume two[2] including the

---

[1] CONV 724/03.

Charter of Fundamental Rights in its entirety as part II of the constitution; the detailed policies and their legal bases as part III and the general and final provisions of the constitutional treaty as part IV was published one day later. Also made public were the draft texts of part II[3] and part IV[4] with explanatory comments, and an overview[5] of those sections of part III which had been modified by the Praesidium or which were new in relation to existing treaties and which had not so far been discussed by the Convention.

The mass of texts was a big media event. It was the first time that the press and public had an overview of what the Convention was seeking to produce and could balance the claims made about the constitutional treaty with its provisional contents. However, the Praesidium had failed to meet its target of publishing a fully revised text because it was split and incapable of agreement. The articles of title IV of part I on the institutions were unchanged from the original version published after its meeting of 22–23 April.[6]

In the previous week's marathon, the Praesidium had agreed revised articles on economic governance, the budget, the implementation of Union action, justice and home affairs, the definition and objectives of the Union, the treaty's general and final provisions, external action, the incorporation of the Charter, the Union's neighbourhood policy, Union membership and new legal bases in part III that would define policies on energy, civil protection, intellectual property, civil administration, space and sport. A disingenuous cover note explained the missing institutional articles.[7] It promised a revised version of title IV 'at a later stage, as these thoughts mature'.

The end-May drafts managed simultaneously to offend supporters of greater European integration, those who want a more intergovernmental Union and conventionnels of a religious persuasion – suggesting that Giscard and the Praesidium must have got something right. When the part I appeared on 26 May, it left the overall impression that Giscard had persuaded the Praesidium to back away from some of the more integrationist aspects of

---

[2] CONV 725/03.
[3] CONV 726/03.
[4] CONV 728/03.
[5] CONV 727/03.
[6] CONV 691/03.
[7] It said: 'The very numerous amendments received and the comments made at the plenary on these articles often go in opposite directions, particularly on central questions, including the three linked questions highlighted in the note of 23 April (representation in the European Parliament, definition of the qualified majority, and composition of the Commission). The Praesidium therefore thinks it would be appropriate to devote more time to discussion and thought on those subjects.'

earlier drafts. Foreign and tax policy remained intergovernmental with unanimity the general rule in these areas.

The assessment swung the other way when the second volume appeared on the following day. This revealed a substantial extension of the European Parliament's powers of codecision with the Council (henceforth to be known as ordinary legislative procedure) from 34 to 70 policy areas and the application of qualified majority voting in the Council of Minister's in place of unanimity in more than 20 procedures.

Some decisions suggested that Giscard and the Praesidium had applied the principle that 'the squeakiest wheel gets the most grease' in response to the thousands of amendments. Reflecting intense lobbying from several countries, but especially the personal intervention of Tony Blair during a visit by Giscard to 10 Downing Street on 19 May, the word 'federal' was dropped from the first article. The well organised and vocal social lobby gained greater recognition for social and employment policies in the updated drafts. Unice, the consensually inclined European employers' federation which had observer status in the Convention, was chagrined to see 'competitiveness' dropped from the Union's objectives despite having lobbied hard, and at first successfully, for its inclusion in the first draft articles published in February.

15.2 THE REVISED PART I

With 59 articles, the draft part I now had 13 articles more than promised in the October 2002 'skeleton'.[8] The Praesidium made significant changes, notably to the opening articles, defining and stating the objectives of the Union and clarifying its competences vis-à-vis the member states. The first three articles of the Praesidium's first draft[9] had attracted no fewer than 435 amendments, so extensive rewriting was to be expected.

The first paragraph of article I-1[10] entitled 'Establishment of the Union' replaced 'federal' by the ugly, but less politically charged wording

---

[8] CONV 369/02.

[9] CONV 528/03.

[10] Draft articles from the end-May drafts until the end of the Convention were prefixed with Roman numerals denoting the part of the constitutional treaty to which they belonged. The order of articles in part I stayed unchanged from 26 May although their contents were revised and the style of numeration was changed again in the final text of 18 July to article 1, article 2 etc. Articles in parts II, III and IV continued to have prefixes in Roman numerals in the final text. The order of articles parts III and IV was subject to further change, so that references to the individual articles in parts III and IV of the treaty will continue to be followed at the first appropriate point by the number of the article in the final treaty text in square brackets.

'Community way'. In response to the concerns of the UK's Peter Hain and the Swedish and Irish government representatives, it was made clear that the Union's powers were conferred by member states. The new opening sentences of article I-1 of the draft constitutional treaty were therefore functional rather than majestic.

> Reflecting the will of the citizens and States of Europe to build a common future, this Constitution establishes the European Union, on which the Member States confer competences to attain objectives they have in common. The Union shall coordinate the policies by which the Member States aim to achieve these objectives, and shall exercise in the Community way the competences they confer on it.

Franklin or Madison, this was not.

Giscard's dalliance with a new name for the Union (suggesting United Europe – his own favourite – and even the United States of Europe, on the grounds that European Union was insufficiently lyrical) was stymied when the Praesidium insisted on 'European Union'. An earlier reference to the 'peoples' and states of Europe was changed to 'citizens and states' on the grounds that this better reflected the EU's dual legitimacy.

Several conventionnels, including the French, Belgian and German foreign ministers and Gianfranco Fini, the Italian deputy prime minister, wanted the goal of 'ever closer union' included in article 1. The Praesidium resisted this and contrary to expectations, Giscard even kept the phrase out of his draft preamble published a few days later. The new article I-1 also omitted any reference to the Union's symbols (its flag, money and anthem) which was an integrationist goal and high on the wish-list of conventionnels from France.

Revised article I-2 on the Union's values tidied up the earlier text. The Union was now 'founded on the values of respect for human dignity, liberty, democracy, the rule of law and respect for human rights' which were common to Member States and found 'in a society of pluralism, tolerance, justice, equality, solidarity and non-discrimination.' The revised article incorporated the ideas of equality and non-discrimination in response to amendments. As before, there was no reference to God or Christianity as sought by the Catholic and other churches.

Article I-3 on the Union's objectives was extensively rewritten reflecting many amendments. The new version stressed that the area of freedom, security and justice and the single market were benefits for EU citizens. It included a reference to the social market economy and highlighted a high quality environment and linguistic diversity, while deleting 'discovery of space', one of Giscard's pet proposals. The reference to policies 'generating high levels of competitiveness', sought by Unice in earlier drafting, was consigned to part III. The passage on the Union's relations with the rest of the world was rephrased to make it more outward looking and amplified to include such goals as security, free and fair trade and human rights.

A new article I-4, entitled 'fundamental freedoms and non-discrimination' was inserted, partly at the behest of the president of the European Court of Justice. This singled out the four fundamental freedoms of free movement of persons, goods, services and capital, and freedom of establishment, which originally were confusingly included among exclusive competences of the Union, and stressed that they are guaranteed. The second paragraph reproduced unchanged the previous article 6, barring discrimination on the grounds of nationality.

A new article I-5, defined 'Relations between the Union and the Member States'. It reflected the debate in two special plenary sessions on 5 and 26 March and took elements previously in draft articles 1, 8 and 9. The new article gave prominence to regional and local self-government, which was an important aim of Giscard's ally Teufel, although the result was expressed in somewhat fractured English. Thus the Union was enjoined to 'respect the national identities of its member states, inherent in their fundamental structures, political and constitutional, including for regional and local self government. It shall respect their essential State functions ...' Relocating the idea of loyal cooperation from the title dealing with competences, a second paragraph said 'the Union and the member states shall, in full mutual respect, assist each other to carry out tasks which flow from the Constitution.' Finally the member states were obliged to 'facilitate the achievement of the Union's tasks and refrain from any measure which could jeopardise the attainment of the objectives set out in the Constitution.' Article I-6[11] giving the Union legal personality stayed unchanged.

The articles in title II on 'Fundamental Rights and Citizenship of the Union' were little changed. Besides confirming that the Charter was now part II, article I-7 [12] on fundamental rights made clear the Union 'shall seek accession' (as opposed to 'may accede') to the European Convention for the Protection of Human Rights.

Reflecting their painful birth, the articles on competences were substantially revised. On balance, the changes removed much of the original federal flavour of title III, now entitled 'Union Competences and Actions'.

---

[11] Article 4 in the Praesidium's original draft.
[12] Formerly article 5.

Article I-9[13] on 'fundamental principles' gave greater stress to the idea that Union competences were limited by being conferred by member states following the strong protests from Hain, other UK parliamentarians and Ireland's Dick Roche. Accordingly, the Union would no longer act within the limits of competences 'conferred upon it by the Constitution' but within those 'conferred upon it by the member states *in* the Constitution'. Reiterating the importance of subsidiarity and proportionality in exercising non-exclusive competences, it brought forward from previous article 9 the obligations on EU institutions and national parliaments to apply the rules as laid down in the attached protocol on subsidiarity and proportionality. This protocol and that on the role of national parliaments in the Union were also beefed up somewhat to increase the member states' safeguards against any centralising urges emanating from Brussels.

The editorial changes to I-9 meant article I-10 was much shorter than the previous draft article 9. Renamed 'Union law', it provoked considerable alarm among UK eurosceptics because it made specific reference to the principle of primacy of EU law, which was established by the ECJ in the 1960s but was hitherto absent from Union treaties. However, the reference to competences being conferred by the Constitution was removed, so the article read: 'The Constitution, and law adopted by the Union's institutions in exercising competences conferred on it, shall have primacy over the law of the Member States'.

The Praesidium took account of a large number of amendments with a few limited changes to article I-11 detailing the 'Categories of competence'. Compared with former article 10, the most obvious change, sought by several PES conventionnels and the trade union observer, was to include employment policies with economic policies in the category where 'the Union shall have the competence to ensure the coordination' of Member States' policies.

As requested by several conventionnels, including the UK, Austrian, Finnish, Swedish and German government representatives, article I-12 [14] on 'Exclusive competences' dropped the reference to the four freedoms, which became the centrepiece of I-4.

The Praesidium's response to conflicting amendments on article I-13 [15], 'Areas of shared competence', was broadly to leave well enough alone. The illustrative list of competences was tidied up, so that agriculture and fisheries

---

[13] Formerly article 8.
[14] Formerly article 11.
[15] Formerly article 12.

specifically excluded the conservation of marine resources mentioned in article 12. Social policy was to be limited to 'aspects defined in part III', supposedly to ensure that there would be no expansion of Union competence in this sensitive area, and public health, a controversial element in the original text, was changed to 'common safety concerns in public health matters'.

A broad cross section of member states wanted changes to the original article on coordinating economic policies. The UK, France, Germany and Sweden rejected the idea that 'the Union shall coordinate the economic policies of the Member States...' In response, article I-14 [16] on 'The coordination of economic and employment policies' stated: 'The Union shall adopt measures to ensure coordination of the economic policies of the Member States ... Member States shall coordinate their economic policies within the Union.' The formula used in the first sentence was also applied in a new PES-inspired paragraph covering coordination of employment policies. Further centre-left amendments added another paragraph saying the Union 'may adopt initiatives to ensure coordination of Member States' social policies.'

The Praesidium's original draft on the common foreign and security policy provoked fury on the part of the UK even though it just echoed the Maastricht Treaty in calling for member states' loyalty and mutual solidarity. In the 26 May draft of article I-15 [17] on the 'Common foreign and security policy' the Praesidium not only stuck to its guns, it added that Member States 'shall comply with the acts adopted in this area' to strengthen their obligations under CFSP. Reflecting a large number of amendments, a new first paragraph was added to provide an explicit reference to the Union competence in CFSP and a reference to defence. This said: 'The Union's competence in matters of common foreign and security policy shall cover all areas of foreign policy and all questions relating to the Union's security, including the progressive framing of a common defence policy, which might lead to a common defence.'

Article I-16 [18] was renamed 'Areas of supporting, coordinating or complementary action' to reflect better the fact that legislative competence in these areas lay with the Member States. The list of such areas was modified to delete employment (now in article I-14) and add 'protection and improvement of human health'. Protection against disasters became 'civil

---

[16] Formerly article 13.
[17] Formerly article 14.
[18] Formerly article 15.

protection'. Article I-17 [19] the 'Flexibility clause' was little changed, although the Council of Minister's was to obtain the 'consent' (rather than assent) of the European Parliament for measures taken.

The first part of title V, concerned with *how* the Union would carry out its tasks, was far less controversial than title III about *who* should exercise *what* competence in the Union. Thus the changes to 'The exercise of Union competence' generally constituted a tidying up exercise. However, the Praesidium again rejected the idea of 'organic laws,' championed by Andrew Duff, which would allow constitutional change with super qualified majorities. It argued that an organic law was a legal instrument unknown in some member states and that adding such an unfamiliar act would lessen the clarity of the Union's legal system.

Article I-33[20] on 'Legislative acts' revised the new term for codecision from 'legislative procedure' to 'ordinary legislative procedure' to avoid confusion as the constitutional treaty also provided for a limited number of acts to be adopted differently.

Reflecting many amendments, article I-35 [21] on 'Delegated regulations' was revised to give the European Parliament and Council the power to revoke or 'call back' such legislation independent of each other. The Praesidium also decided to remove sunset clauses from delegated acts on the grounds they could create legal uncertainty.

Title VI on 'The democratic life of the Union' was subject to considerable modification. A new article I-45, expounding 'The principle of representative democracy', amplified and replaced the one sentence article in the original draft providing for political parties at European level. Meeting widespread demands from outside as well as inside the Convention, article I-46[22] on 'The principle of participatory democracy' was expanded to include a requirement for the Commission to carry out 'broad prior consultations with parties concerned' to ensure the Union's actions are coherent and transparent. Article I-47 on 'The social partners and autonomous social dialogue' was also new and responded to the very large number of amendments that wanted the Union to recognise and promote the role of social partners (trade unions and business umbrella groups) at Union level and facilitate dialogue between them.

---

[19] Formerly article 16.
[20] Formerly article 25.
[21] Formerly article 27.
[22] Formerly article 34.

The revised title VII, 'The Union's finances', was noteworthy on two counts. Without specifically mentioning this option by name, article I-53[23] on 'The Union's resources' left open the possibility of creating European taxes by unanimity. A new article I-54 on 'The multiannual financial framework' brought the EU's renamed financial perspective into the Constitution while article III-304 [III-308[24]] set out the details, including a provision that it must last for at least five years. Another important part III article – III-306 [III-310] – set out a simplified budget procedure in which the distinction between compulsory spending, such as agricultural support, and non-compulsory expenditure was dropped, ministerial decisions would be taken by qualified majority and Parliament would have the final word.

Title VIII, comprising article I-56[25] 'The Union and its immediate environment' was altered in response to a PES amendment to ensure the Union's relations with its near neighbours respected the values detailed in article 2 of the Constitution.

Among the generally little changed articles of title IX on 'Union Membership', article I-59 raised the stakes for 'Voluntary withdrawal from the Union' by subjecting an application for withdrawal to scrutiny by the European Council, rather than the Council of Ministers. However, the Praesidium rejected amendments which suggested penalising any state that later wanted to rejoin the Union. The Union, Giscard observed, 'is after all not a prison.' Instead, the text proposed such countries should apply in line with article I-57 detailing 'Conditions and procedure for applying for Union membership'.

15.3 COMMON FOREIGN AND DEFENCE PROPOSALS AFTER IRAQ

The Praesidium's response to the many amendments on CFSP and the lively debate about them in the mid-May plenary session was broadly to change the rhetoric of the articles to please the integrationists while cutting back the plans for more qualified majority voting following pressure from government representatives, led by Hain. There was a strong tilt towards the UK position in the revised drafting, reflecting Giscard's visit to 10 Downing Street on 19 May. A notable casualty of this approach was the provision in the April draft for QMV to apply to joint proposals from the foreign minister and the Commission. Dehaene argued that such joint initiatives would represent the general European interest, but the involvement of the

---

[23] Formerly article 38.
[24] CONV 850/03, 18 July.
[25] Formerly article 42.

Commission aroused British fears of 'communitarisation' of CFSP 'via the back door' and it was deleted.

Rechristened 'Specific provisions for implementing common foreign and security policy', article I-39 of the 26 May draft was couched in rather more forceful language than article 29 of April. Although it looked somewhat fanciful in the light of the Iraq crisis, the revised first paragraph said simply: 'The European Union shall conduct a common foreign and security policy, based on the development of mutual political solidarity among member states, the identification of questions of general interest and the achievement of an ever-increasing degree of convergence of Member States' actions.'

CFSP would be put into effect by the foreign minister and member states, using national and Union resources. These provisions were fleshed out in part III.[26] Among detailed changes, article I-39 was tweaked to make sure that the Council of Ministers would frame the CFSP 'within the strategic guidelines established by the European Council' and that the European Parliament would be 'regularly' consulted on CFSP. Article III-200 [III-205.2] provided for twice yearly debates on CFSP and defence policy in Parliament, whereas the original idea was for annual debates.

Paragraph seven of I-39 specified that the right of initiative would lie with the member states or the foreign minister. An earlier provision that the minister could act 'alone or together with the Commission' was amended to weaken the Commission's involvement to cover proposals from the minister or 'the minister with the Commission's support'.

The article stated that CFSP decisions would be taken by the Council of Ministers or European Council unanimously, except in certain cases, detailed in III-196 [III-201.2] where QMV would apply. Although these exceptions were pared back to accommodate the UK and other governments, QMV would apply, as at present, to the implementation of Union actions or common strategic decisions already adopted by unanimity by the European Council and to the appointment of special representatives.

The rules for abstention, including qualified abstention, stayed unchanged between end-April and end-May. There was also no change to the *passerelle* provision by which the European Council could decide by unanimity without changing the treaties to allow the Council of Ministers to act by QMV in other foreign policy areas. This *passerelle*, which was originally proposed by Peter Hain, stayed mainly because it posed no risk to the intergovernmental nature of CFSP. In its revised version, the article underlined that cases of

---

[26] CONV 725/03.

QMV in external affairs 'shall not apply to decisions having military or defence implications'.

Article I-40 (article 30 in the April texts) giving the 'Specific provisions for implementing common defence policy' was subject to a few revisions. The reference to the Union's operational capability was tweaked to mention civil ahead of military means. Reflecting a joint amendment from Hain of Britain, de Villepin of France and Fischer of Germany, the revised 26 May text banished any idea of a European army by underlining that in tackling its CSDP tasks the Union would use 'capabilities provided by the member states'.

In addressing the enhanced Petersberg tasks, the 26 May text beefed up the references to anti-terrorism activity to stress support for 'third countries in combating terrorism in their territories.' At the request of the UK, Irish, Italian, German and Dutch governments, a reference to military capabilities was added to the name of the proposed 'European Armaments, Research and Military Capabilities Agency'.

Although contentious, the three paragraphs of article I-40 which proposed different forms of enhanced cooperation in the defence area saw only one substantive change with the addition of a reference to close cooperation with NATO in issues of mutual defence against armed aggression.

Article I-42, the 'Solidarity clause', was strengthened considerably. The UK, French and German government representatives obtained tougher language for the fight against terrorism. With support from their colleagues from Ireland, Belgium and Austria, they ensured its scope was extended to natural and man-made disasters in line with recommendations of the working group of defence. In its 26 May version, article I-42 said: 'The Union and its Member States shall act jointly in a spirit of solidarity if a Member State is the victim of terrorist attack or natural or man-made disaster'.

15.4 PART II: THE CHARTER OF FUNDAMENTAL RIGHTS

The Charter, as proclaimed at the December 2000 Nice summit, became part II of the constitution. Apart from some very minor adjustments, the text[27] was as agreed at Nice. There was, however, a lively debate over the so-called horizontal articles (51 to 54) that were included to prevent any extension under the Charter of the application of Union law at the expense of law of the member states.

---

[27] CONV 726/03.

For the UK, Hain made clear he would not accept the Charter in the constitutional treaty without an assurance that its social provisions would not undermine Britain's still relatively liberal employment laws. The discussion turned on the status of the so-called explanations to the Charter, which were drawn up in 2000 and clarified the horizontal issue at that time to the UK's satisfaction. In the 31 May plenary, Hain made the UK's acceptance of the Charter conditional on a satisfactory cross reference to the explanations in the constitutional treaty text, and was supported by Fini of Italy and Roche of Ireland. Commissioner Vitorino said he was working on the issue. Vitorino also made a strong plea for retention of the Charter preamble in the constitution in addition to its own preamble. 'Aesthetically, it may be odd to have one constitution and two preambles,' Vitorino quipped. 'But in China they have one country and two systems. So Europe can be different too'.

15.5   PART III: THE POLICIES AND FUNCTIONING OF THE UNION

Although presented to the conventionnels as a technical rather than a political exercise, the part III[28] articles came as a surprise. The decisions to make a rule of 'ordinary legislative procedure' (codecision) in the Parliament and qualified majority voting in the Council of Ministers resulted in quite sweeping changes.[29] MEPs would have equal legislative powers in 70 rather than 34 policy areas while the national veto would disappear in more than 20 procedures. Some shifts to QMV – such those covering EU staff regulations – were of minor significance. Others were not. Sensitive areas to be brought under majority voting included the protection of employees' rights for those fired unjustly, social security measures for migrant workers and uniform protection of intellectual property rights in the single market. The communitarisation of the Union's area of freedom security and justice saw QMV brought in for legislation on border controls, asylum and immigration policies, judicial cooperation and the setting of minimum rules for the definition of offences and penalties in cases of particularly serious cross-border crime. Some of these issues went to the heart of traditional sovereignty.

In seeking to extend QMV and other Union powers, the Praesidium applied a generous interpretation to the results of working groups and earlier plenary debates. Thus it proposed enabling legislation to create a European Public Prosecutor's Office by unanimity in III-170 [III-175][30] even though there was no consensus in support of the idea in the Convention. Similarly, in the

---

[28] CONV 725/03.
[29] CONV 727/03, ANNEX VIII.
[30] For full text of III-175, see Documentary Annex.

field of taxation, the Praesidium ignored the protests of the UK, Sweden and Ireland and opened a window to QMV. Article III-59 [III-62][31] proposed that the Council of Ministers, acting unanimously, could decide that harmonisation measures concerning turnover taxes, excise duties and other indirect taxation related to administrative cooperation or tax fraud. Once taken, that decision would allow it to act by QMV when adopting legislation laying down appropriate measures to deal with the problem. With article III-60 [III-63], the same restricted *passerelle* procedure would apply to harmonisation measures for administrative cooperation or combating tax fraud in the case of company taxation, provided such action was necessary to ensure proper functioning of the internal market or avoid competitive distortions.

The 27 May text of part III also contained the first articles covering economic governance in the Union. Again the Praesidium brushed aside the reservations that had rendered inconclusive the working group on economic governance. The eurogroup was formally recognised for the first time, to the irritation of the UK. Article III-86 [III-88][32] gave the eurozone countries scope to adopt measures among themselves on economic policy guidelines, budget discipline and multilateral surveillance. A protocol was attached to the articles which provides for an elected president of the eurogroup with a two year tenure. The economic governance articles boosted the role of the Commission, giving it, in article III-73 [III-76.5], the ability to send an opinion to a delinquent state under the excessive deficit procedure and, under article III-68 [III-71.4], the power to send a warning to a member state in breach of the Union's broad economic policy guidelines.

Part III consisted of no fewer than 339 articles. Although around three-quarters of the articles were taken over unchanged or only slightly modified from the existing treaties and gathered together into coherent groups, this section of the draft constitutional treaty dealing with policies and legal bases was evidently much more than a 'tidying up' exercise.

15.6   PART IV: GENERAL AND FINAL PROVISIONS

The Praesidium was so obviously satisfied with the Convention that it decided in article IV-6 [IV-7][33] of the general and final provisions[34] that future amendments to the treaty establishing the constitution should in

---

[31] Full text of III-62 and III-63 in Documentary Annex.
[32] Full text of III-88 to III-90 in Documentary Annex.
[33] Full text of IV-7 in Documentary Annex.
[34] CONV 725/03.

general be studied by a Convention, with the same components as the present one. The Convention would make a recommendation by consensus to a subsequent intergovernmental conference of the member states. Only in the event of minor changes would the matter be referred directly to member states' representatives in a mini-IGC.

There were already considerable doubts among the Convention members about the feasibility of securing unanimous support and ratification in each of the member states for amendments to the eventual constitutional treaty as well as for its approval. However, the Praesidium proposed no changes in procedure at this stage.

Thus, article IV-7 [IV-8] stuck to the existing rules for adoption that require all member states to ratify Union treaties in accordance with their constitutions. However, if, two years after signing the final treaty, one or more countries experienced problems with ratification and four-fifths of member states had already ratified, the problem would then be referred to the European Council.

15.7   GISCARD'S PREAMBLE

After receiving piles of paper in the first two days of the week, the conventionnels were sent a brief missive on 28 May containing the Praesidium's draft preamble.[35]

More accurately, it was Giscard's preamble with his fingerprints all over it, from a quote of Thucydides in ancient Greek at the top (translated as: 'Our Constitution is called a democracy because power is in the hands not of a minority but of the whole people') to a paragraph on the bottom in which the representatives of member states who would sign the text expressed their gratitude to the members of the Convention for having prepared it.

The text sat ill with Giscard's earlier ambition of giving the united Europe of 25 and more member states a lyrical text that eager teenagers would learn by heart. His *oeuvre*, released just before the Ascension Day holiday as he was travelling to Aachen to receive the prestigious 'international Charlemagne Prize' in recognition of his work on the constitution, was justifiably criticised for being wordy and pretentious.

It was also politically contentious. Rather than include the ringing phrase 'ever closer union', beloved by integrationists, Giscard's preamble suggested

---

[35] CONV 722/03.

instead that 'the peoples of Europe are determined to transcend their ancient divisions, and, united in *an ever closer fashion*, to forge a common destiny'. Despite pressure from the Christian wing of the European People's Party and the Vatican, Giscard pointedly omitted a reference to Christianity or any other specific religion in his text. Instead, it made just passing reference to Europe's 'cultural, religious and humanist inheritance' and the 'spiritual impulse always present in its heritage.' Starting with its quote from Thucydides, the preamble was very much a hymn to humanism and democracy. In seeking to encapsulate 2,000 years of European history, it omitted all reference to the dark ages, the middle ages and the centuries when Christianity suffused Europe's politics and culture. There was no mention of the world wars, dictatorships and genocide of the 20th century.

Skipping as it did from the 'civilisations of Greece and Rome' to the 'philosophical currents of the Enlightenment', Giscard's preamble told its readers more about the author's perception of himself than the historical roots of the constitutional treaty. Here was Renaissance man, putting his own stamp on Europe. However, it was far from clear at this stage whether the preamble would ever be used because agreement on the constitutional treaty looked remote.

CHAPTER 16
Managing the Splits

16.1 CRISIS IN THE PRAESIDIUM

The Convention was in crisis because of a split in the 13 strong Praesidium, the very body that was supposed to steer it to success. At the end of May, consensus on a constitutional treaty appeared remote indeed.

The crisis came to a head on 22 May, in the middle of the three day Praesidium session to finalise the revised drafts. Heartened by the mid-May plenary session, Spain's Alfonso Dastis balked at the proposals to scrap the Nice Treaty provisions on voting weights in the Council of Ministers. His revolt prompted other Praesidium members to object to other proposed changes to the Nice Treaty which had been unveiled in the Praesidium's name by Giscard to the 24 April plenary.

The Spanish problem had festered since Giscard first proposed a double majority system for qualified majority voting in the Council, a slimmed down Commission and a somewhat reduced European Parliament. Dastis, together with fellow Spaniard Méndez de Vigo, registered opposition to the changes to the Nice settlement during the late April meeting of the Praesidium. Ana Palacio's strongly worded amendments to the institutional articles were a signal that Spanish opposition would not go away. Stepping up the rhetoric, Dastis warned in the 15 May plenary session that reopening the Nice settlements on voting weights in the Council and seats in the Parliament would lead to 'no agreement in the Convention' and a 'long and difficult Intergovernmental Conference' afterwards. Reinforcing these threats and stiffening Dastis with frequent phone calls was José Maria Aznar, Spain's prime minister. Under pressure from the Socialist opposition at home because of his support of the war in Iraq, the last thing Aznar needed was a decision in the Convention that would undermine his success in Nice of securing Spain's position as one of the Union's big powers.

To make matters worse, the Presidium's discussion on the institutions during its three-day session in May was badly orchestrated, allowing Dastis to rally other members against changing the Nice agreements. The meeting began by looking at the proposals to restructure the distribution of seats in the European Parliament. At this point, Dastis complained about the bid to alter

Nice and unveiled his implacable opposition to the proposals on Council votes. By linking the two issues, he prompted Henning Christophersen and John Bruton to query the plans to overturn the Nice settlement on the Commission. The already fragile consensus behind the late April institutional articles threatened to unravel completely. Doubts about the composition of the Commission raised questions about the foreign minister and the minister's role in the Commission. This in turn prompted questions about the long-term presidency of the European Council and the entire institutional architecture contained in the Praesidium draft. With the Praesidium split, and two government representatives openly opposing the draft provisions on the institutions, the decision was taken to leave the existing institutional chapter unchanged in the revised part I of 26 May.

The move not only exposed the Praesidium's divisions. The do-nothing decision offended conventionnels who had submitted amendments to the original drafts. But by this stage, both the plenary and the Praesidium were becoming side-shows. When the Praesidium met again on 28 May it decided that the plenaries of Friday, 30 May and Saturday, 31 May should focus on enhanced cooperation, economic governance, the Union's budget and own resources and provide conventionnels with a chance to comment on parts II and III. The Praesidium would meet again after the Saturday session for another discussion of the institutions. But it was also decided that Giscard and his two deputies should set aside Wednesday, 4 June for consultations with the Convention's four component groups.

The decision of the leadership to consult the *'composantes'* showed just how dramatically the dynamics of the Convention were changing. Activity was moving into the corridors and back rooms. The structure agreed at Laeken was falling into disuse. The end-May plenaries were lacklustre affairs. As Amato observed: 'The plenary is discussing important topics, but attention is already on future deliberations.'

Dastis, meanwhile, had pulled off a coup. He had widened the appeal of his crusade to retain the Nice Treaty agreements to include the 16 small and medium countries that, as 'friends of the Community method', had been campaigning against the long-term European Council president and for one commissioner per member state. He also persuaded eight government representatives, including fellow Praesidium member Henning Christophersen of Denmark, to join in a signed appeal[1] to the Convention not to tamper with the Nice institutional package.

---

[1] CONV 766/03.

The nine were a strange bunch. They included the representatives of the UK, Poland, Sweden, Austria, Ireland, Lithuania and Cyprus, and, as Duff remarked, signed the letter 'for different and contradictory reasons'. Christophersen objected to the plan to cut the number of MEPs to 700 from 732. Although the draft promised to protect small state interests by saying national representation in the Parliament would be 'degressively proportional' to population with a minimum threshold of four MEPs per member state, the proposed cut in the total number of MEPs meant problems for certain small member states. Those with coalition governments, for example, would not be able to have enough seats in the Parliament to ensure a suitable share out of committee posts among the political parties.

Ireland's Dick Roche was primarily concerned about the proposals for the slimmed down Commission and the absence in the draft articles of the Nice Treaty assurances that the reduced college would be 'chosen according to a rotation system based on the principle of equality'. Poland signed because it was in the same position on voting weights as Spain. The UK's position was the result of a deal between Peter Hain and Dastis to secure Spain's support for maintaining the national veto on tax and social security policies. As members of the coalition of 16 small to medium sized countries, the other signatories were deeply suspicious of Giscard and his perceived tendency to back the interests of the big EU members. The accession countries, in particular, did not want to reopen the Nice agreements which were part of the membership agreements they negotiated with the Commission and were being put to their electorates in referendums.

The letter of the nine was circulated among conventionnels on 30 May. While acknowledging that Nice 'was not perfect', they warned that reopening the Nice settlement would result in the Convention having to submit options to the following Intergovernmental Conference, with the inevitable consequence of limiting its influence over the IGC.

The spectre of options had stalked the Convention since Farnleitner of Austria raised the possibility in the mid-May plenary. Four days after that session, Olivier Duhamel circulated an emotional appeal[2] to his fellow conventionnels warning that options would not only signal the Convention's failure but would fail to deliver the goals sought by 'the British government and the representatives of the less populated states'. Asserting that many Convention members were open 'to various compromises on the unsolved questions,' Duhamel declared: 'But let us proclaim high and strong that we refuse the options. Let us extirpate this venom before it is spread. Let us say with one voice what reason imposes. A constitution, yes. Options, no.'

---

[2] CONV 752/03.

16.2 THE EUROPEAN COMMISSION: MISSING IN ACTION

There were some important absentees from the battlefield as the crisis gathered. Many conventionnels pinned their hopes on a compromise from the original six member states amid reports that they were hatching a text that would bridge the differences. The idea was politically appealing. The original six contained member states that were big and small and from north and south and politically from left and right. The symbolism of their giving a lead would be of incalculable benefit. Yet despite intense contacts between the conventionnels of the six with the foreign policy aides of the national leaders, the efforts came to nothing.

Also striking was the absence of any attempt by the Commission to broker a compromise in the fevered activity of the Convention's final weeks. Such a move would have been expected of the Delors Commission a decade earlier. But the Prodi executive had its own corner to fight as the Convention's close drew near.

The Commission never recovered from the bungled launch of Penelope the previous December. Its problems grew rather than declined in the weeks that followed that fiasco. Barnier and Vitorino suffered setbacks in the college, which weakened their standing in the Convention and Praesidium when the news seeped out. Thus, the college ignored the warnings of its two conventionnels that the Commission's strong line in support of the Community method for foreign policy was too radical for acceptance by the Convention. It spurned the Benelux idea for the Commission president to chair the General Affairs Council, annoying Jean-Luc Dehaene who thought he had Barnier's support for the plan. It failed to back Barnier and Vitorino, who wanted the Commission to produce a new paper in spring 2003 to build on the message of 'Peace, Freedom, Solidarity', again irritating Dehaene who backed the idea.

The tide of sympathy for the Commission in the Praesidium ebbed. The attempt by the two commissioners – on instructions from Prodi – to negotiate articles on competences that conformed with Penelope cost a lot of good will. Dehaene was irritated that Barnier and Vitorino were unable to deliver support for ideas that he thought would benefit the Commission. Changes in the Praesidium depleted its pool of natural Commission supporters. Because of her duties as foreign minister, Spain's Ana Palacio, was less in evidence. Her alternate and eventual replacement, Alfonso Dastis, lacked the Brussels hinterland of the former MEP. Athens' substitution in spring 2003 of MEP George Katiforis by the Greek foreign minister George Papandreou also brought a more independent view of the Commission into the Praesidium. John Bruton, who at one time drew heavily on advice from the Commission, was more independent following his success as chair of the working group on freedom, security and justice.

The Commission's ability to mould the final outcome of the Convention declined sharply after it backed the small country side over the future size of the Commission and the permanent president of the European Council in the row between big and small member states. During March and April, the representatives of the small and medium sized governments appeared to be the coming force in the Convention and, as 'Friends of the Community Method', included in their platform a demand for one commissioner per member state.[3]

The Commission's position on the size of the college was ambiguous during 2002. Romano Prodi and the college had backed one commissioner per member state as the correct way of dealing with the 'big bang' enlargement. But Prodi also floated the idea of an inner cabinet of senior Commissioners in the summer of 2002 and the Commission's official document of December appeared to favour a small Commission in the interests of efficiency. Both Barnier and Vitorino believed a small Commission would be a strong Commission.

But when Giscard presented his April drafts on the institutions, the Commission came out clearly for one member per member state. The two commissioners supported this position in the Praesidium meeting of 23 April, when the Praesidium opted for a smaller Commission with a maximum of 15 members. On 30 April, the Commission discussed the Praesidium's proposals on the institutions at length. It reported[4] that 'the college expressed its preference to have one commissioner per member state' but also made clear that a large Commission could only function as a team by allowing its president to make the necessary divisions of responsibility in its internal organisation. It also opposed the stable presidency of the European Council.

From this point, Prodi was publicly identified with policies diametrically opposed to those of the Praesidium and there was no chance that the Commission could ever play a mediating role in the final crucial weeks of the Convention. The Commission's problems grew when the protagonists of one commissioner per member state among the member states began to fall away. In mid-May, the Benelux countries switched to supporting the Praesidium.[5] Albeit reluctantly, a majority of the other small and medium

---

[3] See the end of March contribution from the representatives of 16 small and medium sized countries entitled 'Reforming the institutions: principles and premises', CONV 646/03.
[4] Commission press release IP/03/611.
[5] CONV 732/03 .

sized member states fell into line with the Praesidium plans for a smaller Commission in the final stages of the Convention in June. That was when the Praesidium agreed that the Commission appointed in 2004 would be constituted in line with the Nice agreement and have one member per member state, and that from 2009 the future 15-member Commissions would work on a system of equal rotation. When the government representatives in the Convention met on 12 June for the last time before Thessaloniki only five still insisted on one commissioner per member state with full voting rights.

After Thessaloniki, an unrepentant Prodi vowed to carry the fight for one commissioner per member state to the IGC[6] and as the intergovernmental conference got underway appeared to be staging a successful fight back. But the consensus that emerged on 13 June marked an unhappy end to an unhappy Convention for the Commission president. In the opening session of the Convention, Prodi promised the Commission would 'make a full and enthusiastic contribution, drawing on all its own experience and its expertise.'[7] Instead, the Commission had been reactive rather than proactive and was left outside the June consensus as far as its own future structure was concerned.

So what went wrong? The Commission certainly suffered no lack of resources. The number of Commission staff working on the Convention was greater than the Convention secretariat. But they were split into different groups. Some worked with the commissioners in the Convention, others were among Prodi's staff, others in the Commission's group of policy advisors headed by Ricardo 'Ricky' Levi while, operating in secrecy, was the group around Francois Lamoureux that produced Penelope. These groups seemed unable to work together.

Matters were not helped by a clash of personalities between Giscard and Prodi. Giscard had little time for Prodi and made no attempt to conceal his feelings. Prodi repaid the compliment. They conducted a dialogue of the deaf. For much of May, the two were embroiled in a squabble over where, when and how to stage a public debate over the institutions. This followed a challenge from Giscard to Prodi[8] to defend his position on the stable presidency of the European Council 'in a public debate in a large European city' of Prodi's choice and put the issue to the judgement of the assembled

---

[6] 'Europe and the Constitution: Letting the people have their say'. Speech/03/346 at the University of Bologna, 5 July 2003, available among Prodi's speeches on his web page on the Commission website at http://www.europa.eu.int.
[7] Speech/02/88, 28 February 2002, CONV 4/02.
[8] In a letter of 7 May.

populace. Although Prodi's spokesman promised 'ice cream and fireworks for everybody', the challenge came to nothing after Prodi came back wanting to address the Convention and declined an offer, made by Erwin Teufel with the friendly encouragement of the Convention secretariat, for the debate to take place in Stuttgart, the capital of Baden Württemberg.

More broadly, the Commission appears to have misread the small member states' analysis of what constituted a better deal for them. A 15 strong Commission looked less unattractive to several of the small member states once the Convention Praesidium conceded the principle of equal rotation for membership of the college. Such a system promised the smalls a fair shot at the top Commission jobs, whereas they would have no such guarantee in a large Commission in which the Commission president would choose how to divide responsibilities.

Indeed, Prodi may have been the author of his own misfortune through publicly coupling the idea of the large Commission with an insistence that its president be a powerful figure who would take responsibility for allocating portfolios, designating vice-presidents and asking for the resignation of Commission members. [9] Although elected by the Parliament, the Commission president would, under the terms of the Praesidium's proposals, be nominated by the European Council 'deciding by qualified majority.' From the viewpoint of some small member states, it was all too easy to imagine the successful candidate for the Commission presidency, once installed, selecting the inner circle commissioners from the large countries which had voted in the European Council to nominate him or her for the post. Such a course would, it is true, run counter to the spirit of the constitutional treaty. But it would be in line with the practices of the European political market.

16.3   BRITAIN OPTS FOR A SINGLE TEXT

Hain's signature on Dastis's round-robin was deeply disappointing for Giscard. He convinced himself after his first meeting with Blair that the prime minister was pro-European in a way that no recent UK leader had been. Giscard had been solicitous of Hain and the UK position throughout the Convention. On the few occasions that Hain did not attend a plenary, Giscard could be heard asking Kerr: 'Où est Hain?' As he once told *Le Monde*: [10] 'I am doing my best so that our text of the constitution is compatible with the demands of Britons desirous of participating in the life of Europe.' When Giscard met Blair in London on 19 May to sort out the

---

[9] IP/03/611.
[10] Edition of 14 March 2003.

UK's non-negotiable positions, the double majority in the Council of Ministers was not among them. Giscard, however, had a promise to remove the word 'federal' from article 1 up his sleeve. During the three day Praesidium meeting that followed, Giscard got rid of the 'f-word' and retained unanimity in foreign policy. He had delivered and he felt betrayed.

In fact, Hain did the deal with Dastis without Blair's knowledge. Hain reasoned that as long as the Convention delivered the stable European Council presidency and respected the UK's other 'red lines', it did not matter much to the UK whether the Convention opted for the Nice Treaty agreements or Giscard's institutional proposals. Hain's own feeling was that reopening Nice was akin to opening Pandora's box. The price for securing an ally against a very unwelcome extension of QMV appeared low.

Looking at conditions in Britain, it is easy to understand why Hain wanted an insurance policy. After long quiescence and neglect, the British tabloid press had discovered the Convention. The right-wing, middle class *Daily Mail* was first off the blocks. 'A blueprint for Tyranny' screamed its front page on 8 May. 'Stealthily and slyly, a European constitution is today being created that will destroy Britain's independence, indeed its very identity.' The constitution in preparation 'would mark the end of everything we understand by the terms Britain and Britishness. There will be no more national sovereignty, no more meaningful elections to Westminster, no freedom independent of our European partners.'

The Mail was always viscerally opposed to the Blair government. Not so Rupert Murdoch's *Sun*, the daily with the biggest circulation in Britain. Blair had wooed the *Sun* before his landslide election in 1997 and the paper claimed the credit for his victories. On 15 May, with 'Save our country' emblazoned across the UK's Union flag, and pictures of Queen Elizabeth I, Admiral Lord Nelson and Winston Churchill across the top of its front page, the Sun summed up Britain's achievements of the past five hundred years. '1588 we saw off the Spanish. 1805 we saw off the French. 1940 we saw off the Germans.' Below, next to an unflattering picture of the prime minister, the headline read: '2003 Blair surrenders Britain to Europe'.

Hain, in Brussels for the mid-May plenary, dismissed the press coverage as 'hogwash'. For the government in London, the tabloid fury resulted in unwelcome political pressure for a referendum on the outcome of the IGC following the Convention. In the Convention, however, the furore probably helped Hain's negotiating position.

UK 'bottom lines' proliferated. In mid-May, they included the elected long-term president of the European Council, national parliaments policing subsidiarity; incorporation of the Charter in such a way as not to change domestic law; foreign policy subject to unanimity with governments in control; **tax** and social security legislation subject to unanimity; no legislative Council and no European public prosecutor. In the end-May plenary sessions after publication of the revised part I and parts II, III and IV, Hain added more red lines. He rejected reinforced cooperation in foreign and security policy. Debating economic governance, he insisted the Commission and European Parliament should have no additional powers to coordinate economic policies; that there was no reason to strengthen the Eurogroup and that control of the Union's own resources should remain with the member states.

'All agree that QMV and codecision should be the norm,' Hain declared to a startled plenary session, before bluntly ruling out QMV for legislation under article III-18 [III-21] on social security for migrant workers and articles III-59 and III-60 on tax. On social policy, he charged that proposals to scrap the national veto in III-99 [III-104.3] went 'way beyond the consensus' in the social affairs working group. Accordingly, he rejected QMV for minimum standards for the protection of workers when their employment contract is ended, codetermination in the workplace and conditions of employment for third country nationals on the grounds that the Nice Treaty, which retained the veto in these areas, had yet to be tested. Moreover, Hain 'still had problems' with article III-166 [III-171] prescribing QMV for legislation on judicial cooperation in criminal matters. It could change the fundamental principles of the British legal system, including *habeas corpus*.

Hain was supported on social and tax issues by Ireland's Dick Roche. But he fell foul of the many MEPs from the EPP and PES who felt that the moves to QMV in part III did not go far enough. Anne Van Lancker, the Flemish Socialist MEP and tireless creator of initiatives to boost the social component of the constitution, complained bitterly about the retention of QMV in fiscal matters. Elmar Brok, the leader of the EPP caucus in the Convention, called for more QMV in foreign policy and accused Britain alone of stymieing the ambitions of the French and German governments. Commissioner Barnier called for the restitution of QMV for joint proposals in foreign policy of the foreign minister and the Commission.

Hain's remarks provoked outrage – both real and feigned – among many conventionnels. The Austrian government's Farnleitner charged that the UK's insistence on a veto in foreign policy 'could blow up the Convention'. As Farnleitner would later indulge in high profile brinkmanship on behalf of the smalls, his remarks served only to highlight how confused conditions were. The Convention had become a negotiation that was being conducted at many different levels: in numerous bi-lateral 'confessionals' and group meetings outside the plenary hall, and over mobile phones with the aides of national leaders who were attending the 300th anniversary celebrations of the Russian city of St Petersburg. Events in Brussels were no longer transparent. All statements were suspect. Dissembling and double-speak was now the norm. The Convention seemed to be turning into an IGC, with the same propensity for blockages, deadlock and breakdown. Optimism was at a low ebb.

Anybody listening to Hain's plenary statements would conclude that the UK was a major threat to consensus in the Convention. But he was also sending out different, more positive signals. From around the middle of May, Britain was making clear that its preference was to have a single text at the end of the Convention. Hain hinted at this in press briefings and spelled it out to fellow 'movers and shakers' at a Hilton dinner. Duhamel's emotional appeal to reject options showed that not all conventionnels either knew or believed the line. But at the end of the month, Hain's message was that the UK would not make common cause with any group to wreck the Convention. The UK's decision to eschew options would be an important background factor in achieving consensus. For the Netherlands' Gijs de Vries, Hain's indication to the government representatives' meeting during the 30–31 May plenary that London would prefer a deal at the Convention was 'the one positive element of the week.' De Vries was speaking after the 31 May plenary, just as Praesidium members were preparing to devote their Saturday afternoon to yet another discussion on the institutional articles.

16.4 GISCARD PREPARES TO BREAK FREE

Giscard was prepared to play hard ball. While those seeking to retain the Nice agreements claimed to reflect the majority of conventionnels, Giscard and his supporters regarded them as an opportunist coalition, supporting an intellectually untenable agreement for diverse and selfish reasons. 'If we stick with Nice, the constitutional part of the Convention is pointless,' Giscard told reporters on the margins of the 31 May plenary session. He was not prepared to dress up failure on the issue as consensus. 'I will go to Thessaloniki in any case. I will tell them this is what we proposed but there was stalemate in the Convention.'

There was no progress on the specific Nice issues when the Praesidium reconvened on Saturday, 31 May. Yet, despite its ongoing split, the Praesidium was able to produce a revised text of part I on the institutions[11]

---

[11] CONV 770/03.

that was issued two days later and which signalled some capacity for compromise and movement.

True, the new text left unresolved the contentious issues that provoked Dastis to revolt. Thus article I-24 continued to specify that a qualified majority vote in the Council of Ministers should be a majority of member states representing at least three-fifths of the Union's population. Draft article I-19 still contained the Praesidium's original proposal for the European Parliament to have a maximum of 700 seats, with the numbers for each member state set broadly in line with population and with a minimum threshold of four seats per member state. Many amendments supported the Nice Treaty settlement of a maximum 732 seats, divided according to the political agreement reached at the December 2000 Nice European Council.

Articles I-20 on the European Council and I-21 on the European Council Chair retained the stable president, to be elected by the European Council by qualified majority voting for two and a half years, renewable once. Many amendments wanted the existing six-month rotating presidency instead. Article I-21 still gave the European Council the option of creating a board of three of its members to assist the president – a proposal that raised fears of creating a new bureaucracy to rival and possibly undermine the Commission.

Article I-23 retained the proposed legislative Council to pass European laws and framework laws jointly with the Parliament and which was strongly opposed by nearly all member states. Also contentious because of its ambiguity was a provision allowing the European Council to give the presidency of a Council to a member state for at least a year 'taking into account European political and geographical balance and the diversity of all member states.' Less controversial was the passage in I-23 providing for the foreign affairs Council to be chaired by the Union's new 'double-hatted' foreign minister.

But there were changes. One of the most important came in article I-25 which now provided an assurance that the system of one commissioner per member state would be maintained for the life of the Commission to be appointed in 2004. By specifying that a slimmed down Commission consisting of a president and just 14 voting members 'will not take effect before 1 November 2009', the revised article went some way to addressing the concerns of the applicant countries which had rallied behind Dastis and Nice.

The wording of article I-21 on the European Council Chair was changed to assuage worries about an over mighty European Council president encroaching on the international activities of other top officials. The article now specified that he or she would ensure the external representation of the Union 'without prejudice' to the responsibilities of the foreign minister and Commission president.

Those opposing the Legislative Council because it fitted awkwardly with the needs of coalition governments or because its members would quickly lose touch with political developments at home were promised in article I-23 that the ministerial representative could be accompanied by 'one or two representatives at the same level with relevant expertise' to tackle sectoral issues. Articles I-19 and I-22 respectively made clear that the Parliament and Council of Ministers were responsible for the EU budget.

Without fanfare, the text dropped Giscard's idea for a Congress of national parliamentarians and MEPs. This deletion of one of the president's pet projects was a very important signal to the Convention. It showed Giscard could change his position. The big question was whether he could compromise further in the make or break consultations with the Convention's component parts that would determine its outcome.

CHAPTER 17
Countdown to Consensus

The Convention entered its final phase, with its Praesidium paralysed over the ages-old question of how to share out the power of the member states in the institutions of the European Union and with just 10 days to reach consensus on the constitutional treaty ahead of the European Council meeting in Thessaloniki.

Giscard had warned a month earlier [1] that working methods in the Convention's final phase would have to be more flexible. The conventionnels were asked to be in Brussels for two periods of three days each between 4–6 and 11–13 June for a more interactive phase. There would be meetings of the political and component groups to identify and solve problems. Plenaries would be more ad hoc, with breaks into the smaller groups. The president and his two deputies would 'be involved in consultations and contacts, enabling the Praesidium to evaluate progress towards consensus as events unfold'.

17.1 WEDNESDAY, 4 JUNE

The decision of Giscard and his two deputies to approach the Convention's component groups marked a new and decisive phase in the life of the Convention. After its shaky start, the triumvirate had welded itself into a strong and interdependent team. There were only two occasions when its unity appeared threatened: once when Giscard cast doubt on the feasibility of Dehaene's idea of the double-hatted foreign minister and the time when Dehaene objected so strongly to Giscard's leak of his institutional articles. When the crisis enveloped the Praesidium, the three could take over as an effective steering group. Towards the end of the Convention, they were meeting more frequently than the Praesidium – with Sir John Kerr in attendance – and always before each meeting of the Praesidium.

That said, the chances of the Convention agreeing a single text for the IGC appeared bleak when its members converged on Brussels for a three day session starting on Wednesday, 4 June. That day, flanked by Jean-Luc

---

[1] Giscard's letter of 8 May 2003 to Convention members. CONV 721/03.

Dehaene and Giuliano Amato, Giscard met in turn with the representatives of the national parliaments, the national governments, the European Parliament and the Commission's two conventionnels with the aim of listening rather than negotiating.

Meeting with national parliamentarians

The day started well. The trio found the national parliamentarians, which constituted the biggest group in the Convention, in an unexpectedly constructive mood. The group – so often portrayed by its representatives in the Praesidium as an inchoate and incoherent body – had produced a 'non-paper' outlining a potential package deal.

René van der Linden, a Dutch Christian Democrat senator, Lamberto Dini, the Liberal Italian senator, and Jürgen Meyer, a Social Democrat member of the German Bundestag, had organised an ad hoc working group which came out strongly in favour of safeguarding the Community method of decision making in the Union while giving the big countries a stable presidency of the European Council. Their paper envisaged an integral draft constitution with no options, the use of the Convention method for future changes, QMV as a general rule, integration of the Charter of Fundamental Rights in the constitution and enhanced cooperation in defence. It proposed to 'strengthen all sides of the institutional triangle'. Thus the Commission president would be elected by the European Parliament and all member states would be represented in the Commission until 2009 (i.e. for the full life of the Commission to be chosen in 2004). After 2009 there would be equal representation of member states based on an equal system of rotation.

While 'acknowledging the merits' of the EU's rotating presidency, the national parliamentarians were prepared to accept a longer term chair of the European Council on condition he or she would be elected by two-thirds of the member states, the European Council would not be a separate institution or have its own bureaucracy or executive powers, and rotation in other Council formations would be maintained. The chairperson could be a member of another EU institution or hold a national mandate. The paper also backed the idea of a separate Legislative Council for law making and stated that the Council's legislative powers should always be exercised in public.

The caucus had therefore produced an integrationist document that confirmed what Giscard and his staff had begun to suspect: that Praesidium members Gisela Stuart and John Bruton were not representative of the national parliamentarians as a whole. The paper also reflected the increasingly close ties of its authors with like minded conventionnels from the European Parliament, which had been fostered through the big political families.

The production of the non-paper was not wholly transparent or fair: there was some subterfuge to prevent those national parliamentarians more wedded to the nation state or more concerned with the rights of national parliaments from spoiling the party. The trio of van der Linden, Dini and Meyer arranged meetings at very short notice and known only to sympathisers. Hostile or sceptical parliamentarians, such as Lord Tomlinson, a British Labour party conventionnel from the UK's upper house, had little chance of influencing the package of ideas put to Giscard in the name of the national parliamentarians.

Dini reported that Giscard left his meeting with the national parliamentarians 'elated'. No wonder, therefore, that his session with the government representatives afterwards came as a rude shock.

Difficulties with government representatives

The mood of the government representatives was somewhere between the grumpy and the ugly. Dastis had done a good job of pulling together support for the Nice arrangements among the nine signatories of the letter and the 16 friends of the Community method.

In the circumstances, it was unfortunate that it fell to George Katiforis, the Greek government alternate, to chair the meeting with Giscard and his two deputies. Katiforis, an MEP by trade, took the chair in the absence of George Papandreou, the Greek foreign minister and senior Greek conventionnel since earlier in the year. Whatever the merits of other member states sending their foreign ministers to the Convention, the pressures of the Greek EU presidency meant Papandreou was rarely able to be engaged in the Convention's activities.

The meeting got off to a bad start when Giscard requested a restricted session with the senior representatives. He was told that he came as a guest and that alternates and assistants would stay in the interests of transparency. Katiforis then failed to encourage a more constructive tone. He first allowed participants to sit behind cards bearing the names of their countries rather than own names, breaking the habits of the Convention and reinforcing their identity as government representatives rather than individual conventionnels. He then polled the participants for their views on key issues, breaking with the Convention's taboo against voting and emphasising the disagreements with the proposals on the table. Finally he organised a *tour de table* of the more than 20 countries present that was still in progress when a visibly irritated Giscard left the meeting after one and three-quarter hours to join the MEPs, leaving Amato and Dehaene in the lions' den.

The divergences between Giscard and the governments were substantial. In a letter to 'Mr President' faxed later that day on his own initiative, Katiforis reported to Giscard that:

- 18 government representatives backed the six-months rotating president of the European Council against five supporting a full-time elected chair;
- 18 were against reopening the Nice agreements on the weighting of votes in the Council of Ministers, the number of European Parliament seats and the structure of the Commission. If the Commission had to be downsized, equal rotation among member states should apply;
- only two voices were in favour of a legislative Council;
- there was 'virtual unanimity for qualified majority voting' except for two wanting the veto on taxation and one for the veto on the 'the strategy of foreign policy' and on social security.

Some members of the group were later to quibble over details of Katiforis's head count. But the negative implications of the meeting for eventually reaching consensus with Giscard were clear and highlighted in a press conference of the 16 'friends of the Community method' that evening. The most serious threat to hopes for a successful conclusion of the Convention came from Hannes Farnleitner, the Austrian representative, who again called for options instead of a single text in the final draft. He claimed that several colleagues had argued for 'good options' rather than 'a bad compromise.'

Ireland's Dick Roche asserted, with some justification, that neither the Nice nor the Laeken European Council mandates authorised the Convention to deal with institutional issues. For Finland, Teija Tiilikainen expressed doubts over whether a long-term European Council chair could be constrained from becoming a rival to the Commission president. Pointing to the Union's economic power, Farnleitner maintained that one commissioner per member state was not excessive. Roche and Henrik Hololei, the Estonian representative, likened re-opening Nice 'to opening Pandora's box'. Tellingly, however, Hololei added: 'None of us think that Nice is good. It is just that no one has come up with anything better.' He went on: 'The double majority is more transparent. But we can't have Nice *a la carte*. It is illogical to scrap something which was created with so much sweat and tears.'

Although Latvia's Sandra Kalniete began the press meeting claiming the 'group of 16 is more united than ever', Hololei's remarks pointed to a fundamental weakness in their position. The group of 16 was a negative coalition, united only in its opposition to Giscard's institutional proposals. It was never able to come together to produce a comprehensive set of draft articles in their place.

Common ground with MEPs

While the 16 were fulminating in the European Parliament's ground floor press room, Giscard was sitting several stories higher and enjoying a much cosier chat with the Convention's MEPs. He found that most European Parliament Convention members were interested in a deal not confrontation. Publication of draft part III of the constitution at the end of May showed that the European Parliament stood to gain a great deal by the extension of 'codecision', its right to legislate as an equal partner with the member states in the Council of Ministers.

The MEPs, like the integrationist caucus of national parliamentarians, wanted a single text with no options. True, they proposed further extensions of QMV to include tax and foreign policy and, echoing ideas put forward by Dini, proposed super-qualified majority voting instead of unanimity elsewhere. But they also signalled a willingness to compromise. Like the national parliamentarians, they suggested that the Commission retain one member per member state until 2009 but with the eventual constitutional treaty laying down the rules for the period afterwards. In return for having the European Parliament elect the Commission president, most MEPs could live with a long-term president of the European Council provided his or her powers were constrained and limited to providing strategic impulses and coordination. 'This component is not dissatisfied,' declared Klaus Hänsch, the German Social Democrat MEP and Praesidium member, after the meeting.

Giscard and his aides had started the day expecting a relatively easy meeting with the MEPs, some difficulty with the government representatives and chaos among the national parliamentarians. The meeting with the government representatives was far worse than anticipated. But by the time they were heading for their final meeting with the two commissioners in the Convention, they realised that the majority positions and willingness to find solutions of the national parliamentarians and MEPs could provide an alternative route to achieving consensus in the Convention as a whole. As he left the MEPs' room Giscard was asked about his earlier meeting with the government representatives. That component, he sniffed, 'is a minority in the Convention.'

Despite widespread despondency in the corridors of the Parliament building, the day spent by Giscard and his deputies among the Convention's component parts had been unexpectedly positive. It pointed to ways he might circumvent the hostile position on institutional architecture of the government representatives. Until that Wednesday, it had been assumed the Convention's final days would see the governments gaining the upper hand and the MEPs marginalised as negotiations increasingly foreshadowed the power balance in the IGC to follow. Instead, the MEPs and their integrationist allies among the national parliamentarians – linked through the political families – continued to strengthen Giscard's hand to the final day of the Convention. The Convention had passed a decisive turning point.

17.2   THURSDAY, 5 JUNE

After Wednesday's hectic activity, Thursday, 5 June looked set to be relatively quiet. The Praesidium reconvened on Thursday morning. A plenary session was scheduled for the afternoon, but, reflecting the Convention secretariat's determination to keep the initiative in the last weeks of negotiation, was not intended to deal with institutions. Instead, the plenary was scheduled to discuss amendments to the other eight titles of the constitutional part I of the draft text, the protocols of subsidiarity and national parliaments and part IV comprising the constitutional treaty's general and final provisions. Giscard still had to deal with the split in the Praesidium but this was put to one side during the morning. Taking on board the previous day's consultations, the Praesidium tackled some of the less controversial issues that had been raised.

Concessions in the Praesidium; warnings from the plenary

Responding to the mood of the Convention, the Praesidium decided to drop some of the more intergovernmental features of its previous institutional proposals in favour of ideas that were more protective of the existing power balance in the Union's institutional triangle. It abandoned the 'board' or 'bureau' to support the longer term president of the European Council. It also agreed the European Council president could hold office in another EU institution, while keeping the restriction that he or she could not hold a national mandate. It therefore took on board the hostility of most national parliamentarians, MEPs and the Commission towards having a new bureaucracy attached to the European Council presidency post, while keeping open the (admittedly distant) possibility of this being double-hatted with the Commission presidency.

The subsequent plenary was supposed not to deal with institutional issues. And indeed its discussions ranged over other disputed issues such as whether or not to include references to Christianity or God in the final text and the reinstatement of competitiveness among the Union's objectives. But the Convention's mind was elsewhere. There was no way of preventing the previous day's events spilling into the plenary. Recognising this, Giscard adroitly exploited his position as chairman to put the government representatives at a disadvantage.

He did this by giving the floor first to Olivier Duhamel, the French socialist MEP. Duhamel had the air of a '68er' and was one of the few conventionnels with an ability to deliver highly emotional, tub thumping rhetoric. Although very different, the two men had ties that went back a long way and were often to be seen chatting in the margins of the Convention. Duhamel did not disappoint. 'We are deadlocked', he declared. 'Certain people are trying to stop us. Don't let them sabotage our work!' To retain the Nice institutional arrangements was, he said, 'totally absurd'. To propose them as an option was 'equivalent to suicide'. The Convention was not an IGC: it existed for the general European good. It was not set up to 'arbitrate petty quarrels among member states over the number of their commissioners, their MEPs or their votes in the Council.' Such petty details were the preoccupation of IGCs and explained their failure.

Echoing Giscard's point, Duhamel underlined that the government representatives were a minority of 28 out of 105 full Convention members. They might have the final word in an IGC, but the Convention should not allow them to make a mockery of its work, or – worse – prevent it from making the proposals Europe needed. It was the Convention's duty to press on with its task of reforming the Union and the Convention members should make absolutely sure that governments took the blame if they wrecked its work now, or later.

Duhamel's carefully structured outburst was loudly applauded and echoed by others, including commissioner Michel Barnier, EPP caucus leader Brok and Luxembourg parliamentarian Ben Fayot. Supporters of the Nice settlements, such as Ireland's Roche and Austria's Farnleitner, were put on the defensive and their position worsened when late in the evening Dominique de Villepin, the French foreign minister, on one of his fleeting visits to the Convention, weighed in with a characteristically elegant appeal to the Convention to 'reject the status quo' and 'refuse petty compromises and the mirage of options' in favour of 'more Europe'.

De Villepin went on to press the case for a stable president of the European Council and 'a more political and collegiate Commission' – issues which the Spanish government had also supported. De Villepin's remarks were a reminder that the seemingly broad support Dastis had built among member states governments for maintaining the Nice institutional arrangements had weak foundations. Dastis was the representative of a big country but had exploited the big-small country split in the Convention by lining up with the smalls.

Earlier that day, the UK's Peter Hain, who was absent from the plenary because of a cabinet meeting in London on the UK's government's impending decision to stay out of the euro, announced on the record that his alignment with the pro-Nice lobby was tactical. He signed the letter of the nine 'for a clear reason: that unanimity on tax policy was crucial for the UK'. For Hain, a broader deal was 'in reach' which would secure a full-time chair of the European Council, an elected president of the Commission and a foreign minister for the Union. According to Hain, it was 'make up your mind time' for the other governments that continued to oppose these policies in the Convention.

Isolating Dastis in the Praesidium

Further progress now hinged on the Praesidium overcoming its differences. It met on Thursday evening after the plenary finished at 20.30. De Villepin contributed to the eventual success of the meeting by taking Giscard out to dinner. That left Dehaene in charge at the beginning of the meeting. In what one participant later described as 'Jean-Luc's finest hour', Dehaene set out to broker deals that would end the deadlock in the Praesidium over the institutions.

The negotiations started slowly. Dastis presented a text that would have put off all discussion about the Nice related issues until 2009 when it would be up to the European Council to start negotiations on the weighting of votes in the Council of Ministers, the structure of the Commission and the number of seats in the European Parliament. This proposal would, in effect, have delayed a solution long beyond 2009. After this discussion went no-where, it was decided instead to look at the institutions in turn, starting with generally uncontroversial issues such as the European Court. Giscard arrived from dinner in time to deal with the Commission. While making clear his doubts about the idea, he conceded that places in a slimmed down Commission should be given on the basis of equal rotation, as specified in the Nice Treaty.

This concession won over Bruton and satisfied Papandreou. Among Praesidium members, Bruton had always been the most critical of the drafts on the Commission. Papandreou, anxious to secure a successful Thessaloniki summit later in the month, realised that equal rotation of commissioners would be a key element in winning over a significant number of government representatives in the Convention. In the Praesidium, however, both Dastis and Christophersen were insistent that the other elements of the Nice settlement had to be retained in the institutional package.

However, Christophersen's resolve began to weaken when the meeting turned to the number of seats in the European Parliament. Denmark, like many small countries, was worried about the reduced scope for sharing round important parliamentary committee posts among the parties in a coalition government if the total number of MEPS were reduced to 700 from 732. When Giscard suggested keeping the Nice total after 2009, Christophersen realised that he would be able to report a success to his own and similarly concerned governments. He did not give way easily, however, insisting, as one eye witness reported, that the higher number of MEPs be enshrined in the final draft.

At this point the alliance between Dastis and Christophersen began to weaken. Nor could Dastis count on Alojz Peterle, the Slovenian parliamentarian and sole representative of the accession countries in the Praesidium. If representatives from three small countries (Ireland, Greece and Denmark) could accept the new proposals from Giscard and his two deputies, why should not Peterle? Moreover, Peterle, a former Slovenian prime minister who tops the EPP list of Slovene candidates for the 2004 European Parliament elections, had an interest every bit as strong as existing MEPs in steering the Convention to success.

Dastis was therefore alone when the discussion turned to the proposal for replacing the complex allocation of votes per member state, detailed in Nice, by QMV through a double majority of half the member states and at least 60 per cent of the population.

The discussion, as Giscard said later, was 'long, until late at night'. It was agreed that the Nice formula should apply until 1 November 2009. There was also some discussion about an enabling clause by which the move to double majority would only be triggered by a unanimous vote in the Council. But this was dropped in favour of a provision by which the double majority system could be delayed for three years, provided two-thirds of member states supported the idea. Despite these concessions, Dastis was heard to declare he would pursue a policy of non-cooperation for the rest of the Convention if the Praesidium held to the double majority on QMV and threatened there would be no further extension of QMV to other areas of policy. The meeting finished some 90 minutes after midnight.

Giscard's victory in the Praesidium left some issues still unresolved. But it marked an important breakthrough after an exhausting 48 hours of complex and emotionally charged negotiations at many different levels in and around the Convention. The Convention by this time had mutated into a mass of interlocking networks. The meetings on Wednesday between Giscard, Dehaene and Amato with its component parts were followed by a welter of meetings and contacts inside the components, among the political families and in the many informal dining and contact groups that had sprung up in the Convention over the previous 15 months, turning the corridors and bar near the plenary hall into hotbeds of gossip and speculation.

17.3   FRIDAY, 6 JUNE

The component parts reconvened separately on the Friday morning to debate the outcome of the Praesidium while waiting for briefings from Giscard and his aides. At 11.00 am, the three fanned out to separate meeting rooms in the European Parliament. Giscard returned to the group of national parliamentarians in recognition of the crucial change that Wednesday's meeting had brought to his and the Convention's fortunes. Dehaene went to brief the MEPs. It was left to Amato to tackle the most difficult group: the government representatives. To the pleasure of several in the meeting, Amato adopted a stance that appeared more solicitous of their views than that of Giscard two days before.

Giscard outlines the deal

Giscard entered the national parliamentarians' room to applause and proceeded to give an oral report, taking them through the Praesidium's decisions. These were more extensive than the compromises needed to isolate Dastis.

- For the Council of Ministers, the Praesidium proposed a General Affairs and Legislative Council to overcome the strong hostility of member states to the idea of a special legislative Council. Giscard explained that this was not quite equivalent to the German Bundesrat, or second chamber representing the states, because it would have two functions: the General Affairs Council would, in liaison with the Commission, also prepare the European Council meetings. As already planned, there would be a Foreign Affairs Council chaired by the Union's foreign minister. No other Council formations were specified although Giscard said Councils such as Ecofin would be detailed in part III. Whereas the early June draft empowered the General Affairs Council to authorise other formations, this task would now fall to the European Council. The presidency of other Councils would be held by member state representatives on a basis of rotation for at least a year. The European Council would lay down the rules for this annual rotation, which Giscard indicated, could lead to team presidencies.

- As envisaged since the end of April, the European Council would be a separate institution, would meet every three months and have its own president elected by QMV among its members for two and a half years, renewable once. But, confirming the previous morning's Praesidium decisions, there would be no board. The president, however, could hold an EU office. Giscard said national mandates were not to be permitted, because this would be incompatible with the common European interest. National foreign ministers would no longer have an automatic right to attend European Council meetings.

- Qualified majority voting would be the general rule for decisions in the Council of Ministers, except where specified in the constitutional treaty. In line with the previous night's decision, QMV would be a majority of member states representing at least 60 per cent of the Union population and take effect on 1 November 2009. In his oral account, Giscard also said the Praesidium was proposing a 'super-QMV' of two-thirds of member states and four-fifths of the population for issues such as CFSP decisions where the European Council or Council of Ministers did not act on a proposal of the Commission or foreign minister. It appeared at first as if the Praesidium was taking up a Lamberto Dini suggestion for an alternative to unanimity. But this proved not to be the case.

  Giscard also outlined for the first time the controversial idea of a *passerelle* or bridging clause by which the European Council, acting unanimously, could decide thereafter to apply QMV to areas still governed by unanimity in part III of the constitutional treaty. Although unanimity would be a huge hurdle in a Union of 25, the *passerelle* offered greater scope for change in the future than unanimity plus ratification in line with the national constitutions of the member states.

- The new provisions strengthened the Commission and the Commission president by way of far more detailed job descriptions. They made clear, for example, that the Commission would oversee the application of Union law, ensure the Union's external representation 'for areas falling within its responsibility' and initiate the Union's 'annual and pluriannual programming'. The latter provision gave the Commission some leverage over the Union's long-term strategy and was an important concession to opponents of a strong longer-term European Council president. Before selecting a Commission president, the European Council would have to hold 'appropriate consultations' as well as take the results of the previous European Parliament elections into account. Giscard also confirmed that equal rotation among member states for filling places in the college of 15 (including the president and foreign minister) would take over from the Nice formula of one commissioner per member state from 1 November 2009.

- The article providing for an EU foreign minister was left unchanged from the early June draft, in spite of complaints, notably from the UK, that the title 'minister' was inappropriate because the Union is not a state.

- The European Parliament would, Giscard confirmed, keep the Nice total of 732 seats beyond 1 November 2009 when it would introduce the principle of degressive proportionality for the allocation of seats, with a minimum threshold of four per member state. The distribution of seats set at Nice would apply in the 2004 elections while details of the new regime would be agreed unanimously by the European Council, on a proposal of the Parliament, before 2009.

The national parliamentarians responded positively with only one or two exceptions, such as the British labour peer Lord Tomlinson who sought in vain to persuade Giscard that the integrationist bandwagon was not representative of the group as a whole. The MEPs also welcomed the proposals while Amato reported a much better atmosphere in the governments' meeting than on Wednesday. Joschka Fischer said it was a 'day of hope', before characteristically warning that the 'devil was in the detail'. For the EPP's Elmar Brok, the changes to the proposed European Council president were important. There would be no board or bureau, no formal procedure for steering work in other Councils and the possibility of a double-hatted presidency with the head of the Commission.

When Giscard appeared before the press, he forecast the Praesidium would be able to produce a single proposal without options for the EU leaders in Thessaloniki. He made light of the Spanish problem, quoting in jest a 'famous French thinker'[2] who once said 'what is truth on one side of the Pyrenees is error on the other'. On a more serious note, he pointed out that Spanish parliamentarians were not notably hostile to the Praesidium's proposals. Indeed, the new proposals were 'supported by a significant number of representatives in the Convention' and would therefore 'form the basis of a final consensus'.

The Praesidium's package ended the efforts of the six original member states to produce their own proposals. Jean-Claude Juncker, the Luxembourg prime minister, was trying to arrange a meeting of the six leaders early in June and several meetings were held at senior official level. But Germany and France called the venture off after the breakthrough.

Some rumblings of discontent remained, however. Reflecting discussions in the preceding day's plenary session, Brok was one of many MEPs to want QMV to apply to foreign policy. The absence of a specific reference to

---

[2] Blaise Pascal 1623-1662.

Christianity continued to exercise many conventionnels from the Christian Democrat centre-right. Federalist MEPs were especially critical that the *passerelle* should be unlocked only by unanimity in the European Council. The Thursday plenary also witnessed growing pressure, notably among MEPs, for the eventual constitution or constitutional treaty no longer to be ratified by unanimity. Elena Paciotti, an Italian Socialist MEP pointed out that the final text should not be ratified by unanimity 'if we want a constitution worthy of its name'. Unanimity would mean the end result was a constitutional treaty rather than a constitution. 'If there is no change in procedure we will have a treaty which cannot be called a constitution. We cannot lie to the citizens,' she said.

There were also new problems in the Praesidium on Friday afternoon. Giscard had promised that texts of the revised articles would be provided later that day. They were not. The problem was the *passerelle*. Although outlined in some detail by Giscard earlier in the day, there had been no previous discussion of a text in the Praesidium. In a move apparently to 'bounce' the less integrationist members of the Praesidium into agreement, Sir John Kerr produced the first draft texts on the *passerelle* for approval in the closing minutes of the afternoon Praesidium meeting. They were not to be considered that day: instead the Praesidium broke up in some disarray after Gisela Stuart and John Bruton walked out to catch evening planes home.

17.4   COUNTDOWN TO CONSENSUS: WEEK TWO

The hazards of late night negotiation and oral reporting became apparent the following week as conventionnels re-converged on Brussels for the final days before the 13 June deadline. Conflicting accounts of the detail of the Praesidium proposals and the absence of a text until the afternoon of Wednesday, 11 June, fuelled suspicions that Giscard and the secretariat might be seeking to renege on deals done. Equally the lack of clarity sustained hopes in all segments of the Convention that more might be extracted from the last rounds of negotiations.

It was in the latter spirit that the leaders of the big three party caucuses – the EPP's Brok, the Liberals' Duff and the Socialists' Amato – met on the evening of Tuesday, 10 June to put their names to two amendments. This first such concerted action by the leaders of the three political families aimed at enabling the constitution to enter into force if not all 25 member states were able to ratify it and provided for a 'lighter' revision procedure where no shift in competences was planned.

Brok, meanwhile, alerted his party colleagues to 'serious problems' arising from apparent anomalies between the previous week's oral accounts of the Praesidium's agreement and the text due on Wednesday. Duff too was concerned that the Praesidium, when it produced its revised articles in written form, would seek to recover powers for the European Council president at the expense of the Commission.

17.5   WEDNESDAY, 11 JUNE

The Convention's component parts met during Wednesday morning. There were again calls from integrationists in the national parliaments and the European Parliament for more QMV and a stronger Commission vis-à-vis the proposed European Council president to maintain the Union's institutional balance. While several government representatives were reported as willing to accept the Praesidium's proposals, the UK's Peter Hain said they were 90 per cent acceptable, and the rest would have to be negotiated in the IGC. The UK, he warned, would speak out against the *passerelle* clause, which was opposed by 'six or seven' countries in the government representatives' meeting.

Revised articles unveiled

When on the afternoon of Wednesday, 11 June Giscard unveiled revised articles for the whole of part I and the preamble,[3] Duff and Brok called for an early adjournment so the Convention's members could discuss the texts in their component groups.

The Praesidium's revisions went beyond the institutional articles in title IV. Thus, the preamble was modified to excise its cursory and eccentric account of Europe's history as a near seamless progression from the glories of ancient Greece and Rome to the wonders of the Enlightenment. But while it retained the reference to Europe's 'cultural, religious and humanist inheritance' it made no concessions to the powerful Vatican-backed lobby that sought a specific reference to Christianity or Christian values. Nor did the federalist goal of 'ever closer union' make a come-back in the preamble, preference being given instead to the concept of a Europe determined and 'united ever more closely, to forge a common destiny.' One oddity in the preamble was the inclusion of the phrase describing Europe as 'united in its diversity' in inverted commas. This device, Giscard was later to admit, was a way of floating a possible slogan for the new, enlarged EU.

---

[3] CONV 797/03.

Another inclusion was the idea in article I-3 on the Union's objectives that Europe's social market economy should be 'highly competitive'. The objective of economic competitiveness had yo-yoed in and out of successive drafts. Its restoration, after deletion from the late May draft, reflected interventions by several conventionnels in the previous week's plenary, as well as protests from Unice, the European employers' federation which was represented in the Convention as an observer.

In title VII on the Union's finances, article I-54 was amended to make clear that the Council of Ministers would act unanimously when adopting the first multi-annual financial framework following the Constitution's entry into force. This was construed by some as giving Spain an arm-lock over regional fund negotiations well into the future.

Inevitably, the main interest focused on the precise institutional texts. Here there were some surprises. The concept of Super-QMV, requiring support reflecting four-fifths of the Union's population, had disappeared. Instead, draft article I-24 restated existing treaty provisions for Council decision making in cases where there was no Commission proposal. The majorities here would be two-thirds of states and three-fifths of population. In an attempt to draw a distinction between the two types of commissioners, those with votes and in the college were to be called 'European commissioners' and the others, without votes, simply commissioners.

A flurry of interventions before the adjournment showed there were still several issues to clear up. Duff, putting the integrationist argument, raised the issue of easier treaty revision and called for more QMV. Ireland's Dick Roche and the Netherlands' Gijs de Vries argued that the passage on equality of member states was not clear enough in the texts on the Council of Ministers and also called for further clarifications to preserve the Commission's competences. The UK's Peter Hain, Sweden's Lena Hjelm-Wallen and the Danish eurosceptic MEP Jens-Peter Bonde opposed the *passerelle* with Bonde complaining that this 'revolutionary clause' had never been debated in the Convention. Erwin Teufel, the Christian Democrat prime minister of Baden-Württemberg, rejected the *passerelle* on behalf of the German *Länder*. He also called for Christianity to be reflected in the preamble. Testifying to what had developed into a close working relationship between the two men, Teufel's plea on Christianity was backed by Joschka Fischer, Germany's Green foreign minister.

To Giscard's approval, Alain Lamassoure, the ever inventive French centre-right MEP, tabled a proposal that was first promoted by Jürgen Meyer, the German Social Democrat parliamentarian, for a citizens' right of petition to the Commission to be included in title VI on the democratic life of the Union.

The idea was that a petition signed by one million citizens from at least eight member states could induce the Commission to take a legislative initiative.

Earlier the French government's normally clipped and cautious alternate Pascale Andréani surprised many when she told of her 'regret and astonishment' at the draft's failure to ensure that trade policy relating to cultural services, education and health was an area of shared competence and so subject to unanimity. She warned that without suitable clarification, 'this constitution will stand no chance of being ratified in France'. But such discordant notes were few. One other came when Hain reminded the Convention that whatever they decided was not an end in itself. Hain's observation that 'we have a very good basis for negotiation in the Intergovernmental Conference' provoked hisses and murmurs of dissent.

The hisses that greeted Hain were sign that the integrationist parliamentarians in the Convention felt the wind still running in their favour. By dint of careful planning, they were about to play a dominating role in the Convention's final 48 hours.

National parliamentarians and MEPs make common cause

Those national parliamentarians who had not jumped aboard the integrationist bandwagon organised by van der Linden, Dini and Meyer were the first to find out how well organised their colleagues had become. Shortly after the national parliamentarians group had reconvened, an irritated Lord Tomlinson rose to warn of the dangers to parliamentary rights of such innovations as the *passerelle*. He was cut short by the chair, Marietta Giannakou of the Greek parliament, who told him that the group was about to decamp to another room for a joint session with the Convention's MEPs. In vain did Tomlinson protest 'we have agreed to meet but not what we are going to say'. As the meeting degenerated into ill tempered squabbling, the redoubtable Ms Giannakou – herself a former MEP – led her troops over the bridge[4] linking the third floors of the European Parliament's two main buildings in Brussels to a prearranged appointment with the MEPs.

When the plenary reconvened that evening, Inigo Méndez de Vigo, one of the two MEPs in the Praesidium, spoke up for both the MEPs and the national parliamentarians in the Convention. They wanted the Convention to extend QMV and codecision, maintain the institutional balance and examine both the possibility of a less onerous revision in future of the Constitution and the right of citizens to petition the Commission. A visibly pleased Giscard could not resist a touch of irony. Referring to his own idea for a

---

[4] Appropriately called a *Passerelle*.

special Congress of national parliamentarians and MEPs, which he had abandoned because of lack of support from the Convention, Giscard complimented Méndez de Vigo for having set up 'a kind of Congress of your own' before handing the floor to Ms Giannakou.

Picking up from where Méndez de Vigo left off, she then proposed strengthening the Commission and role of the European Parliament in appointing the Commission president by authorising the nominated Commission president to reject certain Commissioners proposed by member states and by allowing the Parliament, after two rejections of a candidate nominated by the European Council, to nominate its own candidate for Commission president.

For Johannes Voggenhuber, the Austrian Green MEP, the afternoon's meeting of the two groups of parliamentarians was 'one of the happiest moments of recent months because it created a chance that the Convention would not simply become an IGC.'

Voggenhuber's hopes appeared fulfilled when George Katiforis reported on the government representatives' meeting. Where the parliamentarians had presented a united front Katiforis reported a mix of views. 'Points of doubt and disagreement remain', he acknowledged. His group was 'virtually unanimous' in asking for 'strictly equal rotation in the presidencies' of the Council formations. 'Some, but not all' wanted deletion of the *passerelle* clause. 'Some' wanted a threshold of five not four members for national representation in the European Parliament. 'Some raise the question of qualified majority, preferring to stick with Nice'.

The integrationist bandwagon rolled further as Brok, Barnier, Duff and Duhamel called to extend the scope of QMV. In response, Giscard was obliged to warn that the Convention, with perhaps 12 hours of real work ahead of it, should not go back over old ground but should focus on three or four key issues to achieve consensus. The most important was the issue of qualified majority voting and whether it should be determined by the double majority system proposed by the Praesidium, or the Nice formula. In addition, Giscard singled out the issue of economic governance in the euro-zone and the *passerelle* from unanimity to QMV. It was up to the component groups to iron out their differences on these issues.

He received unexpected backing from Peter Hain who declared: 'We all have some things we are not happy with'. Hain warned that re-opening basic compromises on the election of the Commission president and the election of the chairman of the European Council could 'blow the whole thing up and we will have wasted the whole of our 15 or 16 months spent getting this together.' All that remained was to set the order of business for the following day. After some to-ing and fro-ing between Giscard, Brok and Méndez de Vigo, it was agreed that the Convention's component parts should again meet the following morning, preceded by meetings of the political families. Giscard, Dehaene and Amato would attend the meetings of the '*composantes*', splitting up as before, after which the component groups would submit a last batch of amendments.

These would be considered by the Praesidium on Thursday afternoon and the results presented to the Convention as a whole in a plenary meeting that evening. The Praesidium imposed one important condition on the amendments: that they should be unanimous submissions of the respective component groups. The change of rules was to benefit the better organised caucus of integrationist MEPs and national parliamentarians who by now had effectively muffled the more nationally inclined members of the national parliamentarians' group. The dominance of the integrationists in the national parliamentarians group was complete the following day, when they disowned Gisela Stuart and John Bruton, their two representatives in the Praesidium.

17.6   THURSDAY, 12 JUNE

Thursday's meetings of the Convention's component parts replicated Wednesday's pattern. The national parliamentarians and MEPs were willing to compromise and able to forge joint positions which became the basis of amendments submitted to the Praesidium. Meeting as usual behind closed doors, the government representatives were split, grumpy and resentful.

Divisions among government representatives

The government representatives were also faced with a rather different Giuliano Amato than in previous sessions. Several complained afterwards that Amato was reluctant to take on board amendments, even when they reflected the views of 18 governments, on the grounds that they were not unanimous. Accounts of the meeting indicated little inclination to change. The UK's Peter Hain strongly attacked the idea of the *passerelle*. Germany's Joschka Fischer, attending his first ever meeting of the group, repeated his plea for super qualified majority voting on foreign policy issues.

Highlighting the underlying divisions between incoming and existing and big and small member states, the representatives of 16 small and medium sized countries (including all 10 accession countries) put their names to a joint statement. But rather than convey unity, the four point statement, from the representatives of Austria, Cyprus, the Czech Republic, Estonia, Finland, Hungary, Ireland, Latvia, Lithuania, Luxembourg, Malta, Poland, Portugal, Slovakia, Slovenia and Sweden, made clear there were additional divisions among the members of this group.

On Council issues, the paper said the presidency of council formations should be held by member states on the basis of strictly equal rotation and rejected the European Council becoming an institution. It said: 'We do not support the creation of a permanent full-time president for the European Council', only to add in the next sentence: 'However, three government representatives have expressed their willingness to examine the idea of an elected chair of the European Council'.

On the composition of the Commission, the paper accepted that it should consist of a president, fourteen voting members selected 'on the basis of a system of strictly equal rotation' among member states and as many non-voting members as to ensure the Commission includes one national from each member state. 'However,' it added, 'five government representatives have insisted on preserving the principle of one commissioner per member state, with full voting rights, all being members of the college.'

On the European Parliament, the paper called for the arrangements of the Treaty of Nice to apply for 2004–2009 and to be changed only in the case of further enlargements, with a minimum threshold of five members per member state. The group held to the Treaty of Nice arrangements on qualified majority voting. 'A significant majority continues to prefer the voting system as included in the present Treaty to that proposed by the Praesidium.'

MEPs and national parliamentarians agree common amendments

Because of the divisions among the government representatives, the national parliamentarians found Giscard in an unexpectedly downbeat mood. Although the Convention had made advances that an IGC would never have achieved, the result was not sufficiently ambitious, he complained. The overall result was disappointing.

He did not understand why there had been such resistance to a stable president of the European Council, when this person would have no more power than Greece's Costas Simitis or Denmark's Anders Fogh Rasmussen, the two incumbents in the present and previous rotating presidencies. The insistence of the smaller and accession countries for perfect and equal rotation in the Commission and was a mistake and would lead to conflict, he warned. It was inconceivable that the Commission should have a college without the participation of big member states for an extended period of time.

Giscard had also been disappointed at the reluctance of so many conventionnels to reopen the Nice compromises on QMV, the Commission and the Parliament. Taking the example of the Parliament, he said an assembly of 732 members was much too big to be effective.

In his meeting with the MEPs, Dehaene heard again the now familiar calls for more QMV, especially in foreign policy; unlocking the launch of the *passerelle* from the requirement of unanimous agreement among member states; an 'easier' procedure for ratifying and modifying the eventual constitution and the incorporation of a right of petition to the Commission by citizens. It was fortunate that the MEPs had Dehaene, a true federalist who nonetheless has a keen sense of the possible, in their midst. Dehaene underlined the great progress made on spreading QMV and codecision and the potential for future progress inherent in the existing proposals for more QMV in combination with the *passerelle*. To press for an easier revision clause at this stage would 'open a can of worms', he warned.

The two sets of parliamentarians agreed on a joint position, covering seven points. Picking up the joint amendments for a revision clause agreed by Amato, Duff and Brok at the beginning of the week, they called for a 'more flexible procedure' to change the constitution in cases where there would be neither a shift of competences nor a change in the Charter of Fundamental Rights. Approval in these cases, which would be in part III, by five-sixths of member states 'would deliver the Union genuine constitutional status'.

They were prepared to accept a permanent president of the European Council provided the president-elect of the Commission could reject candidates for the Commission proposed by the member states; the (junior) Commissioners be subject to the same selection procedure as 'European Commissioners' and the functions of the European Council president would not prejudice those of other Union institutions. QMV should be the general rule, also for common foreign and security policy. *Passerelle* decisions should be taken in the European Council by super QMV. They also proposed that QMV should apply in CFSP to joint proposals from the foreign minister and the Commission and that the Convention should be able to decide individual cases of moving from unanimity to QMV in part III after the Thessaloniki European Council.

In addition, the General Affairs and Legislative Council should decide on further Council formations. The scope of the European Court of Justice should be extended to the whole constitution. European citizens should have a right to petition the Commission along the lines proposed by the Bundestag's Jürgen Meyer and the European Parliament's Alain Lamassoure.

And no European laws should be agreed without approval of the European Parliament.

The joint position was turned into seven specific amendments that were approved by a 'large majority' of the two groups and submitted to Giscard. At the last minute, the joint sponsors, Inigo Méndez de Vigo and Marietta Giannakou, decided not to submit an amendment for a revision clause and instead called for this issue to be considered in the July sessions after the Thessaloniki summit. Giscard later indicated that he would allow this. The groups of parliamentarians then despatched their representatives to that afternoon's Praesidium session. In the case of the national parliamentarians, this was an opportunity for long repressed frustrations to rise to the surface. Stuart and Bruton, according to eye witnesses, were openly attacked by name for having failed to represent the views of the group accurately in the Praesidium. To applause from the majority of the group, Lamberto Dini told the two that they were expected either to defend the amendments or stay quiet, but above all not to be disloyal.

The Praesidium's final offer

Uncertainty persisted until the final night. Just before the penultimate plenary session on the evening of Thursday, 12 June, Hannes Farnleitner, the Austrian government delegate warned of failure.[5] Waving the paper with the demands of the 16 governments on the Union's institutions, Farnleitner threatened that the festive lunch promised by Giscard for the next day would 'become a last supper' unless the president compromised.

The excitement among the conventionnels was palpable when Giscard presented the Praesidium's final batch of amended articles[6] to the plenary at 19.45 hours on Thursday, some 100 minutes later than promised. There were detailed but significant changes to the articles on the European Council, its chair, the Council formations, the Commission and QMV which met demands from the Convention's various component groups.

Responding to demands of integrationist parliamentarians and smaller member states, article I-20 now specified that the European Council 'shall not exercise any legislative function'. In article I-21, the role of the European Council chair was further constrained by a stipulation that the job

---

[5] Farnleitner also took steps in preparation for failure. He scheduled a press conference of the smalls for 11am on Friday 13 June to coincide with the start of the session of the Convention that established consensus on the constitutional treaty. The event was publicised among the meetings displayed on the European Parliament's monitor screens during Friday morning. Farnleitner had second thoughts, however, and took part in the week's closing plenary session.
[6] CONV 811/03.

of ensuring preparation and continuity in the European Council's work would be 'in cooperation with the President of the Commission, and on the basis of the work of the General Affairs Council.' Reacting to one of the key demands of the group of 16 small and medium countries, article I-23 now stated that the presidencies of the Council formations other than foreign affairs would be held by member state representatives on the basis of 'equal' rotation, for periods of at least a year.

Many conventionnels worried that the institutional balance of the Union would be upset unless the dates for new measures taking effect were brought into line. Thus article I-24 on QMV retained the double majority arrangements favoured by all Praesidium members except Spain's Dastis but provided greater precision in stating that these would 'take effect on 1 November 2009, after the European Parliament elections have taken place.' Similarly article I-25 on the Commission made clear that the arrangements replacing the Nice system of one commissioner per member state 'will take effect on 1 November 2009'. Article I-19 on the European Parliament specified that the new distribution of seats that would replace that agreed in Nice in the 2009 elections would apply 'for further elections'. Later Giscard claimed that the decision to delay application of these changes until 2009 played a key part in securing the support of the accession countries for the Convention's final draft text.

The article on QMV no longer contained the possibility of member states agreeing by a two-thirds majority to extend the Nice arrangements on QMV for an extra three years from 2009. In addition, the hopes of the two groups of parliamentarians that the *passerelle* would be unlocked by super QMV rather than unanimity were frustrated.

In article I-25, the duties of the Commission vis-à-vis the European Council and foreign minister were made even clearer with inclusion of a sentence saying: 'With the exception of the common foreign and security policy, and other cases provided for in the Constitution, it shall ensure the Union's external representation'. In the same article, any doubts about the composition of the college of commissioners were eliminated by declaring that it would consist of 'its President, the Minister for Foreign Affairs/Vice-president and thirteen European Commissioners'.

Article I-26 rectified an earlier omission by making clear that those nominated 'as non-voting commissioners' would be submitted for approval by the European Parliament in a body with the President and other members of the college, including the foreign minister. No change was made to the foreign minister's role. But a footnote was added to article I-27 promising the establishment of a 'Joint European External Action Service, to assist the minister'. Germany's Joschka Fischer – who at the time was widely seen as a candidate for the foreign minister's post – had pushed the idea of an EU diplomatic corps.

Jürgen Meyer was rewarded for his persistence with a new paragraph four in article I-46 creating the legal base for citizens' initiatives in the Union. 'A significant number of citizens, not less than a million, coming from a significant number of member states' would be able to 'invite the Commission' to submit a proposal for a law to implement the Constitution. The Praesidium continued to set its face against pressure for a specific reference to Christianity in the Constitution, opting only for a minor revision of the preamble to make clear that the 'values' of the cultural, religious and humanist inheritance of Europe 'are always present' in its heritage.

To rectify grievances voiced by conventionnels from Romania and Bulgaria, the Praesidium produced a draft declaration to deal with the impact on the distribution of parliamentary seats and votes in the Council of Ministers of the two countries possibly joining the Union during the period of the Nice arrangements before 2009. For technical reasons, this necessitated a last minute change to article I-19: this now set the permitted maximum of seats in the European Parliament at 736 against 732 previously.

To the deep irritation of many MEPs and national parliamentarians, the Praesidium also acted to meet a specific UK request for additional assurances that the Charter of Fundamental Rights would not impact on UK labour and social security laws. Peter Hain had called for a cross reference to the so-called explanations to the Charter which were drawn up in 2000 to ensure that the Charter could not lead to any extension of the application of Union law at the expense of those of the member states. Hain got his wish with a sentence concocted by Commissioner Antonio Vitorino which was added to the preamble of the Charter. Harking back to the work of the EU's only previous convention, it said 'the Charter will be interpreted by the courts of the Union and the Member States with due regard for the explanations prepared at the instigation of the Praesidium of the Convention which drafted the Charter'.

The anger among the integrationists partly reflected the realisation that the UK had secured a rather good deal out of the Convention. By dint of repeatedly underlining the 'red lines' over which the UK would not go, Hain had prevented the spread of QMV to foreign and defence policy and all areas of taxation, except by way of a very limited *passerelle* for cases dealing with tax fraud that threatened the single market. The UK had secured its main goal of a long-term president or chair of the European Council.

17.7 PEACE BREAKS OUT

Brok and Duff, the first speakers to respond to the revised articles, were cautious and emphasised in turn the Praesidium's failure to spread QMV to foreign policy and its decision to keep the 'padlock' of unanimity on the *passerelle*. But it quickly became clear that the package of amendments, while full of disappointments for many, contained sufficient to please most conventionnels. Marietta Giannakou, whose chairing of the national parliamentarians group had done much to cement the alliance with the MEPs, caught the mood. 'What is done is probably as much as could be done', she declared.

The prospects for consensus brightened when government representatives from very different philosophies came out in favour of the compromise. Ireland's Dick Roche, who was one of the most outspoken of the group of 16, noted with approval how Amato had taken on board the demands of the small and medium sized countries for equal rotation in the Council formations and more precise job descriptions for the Commission and European Council presidents. Germany's Fischer emphasised how the Praesidium had tackled issues raised in the government representatives' meeting and the resulting drafts allowed the Convention members to meet 'in the middle of the bridge'. Hain appealed to the Convention to think of 'the bigger picture' arguing that the Praesidium's work would enable the Convention 'to attain an historic achievement in coming together and creating the first new single Constitutional treaty for Europe.' The texts were approved by the political families and the Convention's component groups the following morning. The way was clear for the Convention in its final session before the Thessaloniki summit to establish consensus: a remarkable and unexpected achievement when compared with the bleak scenario ten days before.

Friday 13 June

In fact, Giscard chose not to use the word 'consensus' in the plenary of 13 June. He did not have to. Convention members, who only 24 hours before had appeared irreconcilable, rose to praise the outcome of nearly 16 months of hard work and Giscard's chairmanship. In the end, everybody compromised. 'All of us will find certain elements that we are not keen on and others that we very much support,' Giscard told his fellow conventionnels.

First to speak was Méndez de Vigo for the European Parliament. Standing up to praise the 'historic moment', Méndez de Vigo signalled to the hall that the time for disputing the constitutional part of the final text was over. He was followed by René van der Linden for the national parliamentarians. Two hours before, in the meeting of the EPP group, van der Linden had opened his remarks with an appeal: 'Let us not make this result a triumph for the president of this Convention because in the last two to three weeks he has set out to destroy the Convention method,' he said. In the plenary hall, these words were forgotten as van der Linden hailed the Convention as a success, offered thanks to the secretariat and congratulations to Giscard, saying how 'very happy' he and his fellow conventionnels were to have had 'such a president'.

Very few conventionnels expressed reservations or set down markers for the IGC that would follow. One was Ana Palacio, Spain's foreign minister. She made clear Spain had a 'basic reservation', but nonetheless hailed the text as 'a legal revolution without precedent' that 'put an end to 19th century diplomacy where we signed such things behind closed doors.' Another was Hannes Farnleitner of Austria, the second to last to speak from the floor. After giving Giscard a backhanded compliment for his 'authoritarian, purposeful and determined' leadership, Farnleitner said he could defend 95 per cent of the outcome with his 'lifeblood'. But there was five per cent – the section on the institutions – which he would not have voted for, had votes been allowed.

Otherwise, an extraordinary coalition of conventionnels representing governments, parliaments and the Commission, from left, right and centre of the political spectrum endorsed the text and the work of the Convention. A palpable sense of satisfaction suffused the plenary hall of the European Parliament building in Brussels as Convention members outbid each other to hail their achievement with statements as contrived as they were sincere. 'Today is Friday, 13,' declared Alojz Peterle, the Slovenian parliament conventionnel and Praesidium member. 'But it is not black Friday. Indeed, it is one of the brightest days that Europe has ever seen'.

For Germany's Joschka Fischer, the outcome symbolised the success of an enlarged, united Europe that could look the US in the eye. 'We have worked together here, old members and new members, big and small from all parts of Europe,' he said. 'This Convention has demonstrated that, differences notwithstanding, there is not an old and a new Europe but a Europe of citizens and states, a Europe of freedom, a Europe of justice and a Europe of democracy: our Europe!'.

Even Johannes Voggenhuber, the outspoken Austrian Green who had made it his business to criticise and clash with Giscard for the past 15 months, was fulsome in his praise: 'Mr President, you have accomplished your task,' he declared. 'In the end, and against my expectations, you were not the Jupiter of this Convention but acted as its midwife. I thank you and offer you my respect.' Only Jens-Peter Bonde, the Danish MEP representing eight eurosceptics who had submitted a minority report for a 'Europe of democracies', rejected the outcome. But he earned a round of applause as he thanked 'everyone for all the new friendships which have been made in this Convention process.'

After all the plaudits, Giscard stepped down from the dais to address the conventionnels from the Parliament's 'lectern of honour'. 'The result is not perfect, but it is unhoped-for,' he said. The Convention had come far since receiving its mandate from the December 2001 Laeken European Council. After 15 and a half months, the assembly comprising 105 Convention members and 102 alternates from both sides of the former Iron Curtain had, Giscard judged, drawn up 'the basis of a future treaty creating a Constitution for Europe'. He would, he said, present their 'joint opus' to the Union's heads of government in Thessaloniki on 20 June with a word of warning for the 25 existing and new member states in the Intergovernmental Conference (IGC) that would follow. 'The closer you stick to our text, which has been discussed at great length, the lighter will be your task'.

Unexpectedly, the strains of the EU anthem – Beethoven's Ode to Joy – filled the hall. Ushers bearing trays of warm Bollinger champagne followed. The conventionnels could toast their success in producing a single constitutional text without options to put to EU leaders at their summit in Thessaloniki a week later.

17.8 VERDICTS AT THESSALONIKI

The initial response of the leaders of the enlarged EU at the European Council in Thessaloniki was to welcome the draft 'Constitution for Europe'[7] and judge it 'a good basis for starting negotiations in the Intergovernmental Conference' to be convened in October.[8]

In the brief preface to the text submitted to the leaders at Thessaloniki, Giscard and his two deputies recalled that the Convention had been asked to respond to three issues: 'How to bring citizens closer to the European design and European institutions; how to organise politics and the European political area in an enlarged Union; and how to develop the Union into a stabilising factor and a model in the new world order'. Its answer, they said:

---

[7] CONV 820/03.
[8] Presidency Conclusions: Thessaloniki European Council SN200/03.

- proposes a better division of Union and member state competences;
- recommends a merger of the treaties and giving legal personality to the Union;
- simplifies the Union's instruments of action;
- increases the Union's democracy, transparency and efficiency by involving national parliaments more in its affairs, simplifying decision-making processes and making the working of EU institutions more transparent and comprehensible;
- and improves the structure and strengthens each of the Union's three institutions, taking particular account of enlargement.

But the celebrations were accompanied by some discordant notes, prompted largely by the Convention's institutional proposals. Poland and Spain made clear their continued strong opposition to the introduction of a double majority system for QMV in the Council of Ministers. Austria stuck by its assessment that the final product may be 95 per cent acceptable but the remaining five per cent of institutional proposals disadvantaged the small member states and needed to be changed. Although Britain's Tony Blair spoke warmly of Giscard, the UK government underlined that the national veto on issues of tax, social security, foreign policy and defence constituted 'red lines' which could not be crossed. Four countries signalled that they wanted a specific reference to Christianity in the constitution. Poland's Leszek Miller was outspoken on both the Nice issue and that of Christianity in the constitution. It was 'incomprehensible' that the voting system should be changed as 'nothing has happened since Nice' to justify this. As for the preamble, it 'should be a reflection of the European legacy and an element of that legacy is Christianity', Miller said.

Luxembourg's prime minister Jean-Claude Juncker, who had launched a blistering attack on the Convention's text and methods in its final days,[9] continued to be hostile, focussing his criticism on the proposed long-term European Council president. Although Juncker's tone in Thessaloniki was less strident, he, with Poland's Miller and Austria's Wolfgang Schüssel, put diplomatic evasions to one side and chose to broadcast their concerns openly at the summit.

The Thessaloniki summit gave Giscard's draft a fair wind despite these, and other less explicit, reservations. Some leaders, such as Germany's Gerhard Schröder and Denmark's Anders Fogh Rasmussen said they could accept the text more or less as it was written. Guy Verhofstadt, Belgium's prime minister, delivered what one observer called 'an extravagant and extraordinary tribute' to Giscard in his meeting with the leaders. When

---

[9] Published in *Der Spiegel*, the German news magazine, during the weekend after June 13.

Verhofstadt said he would fight for more qualified majority voting, his remarks were seen more as a shot across the bows of Blair than a signal of difficulties ahead. But it became clear that agreeing the constitutional treaty at the IGC would be no shoo-in. The IGC, the leaders agreed, should complete its work and agree the treaty 'as soon as possible and in time for it to become known to European citizens before the June 2004 elections for the European Parliament'. The treaty, they added, 'will be signed by the member states of the enlarged Union as soon as possible after 1 May 2004'. So that the final treaty text could be translated into all the languages of the enlarged Union, the IGC would have to conclude some weeks before 1 May although some countries, notably Germany, were pushing in Thessaloniki for the IGC to finish by the end of 2003.

Two sessions of the Convention remained – on 4 July and 9-10 July. According to the Thessaloniki conclusions these were required to complete 'some purely technical work on drafting part III' detailing the Union's policies and their legal bases. The mandate meant parts I and II of the constitutional treaty were henceforth sacrosanct, while there could be no significant constitutional changes to part IV.

CHAPTER 18
The Convention After Thessaloniki

18.1 TIDYING UP PART III

After the heady emotions of 13 June, it was difficult to escape a sense of anti-climax when the 'conventionnels' returned to Brussels on 4 July for the first of the two extra sessions approved by the EU's leaders at their summit in Thessaloniki.

There was, however, some serious work to do. The Convention members, who had submitted 1,687 amendments to the articles in part III, found them piled high and bound by thick rubber bands on their desks. As Giscard remarked, 'handling the amendments could be a very useful physical exercise at the beginning of the day – provided they are passed alternately from the right arm to the left'. Numerous though the amendments were, Giscard ruled that many cancelled each other out and that none would be accepted which threatened the consensus of 13 June over parts I and II of the constitutional treaty. This meant the Convention was to focus on only a score of issues. The one issue addressed most forcefully in the plenary concerned the extension of qualified majority voting (QMV) beyond areas already agreed. The alliance of national parliamentarians and MEPs that played such a crucial role in securing agreement by 13 June was again in evidence.

In a 'key points' paper, Andrew Duff, the Liberal caucus leader, and Lamberto Dini, who now chaired the national parliamentarians by dint of Italy having the EU's rotating presidency, revived their campaign for more QMV in foreign and security policy and areas of fiscal and social policy. The text had been carefully coordinated with Elmar Brok, leader of the European People's Party caucus, and reflected informal soundings with the Commission and the French and Belgian governments. The final touches had been agreed late on 3 July by a cabal including Duff, Méndez de Vigo, Brok, Hänsch, Dini and van der Linden.

The paper demanded no retreat from the consensus achieved over parts I and II of the Constitution and no dilution in part III from the status established under the existing EU treaties. Other goals included majority voting in CFSP in cases where the initiatives of the foreign minister would be supported by Commission and in the two contentious tax articles for harmonising measures to aid administrative cooperation or the battle against tax fraud or evasion. On an issue that stirred passions among constitutionalists and those wanting more 'social Europe', the key points paper urged QMV for article III-5 [III-8] covering policies against discrimination on grounds such as sex, race, age and religion and in social policy for the protection of workers who had been fired. The paper also suggested a bigger role for the Court of Justice in CFSP, more flexible procedures in part IV for future revision of the Constitution and an assurance that the Parliament must give its consent if member states wanted to hold an intergovernmental conference to change the constitution without first setting up a convention.

The Duff-Dini paper broached other contentious issues, which would play a big part in the Convention's discussions before its final session on 10 July. One of the most sensitive was the German government's insistence that access of third country nationals to the labour market should stay subject to unanimity. It was difficult not to feel a sense of *Schadenfreude* at the uncomfortable position that Germany's Joschka Fischer found himself in. He had been a passionate supporter of more QMV throughout the Convention, lecturing all and sundry on how the Union would seize up unless unanimity were swept away. But rising unemployment at home was reflected in strong support for national immigration controls across a broad cross section of German political opinion. Retaining the veto was a key political goal of the prime ministers of the *Länder*, most of which were controlled by the centre-right opposition. They had made their position clear to Chancellor Schröder. Subsequently, Fischer, Erwin Teufel, the Christian Democrat representative of the German *Länder* in the Convention, and Jürgen Meyer, the Social Democrat Bundestag conventionnel, had written to the Praesidium pressing for unanimity.

Fischer began his remarks on 4 July with a strong appeal to the Convention for more QMV in tax and foreign policy. But with campaigning underway for September's state elections in opposition controlled Bavaria and Teufel sitting close by, he took a radically different line just seconds later. 'Immigration policy is one of the most sensitive areas of home affairs,' he said. 'A generalised shift to QMV is not possible at present for Germany.'

France, another advocate of QMV, also had an area where it wanted to keep the national veto. In an earlier session, Pascale Andréani, the French government alternate, had warned that ratification of the constitutional treaty would be a lost cause in France without retention of unanimity for granting negotiating mandates to the Commission for trade negotiations that concerned the 'cultural exception'. With a phalanx of French conventionnels, she again pressed for changes in the draft text which envisaged QMV for international trade agreements covering services in the cultural, audio-visual, health and education sectors. Her call, she declared, was backed by some 30 Convention members from 11 countries who had submitted amendments for the 'cultural exception' to be treated as a shared competence between the Union and member states, and hence subject to unanimity.

The plenary debate also saw a new effort by the political left to obtain greater support in the constitution for 'services of general interest' – Brussels jargon for the public services which many politicians, notably in France and Belgium, enthusiastically support because of their powerful trade union links and despite their tendency to strike against the general interest at times of maximum inconvenience for the general public.

Conventionnels of all political backgrounds from the eurozone wanted the eurogroup nations to have a greater control over their economic governance. Several integration-minded Convention members urged that the Constitution refer to the Union's symbols such as its flag and anthem. A new push was made by Joschka Fischer and the Netherlands' representative Gijs de Vries to strengthen the role of the proposed, but disputed, post of European public prosecutor.

The session was in fact a busy one for Fischer, who was one of few senior government representatives to have come back to the Convention after Thessaloniki. His presence testified to a backlog of lobbying on his agenda to shift decisions in Germany's favour. Fischer rarely raised issues of national concern in the Convention's plenary, preferring to influence the Praesidium and key players by direct contact in the small VIP rooms dotted throughout the Parliament building or by letter from the foreign ministry in Berlin. His intervention on immigration came after these techniques had failed. He had another aim – to support a declaration which he had encouraged the Praesidium to add to part III, providing for the future creation of a 'European External Action Service' to assist the planned Union Minister for Foreign Affairs 'under the minister's authority'. This EU diplomatic corps would be composed of officials from the Council Secretariat, the Commission and member states' diplomatic services.

The draft declaration caused problems for Brok and other integrationist MEPs. Ever fearful that the Convention was tipping the institutional balance too much towards the member states, they insisted the service should be located within the Commission. Fischer expressed his personal sympathy for Brok's proposal but warned it would not have the backing of those member states which wanted the minister's power base in the Council.

The UK was now represented by the British government's alternate Baroness Scotland because Peter Hain was fully occupied taking charge of new responsibilities as leader of the House of Commons. Deploying a dry sense of humour, she did her best to stem the flow of integrationist proposals. QMV, lauded by Duff for its 'seductive' qualities, should, the baroness said, be resisted 'like other temptations, where to succumb would create unnecessary family disharmony'. Warning the Convention against moving the goal posts, she underlined Britain's determination to retain national sovereignty over tax, foreign policy, defence and criminal law procedure. The Swedish, Estonian, Irish and Italian government representatives also called for continued unanimity on tax policy.

But it was Giscard and Amato who defined the limits to the further expansion of QMV. The debate, Giscard said, reminded him of a typical parliamentary debate on budgetary economies. 'Every body is in favour of economy, but the minute you propose a specific measure there is always someone who says 'not that one, and not for me''. Giscard therefore invited Amato, the constitutional lawyer in the Convention's triumvirate, to outline ways of moving to agreement. Taking issue with the idea that extending QMV was a purely technical matter, Amato said the passage from unanimity to majority voting implied a different institutional balance and was also an emotional question. 'On a number of issues, several member states, national public opinion in several countries and several of our colleagues feel that their identity is at stake, their diversity is at stake, some of their vital interests are at stake. That is a fact of life.'

The cases where more QMV could be compatible with the Thessaloniki mandate for the Convention were therefore limited. One clear instance was to enforce in part III the principles that were clearly stated in part I of the Constitution. 'If part I says it has to be decided by qualified majority, in part III we have to list the cases to which qualified majority applies. Otherwise we betray what we have already approved,' Amato said. Second, there might be cases for the Convention to clarify those texts where uncertainty existed over whether a 'window' had been opened for QMV. Third, following the logic that 'something is not purely technical when it raises political objections', the Convention could move to QMV if no one raised political objections to a proposal. Finally, Amato suggested the Convention might consider moving to QMV for legislation on minimum standards as an interim step where QMV was not politically acceptable for 'fully fledged legislation'.

As the conventionnels prepared to leave for the weekend, Giscard made sure they understood Amato's message. He warned that moving much further towards QMV would 'shatter the consensus', adding: 'I know many cases among different European partners where moving to QMV would provoke very negative reactions.'

18.2   THE LAST TWO DAYS

The Praesidium met on Tuesday, 8 July to draw up amendments in the light of the previous week's discussions and Amato's guidelines. It made some progress. But, in what Giscard conceded was a 'mixed bag' of proposals, it agreed no significant changes towards QMV in foreign or tax policy. It left open the issue of the cultural exception after an hour of wrangling in order, it was said, to gauge the opinion of the plenary.

Its key decision favoured Germany, and proved that Fischer's presence in Brussels the previous Friday had been worthwhile. The relevant article, III-163 [III-168], prescribed QMV for the Union's planned common immigration policy. But Germany secured national control over the access of immigrants to the labour market with the addition of a sentence, making clear that QMV 'shall not affect the right of member states to determine volumes of admission of third country nationals coming from third countries to their territory in order to seek work, whether employed or self employed.'

Eurozone countries were given, in III-85a [III-88] their own powers to strengthen budgetary discipline and surveillance in the single currency area and specify their own economic policy guidelines.

To take account of concerns of some neutral countries over the defence articles, the Praesidium changed the rules applying to 'structured cooperation' in III-208 [III-213], by which member states forming coalitions of the willing could carry out demanding military tasks. These were made subject to the same safeguards, set down in articles III-319 to III-325 [III-322 to III-329], which apply to 'enhanced cooperation' in other policy areas.

This was balanced by a concession to integrationists. A new article, III-324a [III-328] opened the way for countries practicing enhanced cooperation to decide, by a unanimous vote, to move from unanimity to QMV in a manner similar to the bridging clauses or *passerelles* agreed before 13 June for part I. For some less integrationist countries, this decision raised the spectre of the Constitution authorising the creation of an *avant garde* or core group of countries within the Union.

Other amendments were tidying up initiatives. A clause in article III-196 [III-201] would engage the foreign minister in trying to resolve a dispute should any member state invoke the 'vital reasons of national policy' to block a decision in one of the few areas of common foreign and security policy subject to QMV. The Praesidium also opened fractionally the capacity of the European Court of Justice to rule on foreign policy matters by giving it jurisdiction to review restrictive measures against individuals under CFSP.

The Praesidium gave the Parliament the right to be consulted in article III-133 [III-138.3] over measures against discrimination in the area of transport and in III-210 [III-215.3] for cases where the Union seeks rapid access to funds to finance urgent foreign policy measures. Also, the Parliament would be informed about agreements between management and labour at Union level in III-101 [III-106.2] and should the Union ever have to implement the solidarity clause in III-226 [III-231] in the case of terrorist attack or natural or man made disaster. Other changes would encourage young people to take part in the Union's democratic life in III-177 [III-182] and enable European researchers to cooperate across borders in III-141 [III-146]. The latter decision gave some heart to supporters of the 'Lisbon agenda' for making Europe more competitive.

In reaction, there was widespread discontent among Convention members from the national and European Parliaments and the Commission. After the document[1] detailing the changes was distributed, MEPs turned on Klaus Hänsch and Inigo Méndez de Vigo, their two representatives in the Praesidium accusing them of having failed to press Parliament's case when agreeing the amendments. So bitter were the complaints that Hänsch, the German Social Democrat MEP in the Praesidium, had to ask his colleagues 'not to get physical'. As chairman of the meetings of Convention MEPs, the EPP's Méndez de Vigo had always tried to give himself manoeuvring room by shying away from formulating firm conclusions after discussions in the European Parliament group. This time, he drew up a list of points and pledged to fight for them in the plenary.

The alliance of integrationist national parliamentarians and MEPs also responded vigorously. After meeting Amato to discuss the Praesidium's decisions, Duff, Dini and Brok reworked their 'key points' paper of the previous week, listing seven demands 'of pivotal importance'. These were:

- QMV in CFSP when the foreign minister's initiatives were supported by the Commission;
- the External Action Service as a single administration within the Commission;
- QMV for setting minimum standards in article III-5 on non-discrimination;
- QMV for legislation under III-59 harmonising indirect tax measures relating to administrative cooperation, tax fraud and tax evasion;
- greater scope for the Court of Justice regarding CFSP, particularly with respect to agencies such as the proposed European armaments agency;

---

[1] CONV 847/03.

- clarification of the European Parliament's role in international commercial agreements. (The proposed article III-222.7 failed to make clear whether its consent was needed);

- a requirement in part IV article 6 that the European Parliament must consent should a future European Council decide *not* to call a convention to revise the Constitution.

A succession of speakers took the floor in the afternoon plenary session to hammer home these points. Singing from the same hymn sheet were Dini for the national parliamentarians, Méndez de Vigo for the MEPs, Duff, Brok, the Belgian Socialist MEP Anne Van Lancker and the Austrian Green Johannes Voggenhuber for the big political families and commissioner Antonio Vitorino. Some Convention members also reminded Giscard of their call for the Constitution to refer to the Union's symbols. Others wanted it to mention the open method of coordination, the system of benchmarking policies, adopted at the March 2000 summit in Lisbon to facilitate Europe's elusive transformation into the world's most competitive economy by 2010.

But the Convention's integrationists did not have things all their own way. The government representatives were largely opposed to significant change and made their position clear. 'It is now time to stop with ambitions,' declared Ireland's Dick Roche. The UK's Baroness Scotland expressed surprise at the 'non-technical changes' in the latest text, including the proposals for structured and enhanced cooperation and the role of the Court. 'We simply cannot support them,' she said. Henrik Hololei, Estonia's representative, spoke out against attempts in the plenary 'to insert fundamental changes' in the Constitution and urged the Convention instead to stick to the Thessaloniki mandate.

A hush fell over the plenary when Fischer spoke. Here, despite his insistence on national control over Germany's labour market, was the most prominent of the integration-minded government representatives. His remarks were sobering. He told the assembly that he encountered problems persuading the cabinet in Berlin to accept compromises reached in the Convention. With the forthcoming Intergovernmental Conference in mind, the conventionnels, Giscard and the Praesidium should 'not to open up compromises that have been reached to extract a final centimetre'. Fischer went on to plead for solutions to 'two small matters'. One was the cultural exception, for which Pascale Andréani made another robust plea, with the support of several French conventionnels and Latvian, Polish, Austrian members. Fischer's other preoccupation was the status of the Euratom Treaty vis-à-vis the constitution.

The Convention had been unable to reach an agreement over Euratom. Giscard and his secretariat always wanted to leave it alone, arguing that to deal with the 46-year-old treaty would be too difficult and was outside the mandate of the Convention. The Greens originally saw the Convention as a way of ending Euratom's favourable treatment of nuclear power – a policy that had grown out of the technological innocence of the 1950s when the environmental hazards of nuclear power were generally unknown.

In the plenary, Fischer, playing on his status as Germany's foreign minister and the Convention's most prominent Green politician, urged a different approach. He asked for a minor amendment so that Euratom would retain its own legal personality. This demand had earlier been adopted by the Convention's Greens to keep open the option of their amending or killing off Euratom at a later date without having to revise the Constitution. It was accepted by the Praesidium in its final meeting late on Wednesday, 9 July.

18.3   THE PRAESIDIUM MEETS FOR THE LAST TIME

The final meeting of the Praesidium nearly ended in failure over the cultural exception. This was to prove an interesting test of Amato's first rule for extending QMV: that principles clearly stated in part I of the Constitution should be enforced in part III. The Convention initiated a quiet revolution when it agreed – against French objections – that article I-12 should list the common commercial policy, without any qualifying clauses, among the Union's exclusive competences. This decision invalidated those parts of article 133 of the Nice Treaty which placed 'agreements relating to trade in cultural and audiovisual services, educational services and social and human health services … within the shared competence of the Union and its member states' and so subject to unanimity.

Consensus on article I-12 made it impossible to solve the problem by reproducing the Nice Treaty text in the Constitution, as demanded by many, mainly French, conventionnels. This logic was reflected in draft article III-212 [III-217] which ranked trade in services alongside goods as part of the common commercial policy that would be implemented by European laws or framework laws, and therefore by QMV. On the other hand, the Praesidium could hardly ignore the clamour from parts of the Convention for the cultural exception or the behind the scenes lobbying by the French government. Paris's call on national loyalties had prompted Commissioner Michel Barnier to support unanimity in the previous Praesidium meeting even though the Commission's policy was for trade in goods in services to be decided by QMV.

Before Giscard joined the Praesidium, he met Amato, Dehaene, Duff, Méndez de Vigo, Dini and Brok: a group which he called 'the elite'. He had taken to consulting this group after his first meeting early in June with the national parliamentarians which proved to be the vital stepping stone to the consensus on parts I and II. He made clear that there could be no further extension of QMV on tax or foreign policy and that a way must be found in the final consensus to satisfy the French and German demands. As a compromise, the elite agreed that the Convention should send a letter to the member states in the IGC to underline how a large majority of Convention members wanted more QMV for tax policy and foreign affairs.

The government representatives also met, for a rather more ill humoured session. There was considerable criticism of the Praesidium for exceeding the Thessaloniki mandate, and of German and French demands for unanimity in their special areas of interest. No German was present. Pascale Andréani arrived late and did not take the floor.

Before tackling the cultural exception, the Praesidium set about meeting the demands of others. This was both necessary and shrewd in view of the widespread impression that the Convention leadership was doing little else but bend over backwards to deal with the problems of France and Germany. The Praesidium took about 30 seconds to decide on a new article, creating official symbols for the Union. This was placed in part IV because there was no way of reopening part I, but with a recommendation that the IGC move it forwards to the 'constitutional' part of the text. The constitutional treaty would thus recognise the Union's flag of twelve golden stars on a blue background, its anthem based on Beethoven's Ode to Joy and the euro as its currency. May 9th, the day in 1950 when Robert Schuman started the process of European integration with his proposal for a European Coal and Steel Community, would henceforth 'be celebrated throughout the Union as Europe day'. The Union would also have as its motto 'United in diversity', the phrase highlighted by Giscard in the preamble to part I.

It agreed to amend article IV-6 [IV-7] to give the European Parliament the right of approval over whether the European Council in future should decide *not* to call a convention to revise the Constitution. This important amendment, on the wish list of national parliamentarians and MEPs, meant in effect that heads of government would never again be able to call an IGC without first having Parliament's approval. By changing references in article IV-2 [IV-3] from European 'Communities' to 'Community' and deleting the first article from the protocol annexed to the Constitution which amends the Euratom Treaty, the Praesidium met the demands of Fischer, Voggenhuber and the environmental lobby and ensured that Euratom retained its own legal personality.

The Praesidium went only part of the way to deal with Brok's worries about the Union foreign minister's planned European diplomatic corps. It added some words to the declaration on the 'European External Action Service' at the end of the Constitution. This now read[2]: 'To assist the future Union Minister for Foreign Affairs, introduced in article 1-27 of the Constitution, to perform his/her duties, the Convention agrees the need *for the Council and the Commission to agree, without prejudice to the rights of the European Parliament*, to establish under the Minister's authority one joint service (European External Action Service) composed of officials from relevant departments of the General Secretariat of the Council of Minister and of the Commission and staff seconded from national Diplomatic Services.' As the declaration also said necessary arrangements for establishing the joint service should be made within a year of the Constitution's entry into force, the Praesidium effectively left the Union's institutions to sort out whether the service should be based in the Commission or the Council at a future date.

The Praesidium also went half way in response to the strong demands of parliamentarians for QMV to apply to article III-5 [III-8] on anti-discrimination legislation. Taking account of a strong wish by Britain to retain the national veto, it decided unanimity should apply in the Council of Ministers for anti-discrimination laws. But they were to be subject in future to the Parliament's consent rather than consultation. Existing legislation already provided that incentive measures in support of anti-discrimination legislation should be decided by QMV. The Praesidium decided the same procedure could also be used to establish basic principles as well.

A further 'half-way-house' solution concerned the open method of coordination. Although adopted with great fanfare at the March 2000 Lisbon European Council for the Union's economic competitiveness programme, this system of benchmarking had been kept out of the constitutional treaty by purists who feared it could undermine the 'Community method' of decision making in the Union. Rather than take the contentious route and draft a special article for the Constitution, the Praesidium decided to allude to the open coordination method without actually naming it in four articles: III-102 [III-107], III-143 [III-148], III-174 [III-179], and III-175 [III-180], dealing with social policy, research, health policy and industrial competitiveness.

Where each article enjoined the Commission to promote the policy in question, the Praesidium, added that its actions should cover 'in particular initiatives aiming at the establishment of guidelines and indicators, the organisation of exchange of best practice, and the preparation of the

---

[2] Additional text in author's italics.

necessary elements for periodic monitoring and evaluation. The European Parliament shall be kept fully informed'. Not for the first time, the Praesidium opted for language that was practical rather than elegant to resolve a problem.

18.4   BACK FROM THE ABYSS

With the 'all must have prizes' phase of the Presidium's deliberations complete, it turned to difficult issue of the cultural exception.

The Praesidium was divided. Although the majority appeared to favour retaining QMV, it was clear Giscard wanted to accommodate France. First soundings showed that Amato supported unanimity with the tactical aim of solving the issue before the IGC. Dehaene, who was absent, was counted as backing France: he had expressed his support and backing the cultural exception was a traditional Belgian policy. Hänsch and Méndez de Vigo were non-committal.

Barnier had been reined in by the college of commissioners and was now counted as favouring QMV. As a Commissioner, the absent Antonio Vitorino could also be counted as a QMV supporter. Alfonso Dastis backed QMV, partly out of displeasure that the Praesidium was making such efforts to appease France and Germany when it had done nothing the previous month to help Spain in its opposition to the double majority system for determining a qualified majority. Earlier in the plenary, Alojz Peterle, the Slovene, had described the existing text with its provisions for QMV in trade policy as 'well balanced and acceptable'.

John Bruton asked for a better definition of the issue. He pointed to article I-3 on the Union's objectives, which stipulated that: 'The Union shall respect its rich cultural and linguistic diversity, and shall ensure that Europe's cultural heritage is safeguarded and enhanced.' Earlier in the plenary session, Bruton drew a distinction between cultural issues and the audio visual industry. The latter, he pointed out, was 'big business'. Did the Convention 'really want to put the Commission in a position where, when it goes to negotiate on a wide range of issues, it cannot do a package deal that includes something on the media?'

Henning Christophersen, the Danish representative, had a different preoccupation – transport. Speaking also on behalf of George Papandreou, Greece's representative who was absent, Christophersen wanted to retain the language of the Treaty of Nice which prescribed the national veto in the area of maritime transport. The Christophersen problem was addressed by insertion of language,[3] obscure even by EU standards into article III-212 on the common commercial policy. The wording linked trade negotiations on maritime transport to the section of part III dealing with transport policy and convinced the Dane that unanimity in maritime transport was secure. With Christophersen satisfied, the dynamic of the meeting changed. He was now prepared to back the French position and could throw the absent Papandreou into the scales on Giscard's side.

But two things happened to sour the atmosphere. Giscard put pressure on Peterle by wondering aloud whether he was entitled to be part of the consensus in the Praesidium. The Laeken declaration specified that the accession countries could take part in the Convention's proceedings in the same way as member states, 'without, however, being able to prevent any consensus which may emerge among the member states'. This condition had been forgotten in the life of the Convention as the enlargement negotiations were completed and the accession country conventionnels came to play a full role in its proceedings. But Giscard, desperate to have a Praesidium decision in his favour, now revived the Laeken condition in an attempt to remove Peterle from the ranks of opponents to the cultural exception. His move backfired. Méndez de Vigo, who was Peterle's mentor in the centre-right EPP, upbraided Giscard for treating Peterle so unkindly and came off the fence to join the supporters of QMV.

The other disturbing moment came when Gisela Stuart decided to tease the French. She asked for the opinion of the Commission and, on hearing it, said she would be against any change away from QMV if that was the Commission's position. Stuart's intervention made Giscard very angry, not least because, against his own convictions, he had always respected the UK's right to resist the Commission's drive to have tax policy determined by majority voting. Giscard, backed by Amato, countered by asking her whether she wanted the opinion of the Commission on QMV for tax matters and whether she would accept this.

A worried Sir John Kerr crept round the table and passed Stuart a pencil written note 'seriously advising' her not to irritate the president any further. Stuart obliged but the impasse remained. Giscard declared the meeting was over and there would be no amendment to solve the problem of the cultural exception.

---

[3] The relevant sentence reads: 'The negotiation and conclusion of international agreements in the field of transport shall be subject to the provisions of section 7 of chapter three of this title and article III-222'.

The Praesidium had failed to agree – leaving the Convention without consensus on an issue which would certainly become a bone of contention in the IGC. But nobody stood-up or made to leave the room. There was a pause. Hänsch broke the silence. 'We have to have a compromise,' he said. Slowly the Praesidium began talking again. It looked again at Bruton's points about cultural diversity. The crisis was over.

Thanks largely to Bruton, the Praesidium devised a compromise that managed both to satisfy the proponents of QMV in trade policy and the backers of the cultural exception. It agreed a text that opened the way for unanimity in the cultural and audio-visual sectors, but narrowly defined its scope thus ensuring QMV should be the general rule. By stating that the Council of Ministers 'shall also act unanimously for the negotiation and conclusion of agreements in the field of trade in cultural and audiovisual services, *where these risk prejudicing the Union's cultural and linguistic diversity*[4]', the text made unanimity a safeguard and shifted the burden of proof to member states to determine if it is warranted.

The success of this formula was illustrated a few days later in the French daily *Le Figaro*, when in separate articles on the same page, Jean-Jacques Aillagon, the French minister for culture, and Pascal Lamy, the trade commissioner, hailed the new accord. During the lengthy discussions on the cultural exception, Lamy had never allowed his French nationality to weaken his support for QMV on trade issues. In *Le Figaro*, Lamy now argued that the new text was a qualitative leap forward for trade policy because the 'logic of initiative and movement' replaced that of 'veto and retreat'.

18.5   THE EXTENSION OF QMV

Despite Amato's valiant efforts to simplify the Union's policy instruments, decision-making procedures remain complex, making it difficult to work out how far the constitutional treaty extends qualified majority voting among the member states in the Council of Ministers. The challenge is enhanced by the absence of any official document setting out the changes clearly.

However, a close examination of the constitutional treaty yields the following facts. It contains 84 legal bases by which Union laws and framework laws are to be decided by ordinary legislative procedure. This process, hitherto known as codecision, entails approval by the European Parliament and by the Council of Ministers with qualified majority voting. The ordinary legislative procedure has been greatly extended from the 34 areas where it has applied hitherto.

---

[4] Author's italics.

But only 25 of the 84 legal bases have come to be categorised as ordinary legislative procedure because of decisions taken in the Convention to move to QMV from unanimity in the Council of Ministers. The increase to 84 from 34 also reflects the creation of new legal bases and the extension of legislative powers over certain acts to the Parliament.

There are, in addition, some 26 Union laws which must be passed by special legislative procedures, of which nine involve majority voting. Of the non-legislative acts of the Union, which the constitutional treaty categorises as regulations and decisions, 17 have to be passed by qualified majority in the Council of Ministers with the Parliament being consulted, and 26 by QMV in Council without consulting Parliament.

There are, in addition, three legal bases in part III where the Council of Ministers decides by a simple majority;[5] five instances under III-201, paragraph 2, where decisions in the area of common foreign and security policy can be taken by QMV; eight instances of administrative decisions where the Council of Ministers decides by QMV[6] and the nomination by QMV of a new European Commission President by the European Council in article 26 of part I.

Altogether there are 153 legal bases in the constitutional treaty where decision making is by QMV or other forms of majority voting in the Council of Ministers and the European Council. By contrast, unanimity is required in 44 legal bases and as a general rule for decisions covering the common foreign and security policy. The 44 legal bases requiring unanimity among the member states comprise 17 legislative acts of the Council of Ministers, 9 non-legislative Council acts and 17 institutional decisions of the Council or the European Council. The Council of Ministers also has to decide unanimously on the taxation rules applying to MEPs under the law of the European Parliament that lays down the statute of members.

18.6 THE SHIP REACHES PORT

The compromise on trade prepared the way for a triumphant end to the Convention. Revised texts of parts III and IV[7] incorporating the Praesidium's amendments were circulated the following morning. But well

---

[5] III-102 and III-111 to set-up advisory committees on employment and social protection and III-249 to decide rules governing committees.

[6] These range from the imposition and lifting of sanctions against member states which are in breach of the Union's values, through the launching of enhanced cooperation operations to nominating members of the Court of Auditors and agreeing lists of members for the Committee of the Regions and the Economic and Social Committee.

[7] CONV 848/03

before that, the conventionnels converged on the plenary hall in a carnival spirit. They had been given small bound versions of the penultimate draft the day before. These became autograph books, as like children at the end of their first summer camp, the Convention members began rushing round seeking signatures from each other.

It was a time to reflect on more than 16 months of hard graft. The conventionnels had met on 26 occasions in plenary sessions covering 52 days. Those in the Praesidium had come to Brussels for 50 separate occasions with an increasingly time consuming schedule in 2003. The conventionnels had made more than 1,800 interventions in the plenary, produced 386 written contributions to the Convention and a further 773 to its working groups and discussion circles. The Praesidium's draft articles generated some 6,000 amendments.

Flanked by two security guards, one of the secretariat staff had earlier carried a cardboard box into the plenary hall. This contained Wui-Kei, the mythical green ceramic Chinese dragon tortoise which Giscard had made the Convention's mascot the summer before, because of its tenacity and perseverance.

Any fears that the frustrations of the previous day would spill over into the final session were finally dispelled after Giscard began to outline the Praesidium's amendments. Shrewdly, he mentioned the symbols first, and was rewarded with applause from across the hall. The stage was set for a re-run of the enthusiastic, congratulatory speeches that marked the consensus on parts I and II a month before.

Hänsch was asked to speak first, on behalf of the European Parliament. Throughout the Convention's sixteen and a half months, Hänsch had always seen the glass as half full rather than half empty. He did not disappoint. 'The European Parliament delegation says yes to this draft treaty for a European Constitution and we say yes not with caveats or reservations but full of conviction and wholeheartedly because we want our draft to be the Constitution of the European Union'. True the draft was made up of compromises, but these did not represent the lowest common denominator. Instead the Constitution, as agreed, was 'a single coherent whole.'

Dini, who had done so much to turn the national parliamentarians into an effective ally of the integrationists, followed with a pointed challenge to Convention members, and especially the government representatives in the hall. They had 'a moral responsibility to support, together with their respective heads of government, the work that we have collectively agreed upon in the Convention.' Bruton spoke next 'as one of the elected representatives of national parliaments in the Praesidium'. That component, representing 550 million people, 'gave an unambiguous welcome to the work we have completed'. The challenge now was 'to go out from here and explain this Constitution to our people; to ensure that our people feel part of our work and part of our achievement.'

Not even Jens-Peter Bonde, the veteran eurosceptic, could break the spell. There were grumbles as Bonde began with the words, 'Mr President, congratulations on the new superstate'. But these turned to laughter, when his final plea 'for referendums alongside the next European elections' was applauded by just one Convention member. 'Well, that was a sort of referendum,' Giscard observed, to yet more laughter.

Twenty speakers later, it was the turn of the vice-presidents to take the floor. For Giuliano Amato, the Convention had reunified Europe. It had achieved far more than an IGC. In an IGC, a 'no' was a 'sovereign no' and there was no need for the government representative to explain. The Convention, by being transparent, forced anyone saying no to engage in democratic debate. That in turn produced results.

Jean-Luc Dehaene recalled how many had considered the Convention a 'mission impossible' at the time of the Laeken summit. It was now 'mission accomplished'. As advisers to the Belgian prime minister ahead of Laeken, both he and Amato had fretted over whether they should use the word 'constitution' for fear that it was too provocative. Now, 18 months later, people could speak about a 'European Constitution, as the most normal thing in the world'. Switching from Dutch to French, Dehaene predicted that the Convention would soon be seen as a decisive step for Europe. He then turned to Giscard without whose personality 'this Convention would not have been what it was'. Giscard, he said, had presided with authority but without being authoritarian. He had listened and created the consensus. He called on the president to become the defender of the Convention's decisions vis-à-vis the Union's heads of state and government.

It was Giscard's turn to speak. Balancing his microphone precariously on a pile of EU Treaties, he turned to the polyglot and heterogeneous crew before him: 'I am proud to have been your president and to have piloted our vessel, sometimes through the mists, sometimes through the cold and sometimes through the waves. But the important thing is our ship has reached port.' Their voyage had been a journey into the unknown. Now their vessel would embark on a second journey; one less perilous, but not without risk, into the IGC. It was the duty of all conventionnels to watch over its journey and ensure that the Constitution remained as intact as possible.

The Constitution was coherent and without options, Giscard said. It was the product of trade offs between frequently contradictory demands: between federalist and non-federalist, between more and less populated member states, between richer and poorer and between the different institutions. The Convention had succeeded because its members had accepted that their preferred solutions were not always acceptable to others. The result was a consensus that was not just an overall consensus, but one that was balanced in its details. 'Anyone wanting to change this Constitution and the balance achieved could risk distorting, even dismembering our work. In that case, public opinion, and one day perhaps historians would say a fantastic opportunity had been lost.'

Giscard switched into English, 'a language all can understand', to give his valedictory thanks to the Convention members and to Amato and Dehaene, Sir John Kerr and Annalisa Giannella, Kerr's deputy in the secretariat. 'We have succeeded because we have learned from each other,' he said. 'I have learned from all of you, at an age that is normally not propitious for learning'. Admitting to a 'touch of melancholy', Giscard added: 'In one's life, if one is lucky, one is permitted once or twice to make a difference, to touch the hem of history. Together we have had that chance. Together we have taken that chance. We should all be proud of that.'

In a final gesture for the cameras, Giscard pretended to feed some lettuce leaves to Wui Kei, his mascot. He invited the Convention members to sign the document which would be handed over with the Constitution to Italy's President Ciampi and Prime Minister Silvio Berlusconi in Rome the following week. The Convention was over. The Constitution was now the responsibility of the Italian presidency and the intergovernmental conference.

CHAPTER 19
Evaluation and Conclusions

19.1 THE ACCIDENTAL CONSTITUTION

The Convention was a tale of the unexpected until the very end. The 'cliffhanger' in the Praesidium late on 9 July was just the last of many events which could have ended differently – and in failure.

The draft constitutional treaty that was handed to the Italian presidency on 18 July 2003 was certainly not preordained. The Laeken declaration envisaged a final document of more modest ambitions 'which may comprise either different options, indicating the degree of support which they received, or recommendations if consensus is achieved.' The Convention's first big surprise came in the opening ceremony, when Giscard announced that his goal was 'broad consensus on a single proposal' for a 'constitutional treaty for Europe'.

There was also nothing inevitable about the Convention's other key turning points. Work on the first 'skeleton' draft of the constitutional treaty began because of pressure from impatient rank and file members of the Convention, led by an alternate, Maria Berger. The inclination of Sir John Kerr was to leave such drafting until early in 2003, by which time the Commission's 'Penelope' document would have shaped discussions. Even after the 2002 summer break, it was unclear whether the Convention would result in a written constitution, a constitutional treaty, a series of treaty amendments or just recommendations.

There was nothing predestined in the autumn 2002 'invasion of the foreign ministers': the event which changed the dynamics of the Convention, making clear its importance to the outside world, although, to the surprise of many, not quite turning it into an IGC. Would Joschka Fischer of Germany and Dominique de Villepin of France have joined the Convention in the late autumn of 2002, had not Britain – of all countries – taken the Convention seriously from the beginning and posted Peter Hain, an assiduous lobbyist in his own right and backed by hard working team of advisers, to be its conventionnel?

The January 2003 Franco-German paper on institutional reform, in which Germany accepted a stable president for the European Council in return for

France backing a Commission president elected by the European Parliament still has the air of a crude trade-off. This was not the preferred solution of Joschka Fischer, Germany's representative in the Convention and foreign minister of the Union's biggest country. In terms of status, intellectual capacity and charisma, Fischer ranked among the real heavy hitters of the Convention. His own thoughts were moving in the direction of a joint presidency of the Commission and European Council. Only a few weeks before, Dominique de Villepin was voicing doubts about the double-hatted foreign minister. But the deal was done at a higher level than foreign ministers by Jacques Chirac and Gerhard Schröder, with the German chancellor, not for the first time, deferring to the president of France.

The paper was important for several reasons. It determined the structure of all subsequent debate on the institutional issue, even providing the base for Giscard's far more radical ideas at the end of April 2003. Its proposal for a stable presidency of the European Council provided common ground for the big countries, otherwise divided by Iraq, won support from Sweden and Denmark among the smaller nations, and even had some appeal for the Belgian government. Although most small and medium sized countries continued to press for a rotating presidency, the focus of the debate began to shift towards the future composition of the Commission which was an issue where federalists and small country representatives were not necessarily in agreement. For many federalists, a small Commission meant a strong Commission, while a Commission comprising one member per member state risked being a weak executive.

Interestingly, the Franco-German institutional reform paper was the last joint submission to the Convention from Paris and Berlin. It marked the high-water mark of Franco-German cooperation in the Convention. The foreign ministers were to be preoccupied in 2003 with another unpredictable event – war in Iraq.

Giscard's proposals for the Union's institutions, which he had leaked to the press in the late afternoon of 22 April just as he was unveiling them to the Praesidium were another unexpected turning point. It looked for all the world as if he was attempting to set up a *directoire* of the big member states to run the Union. These proposals provoked immense shock and anger in the Praesidium and among the integrationist Convention members from the European Parliament and the smaller member states. The conventionnels fumed in the plenary session as Giscard outlined the modified version of his ideas approved by the Praesidium. Yet the Convention did not break apart. Instead, Giscard's proposals acted as a kind of catharsis, paving the way for compromises between integrationists and intergovernmentalists.

Although Giscard's proposals survived in their extreme form for only a day, enough remained after the Praesidium meeting of 23 April to put the Convention on a new course over the two months to the Thessaloniki summit. Most significant was his idea that a 'double' majority – as defined as a simple majority of member states and three-fifths of the Union population – should determine a qualified majority in the Council of Ministers. Armed with hindsight and an Internet search engine it is possible to find published comments from Giscard that indicated a strong desire to overturn the Nice institutional settlement. But when he made his move, it was completely unexpected and transformed the Convention's dynamics.

A late breaking, wholly unexpected turning point was the alliance at the beginning of June 2003 between the integration-minded national parliamentarians and the members of the European Parliament that gave Giscard the opportunity to reach and determine consensus on the draft constitution. The general expectation was that the Convention would become an intergovernmental conference in its final weeks with the parliamentarians marginalized. If that had happened, the outcome would probably have been failure because Spain, driven by its opposition to revising the Nice Treaty, had immobilised the Praesidium and forged its alliance of convenience with the 16 small Convention states. Giscard was not bluffing when he talked at the end of May of possibly having to go to the European Council in Thessaloniki and admit 'there was stalemate in the Convention.'

Again, with hindsight, it is possible to trace stirrings among the national parliamentarians that indicated an integrationist inclination among some and dislike of being cast as the Convention's wall flowers among others. In some parliamentarians, like Italy's Lamberto Dini and the Netherlands' René van der Linden, these characteristics fused and became a motor for action. At the same time, the MEPs had realised how the draft part III, published in the last week of May, greatly increased their power through its extension of codecision, now renamed the ordinary legislative procedure. They now had a big vested interest in the Convention's success.

The Convention provided the infrastructure for the activists to come together – through the groups of the big political families (the centre-right European People's Party, the Party of European Socialists and the European Liberal Democrats) and informal cross cutting dining clubs of movers and shakers which enabled ideas to flow, policies to crystallise and consensus to form. But these developments had to be exploited and the divided Praesidium circumvented.

Here Giscard and his two deputies – Jean-Luc Dehaene and Giuliano Amato – came into their own, fanning out among the various component groups and finding the grounds for consensus. The cohesion of the triumvirate was not self-evident. The three men had been uneasy colleagues at the start, because Guy Verhofstadt, the Belgian prime minister and host of the Laeken summit, let slip that he wanted the two deputies to constrain Giscard. The appointment of the two was a pure serendipity, dreamed up at the last minute in the Laeken summit after Verhofstadt saw his hopes of frustrating Giscard's appointment as the Convention president dashed. It was a chance decision that contributed greatly to the outcome of the Convention.

To a greater or less extent, these events came out of the blue and helped form the final result. They help explain why the Convention was able to produce its 'accidental constitution'.

Other factors should not be ignored in working out quite why the Convention produced the result that it did. Non-events also play an important part in shaping history. One of the most important – and a rather sad tale – was the failure of the Commission to play a leading role in the Convention as it moved towards a conclusion. Indeed, the Commission, which at the start of the Convention was the standard bearer of small countries and integrationists alike, managed to marginalize itself after its public relations disaster with the Penelope document in December 2002. The confusion thus created split the Commission and left its two commissioners in the Convention looking both foolish and unsupported. At the end of April, Romano Prodi, the Commission president, went on to compound the error over 'Penelope' by backing the small country, pro-Nice camp which was calling for one commissioner per member state, just before the solidarity of this group began to fracture. When the Benelux countries deserted the cause, and the other smalls acquiesced, however reluctantly, in the final settlement, the Commission was left pinning its hopes on the IGC that would follow to undo the Convention's articles on the institutions.

By spring 2003, Giscard and the Convention's secretariat had established a virtual monopoly over the power of proposal. The Commission's last document to the Convention was in December 2002. The last big effort of the Franco-German partnership to shape ideas was the institutional paper of January 2003. The original six founding member states were in close contact and appeared close at times to agreeing a joint position. It never came. The Benelux countries, traditionally a ready source of compromise proposals in EU negotiations, lost momentum, in part because of the changes of government in the Netherlands and partly because Belgium did not share Luxembourg's deep distaste for the long-term European Council president.

Another important non-event was the UK decision, made known during May, to work for a single text rather than options. This decision stopped the efforts to create a bandwagon in support of several options. France too contributed significantly to the eventual success of the Convention by quietly dropping its previous insistence on having equal voting rights with Germany in the Council of Ministers. This had been one of the underlying factors behind the difficulties of the Nice negotiation. France's change of heart, which has to be seen in the context of the two countries drawing closer to protect their interests in a union of 25, meant that the double majority idea had a chance of broad acceptance.

The unexpected is a necessary, but not sufficient, explanation for how the Convention was able to reach the conclusion it did. The Convention was also the story of the people in it and how they came to work together. Giscard, as the plaudits during Convention's final sessions in June and July recognised, deserves much credit for steering the Convention to agreement on a single text.

He did not start with a blue print for the constitutional treaty. But he certainly had a compass for the Convention. He was able to exploit developments, because he had very clear ideas on a number of issues. These included:

- The importance of the European Council and its perceived need for a stable president;
- The need to reshape the Commission, to break the Nice formula of one commissioner per member state in favour of a smaller, collegiate model which in his view would be more effective;
- The need for the Union to adapt more radically to the complex challenges of enlargement than simply relying on the arrangements reached at the Nice European Council;
- The need to simplify the treaties and procedures to increase efficiency and legitimacy;
- The need to decide in the Convention by consensus which Giscard defined.

In steering towards a result, Giscard could count on:

- A flexible hard working secretariat (which was better organised than the Praesidium);
- A concentration in his office of information from all key sources, including the fruits of his bi-lateral diplomacy;
- A well honed personal perspective of what could be achieved, for example, realising the limits to qualified majority voting in the foreign policy area;

- An ultimately pragmatic approach, highlighted by his willingness to junk pet ideas, such as the Congress of MEPS and national parliamentarians;
- Personal authority, so that he was never really challenged by the 'conventionnels';
- A keen sense of timing.

Criticised when appointed as being too old to take the EU into the 21st century, Giscard proved a skilful president during the Convention's 16 months. It became apparent in the Convention's earliest days that Giscard could exercise extraordinary authority. He knew a vast amount about the subject. His experience of the EU stretched back further than any one else in the room. And he had his own sources of information, through contacts with EU leaders in national capitals.

Many would be the conventionnels who complained in corridors and bars about his arrogance, his habit of talking to aides when one or another representative from a small country was speaking and his favouring the bigger member states. But only Johannes Voggenhuber pursued a policy of deliberately needling him in the plenary sessions. Although the Austrian Green was admired for his audacity, he was never able to marshal a revolt against Giscard.

Giscard was fortunate to be able to count on the support of Dehaene, Amato and Kerr. All were very different characters but they emerged as a powerful team, especially in the final weeks of hectic negotiations. By contrast, Giscard never felt really comfortable with the Praesidium. It was not representative of the Convention as a whole. Quite often he would leave its meetings – a ruse that enabled him later to ignore decisions taken in his absence. He felt no qualms about circumventing the Praesidium, as when he drew up his original institutional proposals in April or in the first week of June when he sought out the component parts of the Convention.

Spain's Dastis and his allies representing the 16 small and medium sized countries were outflanked once Giscard and his aides perceived an opportunity to garner support from the national parliamentarians and MEPs. Giscard's new alliance enabled him to snatch victory from looming disaster. The decision to seek out the parliamentarians was based on inside knowledge of the mood in the component groups. Giscard's staff knew that the national parliamentarians, for example, were dissatisfied with their representatives in the Praesidium.

The big political families (and especially the well organised centre-right European Peoples' Party and centrist Liberals) were crucial in the

Convention's final weeks. They provided bridges between MEPs and national parliamentarians. The party frameworks fostered links that became quite close – such as those between Dini and Duff in the Liberal group.

All the leaders of the political families (the EPP's Brok, the Liberals' Duff and the Socialists' Amato) wanted the Convention to be a success. Brok and Duff were passionate integrationists to boot. All three had reached out increasingly to the national parliamentarians in the process of gathering support for amendments to the draft articles produced by the Praesidium since February. From there it was a short step to using the political families as a conduit for transferring know-how and back-up resources from the well organised and well endowed European parliamentarians to their like-minded but less well resourced colleagues from national capitals.

A large number of individual conventionnels constituted the countervailing forces which moulded the eventual consensus. Some, like Andrew Duff, Lamberto Dini, Alain Lamassoure, Peter Hain, and Antonio Vitorino, were active both inside and outside the plenary hall. Others, such as Elmar Brok, Inigo Méndez de Vigo and Joschka Fischer, were more active behind the scenes. Still others, such as Anne Van Lancker, John Bruton and Michel Barnier made their marks in the working groups. Accession country representatives, such as Estonia's Henrik Hololei and Poland's Danuta Hübner, were increasingly prominent as the Convention progressed.

Some conventionnels were driven by idealism. Some by the feeling that to accept failure would be poor recompense for sixteen and a half months of travelling back and forth to Brussels. For those conventionnels of the accession countries who can now look forward to advancing their careers as officials of members of the Union, it was obviously better to have membership of a successful Convention on their resumes.

Even the eurosceptics could not resist associating themselves with the Convention at its close. Four eurosceptic Convention members and four alternates, headed by Jens-Peter Bonde[1], produced a minority report proposing a 'Europe of Democracies' which was forwarded by Giscard to the Italian presidency[2] with the completed constitutional treaty. The minority report rejected the draft constitutional text on the grounds that it failed to meet the requirements of the Laeken mandate for greater democratic

---

[1] In addition to Bonde, the following signed the minority report: William Abitbol MEP (alternate); Per Dalgaard, Danish Parliament (alternate); John Gormley, Irish Parliament (alternate); David Heathcoat-Amory, UK Parliament (member); Esko Seppanen MEP (alternate); Peter Skaarup, Danish Parliament (member); Jan Zahradil, Czech Parliament (member).

[2] Annex III CONV 851/03.

legitimacy in the Union. But, when on the final day in July, the conventionnels were signing the text at the front of the plenary hall, the eurosceptics were placed in a dilemma. Should they sign, and be accused of betraying their position, or not sign, and be forgotten by history? Lord Stockton, a British Conservative MEP who was not one of the minority report signatories, offered a way out of the dilemma: 'I signed the document but didn't sign up to it,' he said. In the end, Bonde and his associates took a deep breath and signed, placing the words 'minority report' in brackets after their names.

Even the eurosceptics had come to the conclusion that it was better to be remembered among the 'founding fathers'.

19.2   THE CONSTITUTIONAL TREATY

But a father to what? The general consensus is that the Convention produced what Giscard called for on that last day of February 2002: a constitutional treaty. Giuliano Amato was in no doubts. Asked just after the 13 June agreement on part I, whether he was proud of his 'baby', Amato replied: 'Yes. I am proud. But I wanted a girl, and we have given birth to a boy'. As he elaborated in an article for *Il Sole 24 Ore*, 'constitution' in Italian is a feminine noun while 'treaty' is masculine.

The result of the Convention's sixteen and a half months of work was a draft, no more. The final constitutional text will depend on how negotiations develop in the intergovernmental conference of 25 new and old member states that has followed. The process of ratification by 25 member states and implementation lies in the future and is hedged with uncertainty. Given that the Convention's work took place in volatile circumstances that became ever more frantic as its two deadlines loomed in June and July 2003, the final text is more than creditable. However, as Giscard acknowledged on 13 June, it is not perfect. Some parts of the constitutional treaty are better than others.

The draft, as finally handed over to the Italian presidency on 18 July[3], marks a huge advance on the existing jumble of treaties. Admittedly, the quality of language could be improved[4] and it is doubtful whether it will appeal, as Giscard has hoped, to the average intelligent secondary school pupil. But it is a text with a beginning, a middle and an end that an ordinary mortal can follow and that result far outshines anything produced by the two most

---

[3] CONV 850/03.
[4] Notwithstanding Giscard's decision to have the Académie Francaise vet the language of the French version.

recent intergovernmental conferences that culminated in the treaties of Amsterdam and Nice.

This is particularly true of the way the text meets in full the mandate laid down in the Nice declaration on the future of the Union. It delivers a clearer definition of who does what, that will make the Union more accountable to its citizens and parliaments and governments in member states. The political approach towards policing subsidiarity offers hope that the idea of taking decisions as close to the citizen as possible will, more than a decade after first being written into the Treaty on Union, at last be taken seriously. The article and protocol on subsidiarity also promise to involve national parliaments constructively in the Union's affairs, which was part of the Nice mandate. Nothing should stand in the way of incorporating the Charter of Fundamental Rights in the treaty, thus providing Europe's citizens with a bill of rights which is necessarily hedged to take account of the laws and practices of the member states as well as those of the Union.

The Convention and the text have done an important service by making clear how much a role the Union now plays in the lives of Europeans. The primacy of Union law has been a fact of life for decades but was never written down in any treaty. Thanks to article 10 it is clearer what sort of Union the member states have joined and helped create. Similarly, the implications for member states of competences shared with the Union are now clear. The discovery in article 11, that 'the member states shall exercise their competence to the extent that the Union has not exercised, or has decided to cease exercising, its competence', may, on reflection, be a statement of the obvious. But for those beyond the Brussels beltway the reach of Union power has the capacity to surprise, if not shock, when on the printed page.

Such clarity is welcome. It promises, in the words of the Nice declaration, to improve 'the democratic legitimacy and transparency of the Union and its institutions' and, to cite the rest of that passage, may even 'bring them closer to the citizens of the member states.' But the Convention's mixed record on getting its message across shows there is still much to do.

Although it operated more transparently than any IGC, the Convention failed to generate the public interest that its organisers hoped. True, its website had an average of 47,000 visits a month, rising to 100,000 in June 2003. But a Eurobarometer poll[5] of 25,000 citizens in the 25 member and accession countries just after the June Thessaloniki summit found that only 45 per cent had heard of the Convention. Only in 10 countries were at least half of those

---

[5] Flash Eurobarometer 142, EOS Gallup Europe.

polled aware of the Convention. The ratings ranged from 81 per cent in Greece, where awareness of the EU was heightened by Greece's six-month presidency, to just 25 per cent in the UK. The situation was no better in the accession countries, even though the Convention could fairly claim to be the first institution of united Europe. Only in Cyprus did more than half the respondents know about its existence: for 57 per cent of Europe's new citizens the constitutional treaty remains a closed book.

Also striking was the lack of interest shown by business in the Convention. True, Giscard had a couple of meetings with the European Round Table of Industrialists, a conversation with Josef Ackermann of Deutsche Bank and addressed the secretive Bilderberg Conference at its meeting in Versailles in May 2003. But whereas churches, wildlife organisations and social NGOs actively lobbied the Convention, there was little sign of business interests hovering around the plenary hall. Meanwhile, Unice, the employers' group with lowly observer status, was in a weak position to counter the vigorous cohort of conventionnels constantly pressing for more 'Social Europe'. The failure of business to connect with the constitutional debate would have been inconceivable in the US. It was doubly surprising given the controversy that surrounds the European 'social model' and the debate over whether its spread is damaging economic growth and job creation.

If the Convention and the draft constitutional treaty are to mark the start of a new relationship between the Union and its citizens, the Union's many actors must rise to the challenge and explain and justify what they are about. This applies especially to the Brussels institutions but also to the member states. The European Parliament faces an early test. It is the main beneficiary of the constitutional proposals among the Union's three main institutions. As in all recent reforms of the Union's treaties, its role in legislating with the Council of Ministers will be considerably enhanced. If, in the 2004 European elections, the Parliament sees a further decline in the voter participation rate from the 49 per cent of 1999 the member states will be justified in asking whether its growth in power is really helping to plug the gap between ruler and ruled.

On the other hand, the Union's member governments cannot neglect their own past conduct. How often has an unpopular policy in the past been blamed on 'Brussels' without any acknowledgement that the country in question has approved and often willed it? The clarity provided by the constitutional treaty should curb such tricks.

The constitutional treaty places new and welcome responsibilities on national parliaments, giving them opportunities to play a role in the life of the Union that go beyond the policing of subsidiarity. Two articles in the draft promise to put national parliaments on their mettle because they have the potential to shift responsibilities from the member states to the Union. These are article 17, the so-called flexibility clause, by which the Council of Ministers acting unanimously can take action not specified in the constitutional treaty. The other is article 24 paragraph 4, the generalised bridging or *passerelle* clause, by which the member states' leaders in the European Council can decide by unanimity to remove the national veto from areas of legislation in part III of the constitutional treaty so that they can be decided by qualified majority voting. In both cases, the national parliaments must be informed, giving them an opportunity to influence the decisions of their own governments.

Such checks and balances will only work, however, if national parliaments pay heed to what is happening at the European Union level. Too often scrutiny of Union affairs is in the hands of experts making up specialist committees. If the constitutional treaty is to deliver on its promise of securing progress for Europe's citizens there must be deeper understanding and more discussion of the Union and its impact in national and regional legislatures.

Some specific elements of the constitutional treaty should help promote a more informed debate about the Union in its member states. Although the text produced by the Convention merits only a middle grade for jargon busting, the efforts of Giuliano Amato and his two working groups are certain to result in the demise of the Union's confusing pillar structure and provide the Union with a legal personality. They have re-christened and rationalised the various acts by which the Union legislates. These steps, although seemingly remote from the preoccupations of every day life, should, over time, clear away much of the mystery and confusion surrounding 'Brussels' for the ordinary citizen.

Other gains in this area include opening the Council of Ministers to public scrutiny when legislating. The commitments to dialogue and transparency in the new section of the treaty dealing with the democratic life of the Union offer hope of more openness although there is clearly scope for more.

More directly, the Convention means that each national parliament in the existing member states will now have four members who know more about the European Union than any of their peers. Similarly, the Convention has provided a crash course in EU politics and institutions to no fewer than 78 Convention members and alternates from the 13 accession and applicant countries as well as their legions of staff. The pedagogic impact of the Convention may eventually prove as important as its protocols on national parliaments and subsidiarity in promoting a European *demos*.

Also important for connecting with the citizen will be practical results in policy areas where the Union gains more responsibility. The consensus reached on making it easier for the Union, with the member states, to deal with asylum, immigration and cross-border organised crime should, once transposed into law, lead to easily comprehensible benefits for Europe's citizens.

Whether provisions for stepping up cooperation on foreign and defence policy with the support of a Union foreign minister have a rapid impact on the general public or world affairs is more moot. Although public opinion polls suggest a more active Union role in these areas would be welcomed, the constitutional treaty sets out to facilitate rather than act. Common foreign and defence policies will only play a bigger role when there is sufficient political will. The divisions over Iraq showed how difficult it can be to generate a common political will among 25 member states.

The willingness to embrace more qualified majority voting was what distinguished the Convention's approach to the justice and home affairs agenda from that on common foreign and defence policies, where unanimity remains the rule.

The European Commission has complained that the constitutional treaty's extension of qualified majority voting is too timid to cope with the management challenges of a Union expanded to 25 from 15 member states. Giscard's final report[6] to the Italian presidency pointed out that some Convention members, while joining the broad consensus on the constitutional treaty, would have preferred more qualified majority voting. One of these was Giscard himself. Asked after the final July session whether he had any frustrations, he admitted that he favoured more ready access to QMV for measures against tax fraud where these would aid the single market. However, he did not press the issue because further progress would be sure to be blocked by the UK, Ireland and Sweden.

At first sight the extension of QMV in the constitutional treaty appears limited. The 25 legal bases, which move from unanimity to QMV under the ordinary legislative procedure, compare with 31 areas which moved to QMV in the Treaty of Nice. The previous treaties of Amsterdam, Maastricht and the Single European Act of 1997, 1992 and 1986 extended QMV respectively to 16, 30 and 12 new and existing policy areas.

But if the constitutional treaty's provisions are implemented, QMV or other forms of majority voting will apply to 153 legal bases altogether, compared

[6] CONV 851/03.

with 44 where decisions must be taken unanimously. In addition, the draft includes bridging or *passerelle*[7] clauses by which decisions can move from unanimity to QMV, albeit under the difficult condition that all member states can agree.

Inside the Brussels beltway, qualified majority voting may appear essential for reasons of efficiency in an enlarged Union. But it can look very different from outside Brussels. Every past extension of qualified majority voting makes the next move to QMV more difficult as legislators come closer to core issues of sovereignty. Joschka Fischer's insistence in the final days of the Convention on national government controls over third country nationals entering the labour market showed how even an enthusiastic federalist had to trim his sails to match domestic political realities. QMV can also have its downsides. It can result in compromises that are so far removed from their original goal as to be wrongheaded and damaging. Some recent directives in the financial services sector have actually reduced rather than increased the openness of the market[8].

In the circumstances, the insertion at the beginning of June of a general *passerelle* clause in article 24, by which the European Council can decide 'on its own initiative and by unanimity' to apply qualified majority voting to policies in part III currently subject to the national veto, may offer an interesting way forward. Although criticised by integrationists as likely to remain inoperable in a Union of 25, it marks a major relaxation of existing rules which require an IGC and ratification in each member states to shift to QMV from unanimity.

Obtaining unanimous agreement to unlock the *passerelle* may be difficult. But it is not inconceivable, given the peculiar chemistry among the leaders who make up the European Council. The Union has a way of adjusting to big issues over time: see, for example, how justice and home affairs are being 'communitarised' whereas ten years such developments would have appeared inconceivable. Who is to say that in 10 or 20 years time – which, *pace* the impatience of integrationists, is a short period of time in the life of nations or a continent – such shifts will not have taken place on matters of foreign policy or tax.

Although the Convention was a broadly integrationist body, it had to reflect and operate in a political environment where integration is not notably

---

[7] Article 24.4, the general *passerelle*; 39.8 and III-201.3 for CFSP measures; III-328 for enhanced cooperation; and the restricted *passerelles* III-62 and III-63 for administrative cooperation measures to combat tax evasion and tax fraud.

[8] For example, the prospectuses directive.

popular. Sweden's September 2003 vote against euro membership was a reminder of this. But within these constraints, the constitutional treaty has provided mechanisms that should enable countries that want to integrate to forge ahead.

After two false starts at Amsterdam and Nice, the Convention may have devised rules for enhanced cooperation that should encourage groups of countries to adopt this 'last resort' mechanism for working together in the furtherance of their own objectives in line with the rules of the Union. The separate rules for enhanced cooperation in the defence sphere may also prove acceptable in the light of the apparent softening, before the IGC and during its early weeks, of UK opposition to the plans of Germany, France, Belgium and Luxembourg for a European military planning capability. Such compromises will be more necessary after the Union's enlargement. They add substance of a sort to the motto of the constitutional treaty: 'United in diversity'.

By contrast, attempts to loosen the procedures for future amendment of the constitutional treaty came to nought. Amato, Duff and Brok had sought on behalf of their party groups to ease amendment procedures for those parts of part III, which do not involve a shift of competences of the Union and member states. The three argued that changes in these areas should be agreed by a five-sixths majority of member states in an IGC instead of by unanimity[9] to avoid gridlock in an enlarged Union. This issue was discussed in June, but time, and the Convention's mandate for changing articles in part IV, ran out with the European Council in Thessaloniki.

The situation was unclear until the very end of the Convention, however. In the plenary session of 9 July, Lord Maclennan of Rogart, the British Liberal Democrat representative of the UK upper house, asked after the fate of the amendment. Amato repeated that he agreed with the initiative but added in a resigned manner that the Convention had no mandate for part IV. The reference to the issue of constitutional amendment in the report sent by the Praesidium to the Italian presidency was correspondingly deadpan. It noted simply that some Convention members would have preferred the procedures for future amendment to go further than the overall consensus.

At the 18 July handover, Giscard praised the draft as a 'finished product with no loose ends to be tied up, no options left open'. This was not strictly true. While there are no options left open, there are some loose ends that should be tidied up.

---

[9] See Chapter 6.1 and CONV833/03.

The Praesidium's report to the Italian presidency drew attention to a very strong demand for greater transparency in the way the Union operates. This followed a campaign by Jens-Peter Bonde which attracted signatures from around 90 per cent of Convention members for an automatic presumption of public right of access to documents.[10]

Some other issues were purely technical, such as the protocols that will need to be reviewed or written to secure legal continuity for the previous acts of the European Community and Union if and when the constitutional treaty enters into force. The 11th hour compromise in July also meant the eventual fate of the Euratom Treaty was left to the member states. But overall, the Convention's achievements, measured against the agenda of the Nice declaration, were impressive. It is less easy to be so positive about the institutional provisions that emerged from the final, fevered fortnight of negotiation in June.

At the 18 July ceremony,[11] Giscard extolled the constitutional treaty for providing Europe 'with stable, democratic and effective institutions'. All three sides of the institutional triangle stood to gain. The European Parliament became 'the Union's main legislature'. The Council would 'have a face and a measure of durability' with a European Council president who 'will organise states' work and will be able to plan for the future and think ahead'. The Commission 'organised so as to fulfil its European role' would 'act as a driving force and the main executive' and 'embody the common European interest'.

The constitutional treaty does indeed promise to strengthen the European Parliament's power and influence considerably. In Thessaloniki,[12] Giscard mentioned that codecision, or the ordinary legislative procedure, would be extended to more than 80 areas of legislation. But do the Convention's results strengthen the other sides of the triangle? For Giscard, the stable presidency of the European Council, the slimmed down Commission and the Union foreign minister counted as significant improvements. The first two achievements were among the first aims that he disclosed after being appointed Convention president.

The European Council chair or president, on which the big member states expended so much political capital, is meant to chair and drive forward the work of the European Council and 'ensure its proper preparation and continuity'. But with the job's scope restricted by successive waves of

---

[10] CONV 830/03.
[11] 'The Rome Declaration', 18 July 2003.
[12] Giscard's oral report to the European Council in Thessaloniki, 20 June 2003.

amendments, how will he or she interact with the other Council formations to ensure that in future an important policy is not neglected as was the case with the decisions on justice and home affairs, agreed at the Tampere European Council in autumn 1999? The only direct control the European Council will have over other Councils will be in being able to decide on their formation and setting the rules of 'equal rotation' of their presidencies 'taking into account European political and geographical balance and the diversity of member states'.

Convention staffers accept there is a lack of linkage between the European Council chair and other Councils, but have argued this will not matter over time. The inescapable conclusion is that the personal qualities of the individual elected by a qualified majority of the members of the European Council will be crucial. Yet the European Council has a mixed record in choosing senior officials for the Union. All can agree that Javier Solana has been a success as EU secretary general and high representative for the common foreign and security policy. But how many would make the same claim for recent choices for the post of Commission president?

There is also a question mark over how the president of the European Council will interact with the president of the Commission. 'I have defended the two headed Europe,' Amato remarked on the day the Convention ended. 'But no animal can live with two heads for too long'. In Amato's view the Union must come at some time to having a joint president of the Commission and the European Council. Amato, like Duff and Dini, would have liked the Constitution to give a target date for a single European president. It was not to be.

Given human nature and institutional jealousies, there is a risk that the president of the European Council, the Commission president and the European Foreign Minister will become involved in demarcation disputes and turf wars, which will do nothing to enhance the Union's standing abroad. The double-hatted foreign minister, with a foot in both the Council and the Commission, may have to resolve conflicts within him or herself. Assuming the proposal for the foreign minister goes ahead, an early test of institutional harmony will be the establishment of the joint 'European external action service', which the Convention suggested should be set up within a year of the entry into force of the constitutional treaty from a combustible mix of officials from the general Secretariat of the Council, the Commission and national diplomatic services.

The provisions for a two tier Commission from 1 November 2009 are also problematic, and Giscard admitted as much at Thessaloniki. One particular difficulty derives from the principle of 'equal rotation', inserted in the final round of negotiations at the insistence of the 16 small to medium sized countries. Giscard wanted to return to the original idea of the Commission as a 'high level college with limited membership responsible for defining and proposing the common European good'. The Convention therefore opted for a college of 15, including the president and foreign minister.

But it also had to satisfy demands for all member states to be represented on equal terms. These will be met until 1 November 2009 by keeping to the Nice formula of one member per member state. Thereafter, equal rotation must be made to work with a college of 15, supplemented by non-voting Commissioners. Article 25 gives the European Council the responsibility for solving this predicament before 1 November 2009 on the basis of two principles:

(a) Member states shall be treated on a strictly equal footing as regards determination of the sequence of, and the time spent by, their nationals as members of the college; consequently, the difference between the total number of terms of office held by nationals of any given pair of member states may never be more than one;

(b) subject to point (a), each successive college shall be so composed as to reflect satisfactorily the demographic and geographical range of all the member states of the Union.

The conditions thus described sit ill with the Convention's aim of simplifying the Union's system of government. But it is barely conceivable that they will ever be applied because opposition among the small and medium sized member states to the Convention settlement on the Commission has increased sharply since the Thessaloniki summit.

Although fine in theory, equal rotation also means that a big country such as Germany, France, Britain, Italy, Spain or Poland could find it is without a voting commissioner for a period of five years. How would the affected country respond, say, to the Commission fining one of its leading companies over a competition case or imposing a fine for an illegal state aid? The risk, as Giscard has acknowledged, would be a college whose legitimacy 'would be challenged, which would weaken the Commission's moral authority accordingly.' There is no easy way out of this dilemma short of scrapping the Convention's recommendation and putting something else in its place. This is certainly what Romano Prodi, the Commission president, and some of the small countries which agreed to be part of the Convention's consensus in June want from the IGC. To judge from the IGC's first weeks it looks as if their wish will be granted.

There are further infelicities in the proposed arrangements for the Council of Ministers. The combined Legislative and General Affairs Council was a botched compromise that satisfied no one. By combining legislative and executive functions it ran counter to one of the Convention's main objectives: simplification. It was unloved even among Convention staffers. Calling it an 'absurd' construction which ran counter to the theory of the separation of powers, one observed: 'Montesquieu must be spinning in his grave'. The proposed Legislative Council had already prompted a surge of well organised protests from sectoral ministries in many member states. Amato admitted, just hours after the end of the Convention, that the Praesidium had made a 'terrible mistake' in merging the General Affairs Council with the Legislative Council. Amato, who prided himself on being the inventor of the Legislative Council, described it as 'the walking dead', having been 'already sentenced to death by a large majority of national governments'. That sentence was formally delivered when the Union's foreign ministers met for the first working session of the IGC in Rome on 4 October. The only outstanding questions are when the axe will fall on the Legislative Council and what will replace it.

A question mark also hangs over Giscard's main achievement during the first fortnight of June of securing measurement of a qualified majority vote in the Council of Ministers by means of the double majority. This was the issue on which the Praesidium split in May and where Spain and Poland have resolved to restore the system agreed at the December 2000 Nice summit. While the concept of a majority of member states and three-fifths of the Union's population is easy to understand and transparent compared with the complex and contrived Nice formula for the weighting of countries' votes, it is moot whether Giscard or the Convention had a mandate to decide on the matter. There was no mention of the voting system of the Council of Ministers in the Laeken declaration.

19.3 THE CONTRAST IN METHODS

Unlike the points raised in the Nice declaration, the institutional issues were never thoroughly aired using the Convention method. The Praesidium produced only one 'reflection paper' on the functioning of the institutions.[13] There were no working groups, not even a reflection circle. It is true that the institutional issues were raised in plenary sessions, but towards the end of the Convention and when time was short. The institutional provisions of the constitutional draft were hard-wired into the Convention by the interventions of the large member states, modified only modestly through chaotic

---

[13] CONV 477/03, 10 January 2003.

procedures inside the Convention and always tempered by the insights of Giscard and Sir John Kerr into what Germany, France and the UK would accept.

Meeting the mandate of the Nice declaration vindicated the 'Convention method' of deliberation and decision by consensus. The process of discussion, refinement of issues in working groups, and formulation of draft articles which were subject to further discussion on the basis of amendments, was successful.

This contrasted with the approach taken to deal with the institutional questions where gamesmanship was at a premium from the moment Giscard leaked his own draft articles on 22 April. It was with gusto that Sir John Kerr resorted in the Convention's closing weeks to tricks learned through decades of negotiation in smoked filled rooms. The secretariat focussed on keeping control of the agenda, holding back documents, never letting opposition groups consolidate, and creating a climate in which the most enthusiastic partisan among the conventionnels would eventually settle for a compromise. Although entertaining to behold, the secretariat's handling of the institutional issues resulted in a consensus that was less convincing and therefore flawed. The tactics owed nothing to the 'Convention spirit' which Giscard had demanded in his opening address.

One of Giscard's earliest decisions was to allow no votes in the Convention. It appeared a stroke of genius. He alone would determine what consensus was and consensus remained a riddle even after the Convention members had cleared the hall on 13 June. The day before, the group of MEPs tried to find out from Dehaene what consensus might mean. 'What is consensus?' Dehaene mused. 'My answer is that the day you define consensus, you'll never again find it. It is really something you can't put your finger on. We shouldn't try to translate it into mathematical equations.' Giscard didn't even use the word consensus during the final session, reserving for the press afterwards his judgement that support for the draft was 'virtually unanimous.'

But nebulous consensus only translates into virtually unanimous support if all participants feel they have been treated fairly. Giscard took great pains to meet British objections, so that Tony Blair, writing in the September 2003 British white paper on the constitutional treaty, [14] could describe the Convention's end product as 'good news for Britain'. He made a major effort in the July session to settle Germany's difficulties over immigration and France's insistence on the 'cultural exception' with the result that France

---

[14] The British approach to the European Union Intergovernmental Conference 2003, Cm5934.

and Germany put themselves in the vanguard of countries willing to accept the final draft, virtually unchanged. But Giscard was far less solicitous throughout the Convention of the smaller states and accession countries.

The consensus on 13 June came at the cost of some hurt feelings and bruised egos. It is damaging for the Union that the split between big and small member states, that entered the EU's bloodstream during the French presidency in the second half of 2000, persisted and became worse during a Convention chaired by a former president of France. The fact that small and medium sized countries from either side of the former Iron Curtain were able to make common cause in the big-small country dispute, thus reinforcing the image of the Convention as 'the first constituent assembly on a European scale is scant consolation'.[15]

Giscard's consensus was based on a coalition of parliamentarians. The good news here is that the constitutional treaty can fairly be described as reflecting a Europe of citizens. However, the political reality is that the subsequent IGC is a negotiation among governments, reflecting Europe of the states.

In consequence, several member states and accession states have expressed reservations about the provisions on the institutions in the constitutional treaty and reserved the right to have a proper negotiation in the IGC rather than simply accept the draft text as prepared. Thus Spain's Ana Palacio praised the outcome of the Convention while making clear that the government in Madrid had a 'fundamental reservation' about the system of double majority voting in the institutional texts. Austria's Hannes Farnleitner declared that he could accept 95 per cent of what was agreed, but, if there had been a vote, he would not have voted for the five per cent that covered the institutions.

19.4 A SYNTHESIS THAT WARRANTS RESPECT

These reservations seemed not to threaten the constitutional treaty when the Convention finished the main part of its work in June 2003. In the light of the intervening debate, it is difficult to be so sure. Europe's 'accidental constitution' – the product of so many unexpected twists and turns during the life of the Convention – may yet turn out to be accident prone.

That would be a pity. Even Romano Prodi, an aggrieved and outspoken critic of the Convention's work, has admitted that '90 per cent of what needed to

---

[15] Giscard's description in his speech accepting the Charlemagne prize, Aachen 29 May 2003, available in the speeches section of the Convention website.

be done has been done'. That 90 per cent will surely survive the intergovernmental conference. With luck and good management, there could even be some improvements in the disputed areas of the constitutional treaty and a cleaning up of the language of the many articles in part III that were left untouched for lack of time. Action need not be rushed because many of the institutional changes are not due to take effect before 2009. Giscard's warning that to reopen the text, 'even in part, would cause it to unravel' seems unduly alarmist.

On the other hand, the draft constitutional treaty that emerged from the Convention deserves to be treated with respect. It is more than the usual European Union compromise. The draft is, as Giscard has described it, a 'synthesis', something that strikes 'the necessary balance between peoples, between states old and new, between institutions and between dream and reality.'

The draft produced by the Convention recognises that the Union is rooted in dualities and sets out to reconcile these. It is a Union of states and citizens; a Union of the federal and intergovernmental where states both pool sovereignty and cooperate on policies. It is a Union that has emerged in a bewildering and often accidental manner into something that is less than perfect, often infuriating and capable of great improvement. But capable of improvement it is, and the constitutional treaty produced by the Convention is, both in terms of process and product, evidence of that.

Part VI

Documentary Annex

SECTION A
Giscard's Draft Institutional Proposals of 22 April, 2003
(Articles 14 to 19 plus Article X)[1]

PART I OF THE CONSTITUTION

TITLE IV, THE UNION'S INSTITUTIONS

Article 14: The Union's Institutions

1. The Union's institutions shall aim to ensure consistency and continuity in the policies and actions undertaken in pursuit of its objectives.

2. These institutions are:

    The European Council,
    The European Parliament,
    The Council of Ministers,
    The European Commission,
    The Court of Justice of the European Union,
    The European Central Bank,
    The Court of Auditors.

3. Each institution shall act within the limits of the powers conferred on it in the Constitution and in conformity with the procedures and conditions set out in the Constitution. The institutions shall practice full mutual cooperation.

Article 15: The European Council

1. The European Council, highest authority of the Union, shall consist of the Heads of State or Government of the Member States, together with its President and the President of the Commission. The Vice-President of the European Council and the Foreign Minister shall take part in its work.

2. The European Council shall meet quarterly, convened by its President. When the agenda so requires, its members may decide to be assisted by a minister, and in the case of the President of the Commission, a

---

[1] See Chapter 14.1, 14.2 and 14.3.

Commissioner. When the international situation so requires, the President shall convene an additional meeting of the European Council.

3.   The European Council shall provide the Union with the necessary imperns for its development, and shall determine its general political directions. It shall set out principles and strategic guidelines for the Union's external action. In the area of freedom, security and justice, it shall give guidance for action, legislative and operational.

4.   It shall maintain oversight of the unity, consistency and efficiency of Union action.

5.   Except where the Constitution provides otherwise, decisions of the European Council shall be taken by consensus.

Article 15a: The European Council Chair

1.   The European Council shall elect its President, by qualified majority, for a term of two and a half years, renewable once. The person elected must be, or have been for at least two years, a member of the European Council.

      On issues concerning its common foreign and security policy he shall ensure that the Union at his level is effectively represented in the wider world.

2.   The President of the European Council shall prepare, chair and drive its work ensuring continuity. He shall give an annual report on the State of the Union to a Congress of representatives of the European Parliament and national Parliaments, and participate in its subsequent debate. He shall be assisted by a Vice-President, elected for the same term and by the same procedure. The President and the Vice-President of the European Council may not be members of another European Institution.

3.   The European Council may decide by unanimity, that its President and Vice-President shall be elected by the Congress. In this case, the provisions of Article X, paragraph 7 of Title VI concerning the Congress shall apply.

4.   The European Council Board shall consist of its President and Vice-President, two European Council members chosen in equal rotation, and the Presidents of those formations of the Council defined in Article 17a, paragraphs 3 and 4. The Board shall ensure continuity in the Council's work.

The European Council Board may meet with the participation of the Presidents of the European Parliament and the Commission to ensure consistency across the whole range of Union activities.

Article 16: The European Parliament

1. The European Parliament shall be directly elected by universal suffrage of European citizens in free and secret ballot. The Parliament shall, jointly with the Council, enact legislation, as laid down in the Constitution.

2. Members of the European Parliament shall be elected for a term of five years. Their number shall not exceed seven hundred. Representation of European citizens shall be proportional with a minimum threshold of four members per Member State.

3. The European Parliament shall elect its President and its officers from among its members, for a term of five years.

Article 17: The Council of Ministers

1. The Council of Ministers shall, jointly with the European Parliament, enact legislation and shall carry out executive and co-ordinating functions, as laid down in the Constitution.

2. The Council of Ministers shall consist of a representative of each Member State at ministerial level. Only this representative may commit the Member State in question, and cast its vote.

3. Except where the Constitution provides otherwise, decisions of the Council shall be taken by qualified majority.

Article 17a: Council formations

1. The General Affairs Council shall ensure consistency in the work of the Council of Ministers. It shall be chaired by the Vice-President of the European Council.

2. The Legislative Council shall consider and, jointly with the European Parliament, enact European laws and European framework laws, in accordance with the dispositions of the Constitution. Each Member State's ministerial representative may be assisted by a specialist minister, reflecting the business on the Council agenda.

3. The Foreign Affairs Council shall, on the basis of strategic guidelines laid down by the European Council, flesh out the Union's external policies, and ensure that its actions are consistent. It shall be chaired by the Union's Foreign Minister.

4. The Council shall also meet in the formations of an Economic and Financial Affairs Council, and a Council on Justice and Security. Meeting as General Affairs Council it may decide on further formations.

Article 17b: Qualified majority

1. When the European Council or the Council take decisions by qualified majority, such a majority shall consist of the majority of the Member States, representing at least two-thirds of the population of the Union.

2. Within the European Council, its President and the President of the Commission do not vote.

Article 18: The European Commission

1. The European Commission is called on to give voice to the general European interest. It shall monitor the application of the Constitution, and steps taken by the institutions under the Constitution.

2. Except where the Constitution provides otherwise, Union acts can be adopted only on the basis of a Commission proposal.

3. The Commission shall consist of a President, two Vice-Presidents and up to ten other members. It may call on the help of Commission Counsellors.

4. In carrying out its responsibilities, the Commission shall be completely independent. In the discharge of their duties members of the Commission shall neither seek nor take instructions from any government or other body.

Article 18a: The President of the European Commission

1. Following the European elections, the European Council, deciding by qualified majority, shall put forward to the European Parliament its proposed candidate for the Presidency of the Commission. The Parliament shall reach a view, by a majority of three-fifths of its constituent members, on the candidate put forward by the European Council. If this candidate does not receive the required majority support,

the European Council shall within one month put forward a new candidate, following the same procedure as before.

2. Each Member State shall submit a list of three persons, of which at least one must be a woman, whom it considers qualified to be a European Commissioner. The President-elect, taking account of European political and geographical balance, shall, from among the names submitted, select as members of the Commission up to eleven persons chosen for their competence. European commitment, and guaranteed independence. The President and the persons so named shall be submitted as a body to a vote of approval by the European Parliament. The President shall appoint one of the two Vice-Presidents from among the Commission members so selected.

3. The Commission, as a body, shall be responsible to the European Council and the European Parliament. Under the procedures set out at Art. X of the Constitution, these two institutions may pass a censure motion on the Commission. If such a motion is passed by the European Council or by the European Parliament, the members of the Commission must all resign. They shall continue to handle everyday business until their successors are nominated.

4. The Commission shall work to guidelines laid down by its President, who shall decide on its internal organisation in order to ensure that it acts consistently, efficiently and on a collegiate basis.

5. The President may appoint Commission Counsellors, chosen according to the same criteria as apply for members of the Commission. Their number must not exceed the number of members of the Commission.

Article 19: The Foreign Minister

1. The European Council, deciding by qualified majority, after consulting the President of the Commission, shall appoint the Union's Foreign Minister. He shall conduct the Union's common foreign and security policy.

2. The Foreign Minister shall contribute by his proposals to the development of the common foreign policy, which he shall carry out as mandated by the Council. The same shall apply to the common security and defence policy.

3. The Foreign Minister shall be one of the two Vice-Presidents of the Commission. He shall be responsible for handling external relations and

for co-ordinating the different aspects of the Union's external actions. In this capacity, for these aspects alone, he shall be bound by Commission procedures.

Article X: to be inserted in Title VI on 'The Union's Democratic Life'

1. The Congress of the Peoples of Europe shall provide a forum for contact and consultation in European political life. It shall meet at least once a year. Its meetings shall be public. The President of the European Parliament shall convene and chair them.

2. The President of the European Council shall report on the State of the Union. The President of the Commission shall present the annual legislative programme.

3. The Congress shall not intervene in the Council's legislative procedure.

4. The Congress may be consulted by the President of the European Council or by the President of the Convention on any issue of concern to the Union. It may be called on by the European Council to work up proposals for amendments to this Constitution.

5. One third of the Congress shall be members of the European Parliament: two thirds shall be representatives of national Parliaments. The total shall not exceed seven hundred.

6. The President of the European Council, appointed under the procedure foreseen at Article 15a, shall be installed during a meeting of the Congress convened for that purpose.

7. If the European Council by unanimity so decides, the Congress could become the Electoral College for electing the President of the European Council. The size of each national Parliament's delegation shall then be proportionate to the population of the Member State, with a minimum threshold of four members per Member State, following the arrangements foreseen at Article 16. The Congress shall decide by a majority of its members.

Note: These articles have been transcribed from the institutional text presented by Giscard to the Praesidium on 22 April 2003 and circulated informally thereafter. They should be compared with articles 18 to 27 of the draft constitutional treaty to assess how far the supporters of the 'Community method' succeeded in correcting Giscard's 'big country' and intergovernmental preferences in the seven and a half weeks before the Convention reached its consensus on part 1 of the draft constitutional treaty. As explained in Chapter 14, some of Giscard's ideas were despatched in short order: the European Council vice-president, for example, was an idea that lasted only 24 hours. Others took longer to kill off: Giscard's pet idea of Congress of MEPs and national parliamentarians lingered until the Praesidium meeting of 31 May. There can be no doubt that a good deal of tactical thinking lay behind Giscard's proposals. He set out to shock and galvanise the Convention into action. He therefore included a number of items in his articles that he was happy to discard as the negotiations with the Convention's components developed.

SECTION B
Draft Constitutional Treaty:
Preamble and Part I with Comments

Draft
TREATY ESTABLISHING A CONSTITUTION FOR EUROPE[2]
PREAMBLE

Χρώμεθα γὰρ πολιτείᾳ... καὶ ὄνομα μὲν διὰ τὸ μὴ ἐς ὀλίγους ἀλλ᾽ ἐς πλείονας οἰκεῖν δημοκρατία κέκληται.

Our Constitution .... is called a democracy because power is in the hands not of a minority but of the greatest number

Thucydides II, 37

Conscious that Europe is a continent that has brought forth civilisation; that its inhabitants, arriving in successive waves from earliest times, have gradually developed the values underlying humanism: equality of persons, freedom, respect for reason,

Drawing inspiration from the cultural, religious and humanist inheritance of Europe, the values of which, still present in its heritage, have embedded within the life of society the central role of the human person and his or her inviolable and inalienable rights, and respect for law,

Believing that reunited Europe intends to continue along the path of civilisation, progress and prosperity, for the good of all its inhabitants, including the weakest and most deprived; that it wishes to remain a continent open to culture, learning and social progress; and that it wishes to deepen the democratic and transparent nature of its public life, and to strive for peace, justice and solidarity throughout the world,

Convinced that, while remaining proud of their own national identities and history, the peoples of Europe are determined to transcend their ancient divisions and, united ever more closely, to forge a common destiny,

---

[2] © European Communities, 2003; *Official Journal of the European Union,* 'Information and Notices' series, C 169 of 18 July 2003.

Convinced that, thus 'united in its diversity', Europe offers them the best chance of pursuing, with due regard for the rights of each individual and in awareness of their responsibilities towards future generations and the Earth, the great venture which makes of it a special area of human hope,

Grateful to the members of the European Convention for having prepared this Constitution on behalf of the citizens and States of Europe,

[Who, having exchanged their full powers, found in good and due form, have agreed as follows:]

Note: The Preamble was very much Giscard's own creation. However, the second paragraph was revised in the week before June 13 to remove his highly personal view of European history and is therefore shorter than the original version of May 28 (CONV 722/03) which read:

> Drawing inspiration from the cultural, religious and humanist inheritance of Europe, which, nourished first by the civilisations of Greece and Rome, characterised by spiritual impulse always present in its heritage and later by the philosophical currents of the Enlightenment, has embedded within the life of society its perception of the central role of the human person and his inviolable and inalienable rights, and of respect for law.

The phrase 'united ever more closely' is a substitute for 'creating an ever closer union' in article one of the Treaty on Union. Sir John Kerr was a strong advocate of the change on the grounds that 'ever closer union' committed the EU to constant upheaval that was bad for business and disturbing for citizens. 'United in its diversity' is in inverted commas to signal that it is the Union's motto. This was confirmed by the Praesidium in its final session in July and the phrase appears among the symbols of the Union in article IV-I of the final draft. The passing reference to Europe's religious inheritance is the sole concession to heavy lobbying for an explicit reference to Christianity or god in the constitutional treaty.

PART I

TITLE I: DEFINITION AND OBJECTIVES OF THE UNION[3]

Article 1: Establishment of the Union

1. Reflecting the will of the citizens and States of Europe to build a common future, this Constitution establishes the European Union, on which the Member States confer competences to attain objectives they have in common. The Union shall coordinate the policies by which the

---

[3] See Chapters 6.1; 6.2; 6.4; 13.2 and 15.2.

Member States aim to achieve these objectives, and shall exercise in the Community way the competences they confer on it.

2. The Union shall be open to all European States which respect its values and are committed to promoting them together.

Note: The word 'federal' does not appear in article 1 although it was in the October 2002 skeleton text (CONV 369/02) and the first draft of 6 February 2003 (CONV 528/03). It was replaced by 'Community way'. Its disappearance followed intense lobbying by the UK and others. The government representatives of Austria, Estonia, Italy, Poland, the Czech Republic, Slovenia and Denmark were among those who submitted amendments for its removal. The text submitted by the Praesidium on May 26 proved to be the final version of article 1. It also made clear that the Union acts on the basis of competences conferred by member states. The result of rolling back federal tendencies is a text that is more precise but less elegant than the skeleton which referred to: 'A Union of European states which, while retaining their national identities closely coordinate their policies at the European level, and administer certain common competences on a federal basis'.

Article 2: The Union's values

The Union is founded on the values of respect for human dignity, liberty, democracy, equality, the rule of law and respect for human rights. These values are common to the Member States in a society of pluralism, tolerance, justice, solidarity and non-discrimination.

Note: Deliberately brief, this article also provides criteria for admitting new member states and suspending delinquent members (see articles 57 and 58). The references to pluralism, equality and non-discrimination were added in the 26 May version as a result of amendments to the first draft of 6 February.

Article 3: The Union's objectives

1. The Union's aim is to promote peace, its values and the well-being of its peoples.

2. The Union shall offer its citizens an area of freedom, security and justice without internal frontiers, and a single market where competition is free and undistorted.

3. The Union shall work for the sustainable development of Europe based on balanced economic growth, a social market economy, highly competitive and aiming at full employment and social progress, and with a high level of protection and improvement of the quality of the environment. It shall promote scientific and technological advance.

It shall combat social exclusion and discrimination, and shall promote social justice and protection, equality between women and men, solidarity between generations and protection of children's rights.

It shall promote economic, social and territorial cohesion, and solidarity among Member States.

The Union shall respect its rich cultural and linguistic diversity, and shall ensure that Europe's cultural heritage is safeguarded and enhanced.

4. In its relations with the wider world, the Union shall uphold and promote its values and interests. It shall contribute to peace, security, the sustainable development of the earth, solidarity and mutual respect among peoples, free and fair trade, eradication of poverty and protection of human rights and in particular children's rights, as well as to strict observance and development of international law, including respect for the principles of the United Nations Charter.

5. These objectives shall be pursued by appropriate means, depending on the extent to which the relevant competences are attributed to the Union in the Constitution.

Note: This article tells the reader what the Union is for. It was extensively rewritten in May following a host of amendments. The 26 May version strengthened the language on environmental protection and introduced references to the social market economy, territorial cohesion and linguistic diversity while dropping the discovery of space. The article then stayed largely unchanged although the reference to a highly competitive economy was included in the second week in June.

Article 4: Fundamental freedoms and non-discrimination

1. Free movement of persons, goods, services and capital, and freedom of establishment shall be guaranteed within and by the Union, in accordance with the provisions of the Constitution.

2. In the field of application of the Constitution, and without prejudice to any of its specific provisions, any discrimination on grounds of nationality shall be prohibited.

Note: Introduced on 26 May and thereafter unchanged, paragraph 1 highlights the four 'fundamental freedoms'. Article III-7 says European laws or framework laws may lay down rules to prohibit discrimination on nationality grounds.

Article 5: Relations between the Union and the Member States

1. The Union shall respect the national identities of the Member States, inherent in their fundamental structures, political and constitutional,

inclusive of regional and local self-government. It shall respect their essential State functions, including those for ensuring the territorial integrity of the State, and for maintaining law and order and safeguarding internal security.

2. Following the principle of loyal cooperation, the Union and the Member States shall, in full mutual respect, assist each other in carrying out tasks which flow from the Constitution.

   The Member States shall facilitate the achievement of the Union's tasks and refrain from any measure which could jeopardise the attainment of the objectives set out in the Constitution.

Note: Absent from the February draft, this article was included in the 26 May texts following suggestions of conventionnels in two March plenary sessions. Just as the Union has to respect the member states, so they have to act in line with the principle of loyal cooperation. The 26 May text formed the basis of the final draft article. Late amendments improved its grammar.

Article 6: Legal personality

The Union shall have legal personality.

Note: The only article in part I to retain the language of 6 February, when it was article 4. It signals the end of the pillars and enables the Union to sign treaties, be a member of international organisations and accede to conventions etc.

TITLE II: FUNDAMENTAL RIGHTS AND CITIZENSHIP OF THE UNION[4]

Article 7: Fundamental rights

1. The Union shall recognise the rights, freedoms and principles set out in the Charter of Fundamental Rights which constitutes Part II of the Constitution.

2. The Union shall seek accession to the European Convention for the Protection of Human Rights and Fundamental Freedoms. Such accession shall not affect the Union's competences as defined in the Constitution.

3. Fundamental rights, as guaranteed by the European Convention for the Protection of Human Rights and Fundamental Freedoms, and as they

---

[4] See Chapters 6.5; 13.2 and 15.2.

result from the constitutional traditions common to the Member States, shall constitute general principles of the Union's law.

Note: This important article, which gives the constitutional treaty its bill of rights, was unchanged from 26 May, when the Charter was incorporated at part II.

Article 8: Citizenship of the Union

1. Every national of a Member State shall be a citizen of the Union. Citizenship of the Union shall be additional to national citizenship; it shall not replace it.

2. Citizens of the Union shall enjoy the rights and be subject to the duties provided for in the Constitution. They shall have:

    —   the right to move and reside freely within the territory of the Member States;

    —   the right to vote and to stand as candidates in elections to the European Parliament and in municipal elections in their Member State of residence, under the same conditions as nationals of that State;

    —   the right to enjoy, in the territory of a third country in which the Member State of which they are nationals is not represented, the protection of the diplomatic and consular authorities of any Member State on the same conditions as the nationals of that State;

    —   the right to petition the European Parliament, to apply to the European Ombudsman, and to address the Institutions and advisory bodies of the Union in any of the Constitution's languages and to obtain a reply in the same language.

3. These rights shall be exercised in accordance with the conditions and limits defined by the Constitution and by the measures adopted to give it effect.

Note: At the time of the skeleton, there were suggestions that Giscard wanted to make an issue of Union citizenship. However, the February draft simply reproduced the definition given in the European Communities treaty and the formula was retained through all subsequent drafts. The details in paragraph 2 reproduce rights in title V of the Charter. Detailed provisions appear in title II of part III.

TITLE III: UNION COMPETENCES[5]

Article 9: Fundamental principles

1. The limits of Union competences are governed by the principle of conferral. The use of Union competences is governed by the principles of subsidiarity and proportionality.

2. Under the principle of conferral, the Union shall act within the limits of the competences conferred upon it by the Member States in the Constitution to attain the objectives set out in the Constitution. Competences not conferred upon the Union in the Constitution remain with the Member States.

3. Under the principle of subsidiarity, in areas which do not fall within its exclusive competence the Union shall act only if and insofar as the objectives of the intended action cannot be sufficiently achieved by the Member States, either at central level or at regional and local level, but can rather, by reason of the scale or effects of the proposed action, be better achieved at Union level.

    The Union Institutions shall apply the principle of subsidiarity as laid down in the Protocol on the application of the principles of subsidiarity and proportionality, annexed to the Constitution. National Parliaments shall ensure compliance with that principle in accordance with the procedure set out in the Protocol.

4. Under the principle of proportionality, the content and form of Union action shall not exceed what is necessary to achieve the objectives of the Constitution. The Institutions shall apply the principle of proportionality as laid down in the Protocol referred to in paragraph 3.

Note: An important article in view of the Nice declaration, it was extensively rewritten in May to make clear that member states, and not the Constitution, confer competences on the Union. The reference to regional and local authorities in connection with subsidiarity in paragraph 3 reflects lobbying by conventionnels with regional interests, including Teufel and MacCormick. The article stayed unchanged after 26 May.

Article 10: Union law

1. The Constitution, and law adopted by the Union's Institutions in exercising competences conferred on it, shall have primacy over the law of the Member States.

---

[5] See Chapters 7.1; 7.1; 13.3 and 15.2.

2. Member States shall take all appropriate measures, general or particular, to ensure fulfilment of the obligations flowing from the Constitution or resulting from the Union Institutions' acts.

Note: The Court of Justice established the primacy of Union law in landmark rulings in 1963 and 1964, but the constitutional treaty states it explicitly. This article proved acceptable in its version of 26 May.

Article 11: Categories of competence

1. When the Constitution confers on the Union exclusive competence in a specific area, only the Union may legislate and adopt legally binding acts, the Member States being able to do so themselves only if so empowered by the Union or for the implementation of acts adopted by the Union.

2. When the Constitution confers on the Union a competence shared with the Member States in a specific area, the Union and the Member States shall have the power to legislate and adopt legally binding acts in that area. The Member States shall exercise their competence to the extent that the Union has not exercised, or has decided to cease exercising, its competence.

3. The Union shall have competence to promote and coordinate the economic and employment policies of the Member States.

4. The Union shall have competence to define and implement a common foreign and security policy, including the progressive framing of a common defence policy.

5. In certain areas and in the conditions laid down in the Constitution, the Union shall have competence to carry out actions to support, coordinate or supplement the actions of the Member States, without thereby superseding their competence in these areas.

6. The scope of and arrangements for exercising the Union's competences shall be determined by the provisions specific to each area in Part III.

Note: This article was rewritten in May after many amendments were submitted to the 6 February draft. It then was left unchanged except for paragraph 3 where the Union now can only 'promote and coordinate' economic and employment policies rather than 'ensure the coordination' of these policies. The February version was harder still, saying 'the Union shall have competence to coordinate the economic policies of the member states' and was strongly opposed by many conventionnels.

Economic policy details are set out in title three, Chapter II, section 1 of part III and employment policy details in title three, Chapter III section 1.

Article 12: Exclusive competence

1. The Union shall have exclusive competence to establish the competition rules necessary for the functioning of the internal market, and in the following areas:

    - monetary policy, for the Member States which have adopted the euro,
    - common commercial policy,
    - customs union,
    - the conservation of marine biological resources under the common fisheries policy.

2. The Union shall have exclusive competence for the conclusion of an international agreement when its conclusion is provided for in a legislative act of the Union, is necessary to enable it to exercise its internal competence, or affects an internal Union act.

Note: During its May meeting, the Praesidium removed the 'four freedoms' from paragraph 1 of the 6 February draft and placed them in article 4. The unqualified inclusion of the common commercial policy as an exclusive competence was to prove extremely contentious because it implied that France and other member states would no longer have a national veto over the negotiation of trade agreements covering cultural and audiovisual services. The row over the 'cultural exception' was only resolved during the last meeting of the Praesidium in July. The compromise is incorporated in III-217.

Article 13: Areas of shared competence

1. The Union shall share competence with the Member States where the Constitution confers on it a competence which does not relate to the areas referred to in Articles 12 and 16.

2. Shared competence applies in the following principal areas:

    - internal market,
    - area of freedom, security and justice,
    - agriculture and fisheries, excluding the conservation of marine biological resources,
    - transport and trans-European networks,
    - energy,
    - social policy, for aspects defined in Part III,

- economic, social and territorial cohesion,
- environment,
- consumer protection,
- common safety concerns in public health matters.

3. In the areas of research, technological development and space, the Union shall have competence to carry out actions, in particular to define and implement programmes; however, the exercise of that competence may not result in Member States being prevented from exercising theirs.

4. In the areas of development cooperation and humanitarian aid, the Union shall have competence to take action and conduct a common policy; however, the exercise of that competence may not result in Member States being prevented from exercising theirs.

Note: Energy was first included in the list in paragraph 2 in the 6 February draft and has required a new legal base in article III-157. Amendments to the February draft added territorial cohesion to the list and specified that only 'common safety concerns' in public health were a shared competence. The important policies of research and development and development aid are mentioned separately because, contrary to article 11.2, member states can retain their competences through national programmes, even when the Union is exercising the shared competence. The policy categories in which shared competence apply are to be found in title three of part III where many provisions are unchanged compared with the European Communities treaty. The provisions for the area of freedom, security and justice in Chapter IV of title three of part III are the big innovation.

Article 14: The coordination of economic and employment policies

1. The Union shall adopt measures to ensure coordination of the economic policies of the Member States, in particular by adopting broad guidelines for these policies. The Member States shall coordinate their economic policies within the Union.

2. Specific provisions shall apply to those Member States which have adopted the euro.

3. The Union shall adopt measures to ensure coordination of the employment policies of the Member States, in particular by adopting guidelines for these policies.

4. The Union may adopt initiatives to ensure coordination of Member States' social policies.

Note: Rewritten for the 26 May texts to take account of protests over the 6 February draft which said 'the Union shall coordinate the economic policies of the member states ...', this article required no further amendment.

Article 15: The common foreign and security policy

1. The Union's competence in matters of common foreign and security policy shall cover all areas of foreign policy and all questions relating to the Union's security, including the progressive framing of a common defence policy, which might lead to a common defence.

2. Member States shall actively and unreservedly support the Union's common foreign and security policy in a spirit of loyalty and mutual solidarity and shall comply with the acts adopted by the Union in this area. They shall refrain from action contrary to the Union's interests or likely to impair its effectiveness.

Note: Another article that caused a rumpus when published in February, the 26 May draft did nothing to dilute the expectations of the role of member states – it nonetheless was reproduced unchanged in the final draft treaty. The objectives of the common foreign and security policy are listed in III-193.

Article 16: Areas of supporting, coordinating or complementary action

1. The Union may take supporting, coordinating or complementary action.

2. The areas for supporting, coordinating or complementary action shall be, at European level:

    –   industry,
    –   protection and improvement of human health,
    –   education, vocational training, youth and sport,
    –   culture,
    –   civil protection.

3. Legally binding acts adopted by the Union on the basis of the provisions specific to these areas in Part III may not entail harmonisation of Member States' laws or regulations.

Note: Another article that was left unchanged after 26 May. Sport and civil protection were included on the strength of recommendations from the Christophersen working group and required the creation of new legal bases in III-182 and III-184 respectively. Paragraph 3 establishes the important principle that supporting, coordinating or complementary actions should not result in harmonisation. This reflects the widespread concern before the Convention that these areas were precisely those where 'Brussels' was seeking to increase its power.

Article 17: Flexibility clause

1. If action by the Union should prove necessary within the framework of the policies defined in Part III to attain one of the objectives set by the Constitution, and the Constitution has not provided the necessary powers, the Council of Ministers, acting unanimously on a proposal from the Commission and after obtaining the consent of the European Parliament, shall take the appropriate measures.

2. Using the procedure for monitoring the subsidiarity principle referred to in Article 9(3), the Commission shall draw Member States' national Parliaments' attention to proposals based on this Article.

3. Provisions adopted on the basis of this Article may not entail harmonisation of Member States' laws or regulations in cases where the Constitution excludes such harmonisation.

Note: Based on article 308 of the TEC, article 17 widens the scope for possible Union action from the common market to 'policies defined in part III'. But it builds in new safeguards for member states including the involvement of national Parliaments. The bar on harmonisation reflects Court of Justice case law.

TITLE IV: THE UNION'S INSTITUTIONS[6]

Chapter I – The institutional framework

Article 18: The Union's Institutions

1. The Union shall be served by a single institutional framework which shall aim to:

    —   advance the objectives of the Union,
    —   promote the values of the Union,
    —   serve the interests of the Union, its citizens and its Member States, and ensure the consistency, effectiveness and continuity of the policies and actions which it undertakes in pursuit of its objectives.

2. This institutional framework comprises:

    The European Parliament,
    The European Council,

---

[6] See Chapter 10 for background, 14 covering the genesis of the institutional articles in April 2003 and Chapters 16.4 and 17 for further developments.

The Council of Ministers,
The European Commission,
The Court of Justice.

3. Each Institution shall act within the limits of the powers conferred on it
    in the Constitution, and in conformity with the procedures and
    conditions set out in it. The Institutions shall practice full mutual
    cooperation.

*Note: The Praesidium meeting of 23 April placed the Parliament in its traditional
position at the top of the institutional hierarchy, whereas Giscard's draft of the
previous day put the European Council first. After some prevarication, it was
decided to leave the European Central Bank and Court of Auditors and the Union's
advisory bodies off the list of institutions, while including them in title IV.*

Article 19: The European Parliament

1. The European Parliament shall, jointly with the Council of Ministers,
    enact legislation, and exercise the budgetary function, as well as
    functions of political control and consultation as laid down in the
    Constitution. It shall elect the President of the European Commission.

2. The European Parliament shall be elected by direct universal suffrage of
    European citizens in free and secret ballot for a term of five years. Its
    members shall not exceed seven hundred and thirty-six in number.
    Representation of European citizens shall be degressively proportional,
    with a minimum threshold of four members per Member State.

    Sufficiently in advance of the European Parliamentary elections in 2009,
    and, as necessary thereafter for further elections, the European Council
    shall adopt by unanimity, on the basis of a proposal from the European
    Parliament and with its consent, a decision establishing the composition
    of the European Parliament, respecting the principles set out above.

3. The European Parliament shall elect its President and its officers from
    among its members.

*Note: Although the Convention and Praesidium reversed Giscard's plan to limit the
Parliament to 700 seats, fixing representation by degressive proportionality changes
the institutional settlement of the Treaty of Nice. The new rules will not apply until
2009, however. Detailed provisions concerning the Parliament are in part III, title
six, articles III-232 to III-243 inclusive. The first paragraph makes clear the
Parliament's important role as joint legislator of the Union. As article 26 makes
clear, the election of the Commission president is a less impressive increase in the
Parliament's powers than it appears at first sight.*

Article 20: The European Council

1. The European Council shall provide the Union with the necessary impetus for its development, and shall define its general political directions and priorities. It does not exercise legislative functions.

2. The European Council shall consist of the Heads of State or Government of the Member States, together with its President and the President of the Commission. The Union Minister for Foreign Affairs shall take part in its work.

3. The European Council shall meet quarterly, convened by its President. When the agenda so requires, its members may decide to be assisted by a minister and, in the case of the President of the Commission, a European Commissioner. When the situation so requires, the President shall convene a special meeting of the European Council.

4. Except where the Constitution provides otherwise, decisions of the European Council shall be taken by consensus.

Note: This was a contentious article from the moment on 22 April that Giscard unveiled his vision of the European Council as the 'highest authority in the Union' with a vice-president as well as a president. The Praesidium removed these ambitions on 23 April. The ban on the European Council exercising legislative functions was included in the final set of amendments on 12 June. III-244 has more details.

Article 21: The European Council Chair

1. The European Council shall elect its President, by qualified majority, for a term of two and a half years, renewable once. In the event of an impediment or serious misconduct, the European Council can end his or her mandate according to the same procedure.

2. The President of the European Council:

    −   shall chair it and drive forward its work,
    −   shall ensure its proper preparation and continuity in cooperation with the President of the Commission, and on the basis of the work of the General Affairs Council,
    −   shall endeavour to facilitate cohesion and consensus within the European Council,
    −   shall present a report to the European Parliament after each of its meetings.

The President of the European Council shall at his or her level and in that capacity ensure the external representation of the Union on issues concerning its common foreign and security policy, without prejudice to the responsibilities of the Union Minister for Foreign Affairs.

3.   The President of the European Council may not hold a national mandate.

Note: A stable chair to replace the rotating presidency. The president's powers were reduced in stages from the Giscardian vision of a powerful executive heading a 'board'. The final text tries to enforce cooperation with the Commission president and ensure that the European Council president does not get in a tangle with the foreign minister. By taking out the conditions that s/he should be a former member of the European Council and not be a member of another European institution, the final text (just) holds open the door for a double-hatted Council and Commission president.

Article 22: The Council of Ministers

1.   The Council of Ministers shall, jointly with the European Parliament, enact legislation, exercise the budgetary function and carry out policy-making and coordinating functions, as laid down in the Constitution.

2.   The Council of Ministers shall consist of a representative of each Member State at ministerial level for each of its formations. Only this representative may commit the Member State in question and cast its vote.

3.   Except where the Constitution provides otherwise, decisions of the Council of Ministers shall be taken by qualified majority.

Note: Paragraph 3 is important because it makes clear that henceforth qualified majority voting should be the rule and the national veto the exception in the Council of Ministers, which shares the Community legislator's role with the Parliament. This article stayed virtually unchanged from the very first Giscard draft. Detailed provisions in III-245 to III-249 inclusive.

Article 23: Formations of the Council of Ministers

1.   The Legislative and General Affairs Council shall ensure consistency in the work of the Council of Ministers.

When it acts in its General Affairs function, it shall, in liaison with the Commission, prepare, and ensure follow-up to, meetings of the European Council.

When it acts in its legislative function, the Council of Ministers shall consider and, jointly with the European Parliament, enact European laws and European framework laws, in accordance with the provisions of the Constitution. In this function, each Member State's representation shall include one or two representatives at ministerial level with relevant expertise, reflecting the business on the agenda of the Council of Ministers.

2.   The Foreign Affairs Council shall, on the basis of strategic guidelines laid down by the European Council, flesh out the Union's external policies, and ensure that its actions are consistent. It shall be chaired by the Union Minister for Foreign Affairs.

3.   The European Council shall adopt a European decision establishing further formations in which the Council of Ministers may meet.

4.   The Presidency of Council of Ministers formations, other than that of Foreign Affairs, shall be held by Member State representatives within the Council of Ministers on the basis of equal rotation for periods of at least a year. The European Council shall adopt a European decision establishing the rules of such rotation, taking into account European political and geographical balance and the diversity of Member States.

Note: An article that bears witness to 11th hour compromises. Thus the illogical hybrid of the Legislative and General Affairs Council and the inclusion of sectoral ministers in an attempt to appease the many member states which opposed the idea of a legislative Council. Paragraph 4 preserves the principle of rotation, albeit on a yearly basis. The final round of amendments made clear the rotation would be 'equal'. According to III-245, the European Council must establish the rules governing rotation by unanimity – implying some difficult late night sessions in the future. The Economics and Finance Ministers Council (Ecofin) and that for Justice and Security were in a draft as late as June 2, but then removed.

Article 24: Qualified majority

1.   When the European Council or the Council of Ministers takes decisions by qualified majority, such a majority shall consist of the majority of Member States, representing at least three-fifths of the population of the Union.

2.   When the Constitution does not require the European Council or the Council of Ministers to act on the basis of a proposal of the Commission, or when the European Council or the Council of Ministers is not acting on the initiative of the Union Minister for Foreign Affairs, the required qualified majority shall consist of two-thirds of the Member States, representing at least three-fifths of the population of the Union.

3. The provisions of paragraphs 1 and 2 shall take effect on 1 November 2009, after the European Parliament elections have taken place, according to the provisions of Article 19.

4. Where the Constitution provides in Part III for European laws and framework laws to be adopted by the Council of Ministers according to a special legislative procedure, the European Council can adopt, on its own initiative and by unanimity, after a period of consideration of at least six months, a decision allowing for the adoption of such European laws or framework laws according to the ordinary legislative procedure. The European Council shall act after consulting the European Parliament and informing the national Parliaments.

    Where the Constitution provides in Part III for the Council of Ministers to act unanimously in a given area, the European Council can adopt, on its own initiative and by unanimity, a European decision allowing the Council of Ministers to act by qualified majority in that area. Any initiative taken by the European Council under this subparagraph shall be sent to national Parliaments no less than four months before any decision is taken on it.

5. Within the European Council, its President and the President of the Commission do not vote.

Note: An important article because, from 2009, it replaces the Nice Treaty provisions for the individual weighting of member states' votes in the Council of Ministers with the double majority system that is hotly contested by Spain and Poland. Paragraph 4 is also important: it details the passerelle clause concocted by Sir John Kerr in the penultimate week of the Convention sessions in June as a sweetener for integrationists disappointed that the Convention did not do more to increase the scope of QMV.

Article 25: The European Commission

1. The European Commission shall promote the general European interest and take appropriate initiatives to that end. It shall ensure the application of the Constitution, and steps taken by the Institutions under the Constitution. It shall oversee the application of Union law under the control of the Court of Justice. It shall execute the budget and manage programmes. It shall exercise coordinating, executive and management functions, as laid down in the Constitution. With the exception of the common foreign and security policy, and other cases provided for in the Constitution, it shall ensure the Union's external representation. It shall initiate the Union's annual and multiannual programming with a view to achieving interinstitutional agreements.

2. Except where the Constitution provides otherwise, Union legislative acts can be adopted only on the basis of a Commission proposal. Other acts are adopted on the basis of a Commission proposal where the Constitution so provides.

3. The Commission shall consist of a College comprising its President, the Union Minister of Foreign Affairs/Vice-President, and thirteen European Commissioners selected on the basis of a system of equal rotation between the Member States. This system shall be established by a European decision adopted by the European Council on the basis of the following principles:

   (a) Member States shall be treated on a strictly equal footing as regards determination of the sequence of, and the time spent by, their nationals as Members of the College; consequently, the difference between the total number of terms of office held by nationals of any given pair of Member States may never be more than one;

   (b) subject to point (a), each successive College shall be so composed as to reflect satisfactorily the demographic and geographical range of all the Member States of the Union.

   The Commission President shall appoint non-voting Commissioners, chosen according to the same criteria as apply for Members of the College and coming from all other Member States.

   These arrangements shall take effect on 1 November 2009.

4. In carrying out its responsibilities, the Commission shall be completely independent. In the discharge of their duties, the European Commissioners and Commissioners shall neither seek nor take instructions from any government or other body.

5. The Commission, as a College, shall be responsible to the European Parliament. The Commission President shall be responsible to the European Parliament for the activities of the Commissioners. Under the procedures set out in Article III-243, the European Parliament may pass a censure motion on the Commission. If such a motion is passed, the European Commissioners and Commissioners must all resign. The Commission shall continue to handle everyday business until a new College is nominated.

Note: A battleground between Giscard and supporters of the 'Community method,' this article was subject to extensive amendment in the hectic final fortnight before 13 June. The Commission's supporters ensured there would be a much fuller mission statement compared with the exiguous description of its role in Giscard's very first draft. But the small country advocates of one voting commissioner per member state failed to amend the provision for a slimmed down Commission with two classes of commissioner. The principle of equal rotation of commissioners was added in the final June week. It was also made clear the new arrangements would not apply to the next Commission, to be appointed in 2004, which will have one member per member state as agreed in Nice. The Commission's duties are detailed in III-250 to III-257 inclusive.

Article 26: The President of the European Commission

1. Taking into account the elections to the European Parliament and after appropriate consultations, the European Council, deciding by qualified majority, shall put to the European Parliament its proposed candidate for the Presidency of the Commission. This candidate shall be elected by the European Parliament by a majority of its members. If this candidate does not receive the required majority support, the European Council shall within one month propose a new candidate to the European Parliament, following the same procedure.

2. Each Member State determined by the system of rotation shall establish a list of three persons, in which both genders shall be represented, whom it considers qualified to be a European Commissioner. By choosing one person from each of the proposed lists, the President-elect shall select the thirteen European Commissioners for their competence, European commitment, and guaranteed independence. The President and the persons so nominated for membership of the College, including the future Union Minister for Foreign Affairs, as well as the persons nominated as non-voting Commissioners, shall be submitted collectively to a vote of approval by the European Parliament. The Commission's term of office shall be five years.

3. President of the Commission shall:

   – lay down guidelines within which the Commission is to work;
   – decide its internal organisation, ensuring that it acts consistently, efficiently and on a collegiate basis;
   – appoint Vice-Presidents from among the members of the College.

   A European Commissioner or Commissioner shall resign if the President so requests.

Note: The Praesidium meeting on 23 April ensured that the nomination of the Commission president by the European Council would have to 'take account' of the European elections while his or her election by Parliament would be by simple majority. Giscard's original draft said merely that the European Council decision would be 'following' the European elections and election would require a three - fifths majority in the Parliament.

Article 27: The Union Minister for Foreign Affairs

1. The European Council, acting by qualified majority, with the agreement of the President of the Commission, shall appoint the Union Minister for Foreign Affairs. He or she shall conduct the Union's common foreign and security policy. The European Council may end his or her tenure by the same procedure.

2. The Union Minister for Foreign Affairs shall contribute by his or her proposals to the development of the common foreign policy, which he or she shall carry out as mandated by the Council of Ministers. The same shall apply to the common security and defence policy.

3. The Union Minister for Foreign Affairs shall be one of the Vice-Presidents of the Commission. He or she shall be responsible there for handling external relations and for coordinating other aspects of the Union's external action. In exercising these responsibilities within the Commission, and only for these responsibilities, the Union Minister for Foreign Affairs shall be bound by Commission procedures.

Note: The most readily accepted of the significant institutional changes, despite some qualms about the title of minister from the UK and others, the double-hatted foreign minister is predominantly a Council person. Article 39 of part I charges him or her with implementing the common foreign and security policy and gives the minister the power of proposal on CFSP matters. Article 40 gives him or her power to propose decisions implementing the common security and defence policy. The wide ranging powers and responsibilities of the minister are highlighted by the large number of articles in part III which detail his or her scope of action. These are: III-193 to III-195 inclusive; III-197; III-200 to III-203; III-205 to III-206; III-208; III-210 to III-211; III-213; III-215; III-224; III-227; III-229 to III-231 inclusive.

Article 28: The Court of Justice

1. The Court of Justice shall include the European Court of Justice, the High Court and specialised courts. It shall ensure respect for the law in the interpretation and application of the Constitution.

   Member States shall provide rights of appeal sufficient to ensure effective legal protection in the field of Union law.

2. The European Court of Justice shall consist of one judge from each Member State, and shall be assisted by Advocates-General.

The High Court shall include at least one judge per Member State: the number shall be fixed by the Statute of the Court of Justice.

The judges and the Advocates-General of the European Court of Justice and the judges of the High Court, chosen from persons whose independence is beyond doubt and who satisfy the conditions set out in Articles III-260 and III-261, shall be appointed by common accord of the governments of the Member States for a term of six years, renewable.

3. The Court of Justice shall:

    – rule on actions brought by a Member State, an Institution or a natural or legal person in accordance with the provisions of Part III;
    – give preliminary rulings, at the request of Member State courts, on the interpretation of Union law or the validity of acts adopted by the Institutions;
    – rule on the other cases provided for in the Constitution.

Note: This article changes the name of the Court of First Instance to the High Court. The Court's duties and responsibilities are detailed in III-258 to III-298 inclusive.

Chapter II – Other Institutions and bodies

Article 29: The European Central Bank

1. The European Central Bank, together with the national central banks, shall constitute the European System of Central Banks. The European Central Bank, together with the national central banks of the Member States which have adopted the Union currency, the euro, shall conduct the monetary policy of the Union.

2. The European System of Central Banks shall be governed by the decision-making bodies of the European Central Bank. The primary objective of the European System of Central Banks shall be to maintain price stability. Without prejudice to the objective of price stability, it shall support general economic policies in the Union with a view to contributing to the achievement of the Union's objectives. It shall conduct other Central Bank tasks according to the provisions of Part III and the Statute of the European System of Central Banks and the European Central Bank.

3. The European Central Bank is an Institution which has legal personality. It alone may authorise the issue of the euro. In the exercise of its powers and for its finances, it shall be independent. Union Institutions and bodies, and the governments of the Member States, shall undertake to respect this principle.

4. The European Central Bank shall adopt such measures as are necessary to carry out its tasks in accordance with the provisions of Articles III-77 to III-83 and Article III-90, and with the conditions laid down in the Statute of the European System of Central Banks and the European Central Bank. In accordance with these same provisions, those Member States which have not adopted the euro, and their central banks, shall retain their powers in monetary matters.

5. Within its areas of competence, the European Central Bank shall be consulted on all proposed Union acts, and all proposals for regulation at national level, and may give an opinion.

6. The decision-making organs of the European Central Bank, their composition and operating methods are set out in Articles III-84 to III-87, as well as in the Statute of the European System of Central Banks and of the European Central Bank.

Note: The Convention played safe, so that the article on the ECB and ESCB left unchanged the substance of their tasks, mandate, status and legal regime.

Article 30: The Court of Auditors

1. The Court of Auditors is the Institution which shall carry out the audit.

2. It shall examine the accounts of all Union revenue and expenditure, and shall ensure good financial management.

3. It shall consist of one national of each Member State. In the performance of their duties, its members shall be completely independent.

Note: Situation unchanged in substance here and also in detailed articles III-290 and III-291. However, several EU government representatives, including those of the UK, Germany, the Netherlands and Sweden, wanted to restructure the Court of Auditors and reduce its size from one member per member state.

Article 31: The Union's advisory bodies

1. The European Parliament, the Council of Ministers and the Commission shall be assisted by a Committee of the Regions and an Economic and Social Committee, exercising advisory functions.

2. The Committee of the Regions shall consist of representatives of regional and local bodies who either hold a regional or local authority electoral mandate or are politically accountable to an elected assembly

3. The Economic and Social Committee shall consist of representatives of organisations of employers, of the employed, and of others representative of civil society, notably in socio-economic, civic, professional and cultural areas.

4. The members of the Committee of the Regions and the Economic and Social Committee must not be bound by any mandatory instructions. They shall be completely independent, in the performance of their duties, in the Union's general interest.

5. Rules governing the composition of these Committees, the designation of their members, their powers and their operations, are set out in Articles III-292 to III-298. The rules governing their composition shall be reviewed at regular intervals by the Council of Ministers, on the basis of a Commission proposal, in the light of economic, social and demographic developments within the Union.

Note: There was some criticism of the two bodies from conventionnels but insufficient momentum for change. Detailed articles run from III-292 to III-298 inclusive.

TITLE V: EXERCISE OF UNION COMPETENCE[7]

Chapter I – Common provisions

Article 32: The legal acts of the Union

1. In exercising the competences conferred on it in the Constitution, the Union shall use as legal instruments, in accordance with the provisions of Part III, European laws, European framework laws, European regulations, European decisions, recommendations and opinions.

    A European law shall be a legislative act of general application. It shall be binding in its entirety and directly applicable in all Member States.

    A European framework law shall be a legislative act binding, as to the result to be achieved, on the Member States to which it is addressed, but leaving the national authorities entirely free to choose the form and means of achieving that result.

    A European regulation shall be a non-legislative act of general application for the implementation of legislative acts and of certain specific provisions of the Constitution. It may either be binding in its

---

[7] See Chapters 7.4 and 13.6.

entirety and directly applicable in all Member States, or be binding, as regards the result to be achieved, on all Member States to which it is addressed, but leaving the national authorities entirely free to choose the form and means of achieving that result.

A European decision shall be a non-legislative act, binding in its entirety. A decision which specifies those to whom it is addressed shall be binding only on them.

Recommendations and opinions adopted by the Institutions shall have no binding force.

2. When considering proposals for legislative acts, the European Parliament and the Council of Ministers shall refrain from adopting acts not provided for by this Article in the area in question.

Note: The fruit of Amato's working group on simplification, this article renames and defines the legal instruments available to the Union. European laws correspond to regulations and framework laws to directives. This article is little changed from draft article 24 published on 26 February.

Article 33: Legislative acts

1. European laws and European framework laws shall be adopted, on the basis of proposals from the Commission, jointly by the European Parliament and the Council of Ministers under the ordinary legislative procedure as set out in Article III-302. If the two Institutions cannot reach agreement on an act, it shall not be adopted.

   In the cases specifically provided for in Article III-165, European laws and European framework laws may be adopted at the initiative of a group of Member States in accordance with Article III-302.

2. In the specific cases provided for by the Constitution, European laws and European framework laws shall be adopted by the European Parliament with the participation of the Council of Ministers, or by the latter with the participation of the European Parliament, in accordance with special legislative procedures.

Note: Ordinary legislative procedure in paragraph 1 is the new name for codecision. Article III-302 is equivalent to article 251 of the TEC. Article III-165 is the special provision in the area of freedom, security and justice which gives the right of initiative to propose an act to a quarter of the Member States, as well as the Commission.

Article 34: Non-legislative acts

1. The Council of Ministers and the Commission shall adopt European regulations or European decisions in the cases referred to in Articles 35 and 36 and in the cases specifically provided for in the Constitution. The European Council shall adopt European decisions in the cases specifically provided for in the Constitution. The European Central Bank shall adopt European regulations and European decisions when authorised to do so by the Constitution.

2. The Council of Ministers and the Commission, and the European Central Bank when so authorised in the Constitution, adopt recommendations.

Note: Non legislative acts are European decisions and European regulations as defined in article 32, paragraph 1. They implement legislative acts and some specific provisions of the constitutional treaty. This article details which institutions can adopt non-legislative acts and in what circumstances.

Article 35: Delegated regulations

1. European laws and European framework laws may delegate to the Commission the power to enact delegated regulations to supplement or amend certain non-essential elements of the European law or framework law.

    The objectives, content, scope and duration of the delegation shall be explicitly defined in the European laws and framework laws. A delegation may not cover the essential elements of an area. These shall be reserved for the European law or framework law.

2. The conditions of application to which the delegation is subject shall be explicitly determined in the European laws and framework laws. They may consist of the following possibilities:

    –   the European Parliament or the Council of Ministers may decide to revoke the delegation;
    –   the delegated regulation may enter into force only if no objection has been expressed by the European Parliament or the Council of Ministers within a period set by the European law or framework law.

    For the purposes of the preceding paragraph, the European Parliament shall act by a majority of its members, and the Council of Ministers by a qualified majority.

Note: An important innovation to overcome problems imposed by the lack of secondary legislation in the Union. When delegated regulations were proposed in the 26 February draft articles, the Praesidium stressed that it was always the legislator which decided on a case by case basis by way of the law or framework law whether to delegate. The legislator would also determine on a case by case basis the scope of delegation as well as its objectives and content. Two control mechanisms are detailed in paragraph 2.

Article 36: Implementing acts

1. Member States shall adopt all measures of national law necessary to implement legally binding Union acts.

· 2. Where uniform conditions for implementing binding Union acts are needed, those acts may confer implementing powers on the Commission, or, in specific cases duly justified and in the cases provided for in Article 39, on the Council of Ministers.

3. The European laws shall lay down in advance rules and general principles for the mechanisms for control by Member States of Union implementing acts.

4. Union implementing acts shall take the form of European implementing regulations or European implementing decisions.

Note: This article recognises that as a general rule, the Member States implement the Union's acts. Exceptions may arise if there is a need for uniform implementing conditions. In such a case, implementing powers are conferred on the Commission or in CFSP (article 39) cases on the Council.

Article 37: Principles common to the Union's legal acts

1. Unless the Constitution contains a specific stipulation, the Institutions shall decide, in compliance with the procedures applicable, the type of act *to be adopted in each case, in accordance with the principle of proportionality set out in Article 9.

2. European laws, European framework laws, European regulations and European decisions shall state the reasons on which they are based and shall refer to any proposals or opinions required by the Constitution.

Note: This article makes clear that the principle of proportionality governs the choice of a particular legal act for the exercise of competences.

Article 38: Publication and entry into force

1. European laws and framework laws adopted under the ordinary legislative procedure shall be signed by the President of the European Parliament and by the President of the Council of Ministers. In other

cases they shall be signed by the President of the European Parliament or by the President of the Council of Ministers. European laws and European framework laws shall be published in the Official Journal of the European Union and shall enter into force on the date specified in them or, in the absence of such a stated date, on the twentieth day following their publication.

2. European regulations and European decisions which do not specify to whom they are addressed or which are addressed to all Member States shall be signed by the President of the Institution which adopts them, shall be published in the Official Journal of the European Union and shall enter into force on the date specified in them or, in the absence of such a stated date, on the twentieth day following their publication.

3. Other decisions shall be notified to those to whom they are addressed and shall take effect upon such notification.

Note: Details of measures that are essential to guarantee legal certainty.

Chapter II – Specific provisions

Article 39: Specific provisions for implementing common foreign and security policy[8]

1. The European Union shall conduct a common foreign and security policy, based on the development of mutual political solidarity among Member States, the identification of questions of general interest and the achievement of an ever-increasing degree of convergence of Member States' actions.

2. The European Council shall identify the Union's strategic interests and determine the objectives of its common foreign and security policy. The Council of Ministers shall frame this policy within the framework of the strategic guidelines established by the European Council and in accordance with the arrangements in Part III.

3. The European Council and the Council of Ministers shall adopt the necessary European decisions.

4. The common foreign and security policy shall be put into effect by the Union Minister for Foreign Affairs and by the Member States, using national and Union resources.

---

[8] See Chapters 8.1; 14.5 and 15.3.

5. Member States shall consult one another within the European Council and the Council of Ministers on any foreign and security policy issue which is of general interest in order to determine a common approach. Before undertaking any action on the international scene or any commitment which could affect the Union's interests, each Member State shall consult the others within the European Council or the Council of Ministers. Member States shall ensure, through the convergence of their actions, that the Union is able to assert its interests and values on the international scene. Member States shall show mutual solidarity.

6. The European Parliament shall be regularly consulted on the main aspects and basic choices of the common foreign and security policy and shall be kept informed of how it evolves.

7. European decisions relating to the common foreign and security policy shall be adopted by the European Council and the Council of Ministers unanimously, except in the cases referred to in Part III. The European Council and the Council of Ministers shall act on a proposal from a Member State, from the Union Minister for Foreign Affairs or from that Minister with the Commission's support. European laws and European framework laws are excluded.

8. The European Council may unanimously decide that the Council of Ministers should act by qualified majority in cases other than those referred to in Part III.

Note: This article puts in treaty language the main conclusions of the Dehaene working group on external action and puts emphasis, after the experiences with the war in Iraq, on encouraging consultation, cooperation and convergence. It is little changed from the 26 May version, which strengthened the original 23 April text. The European Council has the key role in determining strategy. As a general rule, decisions are taken by unanimity. Although it will be difficult to unlock, paragraph 8 provides a passerelle by which the European Council can decide unanimously that the Council of Ministers should take more CFSP decisions by QMV.

Article 40: Specific provisions for implementing the common security and defence policy[9]

1. The common security and defence policy shall be an integral part of the common foreign and security policy. It shall provide the Union with an operational capacity drawing on assets civil and military. The Union may use them on missions outside the Union for peace-keeping, conflict

---

[9] See Chapters 8.2; 14.5 and 15.3.

prevention and strengthening international security in accordance with the principles of the United Nations Charter. The performance of these tasks shall be undertaken using capabilities provided by the Member States.

2. The common security and defence policy shall include the progressive framing of a common Union defence policy. This will lead to a common defence, when the European Council, acting unanimously, so decides. It shall in that case recommend to the Member States the adoption of such a decision in accordance with their respective constitutional requirements.

    The policy of the Union in accordance with this Article shall not prejudice the specific character of the security and defence policy of certain Member States and shall respect the obligations of certain Member States, which see their common defence realised in the North Atlantic Treaty Organisation, under the North Atlantic Treaty, and be compatible with the common security and defence policy established within that framework.

3. Member States shall make civilian and military capabilities available to the Union for the implementation of the common security and defence policy, to contribute to the objectives defined by the Council of Ministers. Those Member States which together establish multinational forces may also make them available to the common security and defence policy.

    Member States shall undertake progressively to improve their military capabilities. A European Armaments, Research and Military Capabilities Agency shall be established to identify operational requirements, to promote measures to satisfy those requirements, to contribute to identifying and, where appropriate, implementing any measure needed to strengthen the industrial and technological base of the defence sector, to participate in defining a European capabilities and armaments policy, and to assist the Council of Ministers in evaluating the improvement of military capabilities.

4. European decisions on the implementation of the common security and defence policy, including those initiating a mission as referred to in this Article, shall be adopted by the Council of Ministers acting unanimously on a proposal from the Union Minister for Foreign Affairs or from a Member State. The Union Minister for Foreign Affairs may propose the use of both national resources and Union instruments, together with the Commission where appropriate.

5. The Council of Ministers may entrust the execution of a task, within the Union framework, to a group of Member States in order to protect the Union's values and serve its interests. The execution of such a task shall be governed by Article III-211.

6. Those Member States whose military capabilities fulfil higher criteria and which have made more binding commitments to one another in this area with a view to the most demanding missions shall establish structured cooperation within the Union framework. Such cooperation shall be governed by the provisions of Article III-213.

7. Until such time as the European Council has acted in accordance with paragraph 2 of this Article, closer cooperation shall be established, in the Union framework, as regards mutual defence. Under this cooperation, if one of the Member States participating in such cooperation is the victim of armed aggression on its territory, the other participating States shall give it aid and assistance by all the means in their power, military or other, in accordance with Article 51 of the United Nations Charter. In the execution of closer cooperation on mutual defence, the participating Member States shall work in close cooperation with the North Atlantic Treaty Organisation. The detailed arrangements for participation in this cooperation and its operation, and the relevant decision-making procedures, are set out in Article III-214.

8. The European Parliament shall be regularly consulted on the main aspects and basic choices of the common security and defence policy, and shall be kept informed of how it evolves.

Note: Another article that looks ahead, creating a framework into which the Union can grow, should it decide to develop common defence as envisaged in paragraph 2. Given the hurdle created by the need for unanimity in the European Council, paragraphs 5, 6 and 7 are important as they provide for various forms of 'enhanced cooperation' to allow countries that want to forge ahead with more integrated policies to do so. The reference to NATO in paragraph 7 was a late addition to ease the concerns of the UK and several east European accession countries that European defence could weaken the Atlantic alliance. The tasks mentioned in paragraph 1 are the upgraded 'Petersberg tasks' detailed in III-210.

Article 41: Specific provisions for implementing the area of freedom, security and justice

1. The Union shall constitute an area of freedom, security and justice:

   – by adopting European laws and framework laws intended, where necessary, to approximate national laws in the areas listed in Part III;

- by promoting mutual confidence between the competent authorities
of the Member States, in particular on the basis of mutual
recognition of judicial and extrajudicial decisions;
- by operational cooperation between the competent authorities of the
Member States, including the police, customs and other services
specialising in the prevention and detection of criminal offences.

2.   Within the area of freedom, security and justice, national Parliaments
may participate in the evaluation mechanisms foreseen in Article III-161,
and shall be involved in the political monitoring of Europol and the
evaluation of Eurojust's activities in accordance with Articles III-177
and III-174.

3.   In the field of police and judicial cooperation in criminal matters,
Member States shall have a right of initiative in accordance with Article
III-165 of the Constitution.

*Note: Paragraph 1 sets out the new arrangements covering Union and member state
responsibilities after abolition of the justice and home affairs pillar. The first indent
refers to the parts of the policy, including asylum and immigration, being brought
under the Community method. Articles III-164, III-166 to III-168, III-171 to III-174,
article III-176.2 and III-177 move from unanimity to QMV. In paragraph 3, article
III-165 gives the right of initiative to one quarter of member states in the two policy
areas named.*

Article 42: Solidarity clause

1.   The Union and its Member States shall act jointly in a spirit of solidarity
if a Member State is the victim of terrorist attack or natural or man-made
disaster. The Union shall mobilise all the instruments at its disposal,
including the military resources made available by the Member States, to:

(a) –   prevent the terrorist threat in the territory of the Member States;
   –   protect democratic institutions and the civilian population from
       any terrorist attack;
   –   assist a Member State in its territory at the request of its political
       authorities in the event of a terrorist attack;

(b) –   assist a Member State in its territory at the request of its political
       authorities in the event of a disaster.

2.   The detailed arrangements for implementing this provision are at Article
III-231.

*Note: Originally limited to dealing with terrorist threats, the solidarity clause was
beefed up in the May draft to cover natural and man-made disasters as well. Article*

III-231 involves the Commission and the Foreign Minister in preparing cooperation. In a crisis, member states would coordinate in the Council of Ministers with the aid of the Union's defence policy committees and a standing committee for operational cooperation in internal security to be set up under III-162. It will be the job of the European Council to assess regularly threats facing the Union.

Chapter III – Enhanced cooperation[10]

Article 43: Enhanced cooperation

1. Member States which wish to establish enhanced cooperation between themselves within the framework of the Union's non-exclusive competences may make use of its Institutions and exercise those competences by applying the relevant provisions of the Constitution, subject to the limits and in accordance with the procedures laid down in this Article and in Articles III-322 to III-329.

   Enhanced cooperation shall aim to further the objectives of the Union, protect its interests and reinforce its integration process. Such cooperation shall be open to all Member States when it is being established and at any time, in accordance with Article III-324.

2. Authorisation to proceed with enhanced cooperation shall be granted by the Council of Ministers as a last resort, when it has been established within the Council of Ministers that the objectives of such cooperation cannot be attained within a reasonable period by the Union as a whole, and provided that it brings together at least one-third of the Member States. The Council of Ministers shall act in accordance with the procedure laid down in Article III-325.

3. Only members of the Council of Ministers representing the States participating in enhanced cooperation shall take part in the adoption of acts. All Member States may, however, take part in the deliberations of the Council of Ministers.

   Unanimity shall be constituted by the votes of the representatives of the participating States only. A qualified majority shall be defined as a majority of the votes of the representatives of the participating States, representing at least three-fifths of the population of those States. Where the Constitution does not require the Council of Ministers to act on the basis of a Commission proposal, or where the Council of Ministers is not acting upon initiative of the Minister for Foreign Affairs, the required

---

[10] See Chapter 14.6.

qualified majority shall be defined as a majority of two-thirds of the participating States, representing at least three-fifths of the population of those States.

4. Acts adopted in the framework of enhanced cooperation shall bind only participating States. They shall not be regarded as an acquis which has to be accepted by candidates for accession to the Union.

Note: Introduced in the Amsterdam Treaty and developed further in the Nice Treaty, enhanced cooperation was still untested when the Convention met. But with enlargement bringing 10 very different member states into the Union, its time may come. The rules are structured to encourage countries to cooperate inside, rather than outside the Union. The idea is that it should be an instrument of progressive integration, open to all member states, although only one-third of member states are needed to start. Member states in enhanced cooperation benefit from existing Union infrastructure and their citizens enjoy Parliamentary and judicial guarantees. Countries not taking part have an assurance that their interests are protected. If enhanced cooperation catches on, the way will be open to a more varied, multi-speed Union. It cannot apply to the Union's exclusive competences.

TITLE VI: THE DEMOCRATIC LIFE OF THE UNION[11]

Article 44: The principle of democratic equality

In all its activities, the Union shall observe the principle of the equality of citizens. All shall receive equal attention from the Union's Institutions.

Article 45: The principle of representative democracy

1. The working of the Union shall be founded on the principle of representative democracy.

2. Citizens are directly represented at Union level in the European Parliament. Member States are represented in the European Council and in the Council of Ministers by their governments, themselves accountable to national Parliaments, elected by their citizens.

3. Every citizen shall have the right to participate in the democratic life of the Union. Decisions shall be taken as openly as possible and as closely as possible to the citizen.

4. Political parties at European level contribute to forming European political awareness and to expressing the will of Union citizens.

---

[11] See Chapters 9.1 and 13.10.

Note: A greatly expanded version of the original article of the 4 April draft which made only brief mention of political parties at Union level. It highlights the democratic credentials of the European Parliament, European Council and Council of Ministers and gives another airing to the subsidiarity principle.

Article 46: The principle of participatory democracy

1. The Union Institutions shall, by appropriate means, give citizens and representative associations the opportunity to make known and publicly exchange their views in all areas of Union action.

2. The Union Institutions shall maintain an open, transparent and regular dialogue with representative associations and civil society.

3. The Commission shall carry out broad consultations with parties concerned in order to ensure that the Union's actions are coherent and transparent.

4. No less than one million citizens coming from a significant number of Member States may invite the Commission to submit any appropriate proposal on matters where citizens consider that a legal act of the Union is required for the purpose of implementing the Constitution. A European law shall determine the provisions for the specific procedures and conditions required for such a citizens' initiative.

Note: Progressively increased in length, the consultation requirement in paragraph 3 was added in May while paragraph 4 on the citizens initiative was one of the last amendments accepted before 13 June.

Article 47: The social partners and autonomous social dialogue

The European Union recognises and promotes the role of the social partners at Union level, taking into account the diversity of national systems; it shall facilitate dialogue between the social partners, respecting their autonomy.

Note: Added in May after a large number of amendments from across the political spectrum.

Article 48: The European Ombudsman

A European Ombudsman appointed by the European Parliament shall receive, investigate and report on complaints about maladministration within the Union Institutions, bodies or agencies. The European Ombudsman shall be completely independent in the performance of his or her duties.

Article 49: Transparency of the proceedings of Union Institutions

1. In order to promote good governance and ensure the participation of civil society, the Union Institutions, bodies and agencies shall conduct their work as openly as possible.

2. The European Parliament shall meet in public, as shall the Council of Ministers when examining and adopting a legislative proposal.

3. Any citizen of the Union, and any natural or legal person residing or having its registered office in a Member State shall have a right of access to documents of the Union Institutions, bodies and agencies in whatever form they are produced, in accordance with the conditions laid down in Part III.

4. A European law shall lay down the general principles and limits which, on grounds of public or private interest, govern the right of access to such documents.

5. Each Institution, body or agency referred to in paragraph 3 shall determine in its own rules of procedure specific provisions regarding access to its documents, in accordance with the European law referred to in paragraph 4.

Note: Many conventionnels wanted stronger transparency rights. Jens-Peter Bonde, the maverick Danish MEP, gathered nearly 200 signatures in support of all documents being accessible to the public unless the responsible body could muster a two-thirds majority to stop this. He proposed that all meetings on proposed legal acts should be open to the public unless there was a justified exception carried by a two-thirds majority. Also drafts and proposals should be accessible to the public as soon as they were adopted or otherwise available. Giscard drew Bonde's initiative to the attention of the IGC.

Article 50: Protection of personal data

1. Everyone has the right to the protection of personal data concerning him or her.

2. A European law shall lay down the rules relating to the protection of individuals with regard to the processing of personal data by Union Institutions, bodies and agencies, and by the Member States when carrying out activities which come under the scope of Union law, and the rules relating to the free movement of such data. Compliance with these rules shall be subject to the control of an independent authority.

Article 51: Status of churches and non-confessional organisations

1. The Union respects and does not prejudice the status under national law of churches and religious associations or communities in the Member States.

2. The Union equally respects the status of philosophical and non-confessional organisations.

3. Recognising their identity and their specific contribution, the Union shall maintain an open, transparent and regular dialogue with these churches and organisations.

Note: The text reproduces declaration 11 annexed to the Amsterdam Treaty which states the EU respects the status of churches and religious associations or communities in the member states as well as philosophical and non-confessional organisations

TITLE VII: THE UNION'S FINANCES

Article 52: Budgetary and financial principles

1. All items of Union revenue and expenditure shall be included in estimates drawn up for each financial year and shall be shown in the budget, in accordance with the provisions of Part III.

2. The revenue and expenditure shown in the budget shall be in balance.

3. The expenditure shown in the budget shall be authorised for the annual budgetary period in accordance with the European law referred to in Article III-318.

4. The implementation of expenditure shown in the budget shall require the prior adoption of a binding legal act providing a legal basis for Union action and for the implementation of the expenditure in accordance with the European law referred to in Article III-318. This act must take the form of a European law, a European framework law, a European regulation or a European decision.

5. With a view to maintaining budgetary discipline, the Union shall not adopt any act which is likely to have appreciable implications for the budget without providing an assurance that the proposal or measure in question is capable of being financed within the limit of the Union's own resources and the multiannual financial framework referred to in Article 54.

6. The Union's budget shall be implemented in accordance with the principle of sound financial management. Member States shall cooperate with the Union to ensure that the appropriations entered in the budget are used in accordance with the principles of sound financial management.

7. The Union and the Member States shall counter fraud and any other illegal activities affecting the financial interests of the Union in accordance with the provisions of Article III-321.

Note: III-318 prescribes unanimity in the Council of Ministers until 1 January 2007 and QMV thereafter.

Article 53: The Union's resources

1. The Union shall provide itself with the means necessary to attain its objectives and carry through its policies.

2. Without prejudice to other revenue, the Union's budget shall be

3. A European law of the Council of Ministers shall lay down the limit of the Union's resources and may establish new categories of resources or abolish an existing category. That law shall not enter into force until it is approved by the Member States in accordance with their respective constitutional requirements. The Council of Ministers shall act unanimously after consulting the European Parliament.

4. A European law of the Council shall lay down the modalities relating to the Union's resources. The Council of Ministers shall act after obtaining the consent of the European Parliament.

Note: Paragraphs 3 and 4 are complicated. According to the third paragraph, setting the limit of the Union's income (own resources) and establishing possible new resources (including taxes) requires unanimity in the Council and ratification by the member states. But the fourth paragraph subjects the practicalities of revenue raising within the limit to QMV, posing – in London's view – a threat to the UK budget rebate.

Article 54: The multiannual financial framework

1. The multiannual financial framework shall ensure that Union expenditure develops in an orderly manner and within the own resources limits. It shall determine the amounts of the annual ceilings for commitment appropriations by category of expenditure in accordance with the provisions of Article III-308.

2. A European law of the Council of Ministers shall lay down the multiannual financial framework. The Council of Ministers shall act after obtaining the consent of the European Parliament, which shall be given by a majority of its component members.

3. The annual budget of the Union shall comply with the multiannual financial framework.

4. The Council of Ministers shall act unanimously when adopting the first multiannual financial framework following the entry into force of the Constitution.

Note: The multi-annual financial framework controls the development of Union spending within the own resources limits. Article 308 says the financial framework should cover at least five years rather than the current seven years, expiring in 2006. The unanimity requirement was added in the final week before 13 June (reportedly after lobbying by Spain) and will make for an extremely difficult negotiation. Thereafter QMV.

Article 55: The Union's budget

The European Parliament and the Council of Ministers shall, on a proposal from the Commission and in accordance with the arrangements laid down in Article III-310, adopt the European law determining the Union's annual budget.

Note: Article III-310 changes the budget procedure radically. The Commission will submit a draft budget to the European Parliament and Council and it will have only one reading in each institution before going to a conciliation procedure, if necessary. The European Parliament will have the final word on spending in case of a disagreement with the Council. There will be no longer be a distinction between obligatory spending (as on agriculture) and non-obligatory spending.

TITLE VIII: THE UNION AND ITS IMMEDIATE ENVIRONMENT[12]

Article 56: The Union and its immediate environment

1. The Union shall develop a special relationship with neighbouring States, aiming to establish an area of prosperity and good neighbourliness, founded on the values of the Union and characterised by close and peaceful relations based on cooperation.

2. For this purpose, the Union may conclude and implement specific agreements with the countries concerned in accordance with Article III-

---

[12] See Chapter 13.12.

227. These agreements may contain reciprocal rights and obligations as well as the possibility of undertaking activities jointly. Their implementation shall be the subject of periodic consultation.

Note: The values of the Union in paragraph 1 are those in article 2 and are mentioned to set a benchmark for the Union's partner countries. Article III-227 details at length the procedures for negotiating agreements with third states.

TITLE IX: UNION MEMBERSHIP[13]

Article 57: Conditions of eligibility and procedure for accession to the Union

1. The Union shall be open to all European States which respect the values referred to in Article 2, and are committed to promoting them together.

2. Any European State which wishes to become a member of the Union shall address its application to the Council of Ministers. The European Parliament and the Member States' national Parliaments shall be notified of this application. The Council of Ministers shall act unanimously after consulting the Commission and after obtaining the consent of the European Parliament. The conditions and arrangements for admission shall be the subject of an agreement between the Member States and the candidate State. That agreement shall be subject to ratification by each contracting State, in accordance with its respective constitutional requirements.

Note: Paragraph 1 was added in May and is the first reference in a Union treaty to the 'Copenhagen criteria' for Union membership. Paragraph 2 is modelled on article 49 of the TEU but with the added reference to notification of Parliaments. The article merges draft articles 43 and 44 published on 4 April 2003.

Article 58: Suspension of Union membership rights

1. On a reasoned proposal by one-third of the Member States, by the European Parliament or by the Commission, the Council of Ministers, acting by a majority of four-fifths of its members after obtaining the consent of the European Parliament, may adopt a European decision determining that there is a clear risk of a serious breach by a Member State of the values mentioned in Article 2. Before making such a determination, the Council of Ministers shall hear the Member State in

---

[13] See Chapter 13.11.

question and, acting in accordance with the same procedure, may address recommendations to that State.

The Council of Ministers shall regularly verify that the grounds on which such a determination was made continue to apply.

2. The European Council, acting by unanimity on a proposal by one-third of the Member States or by the Commission and after obtaining the consent of the European Parliament, may adopt a European decision determining the existence of a serious and persistent breach by a Member State of the values mentioned in Article 2, after inviting the Member State in question to submit its observations.

3. Where a determination under paragraph 2 has been made, the Council of Ministers, acting by a qualified majority, may adopt a European decision suspending certain of the rights deriving from the application of the Constitution to the Member State in question, including the voting rights of that Member State in the Council of Ministers. In so doing, the Council of Ministers shall take into account the possible consequences of such a suspension on the rights and obligations of natural and legal persons.

That Member State shall in any case continue to be bound by its obligations under the Constitution.

4. The Council of Ministers, acting by a qualified majority, may subsequently adopt a European decision varying or revoking measures taken under paragraph 3 in response to changes in the situation which led to their being imposed.

5. For the purposes of this Article, the Council of Ministers shall act without taking into account the vote of the Member State in question. Abstentions by members present in person or represented shall not prevent the adoption of decisions referred to in paragraph 2.

This paragraph shall also apply in the event of voting rights being suspended pursuant to paragraph 3.

6. For the purposes of paragraphs 1 and 2, the European Parliament shall act by a two-thirds majority of the votes cast, representing the majority of its Members.

Note: The article reproduces in substance article 7 of the TEU and article 309 of the TEC and makes specific reference to the values in article 2.

Article 59: Voluntary withdrawal from the Union

1. Any Member State may decide to withdraw from the European Union in accordance with its own constitutional requirements.

2. A Member State which decides to withdraw shall notify the European Council of its intention; the European Council shall examine that notification. In the light of the guidelines provided by the European Council, the Union shall negotiate and conclude an agreement with that State, setting out the arrangements for its withdrawal, taking account of the framework for its future relationship with the Union. That agreement shall be concluded on behalf of the Union by the Council of Ministers, acting by a qualified majority, after obtaining the consent of the European Parliament.

    The representative of the withdrawing Member State shall not participate in Council of Ministers or European Council discussions or decisions concerning it.

3. The Constitution shall cease to apply to the State in question from the date of entry into force of the withdrawal agreement or, failing that, two years after the notification referred to in paragraph 2, unless the European Council, in agreement with the Member State concerned, decides to extend this period.

4. If a State which has withdrawn from the Union asks to re-join, its request shall be subject to the procedure referred to in Article 57.

Note: The 'exit clause'. The involvement of the European Council in paragraph 2 is to convey the gravity of such a move. However, as paragraph 4 makes clear, there are no special penalties for a state seeking to re-enter.

SECTION C
Draft constitutional treaty:
Preamble of Part II and Selected Articles
from Parts III and IV with Comments

PART II

THE CHARTER OF FUNDAMENTAL RIGHTS OF THE UNION

The peoples of Europe, in creating an ever closer union among them, are resolved to share a peaceful future based on common values.

Conscious of its spiritual and moral heritage, the Union is founded on the indivisible, universal values of human dignity, freedom, equality and solidarity; it is based on the principles of democracy and the rule of law. It places the individual at the heart of its activities, by establishing the citizenship of the Union and by creating an area of freedom, security and justice. The Union contributes to the preservation and to the development of these common values while respecting the diversity of the cultures and traditions of the peoples of Europe as well as the national identities of the Member States and the organisation of their public authorities at national, regional and local levels; it seeks to promote balanced and sustainable development and ensures free movement of persons, goods, services and capital, and the freedom of establishment.

To this end, it is necessary to strengthen the protection of fundamental rights in the light of changes in society, social progress and scientific and technological developments by making those rights more visible in a Charter.

This Charter reaffirms, with due regard for the powers and tasks of the Union and the principle of subsidiarity, the rights as they result, in particular, from the constitutional traditions and international obligations common to the Member States, the European Convention for the Protection of Human Rights and Fundamental Freedoms, the Social Charters adopted by the Union and by the Council of Europe and the case law of the Court of Justice of the European Union and of the European Court of Human Rights.

In this context the Charter will be interpreted by the courts of the Union and the member states with due regard to the explanations prepared at the instigation of the Praesidium of the Convention which drafted the Charter.

Enjoyment of these rights entails responsibilities and duties with regard to other persons, to the human community and to future generations.

The Union therefore recognises the rights, freedoms and principles set out hereafter.

Note: The sentence highlighted in italics was inserted just before 13 June to give the UK extra assurance that the Charter would not lead to legal challenges of its labour and social legislation. The 'ever closer union' lives on in the first sentence, having been excluded from part I of the constitutional treaty.

PART III

NON-DISCRIMINATION AND CITIZENSHIP

Article III-8[14]

1. Without prejudice to the other provisions of the Constitution and within the limits of the powers conferred by it upon the Union, a European law or framework law of the Council of Ministers may establish the measures needed to combat discrimination based on sex, racial or ethnic origin, religion or belief, disability, age or sexual orientation. The Council of Ministers shall act unanimously after obtaining the consent of the European Parliament.

2. European laws or framework laws may establish basic principles for Union incentive measures and define such incentive measures, to support action taken by Member States, excluding any harmonisation of their laws and regulations.

Note: A battleground between federally minded supporters of 'Social Europe' and the UK government representative, the final draft resorts to a familiar type of compromise, which leaves non-discrimination legislation subject to unanimity, but makes 'incentive measures' subject to QMV.

FISCAL PROVISIONS[15]

Article III-62

1. A European law or framework law of the Council of Ministers shall lay down measures for the harmonisation of legislation concerning turnover

---

[14] See Chapter 18.3.
[15] See Chapters 8.4 and 15.5.

taxes, excise duties and other forms of indirect taxation provided that such harmonisation is necessary for the functioning of the internal market and to avoid distortion of competition. The Council of Ministers shall act unanimously after consulting the European Parliament and the Economic and Social Committee.

2. Where the Council of Ministers, acting unanimously on a proposal from the Commission, finds that the measures referred to in paragraph 1 relate to administrative cooperation or to combating tax fraud and tax evasion, it shall act, notwithstanding paragraph 1, by a qualified majority when adopting the European law or framework law adopting these measures.

Article III-63

Where the Council of Ministers, acting unanimously on a proposal from the Commission, finds that measures on company taxation relate to administrative cooperation or combating tax fraud and tax evasion, it shall adopt, by a qualified majority, a European law or framework law laying down these measures, provided that they are necessary for the functioning of the internal market and to avoid distortion of competition.

That law or framework law shall be adopted after consultation of the European Parliament and the Economic and Social Committee.

Note: Articles III-62 and III-63 contain restricted passerelles marking an attempt by integrationists to prise open Union tax legislation to QMV. This 'foot in the door' technique reflects the majority view in the economic governance working group. It remains hotly contested, with the UK, Sweden and Ireland strongly opposed.

PROVISIONS SPECIFIC TO MEMBER STATES WHICH ARE PART OF THE EURO AREA[16]

Article III-88

1. In order to ensure that economic and monetary union works properly, and in accordance with the relevant provisions of the Constitution, measures specific to those Member States which are members of the euro area shall be adopted:

   (a) to strengthen the coordination of their budgetary discipline and surveillance of it;

---

[16] See Chapters 8.4 and 15.3.

(b) to set out economic policy guidelines for them, while ensuring that they are compatible with those adopted for the whole of the Union and are kept under surveillance.

2. For those measures set out in paragraph 1, only members of the Council of Ministers representing Member States which are part of the euro area shall vote. A qualified majority shall be defined as the majority of the votes of the representatives of the Member States which are part of the euro area, representing at least three-fifths of their population. Unanimity of those members of the Council of Ministers shall be required for an act requiring unanimity.

Article III-89

Arrangements for meetings between ministers of those Member States which are part of the euro area shall be laid down in the Protocol on the Euro Group.

Article III-90

1. In order to secure the euro's place in the international monetary system, the Council of Ministers, on a proposal from the Commission and after consulting the European Central Bank, shall adopt a European decision establishing common positions on matters of particular interest for economic and monetary union within the competent international financial institutions and conferences.

2. For the measures referred to in paragraph 1, only members of the Council of Ministers representing Member States which are part of the euro area shall vote. A qualified majority shall be defined as the majority of the votes of the representatives of the Member States which are part of the euro area, representing at least three-fifths of their population. Unanimity of those members of the Council of Ministers shall be required for an act requiring unanimity.

3. The Council of Ministers, on a proposal from the Commission, may adopt appropriate measures to ensure unified representation within the international financial institutions and conferences. The procedural provisions of paragraphs 1 and 2 shall apply.

Note: Recognition that the euro area should have its own rules with ministers meeting separately from the Ecofin Council. Important as enlargement will put eurozone countries in a minority of member states, at least temporarily. The protocol mentioned in III-89 provides that the Euro Group president should be elected for two and a half years by a majority of participating member states.

POLICIES ON BORDER CHECKS, ASYLUM AND IMMIGRATION

Article III-168[17]

1. The Union shall develop a common immigration policy aimed at ensuring, at all stages, the efficient management of migration flows, fair treatment of third-country nationals residing legally in Member States, and the prevention of, and enhanced measures to combat, illegal immigration and trafficking in human beings.

2. To this end, European laws or framework laws shall establish measures in the following areas:

   (a) the conditions of entry and residence, and standards on the issue by Member States of long-term visas and residence permits, including those for the purpose of family reunion;

   (b) the definition of the rights of third-country nationals residing legally in a Member State, including the conditions governing freedom of movement and of residence in other Member States;

   (c) illegal immigration and unauthorised residence, including removal and repatriation of persons residing without authorisation;

   (d) combating trafficking in persons, in particular women and children.

3. The Union may conclude readmission agreements with third countries for the readmission of third-country nationals residing without authorisation to their countries of origin or provenance, in accordance with Article III-227.

4. European laws or framework laws may establish measures to provide incentives and support for the action of Member States with a view to promoting the integration of third-country nationals residing legally in their territories, excluding any harmonisation of the laws and regulations of the Member States.

5. This Article shall not affect the right of Member States to determine volumes of admission of third-country nationals coming from third countries to their territory in order to seek work, whether employed or self-employed.

Note: The 'German exception,' reflecting fears in Berlin that large scale immigration at a time of high unemployment in Germany could trigger political problems and social unrest. Whereas qualified majority voting is the general rule

---

[17] See Chapter 18.2.

*for asylum and immigration policies, Joschka Fischer fought for, and won, the right
in paragraph 5 for national governments to restrict the inflow of immigrants to their
labour markets.*

JUDICIAL COOPERATION IN CRIMINAL MATTERS

Article III-175[18]

1. In order to combat serious crime having a cross-border dimension, as
   well as crimes affecting the interests of the Union, a European law of the
   Council of Ministers may establish a European Public Prosecutor's
   Office from Eurojust. The Council of Ministers shall act unanimously
   after obtaining the consent of the European Parliament.

2. The European Public Prosecutor's Office shall be responsible for
   investigating, prosecuting and bringing to judgement, where appropriate
   in liaison with Europol, the perpetrators of and accomplices in serious
   crimes affecting more than one Member State and of offences against
   the Union's financial interests, as determined by the European law
   provided for in paragraph 1. It shall exercise the functions of prosecutor
   in the competent courts of the Member States in relation to such offences.

3. The European law referred to in paragraph 1 shall determine the general
   rules applicable to the European Public Prosecutor's Office, the
   conditions governing the performance of its functions, the rules of
   procedure applicable to its activities, as well as those governing the
   admissibility of evidence, and the rules applicable to the judicial review
   of procedural measures taken by it in the performance of its functions.

*Note: The controversial provision for a European public prosecutor. Although John
Bruton's working group was split on the issue and there was no consensus in the
subsequent plenary debate, the Praesidium decided to retain the possibility of
creating the office in the treaty and make it subject to unanimity.*

THE UNION'S EXTERNAL ACTION

PROVISIONS HAVING GENERAL APPLICATION

Article III-193[19]

1. The Union's action on the international scene shall be guided by, and
   designed to advance in the wider world, the principles which have

---

[18] See Chapters 8.3 and 13.8.
[19] See Chapter 8.1.

inspired its own creation, development and enlargement: democracy, the rule of law, the universality and indivisibility of human rights and fundamental freedoms, respect for human dignity, equality and solidarity, and for international law in accordance with the principles of the United Nations Charter.

The Union shall seek to develop relations and build partnerships with third countries, and international, regional or global organisations, which share these values. It shall promote multilateral solutions to common problems, in particular in the framework of the United Nations.

2. The Union shall define and pursue common policies and actions, and shall work for a high degree of cooperation in all fields of international relations, in order to:

   (a) safeguard the common values, fundamental interests, security, independence and integrity of the Union;

   (b) consolidate and support democracy, the rule of law, human rights and international law;

   (c) preserve peace, prevent conflicts and strengthen international security, in conformity with the principles of the United Nations Charter;

   (d) foster the sustainable economic, social and environmental development of developing countries, with the primary aim of eradicating poverty;

   (e) encourage the integration of all countries into the world economy, including through the progressive abolition of restrictions on international trade;

   (f) help develop international measures to preserve and improve the quality of the environment and the sustainable management of global natural resources, in order to ensure sustainable development;

   (g) assist populations, countries and regions confronting natural or man-made disasters;

   (h) promote an international system based on stronger multilateral cooperation and good global governance.

3. The Union shall respect the principles and pursue the objectives listed in paragraphs 1 and 2 in the development and implementation of the

different areas of the Union's external action covered by this Title and the external aspects of its other policies.

The Union shall ensure consistency between the different areas of its external action and between these and its other policies. The Council of Ministers and the Commission, assisted by the Union Minister for Foreign Affairs, shall ensure that consistency and shall cooperate to that effect.

Note: The principles governing the Union's common and security policy, agreed in the Dehaene working group on external action.

COMMON COMMERCIAL POLICY

Article III-217[20]

1. The common commercial policy shall be based on uniform principles, particularly with regard to changes in tariff rates, the conclusion of tariff and trade agreements relating to trade in goods and services and the commercial aspects of intellectual property, foreign direct investment, the achievement of uniformity in measures of liberalisation, export policy and measures to protect trade such as those to be taken in the event of dumping or subsidies. The common commercial policy shall be conducted in the context of the principles and objectives of the Union's external action.

2. European laws or framework laws shall establish the measures required to implement the common commercial policy.

3. Where agreements with one or more States or international organisations need to be negotiated and concluded, the relevant provisions of Article III-227 shall apply. The Commission shall make recommendations to the Council of Ministers, which shall authorise the Commission to open the necessary negotiations. The Council of Ministers and the Commission shall be responsible for ensuring that the agreements negotiated are compatible with internal Union policies and rules.

    The Commission shall conduct these negotiations in consultation with a special committee appointed by the Council of Ministers to assist the Commission in this task and within the framework of such directives as the Council of Ministers may issue to it. The Commission shall report

---

[20] See Chapter 18.4.

regularly to the special committee and to the European Parliament on the progress of negotiations.

4. For the negotiation and conclusion of agreements in the fields of trade in services involving the movement of persons and the commercial aspects of intellectual property, the Council of Ministers shall act unanimously where such agreements include provisions for which unanimity is required for the adoption of internal rules.

   The Council shall also act unanimously for the negotiation and conclusion of agreements in the field of trade in cultural and audiovisual services, where these risk prejudicing the Union's cultural and·linguistic diversity.

   The negotiation and conclusion of international agreements in the field of transport shall be subject to the provisions of Section 7 of Chapter III of Title III and Article III-227.

5. The exercise of the competences conferred by this Article in the field of commercial policy shall not affect the delimitation of internal competences between the Union and the Member States, and shall not lead to harmonisation of legislative or regulatory provisions of Member States insofar as the Constitution excludes such harmonisation.

Note: This article was the subject of difficult negotiations in the final session of the Praesidium. The compromise on the cultural exception is highlighted in italics.

PART IV

GENERAL AND FINAL PROVISIONS

Article IV-1: The symbols of the Union [21]

The flag of the Union shall be a circle of twelve golden stars on a blue background.

The anthem of the Union shall be based on the Ode to Joy from the Ninth Symphony by Ludwig van Beethoven.

The motto of the Union shall be: United in diversity.

The currency of the Union shall be the euro.

9 May shall be celebrated throughout the Union as Europe day.

---

[21] Soo Chapter 18.3.

Note: A high priority for integrationist conventionnels, this article was added on the final day of the Convention. The symbols are seen as a way of bringing the Union closer to Europe's citizens. The Convention added a footnote to say this article would be better situated in part I.

Article IV-7 [22] : *Procedure for revising the Treaty establishing the Constitution*

1. The government of any Member State, the European Parliament or the Commission may submit to the Council of Ministers proposals for the amendment of the Treaty establishing the Constitution. The national Parliaments of the Member States shall be notified of these proposals.

2. If the European Council, after consulting the European Parliament and the Commission, adopts by a simple majority a decision in favour of examining the proposed amendments, the President of the European Council shall convene a Convention composed of representatives of the national Parliaments of the Member States, of the Heads of State or Government of the Member States, of the European Parliament and of the Commission. The European Central Bank shall also be consulted in the case of institutional changes in the monetary area. The European Council may decide by a simple majority, after obtaining the consent of the European Parliament, not to convene the Convention should this not be justified by the extent of the proposed amendments. In the latter case, the European Council shall define the terms of reference for the conference of representatives of the governments of the Member States.

   The Convention shall examine the proposals for amendments and shall adopt by consensus a recommendation to the conference of representatives of the governments of the Member States provided for in paragraph 3.

3. The conference of representatives of the governments of the Member States shall be convened by the President of the Council of Ministers for the purpose of determining by common accord the amendments to be made to the Treaty establishing the Constitution.

   The amendments shall enter into force after being ratified by all the Member States in accordance with their respective constitutional requirements.

4. If, two years after the signature of the treaty amending the Treaty establishing the Constitution, four-fifths of the Member States have

---

[22] See Chapters 6.1; 13.13 and 15.6.

ratified it and one or more Member States have encountered difficulties in proceeding with ratification, the matter shall be referred to the European Council.

Note: This article now presumes that a Convention will be called to prepare future revisions of the constitutional treaty. National governments will only be able to organise an intergovernmental conference without a Convention with the express permission of the European Parliament. The article retains the current, difficult procedure of ratification by all member states, the Convention having been unable to agree easier revision procedures for those provisions of part III which do not affect the objectives, values or competences of the Union in the time available.

Article IV-8: Adoption, ratification and entry into force of the Treaty establishing the Constitution

1. The Treaty establishing the Constitution shall be ratified by the High Contracting Parties in accordance with their respective constitutional requirements. The instruments of ratification shall be deposited with the Government of the Italian Republic.

2. The Treaty establishing the Constitution shall enter into force on ...., provided that all the instruments of ratification have been deposited, or, failing that, on the first day of the month following the deposit of the instrument of ratification by the last signatory State to take this step.

Note: The rules for adoption and ratification are unchanged from those in the Treaty on Union.

DECLARATION IN THE FINAL ACT OF SIGNATURE OF THE TREATY ESTABLISHING THE CONSTITUTION

If, two years after the signature of the Treaty establishing the Constitution, four-fifths of the Member States have ratified it and one or more Member States have encountered difficulties in proceeding with ratification, the matter will be referred to the European Council.

The May draft of article IV-8 included this provision as a third paragraph. It stands in the final version of the constitutional treaty at the very end as a declaration.

Name Index

Other publications by EuroComment

We are confident that you will have found the present book by Peter Norman informative, provocative and fascinating. Why not subscribe to EuroComment's other publications?

The European Council Commentaries

The European Council is at the core of the European Union's system of government. These commentaries, based on a wide range of published and unpublished material, as well as countless interviews, are designed to help readers keep track of the most important decisions and developments in the Union. Written in a lucid and lively style, they are also reference works that will retain their interest and value for a long time to come.

Commissioner Chris Patten wrote of the series in the following terms:

> As European Councils have progressively taken centre stage, both institutionally and in providing strategic impetus to the Union, it has become increasingly important that they should be properly recorded – for immediate purposes and for posterity. I suspect that the series launched by Peter Ludlow will quickly become indispensable.

For information about how to subscribe, see the order form on the opposite page.

The Briefing Notes

The Briefing Notes provide authoritative analyses of important developments or issues in the politics of the European Union. Standard features include coverage of every European Council meeting and each incoming Presidency. Other subjects dealt with in the first eighteen months included the European Convention, EU-US relations, the EU and the war in Iraq, economic policy coordination and the IGC.

Each note is between twenty and thirty pages long and is only available electronically. The annual subscription for a guaranteed minimum of ten papers is € 75 per reader. Institutional subscriptions are also possible and are calculated on the basis of the estimated likely readership in the organisation concerned.

For further information, contact info@eurocomment.be

European Council Commentary Series

EuroComment's European Council Commentaries are available individually or through a subscription. To order fill in and send us the form below or visit our website: http://www.eurocomment.be

Name .... Company ....

Telephone .... E-mail ....

Bill To .... Deliver To ....

....

....

....

VAT Number if applicable: ....

Current Titles	Price	Qty	Total
The Laeken Council; 243pp	30 €	....	....
The Barcelona Council; 275pp	30 €	....	....
The Seville Council; 195pp	30 €	....	....
Future Titles			
The Making of the New Europe; July-Dec 2002; 400pp	50 €	....	....
The Limits of European Integration; Jan-June 2003; 400pp	50 €	....	....
*Postage			....
Sub-total A			....

Take out a 12-month subscription and save 25 € on the next two titles in the series.

Item	Price	Qty	Total
12 month subscription to the next two titles	75 €	....	....
**Postage			....
Sub-total B			....

*Postage destination & charges per book
Belgium € 6, EU Countries € 8.50, Rest of World € 12.50
**Postage destination & charges per subscription
Belgium € 12, EU Countries € 17, Rest of World € 25

TOTAL ORDER VALUE (A+B)	

Credit Card Payments:

○ Diners Club   ○ Euro Card   ○ Master Card   ○ Visa

Card number .... Expiry date ....

Name on card ....

Registered address ....

Send the completed form to: *EuroComment, Avenue Louise 113, 1050 Brussels, Belgium.* Alternative payment methods are available. For more information, please contact EuroComment at info@eurocomment.be